THE CAMBRIDGE GUIDE TO MIXED METHODS RESEARCH FOR THEATRE AND PERFORMANCE STUDIES

We often know performance when we see it – but how should we investigate it? And how should we interpret what we find out? This book demonstrates why and how mixed methods research is necessary for investigating and explaining performance and advancing new critical agendas in cultural study. The wide range of aesthetic forms, cultural meanings, and social functions found in theatre and performance globally invites a corresponding variety of research approaches. The essays in this volume model reflective consideration of the means, processes, and choices for conducting performance research that is historical, ethnographic, aesthetic, or computational. An international set of contributors addresses what is meant by *planning* or designing a research project, *doing* research (locating and collecting primary sources or resources), and the ensuing work of *interpreting* and communicating insights. Providing illuminating and necessary guidance, this volume is an essential resource for scholars and students of theatre, performance, and dance.

TRACY C. DAVIS is Barber Professor of Performing Arts at Northwestern University. She has published over a hundred articles in arts, humanities, and social sciences journals; has edited and authored a dozen monographs on theatre history and historiography, the history of the book, and cultural studies; and has wide experience in editing book series and advising doctoral students.

PAUL RAE is Professor of Theatre Studies and Head of the School of Culture and Communications at the University of Melbourne. He is the author of *Theatre & Human Rights* (2009) and *Real Theatre* (2019), and a former editor of the journal *Theatre Research International*. He researches and publishes widely on contemporary theatre and on the performance cultures of the Asia-Pacific region.

'This collection feels like a masterclass with the leading teachers of research methods in our field. It gathers contributions from an international group of distinguished scholars, assembling them in a dynamic organizational structure.'

Shannon Jackson, University of California, Berkeley

'This field-defining volume is a sorely needed clarion call. Those of us working in theatre and performance studies too rarely consider "how research comes into being". What we need is fresh energy and new direction concerning methodologies. These essays, theoretically abundant and transnational in scope, offer just that and will reinvigorate the field for years to come.'

Douglas A. Jones, Duke University

'Sophisticated, pragmatic, and eminently readable, this *Guide* will be a core text in all methods and methodologies courses in theatre and performance studies, and will be required reading for anyone doing research in the field: archival, embodied, ethnographic, interdisciplinary, cross-cultural, practice-based, unconventional, or any mixture of the above.'

Ric Knowles, University of Guelph

'A must-read for theatre and performance scholars and artists. Excellently curated with great attention to practical, theoretical, and pedagogical uses, this book provokes thinking through what we mean by "performance as method" in theatre and performance studies research. Researchers seeking ways to decolonize thinking, activate Indigenous approaches, and integrate methodologies of inclusion in their work will find gems of ideas in this collection.'

Jazmin Llana, De La Salle University

'This is a terrific volume. Including a wide range of academic voices, the book invites researchers to experiment with methods and working processes that are sited, situated, and contextually located. It is critically astute, well balanced, and thought-provoking, and will inspire and inform scholars for years to come.'

Helen Nicholson, Royal Holloway, University of London

'A smart, rigorously conceived, and eminently readable collection that reveals how thinking about methods takes us right to the heart of what and how we research in theatre and performance studies. I expect this book will inspire scholarship and guide teaching for years to come.'

Heike Roms, University of Exeter

THE CAMBRIDGE GUIDE TO MIXED METHODS RESEARCH FOR THEATRE AND PERFORMANCE STUDIES

EDITED BY

TRACY C. DAVIS

Northwestern University

PAUL RAE

University of Melbourne

CAMBRIDGE
UNIVERSITY PRESS

CAMBRIDGE
UNIVERSITY PRESS

Shaftesbury Road, Cambridge CB2 8EA, United Kingdom

One Liberty Plaza, 20th Floor, New York, NY 10006, USA

477 Williamstown Road, Port Melbourne, VIC 3207, Australia

314–321, 3rd Floor, Plot 3, Splendor Forum, Jasola District Centre, New Delhi – 110025, India

103 Penang Road, #05–06/07, Visioncrest Commercial, Singapore 238467

Cambridge University Press is part of Cambridge University Press & Assessment, a department of the University of Cambridge.

We share the University's mission to contribute to society through the pursuit of education, learning and research at the highest international levels of excellence.

www.cambridge.org
Information on this title: www.cambridge.org/9781009294881

DOI: 10.1017/9781009294904

First published 2024

A catalogue record for this publication is available from the British Library

Library of Congress Cataloging-in-Publication Data
NAMES: Davis, Tracy C., 1960– editor. | Rae, Paul, editor.
TITLE: The Cambridge guide to mixed methods research for theatre and performance studies / edited by Tracy C. Davis, Paul Rae.
DESCRIPTION: Cambridge ; New York, NY : Cambridge University Press, 2024. | Includes bibliographical references and index.
IDENTIFIERS: LCCN 2023040257 | ISBN 9781009294881 (hardback) | ISBN 9781009294904 (ebook)
SUBJECTS: LCSH: Theater – Research – Methodology. | Performance – Research – Methodology. | Mixed methods research.
CLASSIFICATION: LCC PN2037 .C26 2024 | DDC 792–dc23/eng/20231107
LC record available at https://lccn.loc.gov/2023040257

ISBN 978-1-009-29488-1 Hardback

Contents

Figures

Tables

Contributors

RUTHIE ABELIOVICH is Assistant Professor of Theatre Art at Tel Aviv University, specializing in Jewish theatre, sound, voice, and media. She is the author of *Possessed Voices: Aural Remains from Modernist Hebrew Theatre*, co-editor (with Linda Ben-Zvi and Sharon Aronson-Lehavi) of *A Stage of Their Own: Seven American Feminist Plays*, and co-editor (with Edwin Seroussi) of *Borderlines: Essays on Maps and the Logic of Place*. She has published in *TDR: The Drama Review*, the *Theatre Journal*, *Performance Research*, *Theatre Research International*, and the *Journal of Classical Sociology*. In 2020 she received a European Research Council Starting Grant to study popular Yiddish theatre (1880–1920).

NATALIE ALVAREZ is Professor of Theatre and Performance Studies and Associate Dean of Scholarly, Research, and Creative Activities in The Creative School at Toronto Metropolitan University. She is the author, editor, and co-editor of five books, most recently *Theatre & War*, *Sustainable Tools for Precarious Times: Performance Actions in the Americas* (winner of ATHE's Excellence in Editing award), and *Immersions in Cultural Difference: Tourism, War, Performance* (winner of the Ann Saddlemyer book prize). Her research focuses on immersive simulations in the public sphere, Latina/o/x performance, and performance activism in the Americas.

PATRICK ANDERSON is Professor in the Departments of Communication and Ethnic Studies at the University of California, San Diego and a Guggenheim Fellow. He is the author of *Autobiography of a Disease* and *So Much Wasted: Hunger, Performance, and the Morbidity of Resistance*, and the co-editor (with Jisha Menon) of *Violence Performed: Local Roots and Global Routes of Conflict*. His book *The Lamentations: A Requiem for Queer Suicide* will be published in 2024. In 2018, he was appointed by the mayor and city council of San Diego to the Commission on Police Practices, which represents the community in reviewing complaints against the police, officer-involved shootings, and in-custody deaths. In 2020, he completed his death doula certification at the University of Vermont.

AWO MANA ASIEDU is Associate Professor of Theatre Studies at the School of Performing Arts, University of Ghana, where she is currently Dean. Her research interests are in African theatre and performance, audiences, and the sociology of theatre. Her research has been published in *Contemporary Theatre Review*, *Theatre Research International*, *African Theatre*, and *Theatre History Studies*. She has contributed several book chapters, most recently to the *Routledge Companion to Audiences and the Performing Arts*. She is co-editor of *The Performing Arts in Africa: Ghanaian Perspectives*.

JULIUS BAUTISTA is Senior Lecturer at NUS College, Singapore. He received a PhD in Southeast Asian studies (anthropology and cultural history) at the Australian National University, and has published on religious practice in Asia, with a focus on Christian iconography, religious piety, and the relationship between religion and the state. He is the author of *The Way of the Cross: Suffering Selfhoods in the Roman Catholic Philippines* and *Figuring Catholicism: An Ethnohistory of the Santo Niño de Cebu*, editor of *The Spirit of Things: Materiality and Religious Diversity in Southeast Asia*, and co-editor (with Francis Lim) of *Christianity and the State in Asia: Complicity and Conflict*.

LEO CABRANES-GRANT is Professor of Theatre, Performance, and Intercultural Studies in the Departments of Theater and Dance and Spanish and Portuguese at the University of California, Santa Barbara. He is the author of *Lope de Vega and the Uses of Repetition* and *From Scenarios to Networks: Performing the Intercultural in Colonial Mexico*. He has received the Association for Theatre in Higher Education Award for Outstanding Article, the Puerto Rican Institute of Culture Award for Best Play, and the Asunción Drama Award from Pregones Theater in New York. He has also published four collections of poetry, and his plays have been produced in Santa Barbara, Boston, New York, and San Juan. He is a past editor of *Theatre Survey*.

BRANDI WILKINS CATANESE is Associate Professor in the Departments of African American Studies and Theater, Dance, and Performance Studies, and Associate Dean in the Graduate Division at the University of California, Berkeley. She is the author of the book *The Problem of the Color[blind]: Racial Transgression and the Politics of Black Performance* and essays in journals including *Theatre Journal*, *Theatre Survey*, and *Performance Research*. She is a past editor of *Theatre Survey*. Her current work addresses the aesthetics and politics of Black feminist performance and the formal and affective properties of ostensibly post-racial performance.

ANKE CHARTON is Assistant Professor of Theatre at the University of Vienna. Her scholarship focuses on early modern performance cultures, music theatre, and gender studies. She is the author of *prima donna, primo uomo, musico: Körper und Stimme: Geschlechterbilder in der Oper* and has co-edited volumes on theatre historiography and on power relations in the music industry. Recent publications include papers on trans voices, intersectional historiographies, and structural abuse in the classical music sector. Her current book project investigates Siglo de Oro narratives and Spanish theatre, supported by an Elise Richter Grant from the Austrian Science Fund. She holds a PhD from Leipzig University.

ADRIAN CURTIN is Associate Professor of Drama at the University of Exeter. He is the author of *Avant-Garde Theatre Sound: Staging Sonic Modernity* and *Death in Modern Theatre: Stages of Mortality*. He researches modern Western drama and theatre from the late nineteenth century onwards, with an emphasis on experimental forms. Areas of specialization include theatre sound and aurality, theatrical exploration of mortality, and the representation and staging of Western classical music. He was the principal investigator of the Arts and Humanities Research Council-funded research network Representing 'Classical Music' in the Twenty-First Century, which ran from 2019 to 2021, and he co-edited a special collection of the Open Library of Humanities on this topic. He is co-editor of *The Edinburgh Companion to Modernism in Contemporary Theatre*.

TRACY C. DAVIS is Barber Professor of Performing Arts at Northwestern University. Her most recent books are *Liberal Lives and Activist Repertoires: Political Performance and Victorian Social Reform*, *The Routledge Handbook to Theatre and Performance Historiography* (co-edited with Peter W. Marx), and *Uncle Tom's Cabins: The Transnational History of America's Most Mutable Book* (co-edited with Stefka Mihaylova). She has published over a hundred articles in journals dedicated to the arts, humanities, and social sciences. Her unique, multifaceted knowledge of theatre and performance history is a product of contributions to the field as a scholar and author as well as a critic, dramaturg, and historical consultant. She is general editor (with Christopher B. Balme) of the six-volume study *A Cultural History of Theatre*, editor of the monograph series Cambridge Studies in Theatre and Performance Theory, and co-editor of the Palgrave monograph series Transnational Theatre Histories.

EMINE FIŞEK is Junior Group Leader in the Institute for Urban and Regional Research of the Austrian Academy of Sciences, where she is Principal Investigator of the European Research Grant Project 'Theatre and Gentrifications in the European City (2023–2028)'. She is the author of *Aesthetic Citizenship: Immigration and Theater in Twenty-First-Century Paris* and *Theatre & Community*. She has published articles in *Theatre Journal*, *Theatre Research International*, *Text and Performance Quarterly*, *Comparative Drama*, and *French Cultural Studies*. Her current research is on the impact that cultural memory, urban transformation, and international migration have had on theatre in Turkey in the twenty-first century. From 2012–2023, she was Assistant Professor in the Department of WesternLanguages and Literatures at Boğaziçi University in Istanbul.

MAGGIE B. GALE is Professor of Drama and Vice-Dean of Research in the Faculty of Humanities at the University of Manchester. Her research focuses on gender, performance, and historiographic practices. She is co-editor of the journal *Contemporary Theatre Review*, as well as two University of Manchester Press book series: Theatre – Theory – Performance, and Women, Theatre and Performance. Recent publications include *A Social History of British Performance Cultures 1900–1939: Citizenship, Surveillance and the Body*, and two collections edited with Kate Dorney: *Stage Women 1900–1950: Female Theatre Workers and Professional Practice*, and *Vivien Leigh: Actress and Icon*.

NICOLA MĀRIE HYLAND is Senior Lecturer in the Theatre Programme of Te Herenga Waka/Victoria University of Wellington. Of Te Atihaunui-a-Pāpārangi and Ngāti Hauiti descent, she researches representations of Indigeneity in contemporary performance, intersections of gender and race in popular culture, and devised theatre practices. Hyland has worked as a writer, editor, director, cultural adviser, and devisor in Australasia. She has published in *TDR: The Drama Review*, *Theatre Topics*, and the *Contemporary Theatre Review*, and edited a Special Topic edition for the *Australasian Drama Studies Journal*. Recent publications include studies on the contemporary politics of haka, the misrepresentation of Māori women in Shakespeare, and the Pacific feminism of Disney's *Moana.* She is co-editor of *Off Book: Devised Performance and Higher Education* and co-author of a monograph celebrating the history of the influential Māori theatre company Taki Rua. She is currently a co-investigator on an interdisciplinary project exploring affect and emotion in interactive media.

TONY MCCAFFREY is Lecturer in Creative Industries at the National Academy of Singing and Dramatic Art, Ara Institute, Christchurch, New Zealand. He has been an actor, director, and writer for many years and is Artistic Director of Different Light Theatre, an ensemble of learning-disabled artists founded in 2004 that has performed in New Zealand, Australia, the United States, and the United Kingdom. McCaffrey is co-convenor of the Performance and Disability Working Group of the International Federation for Theatre Research. He is the author of *Incapacity and Theatricality: Politics and Aesthetics in Theatre Involving Actors with Intellectual Disabilities* and *Giving and Taking Voice in Learning Disabled Theatre*, as well as a number of book chapters and journal articles.

MICHAEL MCKINNIE is Professor of Theatre at Queen Mary University of London. His research focuses primarily on theatre's relationship with political economy and its role in urban development. He is the author of, among other things, *Theatre in Market Economies* and *City Stages: Theatre and Urban Space in a Global City*, and is the editor of *Space and the Geographies of Theatre*.

DEREK MILLER is John L. Loeb Professor of the Humanities at Harvard University, where he teaches on theatre, dance, and media in the English Department. His research seeks a macro perspective on theatre's material operations, particularly since the nineteenth century, in the United States and United Kingdom. He is the author of *Copyright and the Value of Performance, 1770–1911* and is currently writing a data-driven history of Broadway.

PRARTHANA PURKAYASTHA is Reader in the Department of Drama, Theatre and Dance at Royal Holloway, University of London. Her monograph *Indian Modern Dance, Feminism and Transnationalism* won the de la Torre Bueno Prize and the Outstanding Publication Award from the Dance Studies Association. She is co-editor of *The Oxford Handbook of Indian Dance* (with Anurima Banerji) and of *Theatre*

Research International's special issue 'Sounding Corporeality' (with Aoife McGrath, Tereza Havelková, and Marcus Tan). Her current research project explores a decolonial method of reading dance images, engaging historiography, visual culture, and critical theories on race, gender, and sexuality.

PAUL RAE is Head of the School of Culture and Communication and Professor in Theatre Studies at the University of Melbourne. He is the author of *Theatre & Human Rights* and *Real Theatre: Essays in Experience*. He is a past editor of *Theatre Research International* and has published widely on contemporary theatre and on the performance cultures of the Asia-Pacific region.

JULIA M. RITTER is an award-winning dance artist and scholar whose work demonstrates the integration of her training in dance, voice, and theatre with interdisciplinary methods of enquiry. She is the author of *Tandem Dances: Choreographing Immersive Performance*. She has received the Selma Jeanne Cohen Lecture Prize (Fulbright Association) and the André G. Bourassa Prize for Creative Research from the Société québécoise d'études théâtrales (Canada) for her scholarship on dance and immersive performance. Other awards include three Fulbright Scholar Awards and an Individual Artist Choreographic Fellowship Award from the New Jersey State Council on the Arts. Ritter is the recipient of a Presidential Outstanding Faculty Scholar Award from Rutgers University in New Jersey, and serves as Dean of the USC Glorya Kaufman School of Dance.

BEN SPATZ is a non-binary researcher and theorist of embodied practice. They are a reader in drama, theatre, and performance at the University of Huddersfield; author of *What a Body Can Do*, *Blue Sky Body: Thresholds for Embodied Research*, and *Making a Laboratory: Dynamic Configurations with Transversal Video*; and founding editor of the videographic *Journal of Embodied Research* and the Advanced Methods imprint at Punctum Books. They have more than two decades of experience as a performer of contemporary theatre and have been invited to present at more than thirty institutions in seventeen countries. They are artistic director of Urban Research Theater.

KATERINA TEAIWA is Professor and Deputy Director in the School of Culture, History and Language at the Australian National University, Senior Fellow of the Higher Education Academy, and Vice-President of the Australian Association for Pacific Studies. She is of Banaban,

I-Kiribati, and African American heritage, born and raised in Fiji. Teaiwa is the author of *Consuming Ocean Island: Stories of People and Phosphate from Banaba*. She is a founding member of the Oceania Dance Theatre at the University of the South Pacific, and a visual artist with the ongoing research-based exhibition *Project Banaba*, originally commissioned by Carriageworks in Sydney and curated by Yuki Kihara. She is Chair of the Oceania Working Party for the *Australian Dictionary of Biography*, Art Editor for *Contemporary Pacific: A Journal of Island Affairs*, and an editorial board member of the *Journal of the Royal Anthropological Institute* and the *Asia Pacific Journal of Anthropology*.

JONAS TINIUS is Scientific Coordinator and Postdoctoral Researcher in Cultural Anthropology in the European Research Council project Minor Universality: Narrative World Constructions after Western Universalism, at Saarland University, and is an associate member of the Centre for Anthropological Research on Museums and Heritage at Humboldt-Universität zu Berlin. Tinius is the author of *State of the Arts: An Ethnography of German Theatre and Migration* and co-edited *Across Anthropology: Troubling Colonial Legacies, Museums, and the Curatorial* (with Margareta von Oswald) and the two-volume book *Der Fremde Blick: Roberto Ciulli und das Theater an der Ruhr* (with Alexander Wewerka). His research focuses on the social grappling with art, nation, identity, migration, and colonial legacies in institutionalized forms of cultural production (theatres, museums, and galleries).

MELÊ YAMOMO is Assistant Professor of Theatre, Media, and Artistic Research at the University of Amsterdam and the author of *Sounding Modernities: Theatre and Music in Manila and the Asia Pacific, 1869–1946*. He is Co-project Leader and Principal Investigator of the European Joint Programming Initiative on Cultural Heritage project Decolonizing Southeast Asian Archives, as well as of the Sonic Entanglements: Listening to Modernities in Southeast Asian Sound Recordings project funded by the Dutch Research Council. yamomo, winner of the Open Ear Award 2022, is also a composer and theatre maker and is a resident artist at Theater Ballhaus Naunynstraße in Berlin. As artist-scholar, he engages the topics of global and colonial performance histories, sonic migrations, and post/decolonial acoustemologies.

SOO RYON YOON is NRF Academic Professor at the Institute for East Asian Studies, Sungkonghoe University (South Korea). Her research and teaching focus on the racial and gender politics of contemporary Korean and East Asian performance. Her writings have appeared in various journals, including *positions: asia critique*, *Inter-Asia Cultural Studies*, and *Performance Research*, and in the edited volumes *Corporeal Politics: Dancing East Asia* and *History Has Failed Us but No Matter: 2019 Venice Biennale Catalogue for Korean Pavilion*, among others. She received her PhD in performance studies from Northwestern University. Postdoctoral Associate at Yale University and an Assistant Professor at Lingnan University.

Acknowledgements

This project was hatched at a seminar sponsored by the Wenner-Gren Foundation and the Alexander von Humboldt Foundation. Efforts by several graduate assistants advanced the book's preparation, notably Oscar Serquiña, Eloise Mignon, and Alex Knapp. In the latter phases, the Dyason Fellowship enabled the editors to collaborate in person at the University of Melbourne; we are grateful to Jacqueline Doyle, who facilitated arrangements. William N. West and Stefka Mihaylova generously and generatively responded to the Introduction. Finally, Maria De Simone and Jessica Hinds-Bond lent expertise in manuscript preparation. Our thanks to all.

Introduction: Mix and Stir

Tracy C. Davis

At the outset of my course on theatre and performance research methods – a topic I have offered about twenty times – I ask the doctoral students to tally the number of years of education they have completed. In classes averaging a dozen students, some of whom have master's degrees, the tally around the seminar table quickly adds up to over two hundred years. Despite two centuries of diligent and successful studentship, virtually no one has ever taken a course on research methods, though information retrieval skills could stand in for this (among students who took the course in the early 1990s), cultural theory might be understood as this (especially during the 2000s), and practice-as-research (a legitimate but only partial substitute) has sometimes been mentioned (in the years since 2010). To think differently requires a new orientation to the making of knowledge. Two centuries is a lot of time to focus on accumulating knowledge of content – such as theatre history, dramatic literature, and performance theory – rather than on understanding how that content was derived. Most students excel at identifying what scholarship argues yet find it difficult to switch gears and focus on how research comes into being. Given that discovery is the hallmark of doctoral dissertations, I try to guide students to inductively recognize how others' research transpired so that, in time, they may propose their own project, justify a plan for how to do it, feel confident during the research process, and know how to switch up their tactics if circumstances warrant. Transparency about this process is the basic promise taken up in this book. This chapter explains how theatre and performance studies (hereafter, TaPS) research typically proceeds and how approaches combine to reflect the complexity of enquiries. This should ease the way for anyone seeking a firmer foothold by demystifying processes and providing vocabulary for what it is we do when we 'do research'.

Part of the challenge is learning to be precise about how we account for efforts. My course is organized on the book-a-week model – including the latest prize-winning titles – and arrays as many contrasting approaches as possible. Students are charged with determining how the research proceeded. Their statements such as 'the author looked for sources on topic A' receive my rejoinder 'what is *look*?' Likewise, statements such as 'the author analysed the evidence' receive the response 'what is *analyse*?' I state these queries neutrally, yet relentlessly. This Socratic probing continues while everyone chimes in with verbs, trying to rescue classmates and beat the pattern. Finally, when someone pinpoints what they mean by 'collect' or 'read', and 'examine' or 'account', the fog starts to lift. One must 'collect', but *how*? By looking *where*, at *what*, on *which* criteria? Amidst the plethora of the possible, what is done and how is it justifiable? Once something has been 'collected', what are the criteria for noticing things of particular relevance, and thus for 'doing research'? (One *does* what? *Why*? And then one does *what else*?) It may not matter whether the name of a specific tradition can be attached to the thing(s) done, though understanding of that will come eventually; what matters is to be conscious of the steps undertaken, each of which represents a tradition of thought, makes sense in relation to the research question(s), and delimits the enquiry. Theatre and performance research is complex; complex research is *designed*; and to design involves forethought about what are likely to be the best ways to investigate a compelling question and derive explanations. In this book, we call these steps *planning* (the design of a project), *doing* (methods of garnering information), and *interpreting* (methodologies for explaining).

When conducting research, looking for and collecting information differs from construing information into arguments. This is a key insight for humanities projects: there will be a set of activities involving intentional effort to seek and identify stuff (not 'the topic', but something about the topic that a researcher hopes to learn through increments of data) and another set of activities dedicated to understanding and explaining what this stuff adds up to (doing something with the data). For the sake of differentiation, the first kind of activity involves *methods*: ways to gather information relevant to the project, whether that information is just data or, conversely, will later become evidence (data in service of claims). The second type of activity utilizes *methodologies*: analysis (preceding or coextensive with writing) will resemble prior studies' processes of making sense of the stuff that was gathered by deploying theories (these help make narratives about data comprehensible). Methods and methodologies almost invariably exist prior to a novice researcher stepping forth to investigate something. They are 'out there' for us to learn about, understand, selectively use, and ingeniously combine. They structure what and how we research and think. To name what these antecedents are, then to purposefully engage them, is more art than science, and like arts there are techniques – protocols, skill sets, and ethics – necessary to their use. Their skilful (and defensible) use requires practice, though practice is done while learning, in smaller-scale studies that can scale up if the approach is promising. We often attain these capabilities without realizing it, which is a mercy given those two hundred-plus years of effort prior to understanding that we have choices of how to do what we do. Being asked to slow down and define 'looking' and to make considered decisions about 'analysing' holds us accountable: this is tradecraft.

Tradecraft

To know when one deploys a method and when one embarks on a methodology is helpful in a research process, even if it is a rare study that facilitates strictly consecutive deployment. Field research (say, observing a theatre company in rehearsal while taking notes on how artistic decisions are determined, using methods such as field observation, survey techniques, or interviews within the traditions of critical performance ethnography or practice-as-research) must precede analysis (reading notes, collating survey responses, or listening to recordings, and, after many iterations, listing the characteristics of the decision-making process, essential features, and variants). To take this hypothetical example further, once a list of characteristics of artistic decision-making is created, it is subject to methodological understanding in a corresponding intellectual tradition (e.g. content analysis). In tracking trends, the researcher might then want to investigate patterns; the findings could, for example, be accounted for as a system produced through activities representing deeply held cultural concepts or experiences superseding individuals (structuralism); as descriptions of actions and inter-dynamic interactions of sets of people and things (actor-network theory); or as individuals' negotiation of genealogies of practice relating to language or social structure coalescing into institutionalized ways of thinking (discourse theory). There are more possibilities, but the point is that information gathered during field research may be subjected to multiple methodologies (traditions of interpretation), singly or in combination, and this predicates a lot about the conclusions.

Methods are selection criteria that strongly influence how a researcher spends their time. Which choices of methods will most likely facilitate finding what is germane to a question? What kind of vigilance while engaging with others, observing, or reading will result in notes useful for the analysis they will later undergo? If the research incorporates documenting a production, one might gather insight at rehearsals and watch performances. The next goal may be to understand performance vis-à-vis culture, and so a researcher might discuss the production with contributing artists, consult what artists generated in preparation for the production (such as designs), or gather traces of performance reception from digital sites or in archives or libraries. One might even turn their attention to things referred to in the production – such as contemporary events, history, or other cultural knowledge – which are 'not theatre'.

Multi-method as well as multi-methodological approaches may be needed. What is observed, who is engaged, and what is taken down as notes are consequential because the intended methodological traditions of interpretation will require that certain kinds of criteria were prioritized at the earlier stage of enquiry. Because one cannot necessarily know what matters most when setting out to design research, one must rely on skill and experience to ensure that the project's data-gathering method(s) be more efficient and ultimately useful when data is analysed. One can decide between methodologies after the observations are made, but it is impossible to note-take everything and to prepare for every interpretive contingency, especially since insight is likely to occur throughout the process. With a set of (unoptimized) notes in hand, one might then ask: Which choices are conducive to deriving the best explanations? Which characteristics of what is observed should be correlated or contrasted?

TaPS allows eclectic approaches partly because it is the sum of an academic history engaged, successively and variously, with folkloric, archaeological, anthropological, literary, sociological, philosophical, and historical approaches dedicated not only to its own performative products (such as scripts, scores, designs, and other documentation) but also to art or architecture, culture and social behaviour, cognitive processes, governance, trade, and technology (influences that each have their own methods and methodologies that fall into or out of favour over time). In justifying the validity and importance of the live event (and live events from the past), TaPS adopts the premises of other disciplines and takes up the ways these disciplines pursued their insights, yet sometimes radically changes the context. For example, in *Building Character: The Art and Science of Casting*, Amy Cook (2018: 26) acts as a 'disciplinary ambassador' between theatre scholars and cognitive linguists, promoting understanding of the consequences of casting choices. Like many other TaPS scholars interested in cognitive science, she does not do anything empirical: instead, she utilizes semiotics and reception theory to reveal 'where the character's body is constructed from words'.

In different regions and scholarly organizations, TaPS has been defined through allegiance to a particular discipline or approach (McKenzie et al., 2010; Riley & Hunter, 2009). Lately, TaPS has generated its own, distinct, methods and methodologies, such as performance genealogy, (applied) practice-as-research, and critical media history. Collectively, TaPS is a sum of these parts. This allows for a tremendous variety of enquiries, which in turn means a significant burden in understanding the tradecraft of the many traditions of enquiry, along with the opportunity to mix traditions in research design.

Drama, Theatre, and Performance Research

TaPS research sometimes begins with dramatic texts. Whereas a 'close reading' of a play text may focus on genre and form, prosody, literary and linguistic devices, and any other formalist elements (in the New Critical or Russian formalist sense), a practised student of drama 'stages' performance in the mind's eye (and ear) while reading. Anne Ubersfeld (1999: xxi) argues in *Reading Theatre* that reading a dramatic script differs from reading other kinds of texts, for 'the key lies outside itself', in the domain of performance. This is a distinction with a difference that reflects Otakar Zich's contrast between a dramatic work seen from within ('from the viewpoint of its inner relations') and one seen without (from an audience's perspective) (Gajdoš, 2007: 82). For a director or dramaturg, reading a dramatic text might entail noting the potential for double casting, picturing characters' interactions, and connecting the plot to the visual or sonic world that the characters inhabit. An actor may think about what a specific character does and how they express themselves, experience or promulgate the consequences of ideology, and navigate their world. Setting out to do research, a scholar may find it advantageous to try to 'experience' the play from a spectator's vantage, to inhabit one of these theatre makers' identities, or to approximate a historicized perspective with culturally specific knowledge about staging, acting practices, dramatic theory, social history, and formalist norms.

The printing of plays has evolved in ways that presume readers' engagement beyond what is on the page, necessitating a shift towards performative criteria (Peters, 2000; Worthen, 2005; 2010). Dramatic scripts tend to be replete with dialogue and sparing about everything else, yet specific methods become involved in reading practices when, for example, a phenomenological approach investigates the experience of stage time (which differs from both reading time and elapsed time), querying how action unfolds through plot sequencing and how this temporal unfolding is conveyed through design elements, pacing, and visual storytelling. For a researcher, this predicates an infinite set of possibilities for a putative audience's experience, but stops well short of such an experience in the reading. The distinction that arises between the work on the stage and what the playwright calls for in staging is hinted at in Table 1.1.

Though a solely intrinsic approach to textual analysis in any tradition of criticism – psychoanalytic, structuralist, materialist, feminist, postcolonial, and so on – is a likely starting point in research, it is no longer a typical goal in TaPS (Walker, 2006). As scripts are regarded as performance-in-potential, a kind of companion to the mise en scène of performance, or a pale shadow of a complex production genealogy, a performative analysis is likely to occur, emphasizing what could transpire multi-sensorially in production. If productions have occurred, a researcher may also want to ascertain what was experienced and then recorded. There is mediation in all these steps. Eyewitness accounts of performance are not reportage (as with play-by-play real-time sports coverage) but what Patrice Pavis (2003: 9–10) calls 'analysis by reconstruction', whether as evaluative reviews or as descriptions. Even when scholars write about what they have witnessed, they do so after the fact, as historians. Their emphases typically fall upon: (1) what happens on and around the stage, (2) the holistic complexity of the event, and (3) theatre in culture (in which case extrinsic research is engaged).

Table 1.1 schematizes a set of play-related questions to differentiate practices of reading, staging in the mind's eye (and ear), accounting for staged choices, and explicating the event within its cultural setting. The first three types of enquiry – intrinsic, performative, and historical approaches – accord with what Christopher B. Balme (2008: 127) terms the theatrical text, the production (any specific staging of the text), and the performance on a given occasion. These lines of enquiry frequently combine in research projects. If the research highlights, for example, a key production within a project about a director's aesthetic, then the onus may be on specifying the choices in the case study's mise en scène, comparing and contrasting these with other examples from the director's oeuvre, and contextualizing them against other directors' productions of the play, thus incorporating all three approaches (intrinsic, performative, and historical). Each approach gives a focus for data collection (methods), and thus a sense of what to look for. If the researcher has seen the production, they must choose what to do with this knowledge, perhaps combining their own sense of the performance (e.g. notes and memories) with other available sources (such as designs,

Table 1.1 *Theatre and performance studies (TaPS) analysis template*

	Question	Focus for methods	Assumption	Predominant methodologies
Intrinsic (text)	*What characterizes this play as a work on the page?*	Genre, form, style Ideology Plot, sequencing Prosody, speech Setting, characters	Interpretation depends upon the use and combination of formalist elements	Deconstruction Formalism Philology Semiotics
Performative (mise en scène)	*How can the play be staged?*	Characterological inflection, interaction Incorporation of other performance forms Light, scenic, costume, and sound elements Onstage and offstage worlds Stylization, pacing, temporalities	Interpretation is a sensory experience, even as a reading practice, which calls forth imagined performance possibilities	Dramaturgical Phenomenology Semiotics
Historical (case study)	*What staging choices were made in a given production?*	Casting, acting, proxemics Producers' history (company ethos, relation to repertoire, intertheatricality) Production history Specific mises-en-scène: acting, scenography, etc.	Historical location of performance will affect production choices (relative to text) and predicate reception, subject to interpretation and misunderstanding	Performance genealogy Performance reconstruction Semiotics
Extrinsic (reception)	*What does the play have to do with the culture that produced it, and with concurrent concerns?*	'Context' for interpretation of the production Horizon of expectations for audiences Meaning in/for culture Performance as social rite Resonance with concurrent issues	Interpretation involves the 'cultural moment', which is seen differently in retrospect, and the habitus (habits, skills, and dispositions) of the producing and/or receiving culture	Discourse theory Material and object theory Reception studies Resistant critiques Semiotics

illustrations, reviews, and prompt books) to constitute evidence leading to understanding the production's genesis into a particular set of choices and results. Once there is data to work with, research on the case study can be further developed through methodological choices. For example, a post-structuralist approach may regard as 'dead' both the playwright (irrelevant to the autonomous artistic acts of theatre makers) and the director (irrelevant to spectators' critical acts of performance interpretation), whereas a psychoanalytic approach may dig deep into the playwright's and/or director's biography. The fourth approach, extrinsic, focuses on reception and is predicated on the circulating stew of cultural and political preoccupations and knowledge of performance repertoires that inflect how a given performance (or production) is capable of being understood and prompting reactions. Exemplary versions of this approach can be found in Ric Knowles's (2004: 17) case studies in *Reading the Material Theatre*, which model 'precisely *how* audiences produce meaning in negotiation with the particular, local theatrical event', following methodological antecedents by Marvin Carlson (1989) in semiotics and Susan Bennett (1997) in reader-response theory.

For Prague School linguist Jiří Veltruský, drama stands on its own as a work of art yet also transforms into another kind of art work, which he called 'the scenic situation' (Gajdoš, 2007: 87, 89). TaPS offers tailor-made approaches for identifying information about 'scenic situations', as well as approaches adopted from other disciplines. Pavis (2003: 9), who, like Ubersfeld and Erika Fischer-Lichte, is influenced by semiotics, allows for psychological, psychoanalytic, sociological, anthropological, and intercultural approaches to analysis of mises-en-scène. He also delineates phenomenological criteria to enable a spectator to specify an overall sense of a performance developed with 'neither the apparent objectivity of empirical observation, nor the absolute universality of abstract theory', lying between 'detailed yet fragmentary description and general, unverifiable theory, between formless signifiers and polysemic signifieds'. P. N. Campbell (1982: 11–21) refers to the facets of a play's existence (as script, staged work, and received production) as interdependent rhetorics that can strengthen, amend, alter, or oppose (the understanding of) a text. Rhetorics are specific to each play, and unique to each production, yet for them to be understood requires playgoers to have cultural knowledge that lies outside performance. Thus, Campbell considers it valuable to think across multiple categories to discern the full scope of a performance. The last column in Table 1.1 indicates some (but by no means all) of the concerns that may be engaged on behalf of indicative questions about matters extrinsic to the play text, and the methodologies that accord to them. Not all kinds of analysis may be possible or sensible for every circumstance, and frequently the methodologies will be additively mixed to sustain different facets of an enquiry, account for different kinds of information, and craft a more replete account.

Table I.1's schema is useful for approaching many kinds of performance, including non-dramatic (non-textually sourced) types. When one is considering performance art, for example, the focus may be on a case study (without either the antecedent or post facto 'trace' of a script), but formalist and phenomenological concerns of intrinsic and performative analysis still pertain. In this vein, when Patrick Anderson (2010: 91–93) marks 'the break from theatrical conventions signaled and emblematized' in Ana Mendieta's and Marina Abramović's performance art works (which took place in art galleries and the open air), he accounts for aesthetic elements and shows how these bear on extrinsic reception. He argues that the works have a performance genealogy distinct from theatre, and yet, he stipulates, 'I do not mean to consign these artists' work strictly to the domain of body art'; instead, he sees their work 'precisely as performance, in the broadest possible sense of that word'. He attends to the 'social, cultural, and political impact' of works, specifically the way that durationality in performance and spectacularity relates to affect's ability to shift cultural-political contexts. For analytical purposes, such 'impacts' of performance have common grounds with performative, historical, and extrinsic analysis of drama.

Likewise, in her explication of movement in contemporary performance, Rachel Fensham (2021: 3–4) signals a relationship between the performative and extrinsic analyses of Table I.1. 'What' questions translate to 'how' questions predicated on spectators' connecting viewing to meaningful things in their own experience. This can be the essence of an analysis focused on extrinsic concerns. For example, she argues that performance strips down form, allowing for 'macro- and micro-levels of attention at one and the same time, with extension – spatial, rhythmic, haptic – into the world around the self'. This emphasizes the kinds of things a spectator attends to, deploying formalist criteria to experience a work phenomenologically. Attending to how we pay attention to the ways movement functions across a range of registers leads to a set of historically framed but culturally conscious questions: 'in what ways do the learned and specialized techniques of performing bodies contribute to understandings of social and political understandings of movement?'

With a performative (not textual) starting point, close attention to both traditions and choices in performance connects case studies to culture and history with specificity (and through the explanatory work afforded by theory). This framework gives scope for many kinds of resistant critique (queer, feminist, Indigenous, Black, Global South, etc.) that track what Fensham (2021: 142) describes as 'perceptions of movement [that] are both internal and observational, and eminently social and political' for different bodies. Such modes of critique take into account viewers' awareness of 'lived possibilities in patterns of production, consumption and imagination', while also relating to globalization, scaling up the nature of the enquiry (Fensham, 2021: 153). Through case studies of performance, Fensham demonstrates how distinct traditions and locations of interpretation connect the mechanics of movement to subjectivity. Subjectivity, in turn, is integral for applying methodologies related to postcolonial and feminist frameworks, which link formalism to phenomenology and affect studies. Relating production case studies to reception in such ways is a frequent approach, but it is not ubiquitous.

Incompleteness and Unrecoverability

Some TaPS research has entirely different points of departure. For example, Christin Essin's (2021) *Working Backstage: A Cultural History and Ethnography of Technical Theater Labor* has little to no use for the analytical criteria of Table 1.1, for it is about the work of performance-making rather than performance per se. Essin shows how, from the perspective of scholarship, knowledge is gathered 'out there' (whether from live people or their artefacts) and synthesized as new insights for the academic sphere. Essin's niche is the occupational landscape of Broadway's technicians. Her case study contributes to the sociology of work, yet her methods are common in TaPS (interviews conducted over several years, augmented by archival research). Initially, Essin (2021: 22) relied on her own contacts from when she was a technician in regional theatre, but the scope of interviewees expanded as participants suggested and helped recruit additional participants (snowball sampling). From copious interviews, she derived a taxonomy of positions and their hierarchies, built up through profiles of individuals. There is no eventhood of rehearsing, opening, and running a production in these human profiles, but rather tasks, careers, and personal networks. Theatre-making is at the centre, yet performance is rather incidental to the professional ethnography, which widely skirts the idea of production histories (Essin, 2021: 18). Individual informants' testimony facilitates network analysis of a cultural unit (Broadway theatre in general and the history and identity of the New York branch of the stageworkers' union more specifically) in the structuralist tradition, and that is the basis of the methodology. Still, the work of specialists such as dressers and child guardians is revealed as affective labour: here, Essin (2021: 147–51, 172) pivots to affect studies to interpret these jobs, documenting how work in shows such as *Matilda the Musical* (2010) generates this type of labour.

Whereas Essin's approach is to find something knowable, research it, and then explicate it – creating a sense of completeness out of her data – since the 1990s much TaPS research has explored ephemerality, incompleteness, and the limits of the knowable. Odai Johnson excels at this, demonstrating the possibilities for thinking relationally even with the slightest of evidence. For example, in *Ruins: Classical Theatre and Broken Memory*, Johnson (2018: 129) draws on Franco Moretti's (2005) concept of mapping to posit the city of Rome and its ancient performances not as a calendar or typology of events but '*as a process* through which imperial ideology and the topographies of power are enacted, disenacted, and rendered visible' a posteriori. This de-emphasizes the need for clarity of any single source or event in favour of many types of sources connected to social scripts, resulting in 'the palimpsest moments when the [social] script and the subscript create a sort of weirdly coherent bilingual exchange'. Though there are delimiters of place and period, this may be as far from a case study as one can get.

Whereas most researchers seek specific kinds of evidence rather than notice evidence that is lacking, Johnson (2021: 44–5) regards locating 'holes' as a valid discovery of another sort:

> Evidence is the beam work that keeps the discipline [of history] upright. But that reliance also trains the eye to look for what is left, not for what has been left out, eliding the absence to alight on events. But the missing can sometimes be the most interesting part of the record.... A well-structured absence retains traces of the disappeared, like the curated frame of the stolen painting, or the odd staple holes of missing pages.

The staple holes in a document (like the postholes of an early Virginian theatre in another of Johnson's studies, his 2006 *Absence and Memory in Colonial American Theatre*) mark a *former* presence and thus a history for the pages or building foundations that are destroyed, rotted, lost, misplaced, or misapprehended. Holes are evidence of something, and even if that something cannot be seen or known it can be known about through its trace (Johnson, 2006). For Johnson (2018: 4–5), all data is relevant – especially theatre's 'scars, shards, and stumpage, its ruins, and the ruins beneath the ruins' – but not, however, as an empiricist cataloguing project (which would have no interpretive methodology). He embraces non-repleteness, non-replicability, and non-recoverability with an exceptional level of comfort about absence (not merely ambiguity). Still, he will suddenly stop short of an inductive insight. For example, though intrigued by the dualistic opposition of presence and absence, Johnson does not resolve across known and unknown data points to mark a stratigraphic trend. This Derridean approach is not *anti-method* but rather reflects a profound *mixing* of methodologies, utilizing philology to connect language to its deep meaning; object-oriented materialism to consider the pre-history, history, and post-history of something's creation and usage, as well as its disappearance or negative trace; discourse theory's relations between language, social structure, and individual agency to broach institutionalized ways of thinking and being; and network analysis to cleave to descriptions (who or what did something) rather than concepts (society, capitalism, empire, norms, individualism, scapes, etc.). Gaps left unfilled can be resplendent emptiness (Davis, 2004).

In historical research, the sensory unknowability of performances and their reception is a commonplace. For the contemporary period, there are methods aimed at excavating reception directly from audiences. Historians' fascination with the sensory experience of theatre-going is broached by different means. Scott A. Trudell (2020: 370–1), for example, emphasizes aural reception: 'Sound studies offers a helpful model in which written texts act as acoustic records – transcriptions, imitations, or "earwitnesses", a term for representing or recalling sound.' This has been leveraged through approaches faithful to the overlapping of 'writing, speech, dance, musical composition, acoustic performance, and visual art' common to many periods and styles. Judith Pascoe's *The Sarah Siddons Audio Files* takes up this challenge, positing a search for the voice of the actress Sarah Siddons (active 1774–1812). The book documents a succession of approaches to identify, combine, analyse, and synthesize relevant information, dwelling on 'the notes taken by George Joseph Bell', a Scottish jurist expert in mercantile law, 'while he was sitting in Siddons's audience' (Pascoe, 2011: 96; see also Bell, ca. 1806). Because of Pascoe's eclectic approach (not despite it), her discovery maps a kind of resplendent emptiness: she concedes that no matter what she does, and no matter how hard she tries to listen, she – in contrast to Bell – cannot hear Siddons's voice.

Like an entire generation enthralled by Siddons, Bell was fascinated by her declamation. Seventy years before the invention of the phonograph, he sought to 'record' the actress's vocal performance by annotating a script, and Pascoe does what she can with these marks of emphasis and cadence, and descriptions of tonality, volume, and quality. Pascoe found Bell's circa

1806 notations, which were transcribed and published by H. C. Fleeming Jenkin in 1878, invaluable. But for what? Comparing the published transcript to Bell's manuscript, Pascoe (2011: 100) examined Bell's observations on Lady Macbeth 'at snail speed'. Observing how punctuation was (mis) transcribed by Jenkin from Bell, she also noticed a feature of Bell's diction: when accounting for 'reactions to Siddons's acting … he did so in the second person, writing that her anxiety in the banquet scene "makes you creep with apprehension", and that her emotion "keeps you breathless"'. Through equally assiduous attention to the discourse of other ear witnesses, Pascoe tried to summon several historically specific facets of late eighteenth-century playgoers' habitus: scrupulous and undivided attention to key scenes and extensive experience of attending many performers' interpretations as well as Shakespearean recitations within social circles. To simulate the historical habitus within her research process, she dedicated time in the University of Iowa Libraries' media department to listen to a host of actresses' recordings of Lady Macbeth on a panoply of obsolete playback machines. She tried to align this with her own immersive experience in an introductory voice class, where she learned about and attempted mastery of breath control. The intent was to generate knowledge that integrated trace evidence of a phantom performance genealogy by listening to great performers from the era of sound recording, together with attaining embodied understanding of technique.

This incorporation of practice-as-research failed to recover early nineteenth-century theatre-goers' experience of Siddons's aesthetic. A spiralling hermeneutic of data generation and intentional acts of analysis could not approximate an alien consciousness. Bell had Siddons's *voice* in his head, which is exactly what Pascoe could not summon, and he knew what it *felt like* to hear it in contrast to other performers' instruments. These were two wraiths in Pascoe's perceptual quest. She concludes that not even time travel could breach this gap:

> Even if I could be whisked back to 1809 and take a seat in the Covent Garden theater, even if George Joseph Bell was jabbing me with his elbow … I would not be an equal sharer in the pleasures of Siddons's performances because I would not … have a vast dramatic repertoire filed away in my brain, with subfiling for variant performances of particular roles. I would sit like a listening-impaired lump, clutching a sad little clothespin bag of Shakespearean quotations, while Siddons made the rest of the audience resonate like harp strings. (Pascoe, 2011: 103)

Despite the attempts at synthesis and recuperation, not even hearing Siddons's phantasmic voice would give a historically situated experience of its timbre, cadences, and thrilling effects. This is a variant on researching absence: something known to have existed, its qualities described and its minutiae transferred from ear to pen, yet an unrecoverable aesthetic experience (and thus unrecoverable knowledge). The historian's role, in such circumstances, is to accede to the ephemerality and the elusiveness of sonic and affective performance genealogies. Utilizing these mixed methods and methodologies traces the contours of what is unreachable.

Johnson and Pascoe demonstrate how multiple methods can show the contours of information, but it is through methodologies that scholars account for what the gaps convey, which gaps can be plugged, and whether an answer is possible. To comprehend the nature of pluralities (as well as the disjunctions), and account for inexorable and ineluctable uncertainty, is the hallmark of deconstruction. Yet, given that there are limits to all endeavours in knowledge-seeking, how do scholars choose other approaches? What else has post-structuralist theory made possible?

Mixology and the Role of Theory

Graduate school puts a premium on learning 'theory' (an imperative best stated in the plural). Theories are scaffolded upon premises derived from extensive observation, category construction, and reduction. For example, observation of living species and fossilized remains, then recognition of variation and adaptation across many species, led to the theory of natural selection. Once established as an explanatory schema, natural selection could be tested in myriad circumstances and extrapolated to account for phenomena in macro and micro contexts. So, too, in cultural theory, but here there is tradecraft to consider. It is folly to take a theory and slam it on any phenomenon at will: natural selection cannot account for why one performance aesthetic takes hold while others fade away any more than it can explain the rise and ebb of civilizations. Theories are useful for some things, but not everything. As a case in point, Pascoe shows affect theory's limits: the detailed ekphrastic accounts of Siddons's voice from the past, combined with exegeses of later performers' recordings, cannot bring to the surface an empirical understanding of corporeal, expressive, or receptive practices in the twenty-first-century researcher (even if she is equipped with a time machine).

TaPS eclectically endorses the value of qualitative experiential and observation-based methods and methodologies (such as practice-as-research and ethnography) as well as techniques in which theoretical deduction is the basis of understanding (such as material and object analysis, deconstruction, and speech-act theory). All these approaches are theory led, even when empirical. Some approaches combine better than others – socio-semiotics and structuralism, resistant critiques and phenomenology, or critical ethnography and discourse theory – so methodological eclecticism is not random or nominal. The designators of many methodologies in Table 1.2 have the tag word *theory* attached to them – affect theory, actor-network theory, material and object theory – which indicates a body of thought, with suppositions and protocols, that in adoption employs particular criteria to identify and gather evidence (through methods) and test its resilience to explain (through methodologies).

Theories are widely accepted concepts that explain many observed effects about fundamental things – special relativity, heliocentrism, climate change, pervasive gender bias, the social construction of race, all of which are theories whether or not the word *theory* is tagged on – whereas *hypotheses* are tentative suggestions subject to testing. A theory alone does not have propositional force, but an enquiry can proceed when a hypothesis relates a theory to the investigation at hand. For example, critical media history (a theory without the term *theory*) pluralistically accounts for performances' function as a memory machine for human experience, yet an enquiry must posit something about a specific instance or pattern in order to draw out the relational meanings. Scaffolding an argument that validates or challenges how something is remediated out of prior performative instantiations can demonstrate not just that repertoires are recombinative (the theory) but also how they manifest (the analysis resulting from applying critical media history's methodologies to evidence) (Davis & Marx, 2021).

In the humanities, research design may lean on theory predictively, though even with follow-through that engages appropriate methods and methodologies we are unlikely to 'prove' a hypothesis so much as proliferate interpretations. In archive-based work, for example, Maggie B. Gale and Ann Featherstone identify 'evidence-gathering with a view to the destabilization, reorganization or reordering of a historical position or perspective' as an approach to generating 'a *version* of history' (Gale & Featherstone, 2011: 37–8). They stress the value of entering an archive with a parcel of good questions, as well as being open to the serendipity of connecting points of information through a creative process. This inherently creative process is not conducive to proving hypotheses; historical research is fraught 'with the dynamic complexities of memory acquisition and replay' in new contexts (including the influence of new or additional theories) (Gale & Featherstone, 2011: 24). This is not simply a contrast between the empiricism of science and the qualitative bias of the humanities, or an

Table 1.2 *Analytical traditions and their associated methods and methodologies*

Analytical traditions, with key advocates	Tenets	Methods	Methodologies
Actor-Network Theory Bruno Latour John Law Michel Callon Annemarie Mol	Connections and exchanges: people, ideas, things across boundaries, inter-dynamics, and associations Allows for manageable scales of enquiry (especially micro studies)	Focus on human or object 'actors' and the relations between them Micro can mean looking at different scales, local to global – not all small-scale interactions can be observed, so seek evidence of their effects	Focus on descriptions (who/what does what), not concepts (society, capitalism, empire, norms, individualism, fields, etc.) Use 'immutable mobiles' to measure and represent connections (including charts, graphs, and texts)
Affect Theory Silvan Tomkins Eve Sedgwick Lauren Berlant Brian Massumi Sara Ahmed Daniel O'Quinn	Refutes linguistic sources and explanations Eschews causal explanations in favour of fluid mental or somatic activity (feelings/moods/corporeal states/atmospheres) that may not be valorized by other kinds of explanation In performance reception, this can account for a response spectrum that is not based in linguistic narrative, or semiotic comprehension In performance criticism, it privileges experience that is neither under conscious control nor within registered awareness; this may be correlated to politics, wellness, or pathology	Historical researchers look for discursive, iconic, or other expressive accounts Empirical researchers look for emergent, corporeal, or expressive practices Affect escapes or exceeds analytic capture by reason, knowledge, language, and perception, so marking its existence (in others) can be challenging	Exegesis or ekphrasis Affective labour, including performing, may be described relationally or functionally Corporeal repertoires emerge expressively, and can be perceived sensorially as performance Can trace how semiotics gets cultural take-up as social scripts in circulation

Content Analysis Harold Lasswell Bernard Berelson	Evaluate text/language for specific proclivities to infer about message, writer(s), audience, and culture Objective, systematic, quantitative description of communication Particularly useful to analyse media content	For conceptual analysis, code content of published texts, interviews, open-ended surveys, fieldwork notes, conversations, web content, iconic texts, film, etc. Coding 'rules' are determined by researcher Focus at the level of word, sense, phrasing, themes; code for existence or frequency; quantitative results can be generated through software or by hand	Observation and narrative based on relational analysis of coded content Track trends; determine psychological or affective content; make generalizations Cognitive mapping; proximity analysis
Critical Media History *Annalist historiography* Stephen Greenblatt Arjun Appadurai Paul Ricœur Elizabeth Maddock Dillon Jonas Barish Friedemann Kreuder Tracy C. Davis and Peter W. Marx	Draws widely from Marxism, rhetoric, cultural analysis, formalism, reception studies, and resistant critiques Performance history as collage, inclusive of transregional contexts, continual change and recombination, and complex interdependencies Theatre and the wider field of performance are mutually constitutive and recombinative as repertoires Theatre, festivals, gatherings, and rites are co-constitutive of the performative field along with the technologies and ideologies they utilize for communication	Acts of spectating specific to cultures and specific formats for the apparatuses and materials of presentation manifest through practices that frame and shape media Materialist evidence of the sensorium allies through representation with the specificity of location; the social form of performance; and constructs such as nation-state and imperium	Account for how performance functions as a memory machine for human experience and communication to deploy the past and shape understanding Scenography, style, and technique are technologies of sensation derived through dramaturgy and subject to distribution by demographic contact and trade routes Pluralistic accounts Recursivity and remediatization Scales from single events to macrohistory

Table 1.2 (*cont.*)

Analytical traditions, with key advocates	Tenets	Methods	Methodologies
Critical Performance Ethnography Clifford Geertz Norman K. Denzin Dwight Conquergood Della Pollock D. Soyini Madison	Combines theorizing with empirically observed data Ethics in fieldwork are paramount; recognize that methodological choices are political Researcher's standpoint and intersectional identities are implicated	Participant observer, auto-ethnography, oral history, and field observation methods Can involve observation of performance; making of performance; everyday life	Incorporates a multitude of methodological traditions to account for fieldwork observations Qualitative interpretation; active reflection on theories and methods; advocacy; accountability Derives grounded theory Dramaturgical analysis of performance and social rites
Deconstruction Jacques Derrida Paul de Man Jonathan Culler J. Hillis Miller	Exposes unquestioned assumptions within philosophical and literary language, unquestioned metaphysical assumptions, and internal contradictions Metaphysical appeal to presence through *differánce*	'Close reading' focuses on irreconcilable contradictions; boundaries between binaries Look for counter-examples to assumptions and paradigms	Recognize the given paradigm: build 'the structure' then introduce problems (what does not fit, and what contradicts it) Account for plurality Assess assumptions and evident assumed binaries, paradigms Dismantle logics of interpretation
Discourse Analysis Jacques Derrida Michel Foucault Fredric Jameson Julia Kristeva Louis Althusser Michel de Certeau Shannon Jackson	Relations between language, social structure, and individual agency are institutionalized ways of thinking Determines what can be taken to be true/real Language as social practice, reproducing (or subverting) political inequity Subsumes post-structuralist, normative-deliberative, and critical-realist discourse theories Theory arises out of specific contexts	Largely linguistic evidence; includes texts, surveys, quantitative data 'Close reading' attentive to how discourses create and reflect conflict (inclusive of language and other kinds of knowledge) Intertextuality	Relate genealogies of practice to political economy, class, or materialist analysis; connect structures, power, and subjectivity Identify how individual agents negotiate structures; account for context Anti-essentialize: problematize concepts taken as natural Question ontological centre; bring into relation with social control

Formalism *Russian formalism* *New Criticism* *dramaturgical analysis* Caroline Levine	Characteristics of formal analysis are meaningful of themselves: the text or production stands on its own Form offers clues to other types of corroboration	Identify literary figures, grammar, syntax, genres, etc.; performative characteristics (style) Engage surface/depth strategies to explicate multiple levels of meaning (the obvious as well as the hidden)	Demonstrate internal patterning (self-contained self-referential objects reveal interior logics) *What* literature or performance says arises from *how* it says it
Materialism *Marxism and Neo-Marxism* (Raymond Williams, Louis Althusser, Henri Lefebvre, Wendy Brown) *public sphere theory* (Jürgen Habermas, Michael Warner, David Harvey) Jean Baudrillard Jacques Rancière Pierre Bourdieu Bruce McConachie Tracy C. Davis Joshua Chambers-Letson	Ongoing re-evaluation of classical economics (the tradition of Adam Smith, David Ricardo, Karl Marx, John Stuart Mill, and Jean-Baptiste Say) in a spectrum of collectivist and liberal varieties Can be structuralist, post-structuralist, or postmodern in locus Meaning can be totalizing or elusive, saturating experience or eluding its impacts and traces Dialectical materialism Performance can reinforce statist prerogatives or facilitate emancipation and survival	Focus on questions about production, economics, labour, value, and consumption Relations and effects among the state, institutions, and individuals evident through space, investment, representation, and relative privilege and constraints Economic impacts scale from the economy as a whole (concerns such as employment, output, and trade) to micro systems (such as private and intimate life)	Analysis can reveal structural relations of hegemony or a 'hyper-reality' of delusion and simulacra Explanations may be epistemic Knowledge as theoretical practice; social theory may endorse or counter economic determinism Critiques of disparity and failures to achieve social and environmental justice

Table 1.2 (*cont.*)

Analytical traditions, with key advocates	Tenets	Methods	Methodologies
Material and Object Theory *thing theory* (Bill Brown, Maurice Merleau-Ponty) Bruno Latour Gilles Deleuze Pierre-Félix Guattari Karen Barad Timothy Morton Robin Bernstein Andrew Sofer Natasha Korda	Alfred Gell attributed 'distributed agency' to art and artefacts, suggesting a theory of 'inferred intentionality'; this counters Latour's tendency towards structuralist networking Connects how people transform the world of physical objects and how that world in turn transforms them Mutual constitution of subject and object, the animate and inanimate, person and thing, and with the ways objects mediate individual and group identities Counters long-standing emphasis on social and discursive construction with the 'textualization' of culture; instead focuses on objects (architecture, books, other human-made artefacts, as well as 'dematerialized' digital and performative media)	Focus on how people make, design, and interact with objects Recognize how everyday practices increasingly acknowledge the embeddedness of 'things' Agency is relational Performance may amplify or reveal the social circulation of meanings through material practices May focus on objects in use, in situ, or in collections (such as archives and museums) to investigate social relations	Aligned with phenomenological approaches to culture, accounts for how objects are mediated with unconscious power Objects situated in relation to belief systems, values, ideas, and assumptions Utilizes description, deduction, and speculation (sensory engagement, intellectual engagement, and emotional registers) to frame hypotheses Challenges assumptions that the object and subject are separable
Performance Genealogy Joseph Roach Diana Taylor Marvin Carlson	Performative events have performative antecedents Posits history and performance as subject to ghosting, recirculation, percolation, and surrogation Repertoires are ongoing embodied practices; archives are their counterparts in cultural memory	Recognize components (e.g. formalist compositional elements such as gestural, thematic, visual, sonic, and structural aspects of performance) Intermedia/intergenre adaptation studies	Comparatively determine lineage and combinatory resemblance, (dis) continuity, returns, and sublimation Performance history (as lineage) Allow for direct (tutelage or archival) and indirect (circulation, vortices) forms of cultural transference

Performance Reconstruction Robert Sarlós Scott Magelssen Mark Franko Ann Hutchinson Guest Rebecca Schneider Kimberly Jannarone *Second Life* *virtual reality* *living museums*	Hypothetical, discursive, or actual 'restaging' of (or through) performance can access otherwise undiscernible social, cultural, and technical information about theatre of the past Reconstruction invariably alters facets, but that in itself is important Fidelity to the original format of performance in its reconstruction matters less than selected facets of performance to focus upon	Comprehensively examine documentation of historical event; or draw on field notes of observed experience Processes of proposing and making theatre (collaborative and experiential), execution of events, and the post hoc analysis of these processes renders data	Account for the site and/or event, holistically or in part (e.g. entire choreography or performance vs indicative acting style) Justify and compare consequences of choices, for example, locale, materials, spatial arrangements, mise en scène, casting in relation to the performance Measure and evaluate 'difference' and speculate on unquantifiable 'incommensurate' contrasts of past and present Applications may include practice-as-research staging (live or simulated staging) Results include physical, diagrammatic, or virtual visualizations; sonic facsimiles; or discursive renderings of sites, events, or choreographies
Practice-as-Research/ Research-as-Practice Augusto Boal Baz Kershaw Helen Nicholson Susan Leigh Foster Lynette Hunter Phillip Zarrilli Ben Spatz	An interdisciplinary research process that leads to and/or reflects upon an arts-related output; draws on arts practice as part of the process; or is otherwise integrated between scholarly methodologies and arts praxis	Knowledge is derived by 'doing' (know what/know how) Generates integral documentation (trace materials that the practice process creates, e.g. script drafts, notes, call sheets, camera reports, continuity notes, costume designs, laboratory reports, treatments, set designs, choreographic notation, sound designs) and external documentation (objects	May involve a hermeneutic 'spiral' of data generation and analysis Privileges the art presentation rather than traditional (written) academic products, though reportage can be in the mode of participant ethnography Reflection on the process is integral to the process
	Influenced by 'action research' (business and education studies), participatory action research, applied theatre, and grounded research	documenting performance encounters, e.g. video, photographs, recordings). Neither stands in for either the practice or the research per se Dramaturgy	Stakeholders in art-making are also stakeholders of knowledge about the practice

Table 1.2 (*cont.*)

Analytical traditions, with key advocates	Tenets	Methods	Methodologies
Reception Theory *phenomenology* Martin Heidegger Roman Ingarden Wolfgang Iser Maurice Merleau-Ponty Stanley Fish Bert O. States Alice Rayner Susan Bennett	Philosophy of experience; direct encounter of human consciousness with the world (or stage world) Description of appearances (not necessarily reality); reality consists of objects and events as they are perceived or understood in human consciousness and not of anything independent of human consciousness Art as mediator between author's consciousness and reader Leisure enables us to perceive aspects hidden from usual viewpoints by habit	Field observation; affective experience; cognition Identify meaning units; schematized perspectives; represented objectivities Study work 'horizontally' through incomplete and perspectival points of views or experiences Reading/experiencing is a duplication of consciousness (real 'me' and alien 'me') May be empirical and quantifiable (e.g. through fMRI (functional MRI) testing) or entirely qualitative Identify interpretive community that shares an institutional context or 'horizon of expectation'	Distinguish reader's/viewer's 'concretization' of the work from the work itself Correlate/distinguish 'aesthetic object' to/from the 'artistic object' Texts' orientations of the possible in relation to experience Correlate internal (or even physiological) facets of spectatorship to forms of observable, unobservable, subjective, or objective facets of experience 'Intentional acts' correlated to 'intentional objects'

Resistant Critiques *Black feminist theory* (Kimberlé Crenshaw, bell hooks, Saidiya Hartman, Hortense Spillers, Barbara Smith) *decolonization of knowledge* (Frantz Fanon, Ngũgĩ wa Thiong'o, Achille Mbembe, Boaventura de Sousa Santos, Fred Moten) *disability studies* (Petra Kuppers, Carrie Sandahl, Bree Hadley) *feminist performance theory* (Jill Dolan, Sue-Ellen Case, Elin Diamond) *Indigenous theory* (Jodi Ann Byrd, Aileen Moreton-Robinson, Dylan Robinson, Linda Tuhiwai Smith, Stephanie Nohelani Teves)	Builds from feminist and gender theory to anti-essentialize, challenge heteronormativity, and explore co-extant subject/object relations in the social world Recognizes the importance of biology, social relations, psychology, materiality, history, and language in conjunction with lived experience Recognizes racialization of bodies, spaces, and institutions; decolonization Performativity connects social, psychological, and representational realms Intersectionality; standpoint theory; environmentalism; postcolonial theory	Identify discursive, legal, and institutional operations of power and oppression (e.g. colonialism, racism, sexism) and dominance (e.g. white privilege, capitalism, patriarchy, heteronormativity), often in combination Focus on ways that power affects, defines, and delimits individuals and groups Identify the implications of structural determinism on thought and action, especially for minoritarian, marginalized, subaltern, or dispossessed communities Identify embodied and cultural decentrings of hegemonic privilege that counter systemic bias	Indebted to deconstructive methodologies, especially with respect to social categories, but also adoptive of other postmodern theories' methodologies Rhetorical techniques of analysis; broad and combinative approaches Storytelling (naming one's own reality) Revisionist interpretations Critique structural inequality Located holistic approaches Transnational/transregional/ supranational solidarities Redress for intergenerational trauma; healing practices 'Critical fabulation' links evidence to narrative, speculation, and intersectional knowledge to generate impossible-to-document histories that represent more replete versions of the past

Table 1.2 (*cont.*)

Analytical traditions, with key advocates	Tenets	Methods	Methodologies
queer theory (Gayle Rubin, Eve Kosofsky Sedgwick, Judith Butler, Michael Warner, Teresa de Lauretis, Jack Halberstam, Lauren Berlant, Adrienne Rich, Sue-Ellen Case, José Esteban Muñoz, Valerie Traub, David Halperin)			
Semiotics Charles S. Peirce Ferdinand de Saussure Roland Barthes Patrice Pavis Erika Fischer-Lichte Keir Elam Marco De Marinis Jiří Veltruský Marvin Carlson Ric Knowles	Communicative processes (intentional and unintentional) based on signs and symbols (linguistic and non-linguistic) Equal concern with processes and signification as communication (generation and exchange)	Identify iconic, indexical, and symbolic signs; these may cohere as systems or stand apart In performance, ascertain para/linguistic, proxemic, kinesic, vestimentary, cosmetic, pictorial, and sonic systems Discern units constituting semantics (relations between signs and the things to which they refer; their denotata, or meaning); syntactics (relations among signs in formal structures); and pragmatics (relations between signs and the effects they have on the people who use them)	Can be applied to texts (drama, scripts), mises en scène (polyphonic synthesis of what is onstage), and performance texts (theoretical model of the observable performance on stage) Socio-semiotics directs attention to specific signifying practices in a culture Accounts for how theatre is experienced, giving a lexicon to separate or conjoined elements contributed by artists and experienced by audiences

Speech-Act Theory J. L. Austin John Searle Daniel Vanderveken Judith Butler Saba Mahmood Martin Puchner	Illocutions describe or commit to a future course of action (this can vary in strength, mode of achievement, propositional content conditions, preparatory conditions, and sincerity) This modifies the 'enactment' of calling something into being (performatives) and attempts at persuasion (perlocutions) with degrees of felicity	Linguistic analysis of discourse Performativity (e.g. in film, social enactments, everyday life)	Reveal normative structures of communication practice (not limited to spoken communication) and discrepancies between utterance and outcome Rather than 'refining' or reconceiving exegetic factors it brings particular aspects into focus
Structuralism Vladimir Propp Claude Lévi-Strauss Émile Durkheim Raymond Williams Richard Schechner Victor Turner Michel de Certeau	Human activity and communication form systems of meaning reducible to law-like behaviour Meaning is produced through practices, phenomena, or activities which serve as signification systems (reproducing deep structures within culture) Emphasizes what structures are as well as how they are produced, reproduced, and perpetuated	Identify a cultural category (e.g. a wedding ritual or locus of knowledge) and break it down into constitutive parts: symbolic objects and activities Observation, participant observation, immersion in community, textual analysis Binary oppositions and basic elements (e.g. plot points, keywords) reveal how human activity is part of a system of signs reducible to law-like behaviour	Interpret meanings identified in associated elements Essentialize the human experience through comparativism of deep structures of human behaviour Biological or deep cognitive structures across humanity determine behaviours cross-culturally Despite local (surface) variants, phenomena are subservient to abstract laws (structures) Everything is within ideology
Textual Philology Karl Lachmann Richard Bentley B. G. Niebuhr Milman Parry W. W. Greg Edward Said Erich Auerbach Jeffrey Masten Sean Gurd Shane Butler	Vernacularity is recuperable through comparative linguistic study Theory of textualized meaning and transmission Lexicography, sociolinguistics, historical linguistics, language geography Works of poetic imagination are products of history	Etymology, textual comparison Track linguistic specificity, diversity, and evolution over time Connect textual analysis with literary criticism and historicism Seek layered structures of texts based on particularized language use and development	Word- and text-based comparison deal with historical development, relationships of language (or languages), and usage Correlate how text or performance generate or reflect meaning (nascent, literal, figurative, affective, etc.) Multi- or interculturalism may align with philological evidence

effect of causal multiplicity in human affairs, but a consequence of virtually everything we assert remaining discursively propositional. Usually, claims to new theorizing are actually hypotheses. Grounded theory has a similar status while being subject to processes of validation internal to a research process based in a specific community as well as testing of the systematic relatedness of concepts, conceptual linkages, variation, broadened conditions, and change factors as benchmarks in the canonical published literature (Creswell, 1998: 210).

The idea of theory guiding choices about research design is widely accepted. Table 1.2 schematically lays out a selection of qualitative approaches prevalent in TaPS, including some conducive to generating grounded theory (critical performance ethnography, practice-as-research, and resistant critiques). Each example is glossed with a few key advocates and tenets that typify the premises of the theory. This is matched with methods of how phenomena/subjects/objects are observed, noted, or processed in order to gather information about them, and then methodologies that utilize what is gathered, accounting for it in research outcomes such as writing, performance, and exhibitions. The possible combinations are endless, and a few examples must suffice to demonstrate how this works.

Two recent full-length studies of play-going – one historical, the other contemporary – illustrate how theories are connected to research approaches and the building blocks of methodologies. In *Common Understandings, Poetic Confusion: Playhouses and Playgoers in Elizabethan England*, William N. West (2021) combines approaches to posit the 'experience' of Elizabethan playgoers and the way this reflected life in early modern London. West makes the most of limited sources through meticulous use of mixed methods, multiple theories, and sundry methodologies. He assembles a lexicon about plays and play-going – including the terms *understanders*, *confusion*, *supposes*, and *non plus*, which all arose during the period – and, utilizing philological analysis, considers the terms' vernacularity in response to beholding and behaving at professional theatres. The instigation of London theatre as a regular and accessible business from 1576 gives a particular and concise timeline through which to track the emergent meanings within a tight geographic area. This is not sociolinguistics so much as an encounter-based approach that aligns the phenomenology of play-going with hermeneutics. Elizabethans actively sought ways to account for what they experienced in the theatre, and West discerns which versions 'fit' in recognition of what Stephen Greenblatt (1988: 1–20) calls 'the circulation of social energy' emergent in this specific context. To help account for this as a process of emergent meaning, West (2021:

10) draws on the philosopher Hans Blumenberg's (2010) concept of absolute metaphors – figures that 'give shape to human engagements with the world and with others' as new meanings emerged from older ones – in conjunction with George Lakoff and Mark Johnson's concept of 'metaphors we live by', which profoundly yet often covertly shape understanding (Lakoff & Johnson, 1980). Thus, Elizabethan theatre created its own framing; through this self-figuration playgoers understood metaphors, and producers figured out how to capitalize on the metaphors. These 'matrices of affect' – an idea that draws on Raymond Williams's 'structures of feeling' – propositionally consolidated to pattern a 'repertoire of behaviors and affects', which, in West's (2021: 14) account, are a history of how playing and play-going developed across the period.

With the addition of each methodology and every theoretical construct, West creates a richer and more nuanced account. He establishes differences, not merely likenesses and correlations, with the goal of finding patterns, not hierarchizing or interpreting them. Instead of seeking formalism within texts, West utilizes texts' sense of formalism emergent in experience. This aligns with Miguel Escobar Varela's (2021: 34) observation that TaPS is invested in understanding what and how theatre means through 'verifiable patterns in the history and current practice of theater performance'. West's (2021: 58, 63) historicist focus identifies, in the act of playing, 'a verbal redistribution of the sensible' (alluding to Jacques Rancière), 'calling attention to how it produces meaning without seeming to', in conjunction with 'material, spatial, cultural, linguistic' circumstances of imagination circulating within and as a result of theatres. Thus, through semiotic and media-specific induction, West identifies how playhouses reinforced structures of feeling, both as a problem for culture (i.e. anti-theatricality) and as an instrument of it. West never conflates a theoretical principle – such as a *dispositif*, absolute metaphor, or structure of feeling – with historical evidence as proof. Rather, he uses these principles to establish relationships between data in an interpretive narrative that recognizes patterns, pluralities, and contradictions in an emergent genealogy of practice derived through the methodologies of philology and content analysis, then deconstruction and discourse analysis.

In scientific investigations, two steps in logical thought – hypothesizing (generating provisional suppositions drawn from known facts) and predicting (forecasting how something will work or behave, based on the hypothesis) – must be linked by a method: something *done* in order to test the hypothesis under specific circumstances. If the expected result is not forthcoming, the prediction is definitely wrong (the hypothesis is less often under suspicion, and the theory even more rarely). Humanistic research works in much the same way; however, there is not an expectation of replicability to establish veracity, for humanities research proceeds on a relational basis and recognizes the subjectivity of a researcher as integral to insights as well as the uniqueness of a cultural situation or moment. No two researchers will derive identical data sets, apply the same method identically, or get precisely the same understanding. Neither the steps taken nor the conclusions drawn are reproducible by another (Escobar Varela, 2021: 23–5), though developing multiple case studies is often tried in order to stand in for replicability.

In contrast with the historical perspective taken by West, the study *Privileged Spectatorship: Theatrical Interventions in White Supremacy* by Dani Snyder-Young (2020) takes a contemporary approach. In this study of performance reception in the United States, Snyder-Young (2020: xxxi) investigates the potential for theatres' programming about race to have effects on predominantly white audiences, and her hypothesis – drawn from Caroline Heim (2016), by way of Erving Goffman – is that 'embodied actions of audience members constitute a performance' recognizable as a repertoire. But what is that behavioural repertoire? Snyder-Young utilizes qualitative participant-observation methods (attendance at performances, post-show talkbacks, and panels) to observe and record audience members' behaviours, their visible markers of racial identification (acknowledging that this does not necessarily equate to their racial identity), and verbal statements (subsequently transcribed). As Chris Rees and Mark Gatenby note, such ethnographic approaches are 'able to link the subjective understandings of individuals with the structural positions within which those individuals are located' (Rees & Gatenby, 2014: 135). (That is also a premise of discourse theory, which is heavily utilized at a later stage of Snyder-Young's research.) Case studies from a variety of cities and theatres over a five-year period consistently confirm Snyder-Young's (2020: xxxv–xxxvi) prediction that white spectators' behaviours and utterances are performatively distinct from those of people of colour, starkly bifurcating the data. This difference correlates to an important observation, evident in the coded content analysis: 'exclusionary responses [from] white audience members … work against artistic and institutional efforts toward inclusion and equity', for at post-show talk-backs audience engagements efforts 'can amplify or interrupt a performance's potential to get audience members to take responsibility for helping to solve the [racialized] problem in the real world'. This has significant consequences. Despite viewing performances that demonstrate the need for decolonization and desegregation, white audiences will avoid looking at their own life choices for how they 'perpetuate and exacerbate white supremacy'. Does this mean that all white spectators will conform to the noted repertoires and that subversion of productions' progressive arguments is inevitable when white audiences predominate? No. Does this signal a *predictive probability* of conforming to the noted repertoires? Yes, at least within the cultural parameters set out in the study, noting the ongoing challenge for artists and publics to disrupt (not just critique) white privilege (Snyder-Young, 2020: 131). Does it mean that despite the racial reckoning in the United States propelled by George Floyd's murder in 2020, white spectators' behaviour remained unchanged? Unknown: this postdates the data collection.

Theory is with us when we deploy methods and methodologies. For example, theory is the constant (if not always welcome) companion of anthropologists using field methods and ethnographic methodologies, and reflecting on methods (as a meta-critique) generates ethical stances (Prentki & Preston, 2009: 63–124). Even in practice-as-research, hypotheses are '*abductive* jumps or kick-starters of a process' (Hansen, 2018: 37), and theory is prominent in practitioners' ability to articulate positionalities (Cahill et al., 2019). These examples represent a few of the many ways to identify relevant information, traditions through which to analyse and relate information, ways in which to explain how knowledge is generated, and the locus of meta-critique.

Epistemologies of Knowing: Artisanal Knowledge

The historiographer François Furet (2001: 270–1) notes that any event, 'if considered in isolation, is unintelligible'. Theory is one means by which scholars subsume knowledge and find intelligibility. Being a cultural insider is another.

In a study of early musical comedies, Peter Bailey (1998: 184) went in search of what made the character type of a naughty (but ultimately nice) ingénue legible to audiences. He wrote that, indicatively, 'implications of prostitution or some kind of sexual buccaneering may help to account for the huge success of the hit song "And Her Golden Hair Was Hanging Down Her Back" that helped *The Shop Girl* to run to nearly six hundred performances in 1894–5'. Meaning came only partly from the lyrics, for it was in performance that the character type was conveyed. Dale Evans gave a sense of the received tradition of the song in the 1944 film *Song of Nevada* (dir. Joseph Kane), smiling, gesturing with her hands, and swaying her hips during the chorus:

But Oh Flo, such a change you know
When she left the village she was shy
But alas and alack she'd gone back
With a naughty little twinkle in her eye.

What gave Flo that twinkling eye is conveyed in the verses, as when she is persuaded to appear in a tableau vivant:

She posed beside a marble bath upon some marble stairs
Just like a water nymph or an advertisement of Pears
And if you ask me to describe the costume that she wears

Pause. In performance, a singer could use aposiopesis, suddenly stopping as if unwilling to proceed with the explanation, then provide the refrain:

> Well, her golden hair is hanging down her back. (McGlennon & Rowenfeld, 1894: n.p.)

For Victorian spectators not equipped to fully understand, the song remained innocent, or perhaps confusing. But those whose visual imagination could summon the scene would see in their mind's eye that Flo appeared unclad in a *pose plastique*, her hair less advantageously arranged than Lady Godiva's on her famous ride. Thus, if they did understand, according to Bailey (1998: 185), the song exploited the genre's '"knowingness", the technique of hints and silences that left the audience to fill in the gaps and complete the circuits of meaning', while hearing and understanding (*entendre*) what is playfully on the verge of signification. 'Flo' may overstep to the equivoque of a double entendre, but the singer-narrator may not. This is how most Victorians understood the song, but how does a researcher come to 'knowingness' about a culture or era not their own? Historical research provides no laboratories for leveraging 'existential conditions and epistemological creativity' to foster an experimental situation (Spatz, 2019: 71).

Queer theory offers a related idea, anti-narrativity, which is key to non-hegemonic epistemologies and thus important for performance reconstruction and analysis. According to Tyler Bradway (2021: 712), by moving attention away from plot and instead towards other 'forms on which narrative depends, such as address, metonymy, description, point of view, and character … suspense, simultaneity, and surprise', narrative can be discovered not working 'on behalf of the normative' but opening 'a condition of possibility for queerness … through which queers forge, experience, sustain, renew, and reimagine relationality'. As a method, ferreting out this strategic formalism means 'conceiv[ing] narrative as an ecology of interdependent forms – aesthetic and nonaesthetic – in contiguous torsion with one another'. This comes full circle to the concerns of Table 1.1, but how can formalist identification lead to semiotic understanding? When a scholar pushes beyond the limits of their own knowledge in search of keys not corresponding to their identity or their experience of signification, the project can be ethnographic, seeking criteria and developing knowledge for thick description, even if the source is textual and the text is historical. Theory per se is not necessarily going to provide the key to social worlds, though theory may explain why social worlds cohere and lock non-belongers out.

In *Wayward Lives, Beautiful Experiments: Intimate Histories of Riotous Black Girls, Troublesome Women, and Queer Radicals*, Saidiya Hartman (2019: xiv) describes such a problem-oriented quest as her endeavour 'to recover the insurgent ground' of young women's lives from 'the journals of rent collectors; surveys and monographs of sociologists; trial transcripts; slum photographs; reports of vice investigators, social workers, and parole officers; interviews with psychiatrists and psychologists; and prison case files, all of which present a problem' of data contextualization. She develops a counter-narrative to her sources, 'liberated from the judgment and classification that subjected young black women to surveillance, arrest, punishment, and confinement', in order to 'exhume open rebellion from the case file, to untether waywardness, refusal, mutual aid, and free love from their identification as deviance, criminality, and pathology' in ways more in accord with the women's own experience. This process allows Hartman to identify who is occluded by Jim Crow racial hierarchy, white supremacist institutions and acts, and gender constraints compounded by racial and sexual intersectionality that preclude first-person perspectives in archived sources. This radical experimentation with critical fabulation to recover subjects hidden in plain sight entails what Hartman (2019: 228) calls 'a practice of possibility' that defies and smashes through all official and tacit barriers. Eventhood and narrative are both subsumed to reclamation.

Boaventura de Sousa Santos (2018: 132–3) notes how such strategies depend on 'artisanal knowledge', or the kinds of knowledge inherent to communities past and present: 'Through such knowledges the groups in struggle become cognitive subjects and cease to be the objects of those alien knowledges that have been used to justify their subjection and oppression.' As in Hartman's practice of critical fabulation, such artisanal knowledges arise from earlier social struggles and are here utilized and resurfaced through a focus on the ways that power affects, defines, and delimits individuals and groups. The goal here is not simply to identify the implications of structural determinism for minoritarian, marginalized, or dispossessed people through deconstruction and discourse analysis, but also to utilize rhetorical techniques and intersectional approaches. This re-centres into narratives what Baz Kershaw and Helen Nicholson call the 'skeleton suggestions' in interpretable spaces (Kershaw & Nicholson, 2011: 6). Artisanal knowledge forces the question of how history (as a discipline and rhetoric) typically effaces certain kinds of experience, and how 'gaps' can be other than silhouettes of epistemological absence. Santos (2018: 136) argues that such epistemologies of the South 'do not disregard methodologies. But they do keep in mind at all times that the social construction of the agents in a struggle is a political act that precedes, exceeds, and conditions the use of methodologies', validating community insiders' knowledge.

TaPS research can engage resistant critique, including decolonization, subaltern studies, de-patriarchization, critical race theory (in conjunction with racialization and de-racialization), critical whiteness studies, critical Indigenous theory, and disability studies. The artisanal knowledge needed for this is often 'a performative kind of knowledge', existing collectively in the commons as 'a mix of knowledge/knower' (Santos, 2018: 140). Robin Bernstein's 2011 book *Racial Innocence: Performing American Childhood from Slavery to Civil Rights* exemplifies this sort of performative knowledge, within the tradition of material object studies known as thing theory. She hypothesizes that childhood is a performance engaged with scriptive things: artefacts that prompt behaviours relating to the social struggles embedded in the objects. Bernstein (2011: 11, 91) examines a range of evidence from the nineteenth- and twentieth-century United States, such as dolls, advertisements, popular performance (including blackface minstrelsy), activity books, and illustrations, seeking patterns for the scripting and thereby generating of 'new' evidence through content and discourse analysis of 'what a thing invited its users to do'. This connects to what Santos (2018: 137) calls empirical, practical, erudite, and scientific knowledge to posit play as historical events in an ecology of knowledge wherein domination and resistance were disavowed yet, in the process, reinforced. Bernstein (2011: 12) analogizes scriptive things in ways akin to a playscript, so 'items of material culture *script* in much the same sense that literary texts *mean*' (i.e. by inviting agential behaviours). Bernstein's prediction comes full circle back to the TaPS analytic terms of Table 1.1: extrinsic analysis of objects' reception explains the structures of feeling as a 'problem-oriented' history that centres both scripts and play, interdependently with a ubiquitous performance genre (onstage and everywhere else too, affecting even children who have no first-hand experience of the full, theatrical, expression of blackface) (see Furet, 2001: 271). This affirms Bernstein's (2011: 201) hypothesis and generates grounded theory: childhood performance immutably connects to white supremacy through the use of toys, dolls, and books, which shape play both for African Americans (servitude and violence) and white people (dominance and mercilessness), within a horizon of events that is infinite but indebted to symbolic interactionism.

Santos (2018: 174) acknowledges the long timeline for completing cultural reparation and restitution that aims to undo entrenched epistemologies uncovered by insights such as Snyder-Young's, Hartman's, and Bernstein's. The poet Dionne Brand (2001: 6) characterizes this kind of self-observation and feeling as 'sitting in the room with history'. This is part of the process – the tradecraft – of research. Rather than being complicit in the academy's destructive forces, disciplined to others' narratives, Christina Sharpe (2016: 13) argues that for diasporic Africans 'the work we do requires new modes and methods of research and teaching' to engage archives' and memories' consequences, unscientifically. New modes of knowledge-making and methodological mixology – particularly arising from critical race theory as well as queer, Indigenous, feminist, and disability studies – embrace theory and method in order to approximate grounded-theory approaches emphasizing 'description, understanding, and explanation' of qualitative data (Jaccard & Jacoby, 2010: 258).

Methods and methodologies for accomplishing path-breaking research are emerging in our midst, bred in specific economic, cultural, and political milieux, like the ever-changing discipline of TaPS. In the chapters that follow, scholars provide reflections on their trials and tribulations, advice, cautionary tales, and new potentialities. Mix and stir.

References

Anderson, P. (2010). *So Much Wasted: Hunger, Performance, and the Morbidity of Resistance*. Durham, NC: Duke University Press.

Bailey, P. (1998). *Popular Culture and Performance in the Victorian City*. Cambridge: Cambridge University Press.

Balme, C. B. (2008). *The Cambridge Introduction to Theatre Studies*. Cambridge: Cambridge University Press.

Bell, G. J. (ca. 1806). Annotated Copy of Mrs. Inchbald's Edition of The British Theatre. Archived in Folger Shakespeare Library, Washington, DC.

Bennett, S. (1997). 2nd edn. *Theatre Audiences: A Theory of Production and Critique*. London: Routledge.

Bernstein, R. (2011). *Racial Innocence: Performing American Childhood from Slavery to Civil Rights*. New York: New York University Press.
Blumenberg, H. (2010). *Paradigms for a Metaphorology*. Trans. R. Savage. Ithaca, NY: Cornell University Press.
Bradway, T. (2021). 'Queer Narrative Theory and the Relationality of Form'. *PMLA*, 136(5), 711–27.
Brand, D. (2001). *A Map to the Door of No Return: Notes to Belonging*. Toronto: Vintage.
Cahill, H., Aitken, V., & Hatton, C. (2019). 'We Need to Talk about Theory: Rethinking the Theory/Practice Dichotomy in Pursuit of Rigour in Drama Research'. In P. Duffy, C. Hatton, & R. Sallis, eds., *Drama Research Methods: Provocations of Practice*. Leiden: Brill, pp. 183–99.
Campbell, P. N. (1982). 'The Rhetoric of Theatre'. *Southern Speech Communication Journal*, 48(1), 11–21.
Carlson, M. (1989). *Places of Performance: The Semiotics of Theatre Architecture*. Ithaca, NY: Cornell University Press.
Cook, A. (2018). *Building Character: The Art and Science of Casting*. Ann Arbor: University of Michigan Press.
Creswell, J. W. (1998). *Qualitative Inquiry and Research Design: Choosing among Five Traditions*. Thousand Oaks, CA: SAGE.
Davis, T. C. (2004). 'The Context Problem'. *Theatre Survey*, 45(2), 203–9.
Davis, T. C., & Marx, P. W. (2021). 'Introduction: On Critical Media History.' In T. C. Davis & P. W. Marx, eds., *The Routledge Companion to Theatre and Performance Historiography*. London: Routledge, pp. 1–39.
Escobar Varela, M. (2021). *Theater as Data: Computational Journeys into Theater Research*. Ann Arbor: University of Michigan Press.
Essin, C. (2021). *Working Backstage: A Cultural History and Ethnography of Technical Theater Labor*. Ann Arbor: University of Michigan Press.
Fensham, R. (2021). *Theory for Theatre Studies: Movement*. London: Methuen.
Furet, F. (2001). 'From Narrative History to Problem-Oriented History'. In G. Roberts, ed., *The History and Narrative Reader*. London: Routledge, pp. 269–80.
Gajdoš, J. (2007). *From Drama Technique to Scenology*. Prague: Amu and Kant.
Gale, M. B., & Featherstone, A. (2011). 'The Imperative of the Archive: Creative Archive Research'. In B. Kershaw & H. Nicholson, eds., *Research Methods in Theatre and Performance*. Edinburgh: Edinburgh University Press, pp. 16–40.
Greenblatt, S. (1988). *Shakespearean Negotiations: The Circulation of Social Energy in Renaissance England*. Oxford: Clarendon Press.
Hansen, P. (2018). 'Research-Based Practice: Facilitating Transfer across Artistic, Scholarly, and Scientific Inquiries'. In A. Arlander, B. Barton, M. Dreyer-Lude, & B. Spatz, *Performance as Research: Knowledge, Methods, Impact*. London: Routledge, pp. 32–49.
Hartman, S. (2019). *Wayward Lives, Beautiful Experiments: Intimate Histories of Riotous Black Girls, Troublesome Women, and Queer Radicals*. New York: W. W. Norton.

Heim, C. (2016). *Audience as Performer: The Changing Role of Theatre Audiences in the Twenty-First Century*. London: Routledge.
Jaccard, J., & Jacoby, J. (2010). *Theory Construction and Model-Building Skills*. New York: Guilford.
Johnson, O. (2006). *Absence and Memory in Colonial American Theatre: Fiorelli's Plaster*. New York: Palgrave Macmillan.
Johnson, O. (2018). *Ruins: Classical Theatre and Broken Memory*. Ann Arbor: University of Michigan Press.
Johnson, O. (2021). 'The Size of All That's Missing'. In T. C. Davis & P. W. Marx, eds., *The Routledge Companion to Theatre and Performance Historiography*. London: Routledge, pp. 43–64.
Kershaw, B., & Nicholson, H. (2011). 'Introduction: Doing Methods Creatively'. In B. Kershaw & H. Nicholson, eds., *Research Methods in Theatre and Performance*. Edinburgh: Edinburgh University Press, pp. 1–15.
Knowles, R. (2004). *Reading the Material Theatre*. Cambridge: Cambridge University Press.
Lakoff, G., & Johnson, M. (1980). *Metaphors We Live By*. Chicago: University of Chicago Press.
McGlennon, F., & Rowenfeld, M. H. (1894). *And Her Golden Hair Was Hanging Down Her Back*. New York: Frank Tousey.
McKenzie, J., Roms, H., & Wee, C. J. W.-L. (2010). 'Introduction: Performance in an Age of Globalization'. In J. McKenzie, H. Roms, & C. J. W.-L. Wee, eds., *Contesting Performance: Global Sites of Research*. Basingstoke: Palgrave, pp. 1–22.
Moretti, F. (2005). *Graphs, Maps, Trees: Abstract Models for Literary History*. London: Verso.
Pascoe, J. (2011). *The Sarah Siddons Audio Files: Romanticism and the Lost Voice*. Ann Arbor: University of Michigan Press.
Pavis, P. (2003). *Analyzing Performance: Theater, Dance, Film*. Trans. D. Williams. Ann Arbor: University of Michigan Press.
Peters, J. S. (2000). *Theatre of the Book 1480–1880: Print, Text, and Performance in Europe*. Oxford: Oxford University Press.
Prentki, T., & Preston, S. (2009). *The Applied Theatre Reader*. London: Routledge.
Rees, C., & Gatenby, M. (2014). 'Critical Realism and Ethnography'. In P. K. Edwards, J. O'Mahoney, & S. Vincent, eds., *Studying Organizations Using Critical Realism: A Practical Guide*. Oxford: Oxford University Press, pp. 132–47.
Riley, S. R., & Hunter, L., eds. (2009). *Mapping Landscapes for Performance as Research: Scholarly Acts and Creative Cartographies*. London: Palgrave.
Santos, B. de S. (2018). *The End of the Cognitive Empire: The Coming of Age of Epistemologies of the South*. Durham, NC: Duke University Press.
Sharpe, C. (2016). *In the Wake: On Blackness and Being*. Durham, NC: Duke University Press.
Snyder-Young, D. (2020). *Privileged Spectatorship: Theatrical Interventions in White Supremacy*. Evanston, IL: Northwestern University Press.

Spatz, B. (2019). 'Molecular Identities: Digital Archives and Decolonial Judaism in a Laboratory of Song'. *Performance Research*, 24(1), 66–79.

Trudell, S. A. (2020). 'Shakespeare's Notation: Writing Sound in *Much Ado about Nothing*'. *PMLA*, 135(2), 370–7.

Ubersfeld, A. (1999). *Reading Theatre*. Trans. F. Collins. Toronto: University of Toronto Press.

Walker, J. (2006). 'The Text/Performance Split across the Analytic/Continental Divide'. In D. Krasner & D. Z. Saltz, eds., *Staging Philosophy: Intersections of Theater, Performance, and Philosophy*. Ann Arbor: University of Michigan Press, pp. 19–40.

West, W. N. (2021). *Common Understandings, Poetic Confusion: Playhouses and Playgoers in Elizabethan England*. Chicago: University of Chicago Press.

Worthen, W. B. (2005). *Print and the Poetics of Modern Drama*. Cambridge: Cambridge University Press.

Worthen, W. B. (2010). *Drama: Between Poetry and Performance*. Chichester: Wiley-Blackwell.

PART I

Planning

Few research projects have a definitive beginning point, but they all begin somewhere, somehow. The chapters in this part focus on conception and planning, indicating ways that a research idea is demarcated and positioned relative to disciplinary and extra-disciplinary kinds of knowledge, for solo-author projects and multi-author research.

Our standpoints – cultural, disciplinary, institutional – are likely to affect how we relate to things, and thus how we realize a topic exists and what is worth pursuing about it. What 'comes first' is everything we are in the world, and what our world is. The chapters in this part are bookended by two conversations between the editors and scholars that explore this idea. The first contextualizes methods in relation to difference. Nicola Mārie Hyland describes how her combination of methods to study a Disney film – an Indigenous 'mana wahine approach alongside a cultural-materialist, auto-ethnographical approach' – aligns with decolonizing critical objectives and yet works as a spiral, involving reading theory, consulting with others, and incorporating experience that includes the 'critical' act of appraising the art. Naming specific methods for a project can 'instil a kind of terror', as Brandi Wilkins Catanese admits, and the decision to mix several methods makes it hard to know when the work is complete. Reading leads to questions, which leads to more reading: this is what both getting started and getting on with it look like, yet, for Catanese, throughout there is a personal orientation to Black feminist theory, which helps her determine what the project requires. Ben Spatz describes their experimental approach recording video in singing sessions, differentiating this from compiling documentation as a way to explore jewish (*sic*) identity across many instantiations, with edited audiovisual publication rather than performance as an end goal. For all three conversants, multiple identities can be brought to bear in the framing and pursuit of research, and, as Spatz puts it, 'when we mix methods, we are mixing worlds'.

Maggie B. Gale explores the reciprocity between things we intuitively sense or know and things we go and try to find out. This is mediated by available resources and – for purposes such as grant applications, abstract submissions, book proposals, and dissertation prospectuses – consciously set in relation to things other people know (what the 'field' says and how our 'research hunch' relates). This is done not once, but over and again as a project develops. Gale exemplifies her insights through historical research about an individual, setting the actress Elsa Lanchester in her artistic, personal, and cultural milieux, recognizing things that affected her (work opportunities, geographic location, and domestic life) as well as things that Lanchester brought about (roles, venues, and forms in which she chose to work) as potential options for framing what to explore in a project. Research, in this case, is about identifying choices made by the historical individual and deciding to shift focus relative to previously published work (including that person's autobiographical writing) to change the received sense of the person, their life, and their work.

Michael McKinnie accounts for ways to get from making hunches about theatre's place in the world to theorizing about it. This, he argues, is where interdisciplinarity is useful: it changes our understanding of what theatre is by changing the terms one can use about how theatre sits in the world. Research proceeds by recognizing a seemingly atypical correlation or commonality (here, from sociology or economics), leading to generalizable statements against which a specific case can be particularized. Through such an approach, an observation can be disaggregated from a hermetic account (singular and contained to theatre per se), connected to cultural sociology, and then reconceived. Following the precedent of cultural sociologist Howard S. Becker, McKinnie calls this process of thought 'tricks': logic statements that frame premises, samples, and potential explanations.

Whereas Gale and McKinnie posit individual researchers in settings uncomplicated by cultural pluralities, Emine Fişek undertakes a thought experiment about what the 'differences' of refugee theatre inaugurate. In the design of a hypothetical study across several contrasting European sites and national contexts, she asks what kinds of questions can frame a multi-researcher project and which combination of methods would be required to conduct such a study. The answer is not monolithic; rather, the researchers' standpoints will necessitate heterogeneity of frames for research, such as national norms or exceptionalities, linguistic monocultures or pluralities, and presumptions about the stability and sustainability of persons who, by definition, cope with volatile and contingent circumstances of migration. Additionally, the policy-dependent conditions for art-making across the European Union (EU) complicate everything for art-makers, and thus also those who study them.

Whereas going to a performance (as a spectator or researcher) does not require institutional review board (IRB) clearance, ethics can have a more oblique relationship with the making and viewing of performance and its connection with communities when oral history, interviews, and other field methods are involved. In the second conversation, concern for vulnerable populations prompts discussion about how two performance scholars approach ethics review protocols and what kinds of concerns are raised by one's status as cultural insider (or outsider). For Patrick Anderson, whether as a member of the Commission on Police Practices for the San Diego Police Department or as a faculty member at the University of California, San Diego, attending to others' sense of empowerment in micro gestures is often where insight lies. Natalie Alvarez, for her part, draws on her research into the efficacy of scenario-based de-escalation training of police responses to mental health crises in Ontario, and speaks to the 'unspoken ideological codes or imperatives at work in such situations'. Both scholars' endeavours are predicated on the centrality of performance to understanding and realigning priorities in cooperation with communities that have their own powerful traditions of oversight.

CHAPTER 1

Methods Dialogue: Difference

Brandi Wilkins Catanese, Nicola Mārie Hyland, and Ben Spatz

Suggested Reading

Hyland, N. (2020). '"I Am Not a Princess": Navigating Mana Wahine in Disney's *Moana*'. *Performance Paradigm*, 15, 7–22.

King, R. S. (2019). 'Radical Interdisciplinarity: A New Iteration of a Woman of Color Methodology'. *Meridians: Feminism, Race, Transnationalism*, 18(2), 445–56.

Spatz, B. (2019). 'Molecular Identities: Digital Archives and Decolonial Judaism in a Laboratory of Song'. *Performance Research*, 24(1), 66–79.

Paul Rae: Hello, everyone. I'm Paul, and I'm British, though I'm beaming in to you from the Wurundjeri land of the Kulin nations in Melbourne, Australia. In Australia, we start these kinds of introductions by acknowledging the elders and families of those on whose land we work, and pay our respects to them.

Tracy C. Davis: I join this conversation from the homelands of the Council of Three Fires (the Ojibwe, Potawatomi, and Odawa, as well as the Menominee, Miami, and Ho-Chunk nations), in Evanston, Illinois, along the shore of Lake Michigan.

Brandi Wilkins Catanese: I come to you from the city of Oakland, which is in unceded Ohlone territory in Northern California.

Nicola Mārie Hyland: Ko Ruapehu Te Maunga, Ko Whanganui Te Awa, Ko Aotea Te Waka Ko Te Atihaunui ā Pāpārangi Te Iwi; Ko Ruahine Te Pae Maunga, Ko Rangitīkei Te Awa, Ko Takatimu Te Waka, Ko Ngāti Hauiti Te Iwi, Kō Nicola Mārie Hyland Tōku Ingoa. Tēnā koutou katoa. My name is Nicola Hyland, I whakapapa to the Te Āti Haunui-a-Pāpārangi, Ngāti Hauiti iwi in Whanganui in the central North Island, but I am in beautiful Wellington, Te Whanganui-a-Tara, which is the traditional homelands of Te Ati Awa, Ngāti Toa Rangatira, and Taranaki whānui iwi.

Ben Spatz: I currently live in Northern England, and I've been thinking about what the equivalent of a land acknowledgement could be here. I'd like to say something about dwelling in an economically depressed area within a former empire and current neocolonial power. But I don't have precise language yet.

Tracy C. Davis: Welcome, everyone. Please say a bit about your choice of the suggested reading material and how that situates you in terms of what you research, and how you research it.

Ben Spatz: The article I shared is one of the first pieces I published after a transformative experience organizing a new kind of theatre laboratory. The project was an investigation of jewish identity, but its methodology was not exactly either critical or auto-ethnographic.[1] I call the approach 'ethnotechnic', meaning that I was looking to experiment actively with jewish identity in relation to other identities, and especially in relation to whiteness, not only in order to understand theoretically how identity works, but also to enact a kind of 'molecular' intervention in identity through what is called practice research, artistic research, or embodied research. In the article, I try to explain what is happening in specific moments of videographic documentation and how this research process overturned some of my assumptions about what it means to research and what the results of research can be. Specifically, I've tried to use artistic research methods to integrate a critical scholarly perspective on contemporary (jewish) identity with my embodied identity and practice, leading to a series of audio-visual publications.

Brandi Wilkins Catanese: I shared an essay by Rosamond S. King that functions for me as a resonant thinking partner: King writes about various women of colour scholars and creative spirits who have influenced her approach to merging literary, historical research with her own creative practice. In my current work on Black motherhood, reproductive justice – an analytical framework that doesn't just focus on safe gestational politics but offers a broader conception of what it is to have the right to choose to parent or not parent and to fight for the right to nurture people into a hospitable world – offers a productive way to understand what's important and feminist and yet frequently not discussed in what many artists are doing. For example, Lynn Nottage is a Black woman playwright, and, though we don't necessarily lead with talking about her plays as feminist, there are instances of frustrated motherhood in many of them. It became clear to me that reproductive justice offers a useful interdisciplinary way of talking about the questions of care and kinship that permeate her work and the work of other Black feminist artists.

I'm trying to look at the ascendancy of reproductive justice as a framework for Black feminist political action, and the way the arts participate in that. I started with the theatre, but I'm also looking at political practice and other modes of aesthetic practice. I'm still in the exploratory phase in that regard, but as I lean in to that social science scholarship it brings up anxiety: I am an avowedly qualitative researcher, and very focused on feelings and other reactions that can't easily be quantified but are intimately linked to the kinds of structural analyses of power that undergird much existing scholarship in the reproductive justice arena. What is required to bring that literature into relation with the things that I want to think and talk about that are in a more decidedly humanistic realm? How do I also step towards it? What might it require me to look for in my cultural objects of analysis? That is the reason that King's piece resonates for me.

Nicola Māri̇e Hyland: I wrote the article 'I Am Not a Princess' against my will. I didn't want to write about *Moana*. I didn't want to engage with it. For a long time, people would say: 'Have you watched *Moana*? Can you tell me what you think about it?' The article came out of a conference paper, and it evolved (or devolved) specifically to engage with the idea of feminism from a Māori perspective, utilizing our feminist discourse, which is the mana wahine approach. I work in the realm of Mātauranga Māori (Māori knowledge): you could describe it as non-traditional Indigenous theory. It's old knowledge; we inherit it through oral histories, archaeology, the palimpsest of performance and contemporary archaeology, and the decolonizing of the archives. The application of this knowledge to 'postcolonial' life is relatively new. Māori academia is maybe fifty or sixty years old at most, and while these ideas are centuries old, how this knowledge is applied and made relevant to today is truly innovative. So old knowledge is applied to contemporary work, weaving these precolonial ideas into postcolonial acts.

That is why the article starts with a riddle: Why does Moana affect me in such a visceral and corporeal way? I don't actually think I answered that question in the article, but I feel it propelled me into my current research, which is more about Māori performance as enacted remembrance and Māori conceptions of affect.

Paul Rae: If you're talking to people who are not working in theatre and performance studies (TaPS), how do you explain what your methods are?

Nicola Mārie Hyland: I find this question quite terrifying. I've never really confronted it, and I feel I've devolved from a well-behaved utilizer of Western theory to somebody who deliberately doesn't structure things in a way that makes any sense to most people in academia. Essentially, my tools are primarily Indigenous. I am heavily influenced by Linda Tuhiwai Smith's (1999) *Decolonizing Methodologies*. Most methods I utilize seek to find new ways to work with old knowledge. However, I write in English, predominantly for a global audience, and my agenda is to reinforce how our culture is still living, energetic, vital, and original. For instance, I always find opportunities to mix in elements of global popular culture, often ironically, to demonstrate the complexity of contemporary Indigenous identity. To articulate ideas from distinct and often contradictory worlds of knowledge (Western and Indigenous) is a delicate negotiation. I'm not a fluent Māori speaker, so there are multiple layers of translation involved in framing a method: bridging the gap between the original language and English – which is never simply literal – to find a hybridized hypothesis.

The provocations for my research often come from a place of anger – a place of 'I don't agree with what you've said about this work' – but I don't want my approach to reading performance to be simply reactive. I'd rather just illuminate it on its own terms, which often involves a process of destabilizing, or unknowing, Western theories and approaches. This was the case with 'I Am Not a Princess', as I was seeking to find a more satisfying method than a Western feminist reading, which led me to apply a mana wahine approach alongside a cultural-materialist, auto-ethnographic approach.

Decolonizing methodologies are also a matter of integrity in my work: while traditional Māori performance is everywhere, very little is written about non-traditional contemporary Māori performance from a Māori perspective, or the ways these modes create meaning on a deeper level beyond entertainment. It is important to point out that practices of performance using 'Māori means' are widely understood and applied in New Zealand. Māori performers have a general set of tikanga (protocols) applied to rehearsal and production that are both common sense and widely practised and, for me, are my default way of doing things. And since the Māori process offers a strong framework for creating devised work, even if I am making such work, I can focus on creating research questions around the politics of the material, rather than the way I work in the room. For example, this year I am working with students to decolonize John Gay's *Polly, an Opera* (1777) through textual adaptation, operating within a tikanga-led rehearsal process. Tikanga creates a kind of cultural safety net around the work from the outset, and also facilitates the conditions for the research, in practice and on paper.

Paul Rae: In practical terms, when you are doing research, what are you actually doing? What are the practical activities that you undertake?

Nicola Mārie Hyland: A lot of reading. One of Smith's ethical frameworks – it's not hers, she just shared it – is the idea of Titiro, Whakarongo, Kōrero, which is watching and listening before you speak. The first thing I do when I approach the performance is to look and listen, paying attention to the way that other people are having a first-hand phenomenological experience. I do have confidants – different people I talk with about language and about feelings – and my research involves measuring my own reaction against other people's before I articulate an analysis myself. Then there is the part that is traditional in the sense that I'm sitting in an office, doing a lot of reading and googling a bit. That doesn't help me that much, and there are a few resources that I head back to repeatedly, such as Hirini Moko Mead's *Tikanga Māori* (2016) or Rachael Ka'ai-Mahuta and colleagues' *Kia Rōnaki* (Ka'ai-Mahuta et al., 2013). It's pretty spiral – not very linear.

Brandi Wilkins Catanese: Nicola, I just want to say I appreciate that you're leading with the fact that this question of 'What are your methods?' can instil a kind of terror. I certainly feel that: when you receive your training in an interdisciplinary programme a definitive methodological orientation is one of the hardest things for your instructors to try to name because they never cover all the methods. They have to pick one or two. Those might, or might not, resonate with you and suit the needs of your project. It's possible to be a credentialed person in the world, trying to do the work that matters to you, but never to be able to say: 'this is the method I name and claim'. For myself, it has often produced a certain amount of anxiety because when I am mixing methods it's hard to know when I'm finished. When have I done enough to be able to say the thing that I want to say, and to feel that I said it with rigour, so it will hold when other people engage with my work?

With that as a preamble, what does it look like when I do what I do? It looks like reading. It looks like writing. It looks like viewing. It sounds like questioning. I often do talk to myself when I'm working alone, so sometimes it's just asking questions out loud. I read something, it begets a question, and I must put the question to the side to keep pursuing the thing I'm working on right now. I do go back to that question and figure out what it illuminates about the thing I'm trying to do, and where I need to get additional information to answer that question and funnel that material back into the primary project. That, in an iterative fashion, is the most basic description of how I do what I do most often.

At the conceptual level, I think of myself as engaging in close reading and in what I call a kind of discourse analysis: not semiotics and textual structure but more broadly the relations of power that structure how particular cultural objects get produced and what their conditions of circulation and consumption are.

When I teach performance analysis, I encourage my students to think sequentially about the what, the how, and the why of a work: first content and context (What's happening and where? Who's watching it?); then execution (What is the skill with which it's done? What ideals of beauty or refinement or accomplishment does or doesn't it achieve intentionally or unintentionally?); and then impact (Why does it matter that this happened in this time, in this place, for these people, or for us today at a remove from the original circumstances of its creation?). In my own work, I often try to march through that same thought process to account for all those things, not in equal measure but in proportion to whatever the project's question requires.

I think another way of answering the question of what your methods are, particularly for humanists in writing-based fields, is really about theoretical frameworks. For me, Black feminist thought is definitely one of the primary frameworks that structures my thinking about the work that I do, especially the 'why' of my work.

Tracy C. Davis: Framing questions is a classic part of qualitative and quantitative research. Brandi, do you find yourself with a large number of questions you then sift through and prioritize? Do you try to get down to one central question?

Brandi Wilkins Catanese: It depends on the project. Some begin with a question: there's some sort of 'why' that strikes me and motivates me. In those instances, the supplementary or subsidiary questions often come up as a result of whatever mode of engagement is required to begin the process of trying to answer that first question. For example, 'Why does Lynn Nottage have so many instances of frustrated motherhood scattered across her body of work?' Sometimes the additional questions are 'What are the other questions I need to ask?' or 'What are the other things I need to know to answer that question?' Sometimes that involves doing due diligence about the artist's body of work and its critical reception. Sometimes there are little questions that feel tangential at the moment that pop into my brain but end up rerouting the work because I suddenly find that the question with which I began is not the most important question, it was just the invitation to show up. The tangential questions can lead me in a different direction and help clarify what methods might be most appropriate to lean on more heavily in order to do right by my research subject.

Ben Spatz: My experience of mixing methods has led me somewhere surprising. For a long time, I experienced two different streams of research – scholarly and artistic – as separate and parallel to each other. This was a problem for me as a scholar, as an artist, and as a person. During my PhD work, the focus was on theory and history, and what that really means is a methodology of reading and writing, a scholarly practice of the humanities in which knowledge is located in written texts. At the same time, I was following another pathway that rejected academia quite strongly, and I was really thinking that the last thing I would ever become was an academic! This other path was influenced by my encounters with the work of Jerzy Grotowski and those who were influenced by him. Grotowski used the term *research* in contexts of art-making and spiritual or esoteric practices, which he called 'ritual arts' or 'art as vehicle' (Schechner & Wolford, 1997: 368). For a long time, I was struggling to bring together these two meanings of the term *research*. How can we understand the generative things that happen in spaces of practice – in a theatre studio for example, or in what Grotowski called a 'theatre laboratory' – as research in a rigorous sense? In the last part of his life, Grotowski postponed the moment of public presentation indefinitely, which to me suggests a turn from questions of representation and communication to questions of methodology. What are practitioners doing, day after day, when they explore particular kinds of embodied technique? How can we understand embodied practices as research in a sense that is not just metaphorical? What are the actual methods and methodologies of embodied research? What are its results and outcomes?

Tracy C. Davis: Ben, your doctoral research and first book, *What a Body Can Do: Technique as Knowledge, Practice as Research* (Spatz, 2015), covered many different communities (yoga, actor training, and theatre-making, as well as observations of everyday life). Are you thinking of them all or of one in particular? Is everybody always doing research?

Ben Spatz: 'Is everybody doing research?' is a good question. I want to say, in a sense, yes. This is part of what happened for me when those two (scholarly and artistic) streams of research came together: the object of research exploded. On the one hand, the artistic stream of research, which I had been exploring through post-Grotowskian practices, highlighted the extent to which knowledge is a matter of doing, part of embodied life, not something separate that is contained in texts. But those theatre laboratory practices can also be isolated from the world in ways that avoid other kinds of difference. They can be patriarchal and extremely white (not that academia isn't). They can be ableist and construct a very narrow image of embodied research. When this focus on embodied practice collided in my work with critical scholarly perspectives, it became clear that the specific materials one practises – for example, songs – can never be separated from the embodied identity of the practitioner. Instead of a division between practice and theory, or body and mind, what appeared was the inextricability of technique and identity. This is what eventually crystallized into a new research method. And what was most surprising to me in this method was the centrality of video recording.

A video camera had never been part of either type of research for me. Theatre laboratory practices historically exclude cameras from the room, creating a strict division between embodied practice and audio-visual documentation. Theatre and performance scholars often have recourse to video, but in a way that almost by definition gives priority to the live event of public performance. When I introduced a video camera into the space of the theatre laboratory, everything changed. It was as if the camera revealed how much both the idea of embodiment and the writing-based disciplines are based on a sustained rejection of audio-visuality. In the lab method that crystallized in 2017, the camera is located at the heart of the practice. It comes inside the space of play, no longer generating performance documentation but facilitating something completely different, a kind of experimental video data. This is similar in some ways to ethnographic uses of video, but it is experimentation rather than fieldwork. In this context, it becomes possible to work with embodiment and identity in a different way – or rather, to reveal in a new way how embodiment and identity have always been explored and reinvented as part of the processes that lead to performance.

During the Judaica project, which is the focus of 'Molecular Identities', I worked for six months with two other practitioner-researchers, Nazlıhan Eda Erçin and Agnieszka Mendel. The main starting point or source material for our work was a set of ethnographic recordings of jewish songs. We would learn the songs and then play with them, at first just the three of us in a studio, then later also with invited guests and in other kinds of sites and spaces. From the beginning, we were rotating through the roles of practitioner (performer), director, and videographer. As we watched the video material coming out of those lab sessions, I realized that something new was happening. The embodied process was like a theatre laboratory practice – exploring songs, texts, and ways of working – but the result was different. We weren't making a performance. There was no intention to create a repeatable score that could be performed for others. Instead, each moment in which our bodies and identities collided and interacted with particular songs, texts, objects, and places was inscribed in a kind of experimental video data, which could then be edited into new forms of audio-visual publication.

We are still in the process of working through this video material. What I can say at this point is that the process drew heavily on both scholarly methods and artistic methods, but when it crystallized, it brought those two streams together in an unexpected way.

Tracy C. Davis: As you mix methods and methodologies in terms of a sequence of acts and engagements, how is it that, additionally, you strategically work with worldviews and epistemologies that bring to the fore certain kinds of knowledge and understanding? How does that feel? How does your affective response factor in when it's both your starting point and, in some cases, the entire focus?

Nicola Mārie Hyland: For me, it's a relationship between freedom and boundaries. Having an Indigenous standpoint gives me more freedom to articulate things, but it creates boundaries that can protect me and my ideas. There are things that I will refuse to write, and things that I feel really ballsy about saying, because my positionality is becoming increasingly explicit and fundamental to what I'm writing. Having an Indigenous standpoint also means I do not need to speak about the things that I don't know. Mostly it's common sense, and I very rarely get the answer to things from anywhere apart from my own Mātauranga Māori knowledge. It's an amazing, affective experience when I solve a riddle (or I think I have) – a riddle that emerges from my experience of watching or participating in performance. It is something deeper than, but similar to, the question of 'Why did I feel that way about this piece?' If I can articulate in words, in some way, the feeling of being fully overwhelmed by performance, in a way that I can't understand at all while I'm experiencing it, it's so fulfilling. In some ways, solving the riddle kind of replicates that affective response from the original encounter, through finding answers to questions generated by feelings.

Paul Rae: Would you say that it's through your research and your intellectual engagement with these contexts and settings that aspects of your Indigeneity have crystallized for you, or indeed changed and grown?

Nicola Mārie Hyland: Absolutely. It's ironic because not that many Indigenous people are found in academia. In my university only around 2 per cent of the academic staff identify as Māori, and the majority of these are based in Te Kawa a Māui – the School of Māori Studies. So it's uncomfortable finding myself, the lone Māori person, in a typically non-Indigenous space. Part of the struggle is not being able to share questions of method with colleagues who do not and cannot feel the same as I do about work in my field. This is isolating, but also liberating – I experience a performance, alone, and then have this need to put my head on afterward and to go and try and illuminate that feeling for other people who weren't in the room. This is a kind of archaeological process, a layering. Everything that I produce is part of an ongoing conversation that, when I pass away, should add up to the history of my ideas being put together in relation to the sense of the development of my own fraught cultural identity, operating within the academy. I still feel like a neophyte in a lot of ways, because I've turned away from traditional Western frameworks and am moving towards a much more holistic way of working.

Brandi Wilkins Catanese: Nicola, I was struck by what you said about the multiple positionalities that we bring to our work: who you are in relation to your research questions; the places where you engage in fact-finding and analysis; who you are in relation to the project of knowledge production; and how the fruits of your contemplation end up circulating and towards whom. I too think about this a lot. The parts of me that I can or should bring to the research process – that help me get to know a performance, or a performer, or understand a community in order to be able to say something about what's happening there – might leverage facets of my identity, my ability to move through space and access information, and the ways I make sense of what I encounter in those spaces. I might need to summon entirely different parts of myself and my social, political, and ethical positionality in order to share that work. As you mentioned, there may be things that you discover that you will not share because it's not right for them to move from performance into written form to circulate in a decontextualized way, because that would dishonour the relationships through which the knowledge was gained.

I think a lot about the translation required to move from what I know as a result of the conditions of my coming to know it, into the professional responsibilities of demonstrating what I know in the context of my institutional affiliation, departmental affiliation, and so on. It may be super cool for us to leverage our practitioner selves in order to do the work that we're doing, to ask the questions that we're asking. But depending upon how we earn a living, we might be required to boil that down into the format of an essay that has all these citational practices that are going to validate us to colleagues who decide whether we keep our jobs or earn a new job title. This concern about professional legibility is something I think about a lot in terms of my mentorship of the next generation of students, who are so flexible and eclectic in their interests and their desires, for how to build a life as a scholar. How do you acknowledge the methodological expectations of your field, and experience that acknowledgement in your work as something other than conservatism or conformity? Can we think of it as methodological inclusivity, as a way to make something useful within 'conventional' choices of writing style or citations that is not inherently a betrayal of the expansiveness and complexity that one's subject matter requires, or of the practice of freedom that is necessary to push our field forward?

Ben Spatz: I think methods are profound. They are ontological and epistemological frameworks. When we mix methods, we are mixing worlds. It is parts of ourselves that are being mixed, not only at an individual level, but the worlds that we are part of, that we are, that are part of us. It's been eight years since I started to work on jewishness as an identity: to reflect on it, to read about it, to explore my own upbringing in an auto-ethnographic way, but also, just as importantly, to interact with different kinds of materials in an embodied and artistic way that highlights the complexity and materiality of identity. The Judaica project began in 2012, when I shifted from working with invented, non-lexical songs to working with jewish songs. (In the article, I analyse this shift in relation to whiteness and my own need to examine identity and situatedness more carefully.) But what is a jewish song? There is no simple answer. I eventually became interested in the category of songs that are marked as 'Judaica' in the Smithsonian Folkways record label archive, precisely because there is so little, apart from the genre label, that ties those songs together (Smithsonian, n.d.). Within that category you can find folk singers and professional musicians, religious and profane contexts of performance, recent and very old recordings, and an incredible diversity of locations, cultures, and languages. When I learn a song from a recording and sing it, the meaning of that action is completely different than when the same song is sung by someone who is

Polish or Turkish, Christian or Muslim. Not only that, but the meaning of my own singing action changes from day to day, depending on place and context. All of this is well established in TaPS, in a sense. But analysing a moment of performance is quite different from setting up a methodology to work experimentally with technique and identity.

Paul Rae: All three of you have referred to multiple communities in which you participate and/or locate yourselves. How and where do methods feature in the dynamic relations that you have as researchers with these diverse communities?

Brandi Wilkins Catanese: Building on what Ben said, if we think about methods as ontological and epistemological frameworks, our methodological practices become world-making activities. In other words, in the context of my research, I want to live in a world where questions that anchor the Black feminist tradition are constantly part of public dialogue rather than being ignored. How we ask and answer questions offers modes of connection within and beyond the academy. When I attend a play, sit in on a rehearsal, direct a rehearsal, participate in a post-show discussion, or participate in an academic panel organized under a different disciplinary rubric from my own, an affirmation of these shared values is what enables this satisfying experience of pursuing questions together, of making something new together. When I move into a space where people value different ways of seeking out and producing knowledge, it's a privilege and an asset to have that methodological dexterity that enables me to know I can connect with this different community on a subject that matters greatly to us. We may bring different bibliographies to the conversation, but something is going to offer the way in. It might be a love of ethnography, or a love of many modes of discourse analysis, or the joys of the archive. But methods enable co-presence, collaboration, and connection, across objects of analysis, across social identities, and across disciplinary affiliations, and it's not always a loss to temporarily step away from one set of methods in order to step towards another. There's great benefit in the conversations that come from being fluent in multiple methods.

Nicola Mārie Hyland: I teach a whole range of subjects from a whole range of positionalities. It's a survival mechanism, but it's also a reason that academics can be quite empathetic in conversation, because we're trying to engage with our students' worldviews. My students' worldviews are quite diverse, and we must be open to that. Likewise, it's necessary and strategic but also mutually beneficial to engage with methodologies outside of our own and see their efficacy for what they are in the contexts that they are created.

Paul Rae: We often think of methods as a means to an end that lies beyond the immediate circumstances within which methods are being deployed. Can doing research in an ethical way, within a community environment that one has come into for that purpose, also be an end in itself?

Nicola Mārie Hyland: It is often hard for me to justify doing something for a community when the knowledge that I'm imparting about them is not new to them: they're not learning as much about themselves as other people learn about them. Through performance, they're showing their mana (power), originality, and innovation, yet I'm trying to communicate this to a different community, in a different space. Sometimes writing from a Māori perspective feels like rectifying wrongs – where previous scholarship has analysed Indigenous work using Western ideas – but I think a bigger part is showing respect for what these artists are doing and the pride that comes with seeing their success. Being really respectful of the protocols that they use themselves, and being humble, are really important. It's an arduous task. I lived in Australia for eight years. Coming back to New Zealand, justifying myself and building relationships afresh as a Mozzie (Māori Australian) has taken a long time. Sometimes I feel the burden is quite heavy, and it would be easier to write about people who are not around anymore, but the deeper I go into it and the more that I'm open and sharing about processes, they're recognized as mutually beneficial.

Ben Spatz: By temperament and lineage, I have never felt myself easily part of any large community or social group. I've never seen myself as researching with, much less on, any community. In my book *What a Body Can Do*, I had an intentional strategy not to do primary research on anyone. That book is primarily a theoretical intervention: I reinterpret existing secondary sources by applying a new idea (the distinction between technique and practice). For the most part, I did not rely on primary research, because I don't feel comfortable in that position. I generally do not feel comfortable with the conventional scholarly relationship to an object of study, that of a scholar who writes about or on behalf of a community or artist and who then often becomes responsible for the way they are inscribed into the archive. At the same time, I don't see myself as an artist who makes public works. What I always wanted, and what has started to crystallize for me in this new approach to research, was to be able to move back and forth between these positions – the scholarly and the embodied/artistic, or the subject and the object – which I now understand also as gendered and racialized positions (Spatz, 2020). I am looking for a sense of community and a sense of home, but I know that I can only find this in a situation where these roles are more fluid than they are in either the academic or the artistic contexts I have experienced. I need to be able to enter the vulnerable, embodied flow of the practitioner or performer, but I also need to be able to step back and out from that role, in order to analyse my own practice and that of my colleagues from a critical distance. To me, this possibility of shifting positions is the promise of practice research or artistic research. But more concrete methods are needed to realize this promise fully.

I think of methods as building blocks or leverage points for creating alternative institutions, such as a different kind of university, and alternative worlds. I want to support a generative approach to methods, where people are genuinely experimenting, reclaiming, and reapplying older marginalized methods while also inventing new, as yet non-existent methods.

Tracy C. Davis: Given these significant experiential, affective, cognitive, epistemological, and ontological shifts that occur, how do you think about placing your work? Brandi, from your experience as an editor of *Theatre Survey*, do you have submissions that reflect this, and how do you work with them? How can authors who are doing these kinds of work navigate the challenge of placing their work into the public domain?

Brandi Wilkins Catanese: During my time as part of *Theatre Survey*'s editorial team, I would say that we have been very interested in and open to a certain amount of mixing methods. *Theatre Survey* has standing as a historically driven journal, and obviously there are emphases on archival scholarship or a particular kind of ethnographic or oral-historical fact-finding and rumination that legitimize the work as historical. That, first of all, is certainly something to think about: What is privileged when those are the ways that we qualify work as historical? How do we honour the stated mission of the journal while also being clear that doing so is not about reproducing limiting and exclusionary value systems about knowledge production; that we welcome fresh approaches to historical scholarship on performance? Naming one's divergence from a methodological tradition can be a worthy endeavour. I think the 'why' of methods is incredibly important. It's unfortunate that some methods are seen as so self-evidently worthy that people who use them don't actually have to explain why the methods serve the questions being posed, and also what might be missed by a sort of over-loyalty to those methods. Folks who are mixing methods or bringing methods from one field into another field, where they're not as commonly affirmed, have the responsibility of explanation. That responsibility is also an opportunity that invites us to think about, for example, why first-person voice in a piece of writing is a necessary component of its knowledge production, whether that's about honouring the relationships that enabled one to access the community and the information and wisdom it holds, or some other reason. There's something generative in not just using but contextualizing your use of mixed or unexpected methods. And I think that folks who stick with more traditional approaches would also benefit from taking a little bit of time to share with their readers not just the fact of their commitment to a particular methodology but the benefits of their using it.

Ben Spatz: In 2017, I founded the *Journal of Embodied Research* (*JER*), a scholarly journal that exclusively publishes video articles (*JER*, 2017). There are no established methods for creating video articles, so the question of what makes a robust or rigorous video article is being explored through processes of peer review. As of March 2023, *JER* had published thirty peer-reviewed video articles on topics ranging from performer training, contemporary choreography, and intercultural musical collaboration to performance-based filmmaking, site-specific eco-performance, and reconstructed medieval martial arts. Our special issues have addressed 'embodiment and social distancing' (*JER* 3.2, 2020); a specific form of videographic composition that I call 'illuminated video' (*JER* 4.2, 2021); and most recently 'ecologies of embodiment' (*JER* 5.2, 2022), with guest editors Raffaele Rufo and Doerte Weig.

When I launched the journal, my understanding of the video article form was very open. What is a video article, after all? I felt that a platform was needed to explore this question. Over the past few years, I have come to understand *JER* more specifically as a space in which the relationship between textuality and audio-visuality can be contested and investigated. The whole apparatus of scholarly publishing is set up to support the circulation of textual documents. These days, many online journals allow authors to embed multimedia within a text. But what if that topology is reversed, so that writing is within video? Most submissions to *JER* still include extensive voice-over, but is this necessary? What are the possible configurations and relationships of textual and audio-visual layers within a video article? What does video as a medium for thought allow us to understand differently about writing?

To a large degree, these are methodological questions: how to generate video material, how to watch and analyse video material, how to edit and annotate video material. Asking these kinds of questions changes what we understand as knowledge and who can be recognized as knowing, as knowledgeable. There are connections to be made here with contemporary Black and Indigenous decolonizing methods, which I am learning a lot from now.

Paul Rae: Do we usefully reframe the discussion if we ask not 'What are methods?' but 'When are methods?' In conventional research terms, methods come at the beginning, when you identify your hypothesis and establish the means by which you will explore it. But we know that even if one is explicit about one's planned methods at that point, they may change over time, in response to the situation that person is in and to external events. Perhaps that's particularly acute when we also consider multiple identities and standpoints alongside the question of methods. Can you think of examples where something has prompted a radical reassessment and recalibration of your methodological thinking and reframed it while a project was in process?

Ben Spatz: This may not be the answer you are looking for, but I want to point out that there is often a powerful wall erected between the 'when' of research and the time we experience as parents, as children, as caretakers, as lovers, as disabled, as any aspect of our being that is not counted as professional work. I wonder what would happen if we thought about these time frames more in relation to one another.

Brandi Wilkins Catanese: At this very moment, I'm having a little bit of a focus issue. My eight-year-old is in and out and in and out of the room. So are you coming to say hello? You might as well. This is my eight-year-old.

Brandi's daughter: Hi!

Brandi: Okay, thank you very much.

Paul Rae: Earlier on, you saw my sixteen-year-old slinking embarrassedly into the room and then out with the hair dryer.

Brandi Wilkins Catanese: Mine is always fascinated by what I am doing here in front of this machine all day, every day.

Nicola Mārie Hyland: I have an eight-year-old who walks behind me like he's going down an escalator. I can definitely jump on from what Ben was talking about. There's a really strong correlation with identity formation when I'm talking about my positionalities. Indigeneity and motherhood go together in a really strong doubling. For instance, I describe my directing style as maternal – aligned to ideas of the Whaea (mother) figure, which are deeply embedded in mana wahine theory. I've learnt a lot about parenting from methodology, and I've learnt a lot about lecturing from parenting. Particularly during the COVID-19 pandemic, I've learned a lot about the organization of time: theory time and parent time and teaching time. The structure of structure itself is a life force for me: to have something in my life that I have an ability to have agency and control over. You find what becomes important with your research and how to work efficiently. There's this wonderful liminal space between the time that I leave the office and the time that I get home, where I actually have space to think about the things that I want to think about. Then I get home and I feel like I'm not ready to leave that conversation in my head, but there are three young people coming towards me with all of these ideas of their own.

Brandi Wilkins Catanese: Methods are a 'how' that you always grapple with. Particularly for me, methods are always present from an ethical or integrity perspective. If ruminating upon your information is happening with a proper sense of accountability to your thinking partners – the communities for whose benefit you hope to be working – there is never a time when you should feel you have satisfactorily pondered whether the questions you're asking are the right ones or are being asked with the appropriate level of care. There should be ongoing mindfulness about the impact of the where and the how of the circulation of your work. In that regard, the answer to the question 'When are methods?' is that methods are always. There is no time outside of methods. They are always under scrutiny and in development, and that is probably at the root of some of my anxiety about being an eclectic interdisciplinary worker. You never get to stop wondering whether your 'how' is the right how, whether it's good enough, or whether it's sufficient. The 'how' is a responsibility and a challenge. That's the best way I can put it.

Note

1 I lowercase *jewish* and *judaism* to 'mark a corporeal, materialist or phenomenotechnical approach to jewish identity', as I explain in 'Molecular Identities' (Spatz, 2019: 70).

References

JER (*Journal of Embodied Research*). (2017). Open Library of Humanities. Accessed 13 March 2023. https://jer.openlibhums.org/. For issues cited in this chapter see https://jer.openlibhums.org/issues/.

Ka'ai-Mahuta, R., Ka'ai, T., & Moorfield, J. (2013). *Kia Rōnaki: The Māori Performing Arts*. Auckland: Pearson.

Mead, H. M. (2016). *Tikanga Māori: Living by Māori Values*. Wellington: Huia.

Schechner, R., & Wolford, L. (1997). *The Grotowski Sourcebook*. London: Routledge.

Smithsonian. (n.d.). 'Judaica'. *Smithsonian Folkways Recordings*. Accessed 15 February 2023. https://folkways.si.edu/genre/judaica.

Spatz, B. (2015). *What a Body Can Do: Technique as Knowledge, Practice as Research*. Abingdon: Routledge.

Spatz, B. (2020). *Making a Laboratory: Dynamic Configurations with Transversal Video*. Santa Barbara, CA: Punctum Books.

Tuhiwai Smith, L. (1999). *Decolonizing Methodologies: Research and Indigenous Peoples*. New York: Zed Books.

CHAPTER 2

Planning a Research Project: Early Steps

Maggie B. Gale

With its inherent multi-disciplinarity and layers of interpretative complexity, theatre and performance studies (TaPS) offers an overwhelming number of possible points of departure for research. This chapter deals with the potential beginnings of such a process, detailing strategies that might be needed to engage in the 'fore-journey', or planning stages, and, particularly, how to find a research niche. This entails a focus on what might need to be researched to get to the point where it is clear whether there is a viable project, what its scope and scale are, and how it can be productively situated in relation to earlier related research. Identifying a research niche has two essential functions: it facilitates the focusing and refocusing of a research process, and it marks out work as original and significant, explicitly indicating its potential to contribute to a field of enquiry and practice. Just as research involves flexibly utilizing methods and does not always follow a singular direction, a niche is also continually nuanced as research proceeds.

Locating a Niche

In *Beginnings: Intention and Method*, Edward Said (2012 [1975]: xxiii) suggests that 'beginnings are … not always evident' and are inherently bidirectional: to find a beginning we have to reflect on what we already know, in order to imagine or seek out the thing we do not yet know. Suffice to say, the more experienced the researcher, the more that which Said calls 'the already familiar' conditions of the research framework and methodological process can make the researcher overconfident and unoriginal or, conversely, underconfident and risk averse. Whatever the breadth and depth of existing knowledge, the ability to identify what it is you *do not* know is crucial. Historiographer Tom Griffiths (2016: 13–14, 203) refers to 'historical consciousness' as the mindset historians develop in order to find ways of capturing a past that 'is alive and shifting …

both elusive and malleable', and he recalls Hayden White's suggestion that historians must acknowledge the utility of 'focusing on the practice, and not just the epistemology of history'. To find starting points that help outline a potential research project, there is always tension between what we already know and what it is we think we might need to find out: sometimes Griffiths's 'historical consciousness' has a useful role, but at other times the research process can feel intuitive (following a hunch). A hunch might arise in response to something generated by data, or be an intuited response to an event or creative output, or be something that jars with an existing body of knowledge. A hunch is an unproven assertion and might be vague or difficult to articulate, yet it is intriguing enough to pursue. Some hunches will lead nowhere, others will need more time and care to process, and some will be noted and left for future follow-up.

At the beginning of my research career, in the late 1980s (and pre-Internet), the fore-journey of researching required laborious library searching, in person, through paper journals and bibliographies in order to begin to shape and develop a working bibliography (Gale & Featherstone, 2011). This also involved identifying archives without online search tools; negotiating microfiche and reel-to-reel micro-film; finding hard-to-access sources; making use of labour-intensive, expensive processes for ordering materials; and only being able to study out-of-print publications by first travelling to distant locations. All these activities incurred time, labour, and travel costs: by today's standards, they often created impediments to timely and effective research. Now, many primary and secondary materials are more readily accessible. However, the level and quality of accessibility is in constant flux. For my last large-scale research project about the twentieth century, 60–70 per cent of what I consulted in paper form at the start of the process – books, periodicals, and archival holdings – had become newly available in digital form by the end of the seven-year research process (Gale, 2020). But having piles of research materials means nothing unless they can actually be used to formulate and develop the research project itself. The question as to what we do with what we find, and the skill sets needed to do it, is arguably more complex now than it ever has been.

Refined strategizing is needed to prioritize by *relevance*. Experience plays a part here, as well as the relative degree of access attainable (which can vary greatly based on institutional resources). Effective researchers need to engage in a process of what 'mindset' expert Matthew Syed (2019: 137) calls incremental and recombinant thinking: recombination 'is about cross-pollination, reaching across the problem space, bringing together ideas that have never been connected before'. Historians are used to working with data sets that accumulate incrementally, but recombinant thinking – being able to bring together diverse approaches, materials, and applications – sometimes works against what traditionalists might think of as a more orderly approach to research.

Sometimes my own approach to research could be more self-restrained: I am routinely led on by ideas and distracted by potential networks of people or practices. However, that seeming lack of discipline does not necessarily mean lack of method. The trick is to be able to recognize what is or is not a 'research rabbit hole' and whether getting lost – for a moment or two – might be worthwhile. Good research recognizes the productiveness of distraction, whereas poor research refuses any distraction and relies on ordered facts alone. In my early research, I tended to work against what was considered significant, wanting to focus more on non-canonical areas generally assumed to be less worthy. I was interested in women playwrights who worked in the commercial theatre during a period when academics presumed the industry was conservative, bland, and without subversive intent. Established practice at the time led us to believe that while 'amateur' historians might interest themselves in London's West End during the mid-twentieth century, the serious scholar should not do so; neither should they try to make a claim for a feminist identity in work by 'conservative', commercially oriented women artists. For me, however, working against the direction that others travelled was much more interesting and productive. Identifying my research niche was rewarding because I understood how this niche could challenge rigid orthodoxies. Other feminist histories being written in the 1990s were so concerned with tight ideological frameworks that they ruled out documentation and analysis of a lot of women's creative labour. Thus, my resistance to accepted narratives helped me find a niche with the potential to make a feminist historiographic intervention. As a feminist historian, I have always found it necessary to utilize a broad range of theory, methods, and approaches. My early research called on psychoanalytic, political, and social theories of gender contemporaneous to the period of enquiry, alongside theories and histories of labour and of popular culture. I used these as tools to develop critical reflections on women's creative work in the theatre.

Along with accepting that finding your research niche will help you both shape your research and position it in a broader context, it is equally important to build a robust understanding of the contextual basis, however broad or deep, of the creative work you want to explore. However, our reliance on context in research needs to be questioned, as Tracy C. Davis (2004: 204) warns. She writes that despite the way context 'help[s] to convey the immediacy of performances in the past, compensates for their perishability, and conveys their relevance to the past and present', it has a key problem: 'though it is provided for the sake of "completeness", one scholar's criterion for gestalt may be another's idea of irrelevance'. The contexts from which women's theatre labour (and that of other under-represented and under-researched groups) has been erased, raised, and re-erased, never lose significance or complexity. Davis (2004: 206) also reminds us that histories of women's labour in theatre and performance are built upon 'particular foundations' that are flexible and 'implicitly perspectival', not grounded in contextual 'truths'. Sometimes, the 'perspectival' nature of the archives on which our work might rely can present obstacles and challenges. As cultural historian Alison Light (2020: 205) advises, all 'archives are partial … revealing the preoccupations and predilections of those who have created them'. The researcher cannot resolve this sense of 'incompleteness' – whether the fluid nature of context or the perspectival nature of an archive – but can identify it and acknowledge its significance. A useful rule of thumb, even at the earliest stage of research, is that it is wise to triple-check contexts and sources and not assume, when you are told something doesn't exist (an artefact, letter, or recording, for example), that this is always true.

A researcher has to build their own 'archive' of works, contexts, and ideas to consider during the niche-finding stage of a research project. What is not in our 'archive' is often as important as what is. To recognize the potential use of something we were not seeking in the first place – and to train ourselves to see, capture, and evaluate this – is important. A portfolio of starter researcher questions might be: (1) How is my research subject/object shaped by the context in which it was generated? (2) How much of this context is both accessible and useful to detail and understand? and (3) Within this context, how will I recognize when I have found the thing I wasn't actually looking for, which may end up being key to my findings overall?

Identifying a niche places a research project in relation to a field of knowledge and stakes a claim for its potential to make an original contribution to one or more fields with which it is in conversation (Gagnier, 2010; Justus, 2019). Theatre and performance are well suited to critical and historiographical approaches that embrace pluralism, but this presents methodological challenges during the initial research phase.

Scaffolding Elsa Lanchester

Creating a scaffold – an external skeleton used to support an internal edifice – with which to identify, support, and develop a hunch into a more defined research niche is useful. A scaffold can hold up a building, facilitate enhancements during repair, or cover a building while it is completely reconstructed or deconstructed. My own research on the representation and analysis of women's labour in cultural histories of performance can serve as illustration. I am developing a project on the career of Oscar-nominated performer and author Elsa Lanchester (1902–1986), who worked in the United Kingdom and the United States across the avant-garde and mainstream live theatre, and in film and television, from the 1920s until the early 1980s. Lanchester is best known for three things: her marriage to the actor Charles Laughton in 1929; the erratic and not always comfortable nature of her professional partnership with Laughton; and her iconic role in *The Bride of Frankenstein* (1935), James Whale's expressionistic film starring Boris Karloff. Lanchester appears as Mary Shelley in the opening scenes and then returns as 'the Bride' in the closing minutes of the film. Her mummified body comes to life, her huge staring eyes visible between her facial wrappings as she raises her bandaged little finger from the bed, is helped to stand up, screams twice, hisses like a swan when Frankenstein's Monster touches her, and reaches out to Doctor Septimus Pretorius, the ruthless inventor of 'the Bride'. Lanchester was physically supported by stilts to amplify her height, and her hair, with its streaks of wavy white flowing from her temples, was built into an extended 'Egyptian' crown supported by a metal frame attached to her scalp. Her face has a look of extreme shock created in part by the bright, direct lighting. Lanchester's appearance in this role is iconic, in full global circulation. It is a role for which she reportedly spent days in make-up and on set, even though she is on camera as 'the Bride' for little more than a few minutes at the end of the film.

My initial research hunch was shaped by my interest in the professional and personal juxtapositions in Lanchester's career, and the way these might help me read and reflect on other women's performance careers more broadly. I identified a number of contextual beginnings for the project, aware that they may later be accorded different status depending on my findings about Lanchester's life and extensive career. These include the iconic image of Lanchester as 'the Bride', the longevity of her career, her numerous performances across media, and her work as an author. She wrote two autobiographical books: the commissioned *Charles Laughton and I* (Lanchester, 1938), which reads as a kind of self-reflection mixed with observations about both of their personal lives and careers, and *Elsa Lanchester: Herself* (Lanchester, 1983), which has an equally rich quality of detail and self-reflexivity.

A recent biography of Lanchester makes heavy use of these autobiographical works, yet frequently questions Lanchester's motives and indeed her memory of events. With its remit to reposition Lanchester beyond her role in James Whale's 1935 film, Victoria Worsley's *Always the Bride* gives insight into Lanchester's roles and the shape of her professional life (Worsley, 2021). Whilst Worsley's biography – the first on Lanchester – was written without an academic audience in mind, and without use of the substantial archive left by Lanchester in the United States, its appearance means that I have to refine the kinds of questions I need to ask in order to develop the research project. Lanchester's self-defined sense of agency casts her as something of a woman out of time, giving rise to the why, how, and 'so what' of Elsa Lanchester. Worsley's biography undermines Lanchester's 'self-definition' to some extent, and, despite the remit to 'put her story in the spotlight', it emphasizes the ways in which Lanchester tried to avoid being overshadowed by her husband's career, rather than focusing in analytic detail on Lanchester's own work. After Worsley, my sense is now that I might need to focus on two prolific periods of Lanchester's working life: the 1920s (when she ran a bohemian nightclub in London) and the 1940s (when she developed a cabaret act, first in Los Angeles and then through touring). Both periods represent times when her working life was arguably less defined by her connection to Laughton and more defined by her own live performances and producing. Worsley's biography has forced me to think more about what I need to gather and where I might I gather it from, in order to refocus my research niche.

Gathering

A great deal of what has been gathered in the early stages of a research project may not be usable: researchers have to file, store, reuse, or throw away a substantial proportion of what has been accumulated in the process of refinement. Many decide early in the process where and how they are going to narrow down their field of reference. I tend to operate in a kind of overdrive mode of collection, storage, and immersion. This is fuelled by a consumption-driven curiosity, where I am confident I can afford to take some diversionary paths in the hope of discovery. As Gaston Bachelard (2011 [1943]: 1) proposes, imagination 'frees us from immediate images and *changes* them'. In this spirit, imaginative gathering of contextual or factual evidence helps a researcher apply recombinant thinking to their findings. That said, with hard deadlines, sometimes the practice of gathering has to have a strict end date.

Effective research requires an appropriate filing, filtering, and logging system in which information can rest, to be returned to at a later point. The Internet makes available enormous amounts of data, not all trustworthy or easily surfaced (see Bratton & Peterson, 2013). With Elsa Lanchester, there are myriad photos, films, and articles in periodical databases referring to her work in the 1930s and 1940s. She features heavily on a number of cultish websites dedicated to the golden age of horror, where lots of anecdotal evidence is presented as 'truth'. In print, in addition to her two autobiographical books, one of which was recently reissued by demand of her fans (Lanchester, 2018), there is at least one academic article on Lanchester's work pre-film (McWilliam, 2014), and one book of lyrics (Lanchester, 1988). And there is an undigitized archive of her papers in the Margaret Herrick Library, owned by the Academy of Motion Picture Arts and Sciences in Hollywood: thirty-nine linear feet of material arranged in series and bequeathed to the library in 1987. This amount of catalogued material warrants pause. How much time and money will assessing these archival materials necessitate? Lanchester neither came from a throwaway culture nor was formally educated, but she was professionally astute, intellectually curious, and keenly aware of the significance of her work: the footage in the archive is gathered from some sixty years of her own career and from Charles Laughton's. To make full use of the archive will be an extensive and expensive undertaking for me as a UK-based scholar. It may be that a great deal of what is in this archive has been filtered into Lanchester's published works, though unfinished and unpublished works are also listed in the brief contents page. As Alison Light (2020: 202–3) reminds us, memory is 'associated with the work of retention, with hanging on to things, and yet no matter how extensive, an archive cannot represent a life, not even a working life.... Any archive is a selection; there are gaps and silences. Much lands in the bin which should not: some censorship is deliberate but survivals are often arbitrary.' Such considerations need to be weighed up. The archive listings suggest that the majority of contents relate to Lanchester's work from the 1930s onwards, although the 'gaps and silences' may appear as such only because of the 'perspectival' agenda behind the creation of the contents list of a catalogued collection. The assumption that materials from before her marriage to Laughton will be of less interest to prospective users may underpin the contents of the catalogue: in writing the finding aid, the archivist could have underplayed any pre-1929 materials. It could also be that more local avenues might prove useful: the London County Council records might detail the legal case against Lanchester in the 1920s, or the archive at Bedales (the co-educational private school where she taught dance early in her career) could generate materials more immediately helpful in aligning with the emerging scope of my project.[1]

Visiting an archive might be neither possible nor necessary in order to establish a research niche, but a researcher needs to know what kinds of materials could be available, and where and whether they have been catalogued. Here, writing an email to a helpful curator (as opposed to relying on the Internet or old handlists and finding aids) can be fruitful as they may inform you of more useful additional materials. Sometimes, there is no substitute for seeing holdings in person: visiting an archive may transform a project, revealing some vital factor that suggests the existing research scaffold is not viable. The process of gathering at this phase of a research project needs to be extensive, but it does not need to be thorough: you need to know what is available, but you do not necessarily have to address it all head-on at this point. Gathering research information is not the same thing as analysing or critiquing it. Anna Davin reminds us of Carlo Ginzburg's edict that 'the demand for more statistics, more proof, and less speculation or conjecture or indeed imagination' is common (Davin, quoted in Ginzburg, 1980: 6). Worsley provides facts about Lanchester's casting and trajectory of roles, but offers little that is imaginative or conjectural around the circumstances of either her work or her lifelong friendships with other artists and critics. I might, therefore, place more emphasis on the contextual – the world that surrounds and supports an actor's labour – in my emerging research niche.

While you are gathering materials, a 'conjectural paradigm' may involve a multidirectional process: the materials you collect will affect the choice of materials you go on to gather (Davin, quoted in Ginzburg, 1980: 15). Gathering might require a researcher to repeat a cycle of seeking and returning: something logged under one theme or type of data might be better understood in relation to a new finding, and so might be rethought in new terms. Just as Ginzburg (1980: 10–11) notes that a psychoanalyst might 'divine secret and concealed things from despised or unnoticed features, from the rubbish-heap, as it were, of our observations', so too might we need to operate by 'taking marginal and irrelevant details as revealing clues'. Clues can be returned to at any point in the research process, re-found out of seeming insignificance through recombinant thinking in a flexible and adaptable approach.

Here, I am suggesting ways of formulating best practices, but only on the basis that a 'best practice' is merely 'the best so far' and should be permitted to 'evolve through time' (Syed, 2019: 230). For example, in my niche-finding mission on Elsa Lanchester, I returned to her *Charles Laughton and I* some years after first reading it, only to be reminded that she signals her own shift in celebrity status and financial security by referring to the fact that her cook, Nellie Boxall, was dismissed from long-term service in Virginia Woolf's household, then came to work for her and Laughton in Bloomsbury, London. I had completely missed the significance on first reading. The Laughtons' stay in Bloomsbury was an interim arrangement: his film work was in the United States even though he wanted more stage work abroad, and meanwhile Lanchester's main source of employment at this point was live theatre in the United Kingdom. Their Georgian apartment was refurbished by modernist architect Wells Coates (who designed the Isokon Building in London's Belsize Park) and artist John Armstrong (with whom Lanchester had worked in the cabaret club she founded in the mid-1920s, the Cave of Harmony). In this lively and generous household, Lanchester's socialist roots perhaps afforded her a less Victorian attitude towards the servant class, and Boxall's working life must have been very different than when she was employed by Woolf. I returned to Alison Light's *Mrs. Woolf and the Servants* and found a section about this period in Boxall's life (Light, 2007). Light gives a superficial picture of Lanchester, devoid of her radical parents, modernist credentials, work as a performer, and transformation from relative poverty to burgeoning fame and wealth. For Light, Lanchester signifies a bohemian extravagance afforded by rising stardom (in contrast to the relative austerity of Woolf's intellectual and repressive household). This missed link between the three women offers more possibilities for research directions, as does the discovery of the short diary of Laughton's female private secretary from the Bloomsbury period, which is housed in the Bishopsgate Institute in London.

The research process is a kind of feasibility study. While gathering information, you might need more of the kinds of skills and competences micro historians identify. Ginzburg (1980: 12), for example, turns to hunter-gatherers as a model, pointing to attributes we might need to adopt: they 'learnt to sniff, to observe, to give meaning and context to the slightest trace. They learnt to make complex calculations in an instant, in shadowy wood or treacherous clearing.' There comes a point in the gathering process, however, when we have to allow that we have enough material to move to the next stage. Usefully, Bachelard (2014 [1964]: 201) reminds us that the feeling of being in a 'limitless world' can be disorienting: 'if we do not know where we are going, we no longer know where we are'. In the next phase of a project, we ask how we might identify and frame the relationships among what has been gathered, and how these relationships help formulate our niche more concretely.

Connect and Network: Function and Scale

As the process of research unfolds, you have to begin to put the evidence to *work*. Drawing connective lines between things and recognizing their potential place in a network of ideas, or in a sequence of networks, will allow you to sift through and connect seemingly disparate ideas and to identify different modes of critical reading and analysis. Anthropologist Tim Ingold's (2016 [2007]: 46) work on lines is usefully applied here. He suggests we think in terms of threads, traces, and surfaces, finding and making 'cuts, cracks and creases' to break down our discoveries and reading of materials, but also as a way of making further connections. With Elsa Lanchester, for example, I already have an in-depth understanding of UK theatre and performance cultures of the era in which she worked, but I need to familiarize myself with several other spheres: the wider cultural world in which she operated; academic and other writing on those we might now think of as queer artists working in London's bohemian cultural margins of the era; early horror movies; film histories of the 1930s and 1940s; Lanchester's filmography and stage roles (usefully catalogued by Worsley); and the professional and private lives of those artists with whom Lanchester socialized and worked in the United Kingdom and the United States.

In Lanchester's pre-film work in London, we can see direct lines between the art world, avant-garde dance, and the development of post-1918 London cabaret and alternative performance. We can directly relate these to the gendered challenges of the performance job market and issues around state intervention in performance cultures and child labour and performance (both in Lanchester's own work as a child with Isadora Duncan and in her later work with 'street' children). Similarly, we can make connections between Lanchester's socialist credentials, her autobiographic reflexivity, and the manner in which she effectively, and unusually, insinuated herself into the commercial theatre, without formal training or theatrical family connections. We can reformulate a network of the people with whom she worked at different levels of intensity across different media and artistic environs over a sixty-year period, as model/muse, actress, author, partner, producer, and so on. While there is surprisingly little academic work on Lanchester or indeed other female performers from the era with similarly varied and extensive professional profiles (see Gale, 2020), there is a fair amount of work on bohemian London between the wars, and the basic details of Lanchester's cabaret club feature in much of it. There are numerous queer theoretical positionings about *The Bride of Frankenstein* in which assessments of her performance are incorporated. These connections account for the broad field knowledge of my project, but the 'speculative ambition' that underpins my curiosity (as Tim Ingold (2013: 4) labels it) has to be mapped onto the final task. This involves identifying a more focused research niche that will shape and locate my contribution to the knowledge economy of TaPS, both within academia and hopefully beyond.

While the research process itself might reveal an appropriate destination – will it be written up as a conference paper, an article, a chapter, or even a monograph? – it is always good, even at this relatively early stage, to have a sense of the *function* and *scale* of the project. Sometimes research based on an extension of a smaller project will not work: scaling up is not always possible. Conversely, something originally conceived as small scale may in fact be conducive to becoming a larger project. What is a realistic expectation of the contribution your research can make, as well as the amount of time (and other resources) you have to complete it, and what is at stake for you as a researcher? The more experienced researcher may have a level of flexibility in terms of scale and timing that is not available to an early-career researcher, whose ability to assert their research niche may be driven by a sense of urgency.

Assuming that, as Edward Said (2012 [1975]: 3) suggests, a 'beginning immediately establishes relationships with works already existing, relationships of either continuity or antagonism or some mixture of both', even at the hunch stage one can begin to establish a good basis for making an original contribution. With a rough idea of the significance of your object/subject of enquiry, you will likely discover that some of what you considered original thinking was not so: someone else had already done the work. This is not necessarily a negative, for it gives you a strong sense of the 'continuity or antagonism' that will be facilitated by your own work. At first, I was frustrated by the appearance of Worsley's biography of Lanchester, but given that I can work with or against it, this changes how I choose to research a more critical (and focused) study. Worsley's book provoked a tipping point where I could move from knowing what my research was *not*, to knowing what it *might be*, then to knowing what my research niche *is* in terms of its potential readership and impact. I reformulated my focus at this point, with a stronger sense of the intellectual and cultural intervention the research might make.

Alternatively, sometimes a refocus is decided through commission: someone asks you to present at a conference or write for a special edition, and you shape your developing research niche accordingly. At times, only this kind of framework will force you to make a decision about scope, scale, and function, filtering and reorganizing findings to answer the commission. One does this in full knowledge that even after the commission has been fulfilled, the same research might underpin a different and even more significant project further down the line. Recursively, the niche may be redefined, and the process of locating and shaping research findings then begins again.

Note

1 Lanchester refers to the threat of litigation by the London County Council over her management of child labour in her Children's Theatre in the early 1920s.

References

Bachelard, G. (2011 [1943]). *Air and Dreams: An Essay on the Imagination of Movement*. Trans. E. R. Farrell & C. F. Farrell. Dallas, TX: Dallas Institute.
Bachelard, G. (2014 [1964]). *The Poetics of Space*. London: Penguin.
Bratton, J., & Peterson, G. T. (2013). 'The Internet: History 2.0?' In D. Wiles & C. Dymkowski, eds., *The Cambridge Companion to Theatre History*. Cambridge: Cambridge University Press, pp. 299–313.
Davis, T. C. (2004). 'The Context Problem'. *Theatre Survey*, 45(2), 203–9.
Gagnier, R. (2010). 'Twenty-First-Century and Victorian Ecosystems: Nature and Culture in the Developmental Niche'. *Victorian Review*, 36(2), 15–20.
Gale, M. B. (2020). *A Social History of British Performance Cultures 1900–1939: Citizenship, Surveillance and the Body*. Abingdon: Routledge.
Gale, M. B., & Featherstone, A. (2011). 'The Imperative of the Archive: Creative Archive Research'. In B. Kershaw & H. Nicholson, eds., *Theatre and Performance Methodologies*. Edinburgh: Edinburgh University Press, pp. 17–40.
Ginzburg, C. (1980). 'Morelli, Freud and Sherlock Holmes: Clues and Scientific Method'. Intro. A. Davin. *History Workshop*, 9(1), 5–36.
Griffiths, T. (2016). *The Art of Time Travel: Historians and Their Craft*. Victoria, Australia: Black.
Ingold, T. (2013). *Making: Anthropology, Archaeology, Art and Architecture*. Abingdon: Routledge.

Ingold, T. (2016 [2007]). *Lines: A Brief History*. Abingdon: Routledge.
Justus, J. (2019). 'Ecological Theory and the Superfluous Niche'. *Philosophical Topics*, 47(1), 105–24.
Lanchester, E. (1938). *Charles Laughton and I*. London: Faber and Faber.
Lanchester, E. (1983). *Elsa Lanchester: Herself*. New York: St. Martin's Press.
Lanchester, E. (1988). *A Gamut of Girls*. Santa Barbara, CA: Capra Press.
Lanchester, E. (2018). *Elsa Lanchester: Herself*. 2nd ed. Chicago: Chicago Review Press.
Light, A. (2007). *Mrs. Woolf and the Servants: The Hidden Heart of Domestic Service*. London: Fig Tree.
Light, A. (2020). *A Radical Romance: A Memoir of Love, Grief and Consolation*. London: Penguin.
McWilliam, R. (2014). 'Elsa Lanchester and Bohemian London in the Early Twentieth Century'. *Women's History Review*, 23(2), 171–87.
Said, E. (2012 [1975]). *Beginnings: Intention and Method*. London: Granta Books.
Syed, M. (2019). *Rebel Ideas: The Power of Diverse Thinking*. London: John Murray.
Worsley, V. (2021). *Always the Bride: A Biography of Elsa Lanchester*. Orlando, FL: BearManor Media.

CHAPTER 3

Interdisciplinary Acts: Learning about Theatre from the Social Sciences

Michael McKinnie

Interdisciplinarity is hard. Attempted seriously, it means having to work through a lot of thinking from other fields, as well as one's own, and this takes time and patience. Often, we are not trained in the bodies of thought that we engage. Their accepted wisdom, their taken-for-granted intellectual touchstones, their habituated ways of seeing – any or all of these might seem alien from the outside (though, to be fair, one's own field can be equally baffling, even from the inside). The opposite may also be true: in our attempts to get a grip on other fields we may domesticate them, turning them into more assimilable versions of ourselves, the methodological equivalent of what the actor Michael Bryant experienced whilst rehearsing the role of Badger in *The Wind in the Willows* at London's National Theatre in 1990: 'I've been watching these films of badgers and the way they move ... and the thing is they all move exactly like Michael Bryant' (quoted in Bennett, 1991).

There is also the risk of simply getting things wrong. Concepts and theories bring with them their own knotty intellectual histories and politics, and if transposing them from one field to another can be critically generative, it also risks detaching them from those points of origin and formative debates. In the process, important nuances may disappear and critical (and political) stakes may be lost. Concepts and theories may also lose their critical force as they are applied to an increasingly expansive repertoire of phenomena. The result can be a kind of smash-and-grab interdisciplinarity or, simply, misapplication and obfuscation. Even judicious borrowing is no guarantee of success. Concepts and theories from other fields can be perceived as jargon, however well they are explicated or their use is justified.

Interdisciplinarity also tends to sit uneasily within existing institutional practices and structures. Training in interdisciplinary research methods is often informal and ad hoc: doctoral programmes in the English-speaking academy remain predominantly discipline oriented, with all the implications for (say) coursework, methods training, progression, and supervision that follow from this. If interdisciplinarity is periodically in fashion with university research managers and granting bodies, it is often unclear what they mean when they use the term, or how they will address some of the institutional barriers to practising it. And, of course, interdisciplinarity can give off more than a whiff of opportunism when it is used as rhetorical cover for projects and initiatives that are poorly designed or of questionable merit.

So why do it? In part, the answer lies in what type of interdisciplinarity we want to practise. Disciplines evolve by taking up insights, theories, and methods from other disciplines or transdisciplinary fields (urban studies or feminist studies, for example). These other disciplines and fields need not be imagined to be cognate to theatre and performance studies (TaPS). In my case, I have turned to urban geography, as well as to political economy, sociology, economics, and political theory, among others. At times, I have turned to what might be considered transdisciplinary fields: urban studies; social and political thought; postcolonial or diasporic studies; and local, regional, national, or global studies. My aim has often been to develop more complex accounts of theatre's relationship with the state and the market – broadly speaking, between theatre and political economy – and engaging with the social sciences has been a way to do this (McKinnie, 2007; 2017; 2021). Here interdisciplinarity is not so much about initiating new dialogues between theatre scholars and social scientists or proposing new fields of study. Instead, it is more about finding different, and more systematic, ways to think about theatre and its place in the world – structurally, institutionally, and systemically. This involves identifying and delimiting relations between theatre and other social phenomena where these connections are not immediately visible or direct, but where they exist and have material effect. Put simply, interdisciplinarity helps get us from hunches about theatre's place in the world to theories of it.

In order to make this possible, though, in the first place we need to rethink theatre along more relational lines. I turn to the social sciences not so much because social scientists know things about the world that I, as a theatre scholar, do not (though of course it is partly about that). Instead, I turn to them because they make 'moves' with their material that I am unlikely to make with mine, for better or worse. These moves are often unremarkable within their own fields, but, when transposed to analysis of theatre, they suggest different, sometimes counterintuitive, approaches. If moves provide the catalyst for thinking differently, 'tricks' provide formal procedures that help draw out theatre's relationality at subsequent stages of the research process (especially when working with data). For sociologist Howard S. Becker (1998: 4), a trick is 'a specific operation that shows a way around some common difficulty, suggests a procedure that solves relatively easily what would otherwise seem an intractable and persistent problem'. Thinking about theatre structurally, institutionally, and systemically potentially poses a wide variety of problems that we are not always, already, equipped to tackle, so we need to make different moves, and formulate new tricks, to begin to address them.

Moves

Turning to the social sciences throws into relief – and in some ways helps correct for – ways of conceptualizing and observing theatre that are so habituated we may not even be aware of their effect. This applies whether or not social scientists are analysing theatre or other related phenomena. Specifically, turning to the social sciences calls into question our *critical imagery* (how we conceive of theatre itself) and our *patterns of observation* (where, and from what vantage point, we expect to find data related to it). As Becker (1998: 8) puts it, imagery is 'how we think about what we are going to study before we actually start our research' (and, by extension, the stories we tell to explain why our object of study appears the way it does). Theatre scholars often assume, a priori, the exceptionality of our object of study, and so we are often inclined to prioritize characteristics that ostensibly make it that way: most notably, its liveness and its ephemerality. This critical imagery is validated by the experience of being a spectator, to whom these elements are especially important.

Every field has observational biases, in terms of both its predispositions to look for data and its understanding of what the best position for perceiving that data will be. Avoiding these biases is impossible, and there are often good reasons for their existence – the challenge is to acknowledge and control for them. Analyses of theatre are especially susceptible to a form of observational bias that is known in the social sciences as the 'Streetlight Effect' (or, alternatively, the 'Drunkard's Problem'). The Streetlight Effect takes its name from a well-worn joke that goes like this: one night, a policeman comes across a drunk man searching for something under a streetlight. The cop asks, 'What are you looking for?' The man replies, 'I've lost my keys.' They search together and find nothing. The cop asks, 'Are you sure you left them here?' The man replies, 'No, I left them in the park.' The cop says, 'So why are you looking here?' The man responds, 'Because this is where the light is.' The Streetlight Effect accounts for the propensity to look for data where it is easiest to do so, rather than where it is most likely to be found. A theatrical version of the Streetlight Effect can arise if we axiomatically assume that the best place to look for data is onstage, during a live performance, from the position of a spectator (literally, where the light is best). If we have seen a live performance and are able to invoke this experience as a form of critical legitimation, so much the better. But theatre's structures, institutions, and systems (its keys, as it were) may only be partly discernible onstage. In other words, the machine's effects may be apparent, but the full spectrum of social relations it entails – its underlying design, component elements, productive capacity, modes of operation, and more – is only partly evident to spectators.

One potential, if seemingly counterintuitive, move is to ignore what is happening onstage. Or, more precisely, to ignore the particular show that is being performed (though not necessarily the performance itself, even if we might not make it our central focus). I take this move from sociologist Richard Sennett's (1992) *The Fall of Public Man*. Sennett illustrates how moves can be useful even if the argument they originally serve is not entirely persuasive. An argument rarely stands or falls because of a single move, and the potential critical efficacy of a move depends on its new context, not its old one.

In *The Fall of Public Man*, theatre is central to Sennett's theory of a healthy public sphere. 'In a society with a strong public life', he argues, 'there should be affinities between the domains of stage and street; there should be something comparable in the expressive experience crowds had in these two realms' (Sennett, 1992: 37). But Sennett does not try to determine how theatre shapes society, or vice versa. Instead, he is interested in times and places where they are socially coextensive and, by extension, what it means when they are not:

> Therefore, in associating performing arts and social relations, one must be open, simply, to the idea that serious, real, genuine art can assist in understanding a social condition widespread in society. It is equally important to get away from a language of cause and effect. For instance, there are affinities between Parisian stage costume and Parisian street dress in 1750. Instead of asking which determined the other – a meaningless exercise – it is more valuable to inquire what the similarities between stage and street dress, both markedly different from clothing considered appropriate for the home, tell about images of the body in the public. (Sennett, 1992: 38)

A concern with the relationship between theatre and the public sphere is hardly new, whether in the history of European thought or in contemporary performance scholarship (the relationship between theatre and the city is a more recent preoccupation). One can of course debate the merits of

Sennett's argument: no doubt many theatre historians would quibble with his characterization of the Parisian stage in the mid-eighteenth century, and, as Joel Kaplan and Sheila Stowell show in their analysis of how theatre costumes led fashion in late Victorian London, it can sometimes be a highly meaningful exercise not only to identify affinities between stage and street but also to ask how one determined the other (Kaplan & Stowell, 1995).

I am less concerned here, however, with the ultimate persuasiveness of Sennett's argument than I am with some of his moves while making it. First, Sennett's conception of theatre, and the social relations it involves, places a greater emphasis on abstraction and form than many theatre scholars (more likely to see aesthetic concerns) would. The participants in Sennett's theatre events are not particular spectators and performers, but social subjects playing roles, observing conventions, expressing and interpreting signs, and so on. 'There is concrete human experience' here, he argues, but it is 'embedded in this abstract set of logical relations' (Sennett, 1992: 39). Second, Sennett is unconcerned with a question that theatre scholars would almost certainly ask: What particular performances did these people attend? For Sennett, this question is largely beside the point. The individual show would be significant only insofar as its content prompted a distinguishable and attributable reconfiguration of that 'abstract set of logical relations'. While in principle such a scenario is possible, in practice it is rare – change is more likely to occur over time, through multiple and varied performances. Finally, Sennett's theatre is intensively social, but this sociality is intrinsically structural, and its relations unfold without necessary recourse to the content of a particular show. This move unwittingly supplies us with a neat trick, one we might use to think about theatre as a site of structured social relations: the Forget the Show Trick.

Tricks

I take the idea of tricks from Becker's (1998) *Tricks of the Trade: How to Think about Your Research While You're Doing It*. Becker is commonly associated with the 'Chicago school' of sociology (named for both the University of Chicago, which was its institutional home, and the city that often served as its research laboratory). His work extends a qualitative and ethnographic sociological tradition associated with, among others, Everett C. Hughes (Becker's PhD supervisor) and Robert E. Park. To some extent, *Tricks of the Trade* is a guide to research methods in the social sciences, but this generic classification risks implying that *Tricks of the Trade* is less ambitious, and less interrogative, than it is in practice.

Becker (1998: 6–7) sets out to question the 'comfortable thought routines academic life promotes and supports by making them the "right" way to do things'. For him, tricks are 'ways of thinking about what we know or want to know that help us make sense of data and formulate new questions based on what we've found. They help us get all the good we can out of our data by exposing facets of the phenomenon we're studying other than those we've already thought of' (Becker, 1998: 5). Tricks arise in relation to four main problems of critical practice: imagery, sampling, concepts, and logic. I have already mentioned imagery: how we think about what we are going to study before we start our research. Sampling relates to the question of selecting cases, both those that might provide the richest data and those that might challenge what we think we already know about our subject matter. Concepts refer to the general ideas we form about our subject based on what we learn from our imagery and sample. Logic involves identifying our major premises – especially those that seem so commonsensical as to require no explanations or justification – and manipulating them syllogistically (*if we think of X as Y, then Z*), so as to learn more from existing data rather than having to gather additional data.

We can see a trick in action in Becker's own research, even if he does not name it as such. Becker's best-known work is *Art Worlds* (Becker, 2008 [1982]), in which he examines artistic practices as forms of collective activity (including, intriguingly, art forms in which the 'creator' is commonly understood to be a single individual, such as painting). Any artwork, Becker argues, bears traces of that joint activity. At first glance, Becker's approach might seem especially amenable to theatre, since the production and consumption of theatre involve the work of multiple participants, and the signs of their involvement are often clearly evident, either directly (e.g. a cast of actors performing in a crowded theatre) or indirectly (a list of production staff in the programme). But the totality of those signs is never fully discernible in a single time and place, and those perceptible within the live theatre event are not necessarily the most analytically significant, even if their semiotic and phenomenological immanence may imply otherwise (the successful operation of the theatrical event typically encourages a kind of amnesia about other traces that may be less evident, or are only evident elsewhere, but are nonetheless important to the production of a performance).

So what is the trick? At the outset of *Art Worlds*, Becker (2008 [1982]: 2) makes a deceptively useful suggestion: 'Think of all the activities that must be carried out for a work of art to appear as it finally does.' This is the Think of All the Things Trick: identify, as comprehensively as possible, all the activities that had to happen in order for a performance to occur in the way it did (I interpret Becker's 'appear as it finally does' as applying not only to onstage action but to the event as a whole). Inevitably, many of these activities will happen outside the theatre, and will be undertaken by networks of organizations and institutions whose purview is elsewhere. Indeed, these activities may have been undertaken for the purposes of realizing something other than theatre entirely; it does not matter what they were intended to accomplish, just that they impinged in some material way upon the creation of a theatrical artefact, however conceived.

Where we draw the line in terms of which activities matter and which ones do not is a critical judgement call – we could, in principle, make this determination aesthetically, historically, behaviourally, and so on. Among the activities that matter, some will also matter more than others. The Think of All the Things Trick, though, can serve as an imagery trick, a sampling trick, a conceptual trick, and a logical trick. It is especially useful for helping tease out a complex picture of theatre's imbrication with other social institutions and non-theatrical phenomena: its relationship to them, its dependence on them, and its mobilization of them. It also helps us identify relevant scholarship within TaPS and connect it with research from elsewhere that does not address theatre but that may prove useful for understanding theatre's place in the world.

By way of an anecdotal example: in 2013 I was speaking with a staff member at London's Arcola Theatre, which is located in Dalston, East London. He commented that the theatre's box office data indicated a noticeable increase in South London residents buying tickets. A significant contributor to this increase, he suggested, was the fact that two years earlier the Arcola had moved to a new location several blocks south of its original home. The theatre was now located 150 metres (under 500 feet) from Dalston Junction, a long-disused station that had been reopened as a modernized London Overground station in 2010. Prior to 2010, rail connections to Dalston were poor; though the Arcola's original location was close to Dalston Kingsland station, on what was then the North London line, service on the line was notoriously unreliable (and the line itself largely followed an east–west route, so was of little use to travellers from South London). As part of a large-scale public investment programme, spurred in part by the 2012 London Olympics, Transport for London created the London Overground, a comprehensive transportation network that comprised new and existing rail lines extending across the city. Dalston Junction is on an Overground line that extends far south across the River Thames, and branches off to stations across South London. After 2010, a resident of South London could travel to the Arcola much more quickly and easily, without the complications of making multiple train, tube, or bus connections. If we think of all the things that made a performance happen at the Arcola in the way it did, we would likely want to include in our list developments in transportation infrastructure, as well as the substantial public investment these involved and the new patterns of urban mobility they enabled.

The Think of All the Things Trick invites us to think about theatre-going in different ways than we otherwise might. As an imagery trick, it might prompt us to think about how people come to gather as an audience in the first place: where they came from rather than simply who they are, why they are there, or what they are doing. In the process, we might imagine theatre audiences as a problem of economic geography rather than demography, repertoire, or ethnography (though of course it could be all those things too, and at the same time). This would also impinge on any hypotheses we might subsequently formulate. It can also be a sampling trick. Among all the theatres we could potentially select in order to study audiences, the Arcola might be an interesting case to include because, geographically, it seems to be an almost paradigmatically local or neighbourhood theatre (in a city that draws a notable portion of its audiences from beyond London). But if the box office data we gather to test this proposition suggests that our audiences are local to London and yet not quite as tightly drawn as past box office data had indicated, this might prompt us to consider how they travelled to the Arcola in the first place. This takes us to transportation – specifically, because the Arcola is in Inner London, public transportation – and the question of what has changed. As a conceptual trick, it might help clarify useful ways of thinking about what is going on at the Arcola, given our imagery and sample: here, 'infrastructure' might work better than 'gentrification' as a prerequisite for change. And logically, if we think of theatre-going as an infrastructural event, then it highlights the non-theatrical infrastructures on which theatre-going depends, and the different forms of public investment these often involve. We might also think about how theatre-going relates to other social practices this same infrastructure impinges upon (some of which will be artistic but many of which will not). The problem of infrastructure helps us identify potentially relevant scholarship within TaPS that takes it up (such as Boyle, 2016; Jackson, 2011; Schweitzer, 2015; Woolf, 2021) but also points us towards research in other disciplines that examines the politics and poetics of infrastructure, such as in geography (e.g. Cowen, 2014) and anthropology (e.g. Boyer, 2018; Carse, 2016; Larkin, 2018).

We might also begin to formulate tricks to address other research problems. What follows are two logical tricks of my own formulation. Each is inspired by an influential work commonly seen as a landmark or touchstone within a social scientific field, and each speaks to structures, institutions, and systems (and how these inevitably overlap in practice) in some way. The first, the Treat It the Same Trick, emerges from cultural economics: William J. Baumol and William G. Bowen's *Performing Arts: The Economic Dilemma* (Baumol & Bowen, 1966). This trick helps us distinguish theatre from other forms of economic activity. The second, the Treat the Micro as Macro Trick, comes from macroeconomics: John Maynard Keynes's (1973) *The General Theory of Employment, Interest and Money*. This trick uses theatre to help us understand how macroeconomic change happens and gives us a glimpse of what theatre's role within that might be.

The Treat It the Same Trick

When it was published in 1966, *Performing Arts: The Economic Dilemma* arguably inaugurated the field of cultural economics. Its key theoretical contribution endures: the 'cost disease'. It remains perhaps the singular achievement of its field, because the kind of comprehensive empirical and theoretical analysis that Baumol and Bowen undertake of live performing arts industries – primarily but not exclusively in the United States – has yet to be replicated. Why this is the case is open to question. It may be a combination of factors, including the relatively low status of cultural economics within the field of economics; the historical shift within economics towards more quantitative and econometric approaches rather than qualitative ones; and the fact that economics publishing is not book centred. Many of the issues that Baumol and Bowen examine are also now considered more through the lens of public policy than economics.

The cost disease proposes that it is difficult for the live performance industry to realize productivity gains (over time) at the same rate as the wider economy, due to high fixed costs that result from the inseparability of its workers from the goods they produce. (It is easy to see why the cost disease found greater purchase among economists in studies of labour-intensive service industries, such as health care and education, though it was first formulated in relation to live performance.) In perhaps the best-known passage of the book, Baumol and Bowen (1966: 164) argue:

> The characteristic of live performance which precludes substantial changes in its mode of operation is that the work of the performer is an end in itself, not a means for the production of some good.... The immediate result of this technological difference between live performance and the typical manufacturing

> industry is that while productivity is very much subject to change in the latter, it is relatively immutable in the former. Whereas that amount of labor necessary to produce a typical manufactured product has constantly declined since the beginning of the industrial revolution, it requires about as many minutes for Richard II to tell his 'sad stories of the death of kings' as it did on the stage of the Globe Theatre. Human ingenuity has devised ways to reduce the labor necessary to produce an automobile, but no one has yet succeeded in decreasing the human effort expended at a live performance of a 45 minute Schubert quartet much below a total of three man-hours.

The cost disease underlines the fact that, if an actor is both a performer and an industrial technology, live performance always depends on an interplay between artistry and economics. This concept has also been taken up in TaPS, where it has been used to help explain historical shifts in New York's theatre economy during the 1970s (H. Miller, 2016: 61–2) and London's during the 1980s (Hughes, 2015). Its strengths and limitations have also been debated (Boyle, 2017; McKinnie, 2021: 63–6; D. Miller, 2016). It is only possible to formulate the theory of the cost disease in the first place, however, because Baumol and Bowen make two prior moves: they treat live performance as economic rather than an artistic activity; and, having done this, they treat it like any other form of economic activity. If the cost disease is ultimately what distinguishes live performance industries from other industries economically, that distinction only becomes apparent by initially treating them the same. This distinctiveness is an outcome, not a premise, and one made possible by a categorical choice made at the outset.

In the Treat It the Same Trick, we resist the temptation to assume, a priori, that artistry is the most important part of theatre, or that theatre is always already distinctive. Instead, we identify how theatre is like other forms of economic activity: there is a firm (say, a theatre company); labour (actors, technicians, stage managers, ushers); equipment (lighting and sound gear); a plant (the venue); goods and services (the performance itself, programmes, merchandise); and consumers (spectators). By treating theatre the same as other economic enterprises, we gain a fuller picture of its productive – and reproductive – capacity. We might also observe how well coordinated the different elements of this theatrical apparatus are (without always appearing to be so) and how much of it is devoted to ensuring that its theatrical goods are not 'different every night', as it were, but are as much the same as possible, show after show.

Having done this, though, we might also notice that in the theatre a large proportion of production and consumption happen in the same time and place. This characteristic clearly distinguishes theatre from most manufacturing industries, where production and consumption happen at some degree of temporal and spatial remove from each other. The fact that theatre usually involves some sort of public spectacle also distinguishes it from other service industries where production and consumption happen in similarly coextensive and labour-intensive ways: if a public spectacle is desirable in the theatre, this tends not to be the case so much elsewhere; outside of the theatre, 'making a scene' tends to signal the breakdown of the production and consumption process rather than its success. We might also arrive at an alternative account of why co-presence is important: not because it instantiates some form of community, however defined, but because it enables forms of collective semiotic, phenomenological, and semantic efficiency that might otherwise be difficult to achieve. Through applying the Treat It the Same Trick, we begin to tease out theatre's economic characteristics, its affinities with and differences from other industries, and alternative accounts of why these relations matter.

The Treat the Micro as Macro Trick

Theatre scholars often take a determinedly microcosmic approach to performance. We tend to focus on specific instances, and the things that make them unique or different from other specific instances. The purpose of the Treat the Micro as Macro Trick is to understand how theatre is caught up with systemic social forces – especially but not only economic ones – not by treating these forces as wholly endogenous to theatre but by seeing them as operating within and through theatre, though often in ways that are not entirely straightforward or predictable. The Treat the Micro as Macro Trick is in two parts: first, treat the case study as an economic one rather than a theatrical one; second, treat it as macroeconomics rather than microeconomics. In the context of my work, this trick helps surface theatre's relation with broader economic forces, such as the operations of property markets and global finance networks.

The Treat the Micro as Macro Trick is inspired by John Maynard Keynes's *The General Theory of Employment, Interest and Money*, one of the most influential works on modern political economy. We should take the book's title at face value: *The General Theory* is, insistently, a work of *macro*economics. Keynes is interested in general and not special cases, in problems relating to the operations of entire economies, not individual people or households. Throughout *The General Theory*, Keynes turns to familiar, but decidedly non-economic, phenomena to help illustrate macroeconomic logic. These are often examples familiar to his readers from their daily lives, such as the 'Beauty Contest' theory. The Beauty Contest helps explain price fluctuations in equity markets. Keynes (1973: 156) argues that these are not the result of investors accurately assessing underlying asset values (as proponents of the efficient market hypothesis would claim) but are instead the result of investors trying to guess what other investors, in the aggregate, think an asset's value is:

> Or, to change the metaphor slightly, professional investment may be likened to those newspaper competitions in which the competitors have to pick out the six prettiest faces from a hundred photographs, the first being awarded to the competitor whose choice most nearly corresponds to the average preferences of the competitors as a whole; so that each competitor has to pick, not those faces which he himself finds prettiest, but those which he thinks likeliest to catch the fancy of the other competitors, all of whom are looking at the problem from the same point of view.... We have reached the third degree where we devote our intelligences to anticipating what average opinion expects the average opinion to be. And there are some, I believe, who practise the fourth, fifth and higher degrees.

The Beauty Contest is still widely discussed within economics and related fields (Cespa & Vives, 2015; Ilomäki, 2018; Liang et al., 2017; Mauersberger et al., 2020; Stenfors, 2014).

Keynes tells a story about a beauty contest because beauty contests illustrate a much larger story about macroeconomics – methodologically, he reads the micro as macro and, in doing so, reveals something about the operations of capitalism writ large. We can do the same using the Treat the Micro as Macro Trick: How is a single performance a story about capitalism? But we can also do something that Keynes does not. In the Beauty Contest theory, the beauty contest itself falls away once its explanatory power is exhausted. But in the Treat the Micro as Macro Trick, we are still interested in theatre's place within the economy – as a case, not just a hermeneutic. We can also apply the trick to a wide variety of theatrical artefacts: not only individual live performances, but potentially any material involved in the production and consumption of theatre (which could apply it to everything from venues to programmes to published scripts and more). It will work better in some instances than others – tricks are always context dependent – but its potential utility is wider than might first appear to be the case.

In practice, this trick has proven especially useful in relation to 'site-specific' performance. At first glance, site-specific performance appears almost ineluctably micro: its efficacy is premised on achieving spatial particularity and incommensurability (this performance, in this place, will be like no other). But if we treat site-specific performance as macro, a different picture emerges. In London, site-specific performance has, for a long time, been as much about the operation of real estate markets – and the role of developers, finance capital, and the state within them – as it has been about theatre. A show such as HighTide Theatre's production of Beth Steel's *Ditch* (2010), which was staged in the disused railway tunnels under Waterloo Station, is tied up with the commercialization of Britain's historical railway infrastructure, as its owners attempted to monetize this infrastructure to compensate for government cuts to its operating grant (Network Rail ultimately sold off the bulk of its commercial property assets to a partnership of global property investors and private equity). One could take a similar approach to Punchdrunk's *Faust* (2006), whose occupation of a then-empty warehouse in London's Docklands was made possible through the company's partnership with the property development giant Ballymore. The owner of the Bermondsey tobacco factory in which Shunt staged *Money* (2009) was (and is) the corporation Sellar, which is best known for developing the ninety-five-storey Renzo Piano-designed Shard nearby at London Bridge. In all these examples, macroeconomics predicates both the availability and site of the venue and, to a significant degree, the staging parameters and governing aesthetic of the show. Furthermore, these examples raise questions about the operation of global real estate markets and theatre's place within them: site-specific performance is arguably a means to help smooth the transition of property assets from one type to another, while extracting some additional use value in the process. Taken together, these performances are a sign of the growing importance of property in the creation and storage of wealth, for states, private companies, and individuals alike. Some of this story will be particular to London, since the city's property market is especially speculative, but other cities around the world are experiencing their own property booms, with all the inequalities these entail. These macroeconomic forces are global in scale and effect, and theatre is one way to see them unfolding, if we know how and where to look. That's the trick.

Conclusion: Unfamiliar Theatres

My initial hunch in using any of these tricks usually goes something like this: I think this theatrical thing might have something to do with that non-theatrical thing. Although there is always a risk that this relationship is projected rather than actual, more often the problem is that the connections are not immediately apparent or direct – it is one thing to posit the existence of relations between phenomena, theatrical and otherwise, but it is another to figure out how these relations work and why they matter for the study of theatre. We miss connections, or misread them, or miscalculate their significance not so much because of a lack of expertise (or not always because of a lack of expertise) but because our accustomed ways of thinking about, and working with, our objects of study are not wholly suited to the task at hand. Moving from a hunch to a hypothesis – and from positing relations to figuring out, systematically, the forms and significance of these relations – is where interdisciplinarity can be especially useful.

Practising interdisciplinarity is not necessarily comfortable. But this discomfort is often important: rather than identifying outward affinities between theatre and other phenomena – turning Michael Bryant into a badger who acts like Michael Bryant – we are confronted by differences, dissimilarities, and disjunctions, even within our own discipline: There are badgers everywhere, and what do we do about them? Moves and tricks are useful because they make disciplinary gaps generative for studying the real world. They may be most important early in a research process, when they are likely to disrupt our habituated ways of seeing and working, even if this is also when they are likely to feel the strangest. They help generate new insights about cases, not through happenstance but by working systematically with the material at hand. Their formality is especially useful in TaPS, where consciously designed and executed methods are unusual. Of course, the picture of theatre, and its place in the world, that emerges from performing moves and tricks may not be familiar, or even entirely reassuring. But, in the end, that is the point of doing them.

References

Baumol, W. J., & Bowen, W. G. (1966). *Performing Arts: The Economic Dilemma; a Study of Problems Common to Theater, Opera, Music and Dance*. New York: Twentieth Century Fund.

Becker, H. S. (1998). *Tricks of the Trade: How to Think about Your Research While You're Doing It*. Chicago: University of Chicago Press.

Becker, H. S. (2008 [1982]). *Art Worlds*. 25th anniversary ed. Berkeley: University of California Press.

Bennett, A. (1991). 'Diary: What I Did in 1990'. *London Review of Books*, 24 January.

Boyer, D. (2018). 'Infrastructure, Political Energy, Revolution'. In N. Anand, A. Gupta, & H. Appel, eds., *The Promise of Infrastructure*. Durham, NC: Duke University Press, pp. 224–43.

Boyle, M. S. (2016). 'Container Aesthetics: The Infrastructural Politics of Shunt's *The Boy Who Climbed Out of His Face*'. *Theatre Journal*, 68(1), 57–77.

Boyle, M. S. (2017). 'Performance and Value: The Work of Theatre in Karl Marx's Critique of Political Economy'. *Theatre Survey*, 58(1), 3–23.

Carse, A. (2016). 'Keyword: Infrastructure: How a Humble French Engineering Term Shaped the Modern World'. In P. Harvey, C. Jensen, & A. Morita, eds., *Infrastructures and Social Complexity*. London: Routledge, pp. 27–39.

Cespa, G., & Vives, X. (2015). 'The Beauty Contest and Short-Term Trading'. *Journal of Finance*, 70(5), 2099–154.

Cowen, D. (2014). *The Deadly Life of Logistics: Mapping Violence in Global Trade*. Minneapolis: University of Minnesota Press.

Hughes, J. (2015). 'The Theatre and Its Poor: Neoliberal Economies of Waste and Gold in *Les Misérables* (1985) and *Road* (1986)'. *Theatre Journal*, 67(1), 1–19.

Ilomäki, J. (2018). 'Animal Spirits and Risk in Financial Markets'. *Journal of Banking & Financial Economics*, 1, 52–9.

Jackson, S. (2011). *Social Works: Performing Art, Supporting Publics*. New York: Routledge.

Kaplan, J., & Stowell, S. (1995). *Theatre and Fashion: Oscar Wilde to the Suffragettes*. Cambridge: Cambridge University Press.

Keynes, J. M. (1973). *The General Theory of Employment, Interest and Money*. London: Macmillan.

Larkin, B. (2018). 'Promising Forms: The Political Aesthetics of Infrastructure'. In N. Anand, A. Gupta, & H. Appel, eds., *The Promise of Infrastructure*. Durham, NC: Duke University Press, pp. 175–202.

Liang, H., Yang, C., & Cai, C. (2017). 'Beauty Contest, Bounded Rationality, and Sentiment Pricing Dynamics'. *Economic Modelling*, 60, 71–80.

Mauersberger, F., Nagel, R., & Bühren, C. (2020). 'Bounded Rationality in Keynesian Beauty Contests: A Lesson for Central Bankers?' *Economics*, 14(1). https://doi.org/10.5018/economics-ejournal.ja.2020-16.

McKinnie, M. (2007). *City Stages: Theatre and Urban Space in a Global City*. Toronto: University of Toronto Press.

McKinnie, M. (2017). 'Institutional Frameworks: Theatre, State, and Market in Modern Urban Performance'. In K. Solga, ed., *A Cultural History of Theatre in the Modern Age*. London: Bloomsbury, pp. 17–33.

McKinnie, M. (2021). *Theatre in Market Economies*. Cambridge: Cambridge University Press.

Miller, D. (2016). 'Average Broadway'. *Theatre Journal*, 68(4), 529–53.

Miller, H. (2016). *Drop Dead: Performance in Crisis, 1970s New York*. Evanston, IL: Northwestern University Press.

Schweitzer, M. (2015). *Transatlantic Broadway: The Infrastructural Politics of Global Performance*. Basingstoke: Palgrave Macmillan.

Sennett, R. (1992). *The Fall of Public Man*. New York: W. W. Norton.

Stenfors, A. (2014). 'LIBOR as a Keynesian Beauty Contest: A Process of Endogenous Deception'. *Review of Political Economy*, 26(3), 392–407.

Woolf, B. (2021). *Institutional Theatrics: Performing Arts Policy in Post-Wall Berlin*. Evanston, IL: Northwestern University Press.

CHAPTER 4

Mixing Methods in a Multi-Sited, Collaborative Project: Researching Migration, Working with Variation

Emine Fişek

As a theatre and performance studies (TaPS) scholar with research interests in migration and citizenship, I followed the mass arrivals of displaced peoples into Europe that began in 2011 and reached their apogee in 2015–16 avidly and with alarm. This was a period when unprecedented numbers of migrants from across the Middle East fled violence resulting from the Arab Uprisings, the Syrian and Yemeni Civil Wars, and the rise of the Islamic State. For individuals wanting to reach destinations in the European Union (EU), this meant perilous journeys on the Mediterranean or Aegean Seas, or overland through Turkey and the Balkans.[1] While EU member states debated a range of policies designed to enhance continental border security, these migrants languished in overcrowded holding camps, their hopes for permanent sanctuary or resettlement frustrated by rigid migration regimes.[2] Meanwhile, in stark contrast to the reluctance displayed by European states, theatre and performance artists, from Greece to the United Kingdom, responded with urgency. While some performances documented the experiences of migrants, refugees, and asylum seekers, others offered scathing critiques of the EU and developed alternative visions of sociality, care, and responsibility.

From my vantage point in Istanbul, Turkey, this configuration of politics and aesthetics seemed intuitive and yet remote. During this period, Turkey's geographic proximity to (and involvement in) the Syrian conflict made it host to the largest number of forcibly displaced people worldwide.[3] The international emergency occasioned by the influx of refugees at Turkey's borders preoccupied the country's political discourse, and civil society was quick to mobilize in response to the humanitarian crisis. Turkish theatre and performance practitioners, however, were quiet on the subject of the escalating catastrophe. Despite abundant experimentation happening in theatre and performance (Adak & Altınay, 2018: 201–6), a range of political and economic factors constrained the work of artists on this topic. Why did Turkish artists appear so paradoxically out of step with the rest of Europe?

Across Europe, the wide variety of theatre and performance practices that arose in response to the migrant (or refugee) crisis reflect differences in the ways nations experience the relationship between migration and neoliberal globalization, as well as in articulations of European identity and historical responsibility vis-à-vis refugees. Comparative national (and regional) differences in theatre and performance practices provide insight not only into variations in political and aesthetic (mis)alignment across contexts, but also into the local complexities and displacements that have structured responses to this crisis, and ultimately into debates on the viability of a shared, European migration regime. Yet such a complex situation presents researchers with many challenges, both conceptual and practical. Could any single research project hope to discover the causes and manifestations of such differences, including in levels and choices of artistic response, types of artist-migrant alliances, aesthetic approaches, impacts in the sociocultural and political spheres, and resources for documenting theatre and performance? Numerous pragmatic factors compound the challenge. For example, when approaching the European migrant crisis, one individual could undertake national and regional comparative research to some degree, yet engaging with migrants as the study's informants will require knowledge of diverse languages and dialects. Similarly, accessing archival documentation, such as theatre companies' records, will necessitate carefully cultivated, often pre-existing relationships.

This chapter proposes, in a hypothetical manner, that the complexity of theatre and migration in the context of the European migrant crisis could be addressed by a multi-sited, collaborative research design featuring a mixed methods approach. My goal is to demonstrate that the challenges involved highlight methodological issues that even a single researcher, such as a doctoral dissertator, weighs in setting out a multi-contextual project. Typically, TaPS research accounts for both the protocols and the history of the artistic practices, funding schemes, and administration that give rise to productions: scholars study performances' institutional or spatial contexts, encounters between artists and audiences, and varieties of post-performance diffusion. Researching each of these foci involves different methods: that is, distinct kinds of information and ways to ascertain these. Thus, multiple methods combine even in case studies of a single production. As TaPS scholars, we often disavow how methods are brought together, yet when teams of scholars collaborate on a multi-sited project, the consequences of such a disavowal are apt to make for difficulty in determining comparability between discoveries, and to spawn confusion about a project's research questions, objectives, and design/protocol; implicit analytic assumptions and traditions; and organization of day-to-day procedures.

Multi-sited research, in other words, adds orders of complexity. Yet as much as methodological variation and inconsistency characterize the multi-sited research enterprise, the mixed methods that can be used to address discrepancies both within and across sites and cases will remain relevant in any research context. Clarifying choices about, and identifying principles for, mixing methods will be central to tracing the relationship between the hypothetical research project's design and its theoretical commitments and contributions to knowledge about the migration crisis of 2011–16. The following sections elaborate on the use of mixed methods in relation to collaborative dynamics and the determination of research sites and case studies. The final step in the research design's articulation will be to decide *which* mix of methods will collect the kinds of data that will provide answers to the project's basic questions.

Varieties of Collaboration

The feasibility of this hypothetical research project will depend on the recruitment of a team of researchers with appropriate expertise and contacts. Members could hail from disciplinary backgrounds as wide ranging as TaPS, literary studies, communication studies and rhetoric, social anthropology, political science, and urban studies, provided each is adept in performance analysis. Ideally, collaborators will begin by conducting literature reviews on diverse approaches to theatrical representations of international migrancy into Europe during the twenty-first century. While researchers' disciplinary diversity might not hinder agreement about the central focus on performance, it will likely lead to divergence when determining relevant literatures, a factor that might re-emerge when project members debate emphases and traditions for interpreting project findings. One researcher may find it imperative to engage debates on artistic intentionality and political efficacy in recent scholarship on political theatre (Rancière, 2011; Tomlin, 2019), for example, while another may position their study of theatre and performance to intervene in related literatures from which these forms are often absent, such as the scholarship on migration and city-making (Çağlar & Glick Schiller, 2018; Glick Schiller & Çağlar, 2011).

These differences, manifesting during the project's literature review and data-interpretation phases, may mean that collaborators disagree about the kinds of data necessary for realizing the project's objectives, and the balance between different methods by which this data is to be gathered. For example, a project member who wishes to join the conversation on migration and city-making (whose literature is associated with an anthropological tradition that emphasizes long-term ethnographic study) may stress the importance of participant observation, qualitative interviews, or survey methodologies; another project member may instead choose to privilege performance analysis via recorded media, thus working within a medium where ethnographic tools will yield little output. Often, research teams will agree in principle on basics, and decide that either congruence or variety in data-gathering methods and emphases is a strength. Nonetheless, it will be vital for collaborators to talk this through transparently and explicitly: keeping in touch with one another throughout the duration of the research project, expressing and debating ideas, sharing data, discussing evolving concepts along with findings, and exchanging work in progress in all forms are research practices that will run in parallel to data collection and analysis at each site. Consultation will contribute insights to the project's cohesion as well as researchers' challenges, from collecting feedback on critical priorities to negotiating the contours of group identity.

In collaborative research, official and unofficial power dynamics inform these encounters, but questions of power, authority, and agency are further exacerbated when the collaboration is with research participants. In addition to collaboration among members of a research team, TaPS research on migration will likely feature collaborative encounters with the members of the community being researched. For example, studying the Augsburg-based Grandhotel Cosmopolis, a combined refugee accommodation centre, commercial hotel, and communal art space, Anika Marschall (2018) encountered collaboration both within the working principles of this long-term socially engaged performance and as a methodological demand made by the community being researched. Marschall (2018: 148) defines Grandhotel Cosmopolis as a 'durational performative intervention' that constructs collaborative encounters between artists, hoteliers, and interested refugees; since the project's 2012 inauguration, its goal has been to create spaces for prolonged exchange where refugee narratives can be delivered and received without reference to the urgent temporalities of the migrant crisis. Upon contacting the organizers to arrange a visit in 2017, Marschall was asked to participate in the Grandhotel's practice of social commitment by proposing a form of 'knowledge exchange', presenting an offering of some kind that would reciprocate the 'knowledge' she would glean as a researcher. As straightforward as this demand appeared to be, however, Marschall (2018: 154, 156) noted upon arriving in Augsburg that she 'felt quite hesitant to directly approach and talk to people in this very public space and instead [she] actively chose to occupy the role of listener and observer rather than interviewer with set questions'.

In Marschall's situation, the community being researched posited collaborative engagement as a methodological precondition for access. Marschall (2018: 156) noted, however, that the 'part-observational lens and part-participatory engagement behaviour already revealed the many entangled institutional domains of the Grandhotel Cosmopolis', from asylum administration to migration activism to academic research. Collaboration, in other words, risked obscuring the real or perceived differentials of wealth or privilege that structured exchange in each of these contexts, pushing Marschall to question its value as a *given* methodology. As Bradley D. Olson and Leonard Al Jason write, 'The goal of a collaborative partnership is for all stakeholders of a project to have dialogue in an authentic relationship', 'with the aim of full and honest sharing of information' (Olson & Jason, 2015: 369, 403). Ideally, this mode of collaborative research eliminates the felt and real effects of the hierarchy between researcher and research subject, and recognizes research subjects' lived experiences as a form of 'experiential expertise'. Nonetheless, tensions can arise when this expertise does not conform to the theoretical priorities and expectations of the collaborator/researcher. As a result, TaPS researchers focusing on migration can encounter the tensions of collaborative methods at the level of content *and* process, questioning whether migrants are merely 'sources' or fully empowered partners in determining the collaborative performances under scrutiny, as well as whether migrants are merely 'informants' or fully empowered partners in determining their own research outcomes. As the conversation with Natalie Alvarez and Patrick Anderson in Chapter 5 of this volume explores in detail, the ethics of documenting such tensions become far more complicated when power differentials among research stakeholders involve vulnerable populations, and when the onus falls upon researchers to explicate plans for ethical methods before research is conducted.

Determining Sites

If the objective for the hypothetical project is to explore the diversity of theatre and performance practices that emerged in response to the migrant crisis within Europe, which sites will best exemplify this? Choices need to be broad enough to be representative yet limited enough to be practical. The lead researcher would need to undertake a literature review to initially scope the project, and then as collaborators are identified they would need to be consulted. For the sake of argument (and taking the liberty of extrapolating from the secondary literature on this topic), I propose that the following nations would be particularly fruitful for demonstrating heterogeneity: the United Kingdom, Germany, France, Italy, Greece, and Turkey. This choice is already momentous, as it not only delimits the project's geographic coverage but does so by taking the nation-state as the basic unit of analysis, as well as the gross unit of comparison within the EU bloc. What do these choices take for granted about the appropriate scope of 'crisis', 'migration', and 'response', or even 'theatre and performance'? How do they imagine and condition the nature of these phenomena? And how will this affect the project's methods?

Since attention to variation is the guiding impetus behind this project, the frame of the nation-state does make preliminary sense. Each of these nations experienced migration distinctly. Each welcomed, aided, tolerated, or repulsed migrants according to geographic, ideological, and political exigencies. As with Turkey's decades-long EU accession application and the United Kingdom's 'Brexit' referendum of 2015, each nation had distinct agendas for cooperating with or breaking from the EU, both in its reaction to the migrant crisis and in relation to ongoing political trends. Not only did their economic situation affect each nation's capacity to absorb migrants' labour and expertise, the ways in which these capacities were assessed revealed distinct pressure points from anti-immigrant and xenophobic parties. And importantly, each nation had a different funding scenario for the arts and boasted varied infrastructures for showcasing performance; these resources ultimately proved fundamental for nimble left-leaning companies as the crisis unfolded. Charlotte McIvor (2019) underlines precisely this dynamic in her study of the EU's changing arts and culture initiatives in the aftermath of the European refugee crisis. EU policies supporting artistic work on forced migration are fundamental to sustaining migrant and/or minority ethnic artists, McIvor argues, but documenting the impact of macro-level commitments on specific artists and communities is only possible with reference to *local* arts infrastructures and funding priorities. McIvor (2019: 232) proposes a 'comparative *national* approach' that resonates with the demands of my hypothetical multi-sited project: collaborating researchers are responsible for tracing all these site-specific details and curating the body of relevant laws and policies that help explicate how performances came about, what they sought to address, and why (at times) they failed to flourish.

While equating *sites* with *nations* makes practical sense in some respects, this puts pressure on the research question's employment of the 'migrant crisis' framework. Notions of 'crisis' are related to questions of narrative authority: When, under what circumstances, and by whom are certain historical developments identified as unique, unprecedented, and constitutive of a turning point? The 'European migrant crisis' not only assumes a particular narrative point of view (one often associated with the mainstream Euro-American news media), but also adopts these narrators' temporal container as a self-explanatory frame. In contrast, Emma Cox and Caroline Wake demonstrate that the crisis consciousness that has motivated recent TaPS scholarship on migration was already orienting research agendas at the turn of the twenty-first century (Cox & Wake, 2018). Multi-sited enquiry can thus push collaborating researchers to bracket the contestable parameters of crisis by demonstrating the impossibility of a universal timeline (as well as clear geographic or cultural boundaries) for migrant emergency and artistic response.

Studying migration through a nation-state framework poses the additional challenge of situating cross-border collaborations and regional sensibilities for political as well as artistic response. Here, again, national sites are often convenient for organizational and grant-writing purposes, allowing projects to recruit researchers conversant in the dominant cultures and spoken languages of each national context. Yet the political and aesthetic realities of the artists who made the performances, and the geographic contexts of the professional networks among whom they circulate, will often exceed these territorial units. Yana Meerzon, Katharina Pewny, and Tessa Vannieuwenhuyze argue that 'the theatre artist situated at the crossroads of lived experiences of migration and multiple forms of theatre and performance' often employs multilingual forms of expression, including hybridity and code-switching (Meerzon et al., 2018: 258). Even when a production's performance language is singular, the heteroglossia of its *backstage* languages can discredit a monolingual frame. For example, Turkish playwright Berkay Ateş's *Hak* is a solo performance that features Syrian theatre artist Amal Omran, who fled Damascus for Turkey. *Hak* was a Turkish, Belgian, and German co-production that premiered in Cologne in 2014 before coming to Istanbul, where Omran performed in Arabic and Ateş's Turkish script was projected as surtitles. This case study might be included in the project's 'Turkish' site for a variety of reasons, but insisting on a national frame would negate *Hak*'s 'complex web of dramaturgical relations, propositions, and choices' (Meerzon et al., 2018: 259).

In migration studies, Andreas Wimmer and Nina Glick Schiller have long decried the limits of a 'methodological nationalism' that equates migrants' practices and sociability with singular ethnic identities or national territories, negating the hybrid, transnational contexts of migrants' political subjectivities (Wimmer & Glick Schiller, 2003). Caleb Johnston and Geraldine Pratt's study of *Nanay*, a testimonial performance developed from the narratives of Filipina domestic workers in Canada, is an example of methodological transnationalism from a TaPS perspective (Johnston & Pratt, 2019: 127). Starting with a focus on the meanings and resonances that *Nanay*'s 2009 Vancouver premiere generated for audiences, Johnston and Pratt argue that this performance held limited explanatory power when it came to understanding the global care chain, specifically how the Filipino diaspora grapples with migration to North America. To complicate this picture, they document *Nanay*'s journey from Vancouver to Metro Manila, where the piece was first presented to middle-class audiences in an established theatre venue, and then reworked entirely in Tagalog in the context of a migrant-sending community on the city's outskirts. Upon returning to Canada, *Nanay* was refashioned in Whitehorse, where collaboration with Tlingit artists and audience members revealed how racial capitalism positions Filipino labour migration vis-à-vis Indigenous dispossession.

Nanay's transnational and transcultural travels demonstrate the limits of what any single narrative context is able to contribute to our understanding of the *global* forces that affect migrants' lives. As Ric Knowles (2004: 100–1) notes regarding touring or relocated performances more generally, 'meaning is ultimately produced in the theatre through audiences' lived experience … and the social, cultural, and political impact of the theatrical event lives in the ways in which that experience is knitted into the social fabric of the day'. At the same time, however, performances depicting migration are often exemplary milieux for considering tensions between the context-specific nature of theatrical experience and the *multiple* social fabrics at stake in a given production. For Johnston and Pratt (2019), this means that researching *Nanay* involves multi-sited ethnography, the documentation of performance-making processes, and management of the archive that results from the performance's travels. Yet *Nanay*'s travels also demonstrate that methodological transnationalism is less about 'moving theoretical insights from one place to another' and more about the mixed methods that come into play when situating the kinds of knowledge transmission that any single theatre and performance event makes possible (Johnston & Pratt, 2019: 10).

Similarly, a multi-sited research project on performance and migration in the context of the European migrant crisis may find that the frame of the nation-state remains indispensable for research purposes, as the modern bureaucracies of migration (from the granting of asylum to the politics of integration) remain decidedly national in their reach. And yet, registering material and political impacts of the nation-state without automatically assuming that case studies take their political, cultural, and aesthetic cues from it may be what mixed methods makes possible: researchers may supplement the results of their performance analysis or institutional history with information gleaned from semi-structured or oral-historical interviews. The challenge here will be to consider variation not only between different national sites, but also between the implicit assumptions underwriting the choice of different methods for specific cases.

From Sites to Cases

Identifying national contexts is a necessary step in determining the multi-sited project's parameters, yet the concern with sitedness hardly ends there. Theatre and performance practices encompass artistic activities produced in and by national theatre institutions, municipal theatre institutions, public–private partnerships, theatre and performance festivals, not-for-profit theatres, community and neighbourhood theatres, and (particularly since the advent of the COVID-19 pandemic) digital platforms. Retaining institutional variety means that researchers' analytic strategies need to pay consistent attention to the political economy of performance-making, identifying how different funding structures, institutional frameworks, and political and civic ideologies affect the productions in question. Here again, attending to content inevitably means attending to process. Certain methods will harvest a great deal of material in one context, while unearthing far less in another. For example, case studies of productions undertaken by well-funded and institutionalized theatres may draw on robust stores of archival material, whereas others may offer fragmented, less-than-comprehensive, or negligible documentation. Researchers can choose to augment records by conducting semi-structured interviews with artists, but these may prove easier to secure in some contexts than others, depending on whether the ongoing politicization of migration in a given location makes artists reticent to share their views and challenges, even years after the productions, with a project's researchers. Particularly if collaborators from migrant communities were involved with these productions, researchers will have to determine whether interviewing them will compromise anyone's security. Discrepancies will ensue from the material contexts of the project's various case studies, from the availability of archives to the feasibility of ethnographic documentation.

Differences in the pragmatic, political, and ethical dimensions of research design in its preliminary stages have variable stakes. In TaPS research, historicizing, particularizing, and localizing categories of theatre and performance can meet this challenge. To offer a basic example, Sibylle Peters (2010: 154) cautions that the term *performance* does not have ready referents in the German language: researchers conducting their preliminary investigations and identifying case studies for analysis would do well to identify supplementary terms. At times, terminological differences can have political ramifications. I have argued elsewhere that though 'community theatre' is a common analytic rubric in Anglo-American TaPS scholarship, community is neither a frequent discursive trope nor an inevitable political-artistic ideal for theatre in France, where communautarisme (communalism) is a key political charge levelled at hyphenated citizens (Fişek, 2017). A TaPS researcher working with 'community' as a political or aesthetic delimitation, therefore, needs to identify whether this criterion emerges from a characteristic of the site they are studying, or is a result of choices made when defining the project's scope.

Focusing on migration offers further complications. Migration can refer to the experiences of first-, second-, or third-generation immigrant communities settled in a national territory; guest workers, who may live long term in a host country but not qualify for citizenship; seasonal workers, who regularly cross national borders to labour but who cannot settle in these workplaces; and refugees, asylum seekers, undocumented immigrants, and even cosmopolitan expatriates. What unites these categories is a general aura of 'otherness', and in many national contexts, political discourses can amalgamate these populations to stigmatize racialized minorities and advance anti-immigrant agendas. Amalgamations can emerge in artistic projects and scholarly discourses as well, creating dialogue and transformative politics, even as meanings remain in flux. The 'post-migrant' concept commonly employed by creative artists and festival organizers in German-speaking contexts is one example: theatre artist Şermin Langhoff originally employed this term while director of the Ballhaus Naunynstrasse in Berlin's Kreuzberg neighbourhood, where she lobbied for the promotion of diverse artists of migrant origin. Though its meaning is still somewhat 'unfixed and fluctuating', the term has since mushroomed in both the arts and migration scholarship (Stewart, 2017: 57). Yet, as Ayşe Çağlar (2016: 959) argues, insisting on cross-border mobility as *the* defining life experience perpetuates an essentialism that denies migrants and non-migrants 'contemporaneity' and endows those identified as post-migrants with a fixed temporal frame.

How can TaPS scholars researching migration avoid such a trap? Put differently, how might we account for the differing stakes associated with the decision to focus on migration across varied sites? A pragmatic strategy could be to limit the project's focus simply to theatre and performance practices that depict *recent* incidents of cross-border displacement and dispossession, and the changing bureaucracies of asylum in Europe. This strategy will delimit the theatre and performance case studies, but risk obscuring the connectivity between migratory life histories. Consider the case of Athens-based theatre artists Anestis Azas and Prodromos Tsinikoris's documentary play *Clean City* (2016), which features the narratives of five women who have immigrated to Athens from the 1980s on and currently work there as cleaners. *Clean City*'s migratory frame is not focused on the movements characterizing the 2015–16 crisis; its historical background stretches from the collapse of the Soviet Union to the political and economic turmoil across the Balkan landscape. Nonetheless, the production toured throughout Europe during the period of the 'migrant crisis' and was presented as part of the EU-funded EUROPOLY Project, dedicated to countering Euro-scepticism. Including *Clean City* in a project devoted to the migrant crisis would shed light on how past migratory experiences can be employed to comment on present ones, changing perceptions of both categories in the process.

For a case study like *Clean City*, mixed approaches can help circumvent the essentialization of migratory life histories. This could mean starting with a performance analysis of *Clean City*, underlining its focus on the *longue durée* of migrants' experiences with racism in Greece. Meanwhile, discourse analysis of EU arts and culture initiatives, the production's press releases, and performance reviews would demonstrate that *Clean City*'s reception was nonetheless implicated in the cultural climate of the 2015–16 migrant crisis. Here, mixed methods would allow researchers to answer a novel set of questions: Do certain project sites feature paradigmatic narratives of migration? If so, when and how do these paradigms function as gateways for approaching the current crisis? Conversely, has the European migrant crisis itself acquired emblematic status, thus facilitating, empowering, but perhaps also short-changing the telling of other/alternative migrations? Finally, what are the theatrical precedents through which migration has achieved the status of a flexible emblem?

Mixing Methods

At this stage of articulation, the hypothetical project's research parameters (with all complications and caveats intact) are to investigate theatre and performance practices that represent experiences of migrancy, refuge, and asylum emerging across public, private, professional, and amateur arts institutions in six European contexts (the United Kingdom, Germany, France, Italy, Greece, and Turkey) from 2015 to the present. How are artists representing refuge and asylum, and against which historical backgrounds (local, national, supranational) are they framing contemporary migration? How is the language of crisis shaping their political criticisms and informing their visions of political and ethical redress towards refugees and asylum seekers? Which agents, bureaucracies, and institutions emerge in these representations as figures of accountability or witnessing?

With respect to performances (cases) per se, some may be seen live by researchers (perhaps in multiple sites), others may be viewed through recorded media, and possibly others will be studied only through their 'material and immaterial traces' (Roms, 2019: 226). Sources such as scripts, designs, press releases, and reviews will augment researchers' notes from the live events or video/digital documentation. Supplementary research will utilize personal, digital, and institutional archives housing the traces of theatre and performance practices that have addressed refuge and asylum during recent years, whether or not these are fully developed as cases. Finally, given the project's emphasis on how the rubric of the European migrant crisis is negotiated across European national contexts, semi-structured interviews with theatre and performance artists will chronicle how they frame and conceptualize their aesthetic-political choices. Performance analysis will thus combine with production history and institutional history to address what is distinctive about theatre's 'take' on refuge and asylum.

Employing these methods in combination means distinguishing between research that simply utilizes multiple methods for gathering information (e.g. viewing, consulting archives, and interviewing) and *mixed methods research*. Advantages accrue to the latter; Jennifer C. Greene (2015: 608) argues, for example, that mixed methods research involves placing 'different logics of inquiry, different ways of knowing, and thus different perspectives on understanding important social phenomena' in conversation with one another, pushing the researcher to think through *difference* at an analytical level. Here, this would mean acknowledging the very different ways that performance observation, archival research, and semi-structured interviews produce knowledge, and thus the varied ways in which the researcher will account for it. While archival researchers trace how their archives have become authoritative sites (e.g. in whose interest they function and how their knowledge is valorized) and frame their findings with reference to the nature of that authority, researchers conducting qualitative interviews recognize how embodiment and co-presence affect the ways that narratives and meanings are co-constructed by individuals operating in particular contexts. These 'ways of knowing' are joined in their critical attention to the workings of power and ideology, but the target of their self-reflexivity necessarily differs. As a result, the researcher using these methods in combination must 'meaningfully engage with difference precisely through the possibility of mixing at multiple levels', including both the practical level and the level of conceptualizing project gains (Greene, 2015: 607).

Performance Analysis

If the hypothetical project's most basic question concerns *how* theatre and performance artists in Europe represent experiences of refuge and asylum, the empirical data will include the use of spoken and gestural language, performances of affect, and the choice of visual and sonic elements evident in the performance, the promptbook, or printed/published scripts. However, using performance analysis poses two additional questions: Which analytic tradition will the researcher use to notate a given performance, and which critical-theoretical frameworks will inform the analysis of this notation? In other words, the decision of how to 'read' the performance is permeated with methodological choices, which can be singular (e.g. semiotics) or multiple (e.g. semiotic and phenomenology), with cultural implications for the hybridity.

Emma Cox (2017: 479) offers a striking example. Canvassing a range of journalistic, activist, community, and artistic practices responding to the arrival of refugees en masse in Europe, Cox identifies a persistent trope: the depiction of refugee collectivities through visual representations of ceremonial transit. As 'a mode of looking and responding', *processional aesthetics*, Cox argues, is at work not only in the ways that journalists, civil society activists, and artists alike frame refugees' subjectivities (as inherently collective, beleaguered, and aestheticized) but also in the embodied practices refugees develop in response. Cox thus begins with a semiotic strategy identifying a particularly charged sign – that of the refugee processional – across a series of disparate sites operating with both pro- and anti-migrant motivations. She then argues that activist performance practices like the Gatwick Detainees Welfare Group's *Refugee Tales* (based out of Crawley, United Kingdom) do not simply signal meaning through their adoption and reproduction of the processional form, but use this form as the basis for an embodied practice of solidarity.

The *Refugee Tales* project mimics the Chaucerian pilgrimage and involves the ambulatory presentation of personal testimonies from refugees who have experienced indefinite detention in the United Kingdom. Cox demonstrates that these processional acts, which involve the witnessing of fellow pilgrims, borrow from a ubiquitous representational mode but are not merely representational in their meaning-making capacities. The pilgrimage's three-dimensional materiality, its sensory power, and its visceral, affective experientiality require other strategies of documentation, like participant observation. Here, the turn to mixed methods occurs as a direct result of the form of *Refugee Tales*; Cox (2017: 489) observes that a semiotic analytic tradition will not suffice in accounting for the performance's 'affective envisioning', even as she notes that her own interest highlights the symbolic display involved in processional solidarity. The data that Cox gathers through a semiotic reading results in a theoretical framing nourished by critical thinking on the representations of the suffering Other: she draws on Judith Butler's discussion of frames of recognizability in *Frames of War* (Butler, 2010) to understand the forms of spectatorship generated by the refugee procession.

Archival Research

The immediate focus of the hypothetical research project is the recent past, yet I have suggested that the sites and cases of performance practices need to be examined in light of transformations in public discourse surrounding migration. But where and how will the researcher locate precedents? Whereas the theatre 'archive' harbours strong connotations of site specificity, calling to mind dusty boxes of documents tucked away in the corners of theatre institutions, I use the term *archive* to refer to the range of material remains that allow reconstruction of a performance event from the not-too-distant past, including materials produced by the artists themselves (rehearsal notes, personal notes, and correspondences kept by the actors; set designs and models; posters, playbills, programme notes, and other publicity materials generated by the theatre company; commercial photographs; and oral recordings) and materials produced by audience members and critics (blog posts, critical-journalistic reactions, artists' interviews, recordings of post-performance talkbacks, and social media involving the general public as well as specific immigrant communities). As this list makes clear, the contemporary archive is often an 'assemblage' located with multiple individuals (Gale & Featherstone, 2011: 17). The assemblage can be tracked across regularly curated web archives, the haphazard and infrequently maintained online catalogues of newspapers, and the webiverse. Despite their differing locations and magnitude, each of these archives is created by agents exercising idiosyncratic criteria for selection and preservation; their choices develop in relation to the availability of financial and human resources, and decisions are animated by an imaginary about target audiences, readers, and 'users' (including 'cultural influencers'). When collecting material from these varied sites, the goal is not to access a transparent, unmediated truth (what 'really happened') but to consider the criteria, principles, and biases that appear to have shaped the archive, as well as the ways that these choices translate into the research process.

Digital platforms offer alternative kinds of archives and research engagements. Founded by scholar, dramaturg, and curator Szabolcs Musca, New Tides Platform (NTP) is an independent organization that seeks to create a space for collaboration between academic researchers, arts practitioners, and the creative industries. In 2019, together with the related Migrant Dramaturgies Network, NTP co-produced 'Migrations: Harbour Europe', defined as a 'performance and community outreach project featuring three contemporary plays on migration by emerging international playwrights, and a series of conversations and debates' (see NTP, 2019). The three chosen plays – *Genesis* by Chiara Boscaro, *The Sea Is My Nation* by Hala Moughanie, and *Closed Lands* by Simon Grangeat – were workshopped and presented in collaboration with LegalAliens Theatre, a female-led ensemble of international theatre artists based in North London. NTP's website links to LegalAliens Theatre's SoundCloud page, which features seven short recordings from the debates that followed the presentation of Moughanie's play (LegalAliens Theatre, n.d.). The recorded conversations feature key questions in the representation of refuge: When representing contemporary migratory experiences, what are the advantages and disadvantages of verbatim aesthetics? Does playwrights' use of anti-realistic strategies automatically guarantee an ethics of care? And, what are the varying visions of empowerment that audiences bring to bear on refugee testimonies?

These recorded conversations present the researcher with a wealth of information on the event's ideological thrust and social ethos. At the same time, the researcher is compelled to apply the very same questions to the archive's format: What are the advantages and disadvantages of the digital medium? Listening to audience members debate their reactions to Moughanie's play is a tactile experience; certain speakers sit closer to the recording device, other voices drift in from further afield, and a chorus of assenting murmurs rises and falls when a spectator makes a point shared by others. The sensory power of these anonymous, disembodied voices has a direct impact on the researcher's perception of audience reactions, yet, much like verbatim accounts of migratory experience, LegalAliens Theatre's SoundCloud page offers a mediated simulation of authenticity. A researcher approaching this auditory archive will necessarily question the curatorial imagination underlying its formation, and consider what these choices reveal about the kinds of cultural consumption that NTP and LegalAliens Theatre both anticipate and, in turn, produce. These fragmented conversations can be reflective of unanticipated technological failures or the serendipitous availability of recording devices on a given occasion; they may also be the result of deliberate acts of archive formation. Often, researchers will seek to supplement perceived gaps in a fragmented archive via additional methodological strategies, such as semi-structured interviews. In a research project balancing multiple case studies, variances and outright discrepancies in archival data can be productive precisely because multiple analytical methods are required to account for them.

Semi-Structured Interviews

Qualitative research interviews are often framed through archaeological metaphors. Employed by researchers to 'excavate' experiences that are not evident in a performance or its material remains, the semi-structured interview, in particular, can seem like a transparent window into artistic intentionality. Unlike the unvarying length, uniform questions, and fixed structure associated with a standardized survey, the semi-structured interview begins with basic, guiding, but open-ended questions, thus allowing both interviewee and interviewer to react to the exchange as it transpires. This open-ended format contributes to the sense that interviewees produce an unmediated torrent of thoughts and feelings, but scholars of qualitative research frequently caution about relationality and context in the interview's production of knowledge. Irving Seidman (2013: 86–9) warns that even the most open-ended questions can *presume* rather than *solicit* knowledge, and Charles L. Briggs (2003 [1986]: 102–3) adds that 'the communicative structure of the entire interview affects the meaning of each utterance', suggesting that interviewers need to remain alert to the interlocutor's (often implicit) communicative norms.

These sensitivities become especially fraught in research on political theatre and performance, with further resonances in TaPS scholarship on migration. The significance of communicative norms, structures, and presumptions are foregrounded in Alison Jeffers's writing on global refugee theatre and performances. Jeffers argues that contemporary definitions of *refugee* are indelibly marked by the categories and conceptions of the 1951 UN Refugee Convention. Asylum seekers who want to acquire refugee status must prove that they have fled individualized persecution in their home country, and further demonstrate that they would be subject to continued persecution if they were to return. Supplying this proof often requires conventional narrative tropes, but Jeffers (2012: 30–1) argues that 'the story alone is not enough and it must be rehearsed to create a credible *performance*, convincing in the telling as well as in the construction'. Jeffers labels the genre of self-fashioning that emerges in response to this imperative a *bureaucratic performance*, adding that refugee performances are essentially underwritten by the communicative structure of the refugee's interview and application process. That refugee performance is 'conditioned or marked by' bureaucratic performance does not imply, however, that performers cannot transcend these genres, revert their expectations, and challenge their limitations. Rather, Jeffers's argument is that refugee performers are often forced to live with the tensions created by this necessary negotiation.

This has a bearing on TaPS researchers conducting qualitative interviews with migrant artist-informants. In my own research with migrants involved in performance-based immigration activism in France, I often interviewed undocumented artists (Fişek, 2017). Our semi-structured interviews began with assurances of confidentiality, illustrated with reference to guidelines from my home institutions' Institutional Review Boards (IRBs). I was mindful of and often sought to address how the bureaucratic language of informed consent could mirror the language of international law, putting interviewees on edge. I was less attuned, however, to how my interviewees might respond to these parallel communicative norms. Much to my surprise, my interlocutors often waved my precautions away, and granted permission to record and publish their true names. In these moments, the qualitative interview method highlighted contrasts between my ethical anxieties as researcher and the agency and desires of informants (Fişek, 2017: 30). As the following section details, such contrasts can often be resolved reciprocally through dialogue and collaboration. This process revealed my own implicit commitments to certain ideas of refugee authenticity, an insight that ultimately pushed me to rethink my 'reading' of the performances in question.

Scaling Up, Scaling Down

The political economy of much humanities and social science research is such that the funding structures necessary for realizing long-term, multi-sited, and collaborative academic research are slim (if not non-existent) and yet highly prized. Nonetheless, the lessons of multi-sited, collaborative research design are generalizable. In the spirit of estranging the familiar, the intentionality of research design outlined for this hypothetical multi-sited and multi-collaborator project also has direct bearing on single-researcher studies. Multi-sited projects have a propensity to throw research questions, assumptions, and blind spots into high relief, but a research project does not need to be multi-sited to defamiliarize its starting questions, or to warrant careful deliberation about each site. Similarly, where collaborating researchers engage in conversation to make difference explicit, an individual researcher would do well to make explicit their plans and rationales for selecting and combining methods, discuss these plans with experienced researchers, and modify and recalibrate the plans accordingly.

TaPS researchers gravitate towards certain preoccupations – each of which has various methods of investigation – and try to engage them comprehensively, yet pragmatic, political, or even ethical considerations exponentially complicate the study of aesthetic products and experiences. In this chapter, I have argued that heterogeneity in data-gathering methods is an inevitable dimension of the multi-sited research enterprise, and that one way to embrace and address this complexity is to combine multiple methods. Whereas the initial promise of mixed methods is to deliver a large pool of data necessary to answering a research question, the subtler contribution of the mixed methods approach is to make manifest the *differences* embedded in the knowledge generated. The takeaway for single-researcher studies is that this knowledge is not without consequences, as well as potential benefits.

Notes

1 As 2016 drew to a close, the United Nations' (UN's) emerging numbers indicated that the year would be the deadliest on record in terms of lives lost during Mediterranean crossings. The UN Refugee Agency (UNHCR, n.d.b) confirms that the period of 2015–16 features peaks both in the total number of arrivals and in the number of dead or missing refugees.

2 Perhaps the most visible of these camps was the 'Jungle', the series of informal refugee encampments that had formed on the outskirts of the French port town of Calais since the early 2000s. Close to ten thousand refugees were sheltering in the Jungle when the French state announced the site's final destruction in

October 2016, dispersing these individuals across sites in France and reigniting heated debates between France and the United Kingdom as to their shared responsibilities towards camp inhabitants (Schofield, 2016).

3 As of June 2023, Turkey remains at the top of the UNHCR's (n.d.a) list of major hosting countries.

References

Adak, H., & Altınay, R. E. (2018). 'Introduction: Theatre and Politics in Turkey and Its Diasporas'. *Comparative Drama*, 52(3–4), 185–214.

Briggs, C. L. (2003 [1986]). *Learning How to Ask: A Sociolinguistic Appraisal of the Role of the Interview in Social Science Research*. Cambridge: Cambridge University Press.

Butler, J. (2010). *Frames of War: When Is Life Grievable?* London: Verso Books.

Çağlar, A. (2016). 'Still "Migrants" After All Those Years: Foundational Mobilities, Temporal Frames and Emplacement of Migrants'. *Journal of Ethnic and Migration Studies*, 42(6), 952–69.

Çağlar, A., & Glick Schiller, N. (2018). *Migrants and City-Making: Dispossession, Displacement, and Urban Regeneration*. Durham, NC: Duke University Press.

Cox, E. (2017). 'Processional Aesthetics and Irregular Transit: Envisioning Refugees in Europe'. *Theatre Journal*, 69(4), 477–96.

Cox, E., & Wake, C. (2018). 'Envisioning Asylum/Engendering Crisis: Or, Performance and Forced Migration Ten Years On'. *Research in Drama Education: The Journal of Applied Theatre and Performance*, 23(2), 137–47.

Fişek, E. (2017). *Aesthetic Citizenship: Immigration and Theater in Twenty-First-Century Paris*. Evanston, IL: Northwestern University Press.

Gale, M. B., & Featherstone, A. (2011). 'The Imperative of the Archive: Creative Archive Research'. In B. Kershaw & H. Nicholson, eds., *Research Methods in Theatre and Performance*. Edinburgh: Edinburgh University Press, pp. 17–40.

Glick Schiller, N., & Çağlar, A., eds. (2011). *Locating Migration: Rescaling Cities and Migrants*. Ithaca, NY: Cornell University Press.

Greene, J. C. (2015). 'Preserving Distinctions within the Multimethod and Mixed Methods Research Merger'. In S. Hesse-Biber & R. B. Johnson, eds., *The Oxford Handbook of Multimethod and Mixed Methods Research Inquiry*. Oxford: Oxford University Press, pp. 606–15.

Jeffers, A. (2012). *Refugees, Theatre and Crisis: Performing Global Identities*. Basingstoke: Palgrave Macmillan.

Johnston, C., & Pratt, G. (2019). *Migration in Performance: Crossing the Colonial Present*. New York: Routledge.

Knowles, R. (2004). *Reading the Material Theatre*. Cambridge: Cambridge University Press.

LegalAliens Theatre. (n.d.). 'Profile page. SoundCloud'. Accessed 27 February 2023. https://soundcloud.com/legalalienstheatre.

Marschall, A. (2018). 'What Can Theatre Do about the Refugee Crisis? Enacting Commitment and Navigating Complicity in Performative Interventions'.

Research in Drama Education: The Journal of Applied Theatre and Performance, 23(2), 148–66.

McIvor, C. (2019). 'When Social Policy Meets Performance Practice: Interculturalism, the European Union, and the "Migratory and Refugee Crisis"'. *Theatre Research International*, 44(3), 230–47.

Meerzon, Y., Pewny, K., & Vannieuwenhuyze, T. (2018). 'Introduction: Migration and Multilingualism'. *Modern Drama*, 61(3), 257–70.

NTP (New Tides Platform). (2019). 'Migrations: Harbour Europe'. February 2019. Accessed 9 August 2023. www.newtidesplatform.org/migrations-harbour-europe-2019.

Olson, B. D., & Jason, L. A. (2015). 'Participatory Mixed Methods Research'. In S. Hesse-Biber & R. B. Johnson, eds., *The Oxford Handbook of Multimethod and Mixed Methods Research Inquiry*. Oxford: University of Oxford Press, pp. 393–405.

Peters, S. (2010). 'The Performance of Performance Research: A Report from Germany'. In J. McKenzie, H. Roms, & C. J. W.-L. Wee, eds., *Contesting Performance: Global Sites of Research*. Basingstoke: Palgrave Macmillan, pp. 153–67.

Rancière, J. (2011). *The Emancipated Spectator*. 2nd ed. Trans. G. Elliott. London: Verso Books.

Roms, H. (2019). 'How and Why Are Performances Documented?' In M. Bleeker, A. Kear, J. Kelleher, & H. Roms, eds., *Thinking through Theatre and Performance*. London: Methuen Drama, pp. 225–42.

Schofield, H. (2016). 'What Next after the Jungle?' BBC.com, 24 October. Accessed 9 August 2023. www.bbc.com/news/world-europe-37731180.

Seidman, I. (2013). *Interviewing as Qualitative Research: A Guide for Researchers in Education and the Social Sciences*. 4th ed. New York: Teachers College Press.

Stewart, L. (2017). 'Postmigrant Theatre: The Ballhaus Naunynstrasse Takes On Sexual Nationalism'. *Journal of Aesthetics & Culture*, 9(2), 56–68.

Tomlin, L. (2019). *Political Dramaturgies and Theatre Spectatorship: Provocations for Change*. London: Methuen Drama.

UNHCR (UN Refugee Agency). (n.d.a). 'Figures at a Glance'. Accessed 27 February 2023. https://urldefense.com/v3/__https://www.unhcr.org/about-unhcr/who-we-are/figures-glance__;!!DqoX2DkFhyF93HkjWTBQKhk!SCeRQ3KzOxFrulPBKLC3KaKDdFhOuhoxaMtOymzwkAmGaB7HAakvXhW25NQVDspz6RJeIpPx8Gi8W85idnWKV4iL9YGeX9c$.

UNHCR (UN Refugee Agency). (n.d.b). 'Mediterranean Situation'. *Operational Data Portal: Refugee Situations*. Last updated 26 February 2023. https://data.unhcr.org/en/situations/mediterranean.

Wimmer, A., & Glick Schiller, N. (2003). 'Methodological Nationalism, the Social Sciences, and the Study of Migration: An Essay in Historical Epistemology'. *International Migration Review*, 37(3), 576–610.

CHAPTER 5

Methods Dialogue: Ethics

Natalie Alvarez and Patrick Anderson

Suggested Reading

Conquergood, D. (2002). 'Lethal Theatre: Performance, Punishment, and the Death Penalty'. *Theatre Journal*, 54(3), 339–67.
Taylor, D. (2009). 'Afterword: War Play'. *PMLA*, 124(5), 1886–95.

Paul Rae: Ahead of this discussion, each of you circulated an article to contextualize this conversation. What does your selection tell us about what is particularly important to you when it comes to considering ethics within performance research?

Patrick Anderson: Dwight Conquergood was my mentor and afterwards my friend, until his death in 2004. 'Lethal Theatre' demonstrates how to blend critical engagement with theory alongside engaged activist work. The essay begins with a re-examination of Michel Foucault's insistence that, at the time *Discipline and Punish* was published in 1975, state-sanctioned executions were no longer designed as mass spectacles. Conquergood (2002: 342) then describes his own participation in anti-death penalty protests at a federal prison in Terre Haute, Indiana, and carefully argues that state-sanctioned executions in the contemporary United States are explicitly crafted and staged as performances of the state's 'monopoly on violence'. The essay doesn't shy away from narrativizing Dwight's own appearance at protests, or his perspective on the death penalty and spectacles of state-sanctioned executions. But it blends that positioning with a deft reading of precedents in scholarly work, and deeply historical understandings of that work. He situates himself as a historical being who changes over time. This represents astute, methodical, slow scholarship united with an activist approach to what he calls lethal theatre. And it's humble: situated within an understanding of critique as intimately human. I think of that as the heart of research ethics.

Natalie Alvarez: Patrick, the humility you highlight in Dwight's work opens the door to a critical aspect of ethical research for me: the admission of doubt and uncertainty in the face of ethical quandaries. In the conclusion to my 2018 book, *Immersions in Cultural Difference: Tourism, War, Performance*, I wrestle with the ethical implications of claims of knowing or 'understanding' across difference, and reflect on uncertainty, inadequacy, and humility as the starting point for ethical practice. My field research required that I embed myself in scenarios that demanded a vulnerability as researcher, and a rejection of any position of expertise or authority over what I was witnessing.

I chose Diana Taylor's 'War Play', the afterword to a special issue of the journal *PMLA* on war, because it encapsulates what draws me to what she calls 'scenario thinking' and scenario-based enquiry in my own research. Taylor examines how the embodied practices of performance – elements of role-play, rehearsal, and re-enactment, as well as the mise en scène of staged environments – are used to imagine warfare, conceptualizing the territory and 'theatres' of war and the 'enemies' within. Beyond warfare, Taylor traverses a vast terrain of examples and demonstrates how pervasive scenario thinking is in the public sphere. Scenarios operate as a 'what if' exercise, instrumentalizing performance to stage, imagine, and prepare for all kinds of possible futures. Taylor (2009: 1888) expresses her concern for the 'largely unexamined' ways in which the tools of our field are being used in the waging of war. This is a call to TaPS scholars to train their attention on how the performance paradigm is being instrumentalized in warfare and beyond, in ways that raise serious ethical concerns. But it also serves as a reminder of how performance itself is a vital method of analysis – a way of unveiling what, exactly, participants are being compelled to enact and the otherwise invisible but potentially coercive scripts of those enactments. Performance as a method of analysis can identify the ways these scenarios are, as Taylor says, 'killing us' (2009: 1889).

In my research on scenario-based training environments, I am interested in what scenarios habituate in bodies and bodily behaviours. What hidden assumptions or ideological codes are at work? What is reinforced or naturalized about certain structures, especially colonial structures? I also appreciate how Taylor (2009: 1894) opens the door to the possibility that performance can be the means by which participants outstep how these scenarios are 'killing us': scenarios can enact a prefigurative politics that allows participants not only to envision a 'better world' but to bring it into being through bodily action; to 'see ourselves acting', as she says, with greater agency over possible futures. In this way, scenarios, for me, harness the potential of mimesis as a political practice and demonstrate how performance blurs the lines between method and action.

Paul Rae: Very quickly, we have got to what is at stake both in your work and in the papers you submitted: death. This is what makes the question of ethics particularly pressing, and it is only exacerbated by the ambivalence around the uses of performance that also runs across your work. In order to get at the implications of both of these elements for method and methodology, would you describe the methods you use?

Patrick Anderson: I am constantly attempting to track power, understood in its most general terms as the ability to make or help someone do something they couldn't or wouldn't do on their own. In my previous books, this has taken two methodological forms (Anderson, 2010, 2017): first, examining the specific policies and procedures by which self-starvation has been defined, managed, and contained within the domains of the clinic, the prison, and the gallery; and second, attempting to understand the contemporary experience of life-threatening illness within a complex of medical and social institutions that function primarily by treating the ill body as an object to be observed, treated, and managed. In my current research, I am embedded in an ethnographic study of ostensibly public institutions – law enforcement agencies and city governments – and their disparate effects on under-resourced Black and Brown neighbourhoods.

So, when I start, I try to listen without distraction and read very closely, and this continues throughout the research project. I begin with structure and practice, and I ask: What are the institutions through which those practices move? If I'm working with a given body of thought, a set of writings, an author, I focus on the structure of that thought, both its position in time – what came before it, what influenced it, what came after – and also the internal structure of the argument itself. It is at such points in one's thinking, of course, that attention must be turned to the mechanics – the machinery – of the institution itself. Which policies dictate (and make possible) specific kinds of human behaviour? How have specific procedures – and their calcification over time – constructed and reproduced a social world whose precise features are defined by power imbalances, disproportionate vulnerability to suffering, and concentrations of wealth and prestige?

In a very real sense, what we called 'the Method' in acting classes applies more to me as a scholar, I think, than it ever did when I was an actor. I try to pay attention to the people who are engaged in whatever practices I'm focused on, and the people who live within whatever structures or institutions I'm focused on. I try to imagine myself not in a strictly empathic mode but in a 'magic if' kind of mode – which is to say, I try to imagine myself in a position that would necessitate those practices, or make them seductive to the inhabitants of those environments. I try to understand the specific mechanics of a given institution: the day-to-day, unnoticed, seemingly unimportant behaviours and activities by the people who live within that institution, that make it exist; the virtuosities that make it thrive. Then I try to learn about the behaviours themselves: whatever it is, within the institution, that permits *it* to survive and that permits *people* to survive. I try to figure out what those are, understand them as protocols, and then use them to frame my own attempts to understand the larger picture of the institution itself.

Tracy C. Davis: Patrick, let's get more concrete. You get up in the morning, you're going to do research, what is it you *do*?

Patrick Anderson: I'll give you two specific examples. The research I'm doing now is founded on my role on the Commission on Police Practices, a community review board that is empowered to pursue oversight of the San Diego Police Department. The day-to-day work involves combing through files documenting police-involved shootings, in-custody deaths, and community complaints, and arriving at a determination as to whether discipline should be enacted or charges should be brought against that officer. I begin by reading the complaint itself. I then move through every evidentiary piece of that file, watching it or reading it as many times as I need to, in order to understand, in any given moment, who was free to leave, who was calling the shots, who had access to any kind of technology that could cause harm to the people around them, and who was making decisions about what happened more generally to the bodies of the people on the scene – whether they were detained or arrested, whether force was used against them, and so on.

I have deliberately attempted to nurture in myself a similar approach to the day-to-day work of being a faculty member within a university. In faculty meetings, for example, I try to pay attention to who feels empowered to speak without asking if they can do so, asking if they can take a turn. I try to pay attention to who's taking up the most amount of time with speech or space with their bodies, where people are sitting around the table, who feels that they need to take notes, who feels that they need to ask for clarification, and who answers those questions. I try to pay attention to the minutiae of power, moment-to-moment, infinitesimal interactions, micro gestures of power.

Paul Rae: Neither of these examples would conventionally be called 'research': the first seems like a civic duty, and the second concerns the day-to-day business of academic life. Are you deliberately *not* making a distinction between the times when you are 'conducting research into performance' and how you are 'doing your job'?

Patrick Anderson: I am *definitely* not making a distinction. I would say I am *insisting* on not making a distinction. Methodology, after all, is really a question of *labour*: What work are you doing? What tools are you using? What skills do you need to learn before you can do it? What access to expertise do you need in order to do it well? Who will benefit from the doing of this labour, and who may be harmed by it? These are all questions that focus our attention upon the ethics of method. But they are also questions that we should ask ourselves in all of the other venues of faculty life: department meetings, curriculum planning, hiring and promotion reviews, publishing, campus strategic planning, what goes by the name of 'equity, diversity, and inclusion' work, teaching, and, above all, 'community engagement' with people who live in our university towns.

Natalie Alvarez: I really like this challenge you've posed, Tracy, of actually describing what we *do* moment to moment. The difficulty for me is in talking about methods in a systematic way because they're so contingent on the phenomenon: the way I'm situated, the bodies in the room, the relationships. The methods radically change depending on the circumstances and the nature of the questions being asked.

For *Immersions in Cultural Difference* (Alvarez, 2018), I conducted ethnographic field research at sites involving immersive simulations in military training and tourism contexts. This work required embedding myself as a participant observer in these immersive environments, and this dyadic positioning required that I participate in the scene while actively listening, being attentive to the micro movements and micro encounters that happen in the field, and examining what impinged on them. I ask: What are the unspoken ideological codes or imperatives at work in such situations, and which discursive practices are justifying certain courses of action and operating as tacit givens? I conducted interviews in the field alongside a process of observing and documenting; and through a thick description of what I was observing, theories or concepts began to constellate that helped me dig more deeply into the problems that were emerging, to identify what was unreflective about these engagements and better understand the oppressive powers and structures at work. What I do in practice has many alignments with grounded-theory coding methods: extant, predetermined theoretical concepts are not *applied to* the data collected from interviews and field notes; instead the process requires acute attention to empirical detail, identifying patterns and new formulations that *emerge from* the data. This process bears many similarities to the ways in which an actor might verb a text. I think that prior training prepared me well for this method of data analysis.

Some of the ethnographic field research required a more intensive degree of participation, which presented its own ethical challenges. For example, in a mock insurgent training camp for US special forces, I was required to take on the role of an Afghan insurgent alongside US special forces as part of a counter-insurgency exercise designed to 'inhabit the cultural mindset' of the 'enemy-other' in order to better anticipate and extinguish the threat they pose. The presumptive intimacy and violence of this exercise, suggesting that soldiers could somehow step into and inhabit a 'cultural mindset', exposed how a totalizing coalescence of us versus them gets consolidated in practice even as soldiers are imaginatively crossing the threshold of cultural difference, ostensibly to 'better understand' the 'enemy-other'.

My current research requires quite a different methodological approach. The goal has been to design and measure the efficacy of a scenario-based training programme to improve police response to individuals in mental health crises. This was a four-year, collaborative, longitudinal, mixed methods study. Our team designed a training programme that begins with a series of scenarios, informed by Forum Theatre, in which officers effectively step into and 'rehearse' a staged scene involving an individual in mental health crisis. A person with lived experience of mental illness, a mental health professional, and a de-escalation trainer press the pause button on the scene at critical moments, offering insight into effective de-escalation strategies. The idea is that through rehearsal and repetition, de-escalation competencies can become habituated in the body, integrated into the officer's muscle memory and repertoire of decision-making. Officers then move on to a high-intensity circuit of scenarios where they are assessed on their de-escalation competencies. We conducted pre- and post-programme evaluations to measure whether this scenario-based training brings about intra-officer improvements in effective de-escalation and responses to people in mental health crises. Our preliminary analysis of the data to date suggests that the training curriculum leads to marked improvements in officers' demonstrated competencies; and the programme has since led to the development of a standardized curriculum and assessment protocol for officers across Ontario. But what's been most exciting about this project is that community members, people with lived experience of mental illness, mental health advocates, and anti-racism specialists have been involved in its design and delivery. For me, this project has uncovered the potential of research to blur the lines between method and action by intervening in systems that have perpetuated harmful and unfair practices with the active involvement of community members who are most affected by these practices.

Paul Rae: You both currently conduct research in settings where institutional structures figure prominently. Academic research ethics have their own such structures, sometimes known as Institutional Review Boards (IRBs), which scrutinize research protocols and provide ethics approval for projects. Where and how does ethics formally enter into what you do, in terms of such structures?

Patrick Anderson: I'm not sure exactly what you mean by 'formally enters'. Ethics approval is an ongoing process, and should never be considered 'closed', in my opinion. Of course, there are university-based IRBs from which approval must be sought before the formal period of research may begin. But there are many other venues in which the ethics of a specific project need to be negotiated in conversation with others – a sort of IRB committee within communities with whom one is working. In my current work, there are people within the city government and within the police department who dictate how our work may and may not proceed. Perhaps more importantly, there are many people in the community – leaders of local groups, for example, but also respected people in every neighbourhood – from whom I seek constant consultation, in order to ensure that my research does not harm communities that have experienced radical over-policing and police violence. Every group has a process: a formal approval letter from an IRB committee, a nod from an auntie or grandmother, a welcome from a tribal council, a confidentiality agreement that one must sign and to which one is beholden, an accountability session held late at night, when everyone is tired but the kids have finally gone to bed. I would suggest that these are all equally rigorous and important ethical checkpoints. In my own work, I try to keep myself equally accountable to all of them – which means actively seeking out where this kind of process exists within a given community and respecting its standards.

Tracy C. Davis: As you respect community standards, you must also satisfy your university's criteria for ethical conduct of research. Natalie, would you elaborate on your experience?

Natalie Alvarez: A concern for me in the IRB process is that the language used in IRB applications lends itself to a paternalistic and asymmetrical power relation in which the researcher operates independently of the participants to determine, in a kind of a priori fashion, what constitutes risk for *them* and how best to protect *them* from harm (protecting, in turn, the institution from liability). When I was an early-career researcher, it wasn't until I was in the field that I discovered how partial and incomplete the IRB application is in terms of the totality of considerations that inform ethical conduct. There is little in the IRB framework that directs researchers towards ethics as a *process* that is determined *by* and *with* the participants and communities with whom the researcher works.

I think performance-based research lends itself to responsive and holistic approaches to ethical conduct since, by virtue of working in performance contexts, we are more often than not going to find ourselves working with and alongside others, developing collaborative working relationships over time, and in situations that are fluid. A performance orientation can inform a processual approach to ethics that is continuously adjusted based on what's happening in the room, on deepening trust, and on an attentiveness to risks as they emerge moment to moment in concrete practices, which cannot always be accounted for in advance.

Although the origins of the IRB lie in institutional responses to instances of egregious abuses – such as Nazi medical experiments on captured soldiers and civilians during the Second World War, and the Tuskegee syphilis studies on African American men that ran from the 1930s to the 1970s – Eve Tuck and Monique Guishard have offered a sobering critique of the institutions' ambitions. They suggest that the IRB was historically a reactive mechanism that did not address the root cause of these abuses, question the fundamental power differentials at work in scientific enquiry, or address the ways in which research methods were complicit in settler colonialism and white supremacy (Tuck & Guishard, 2013). Their work compels researchers to face their own complicity in these claims. A question I've returned to often with research collaborators is: Who does the work ultimately benefit? That is, how do I, as a researcher, contend with the reality that my publications, which unavoidably extract knowledge from the communities they are ostensibly designed to serve, support my own academic advancement and job security? There seems to be an intensified turn to activism in TaPS scholarship, and I wonder whether this is symptomatic of a need to feel that the work can serve and contribute to those it is 'about' in some fundamental, material way, but also of a need to ameliorate this anxiety that research is always at risk of being complicit in the institutional logics of settler colonialism.

The scenario-based de-escalation curriculum and evaluation framework for police in Ontario is the closest I have come to feeling that my research is having a material impact, intervening in police violence in response to individuals in mental health crises. I conduct this research alongside my volunteer work with a not-for-profit organization that is in the process of launching a non-police response to individuals in mental health crisis in the city of Toronto. From the outside, these joint efforts might seem contradictory: the first might be perceived as a reformist approach to the problem, while the latter is abolitionist. But for me, intervention now requires working both *within* institutions to effect paradigmatic shifts in the immediate reality of policing and *outside* these institutions in grassroots initiatives to bring alternatives into being.

Patrick Anderson: There's another way in which ethics become a pressing concern for me, and it's quite different from what we've talked about so far. Some kinds of research involve spending time in institutions where we would like to see radical and transformational change. For example, I do not believe policing should in any way resemble its current form. And yet, I am spending countless hours – dozens of hours every month – with police officers and police files, paying respect to the ethics evaluators of the police department itself. I sign the confidentiality statements, I understand I can be prosecuted for releasing certain information, and I have agreed to play by those rules. Yet I hope, I dream, that the research I produce out of this work will contribute to a movement that eliminates policing in its current form and reimagines public safety completely.

The ethical quandary is a general one, infusing every formal and informal interaction I have in those rooms. I don't lie to anyone when asked direct questions, and I have made the decision not to break the rules, not to secretly release information that we have access to and that I have agreed not to disclose. Will there ever be a point in the future when I have to reconsider that for some pressing reason? I think about this every time I step into the soundproofed, locked offices where I review video that records trauma, in some cases deadly trauma. Every time we re-review a file, we have to sign another confidentiality form. Every time I sign my name, I'm faced with this decision: can I hold myself to this confidentiality agreement without sacrificing my values, my morals, my ethics? It feels unresolvable every time I sign, and the resolution, for me, is to invest in the longer-term goal of profound change by understanding the work itself as *slow* and many generational. It is at times a profoundly uncomfortable quandary.

Natalie Alvarez: Patrick, have you found yourself in conversations with police officers or staff sergeants with whom you're working and had to put on a face or front? Or are you quite open about your politics?

Patrick Anderson: I should biographize for a moment. I grew up queer in the Deep South of the United States, so I was trained in everyday performance from an early age. As Victor Turner (1982: 93) would say, this was not performance as faking, but performance as *making*: for a queer child and teenager in an extremely hostile environment, everyday performance was a mode of survival. In other words, I learned, and continue to learn, the delicate art of balancing my own self-expression with the need to *keep existing* (for lack of a more sophisticated phrase) within institutions that one desperately longs to overhaul (or, as in childhood, escape). I remember a conversation with our chief of police during training for this board. I did not hedge when I posed questions to him, but neither did I proceed by framing those questions as being personally about him. I didn't go so far as to say 'I hope my presence here leads to the loss of your job', but neither did I pretend to have any commitment to a shared understanding of what the problems are, or how we might solve them.

Natalie Alvarez: We've each highlighted in different ways the flaws and limits of the IRB process and its relation to the institutional logics of settler colonialism. But, for the sake of argument, we may need to disentangle, for the moment, our discussion of the inherent flaws of the IRB specifically, from a discussion about the intertwined relationship of methods and ethics more broadly. I'm personally wary of reducing a reliance on methods to merely a 'professionalizing process' since it risks undermining decades of work by feminist, Indigenous, queer, and critical race scholars that has focused on methodology precisely because it is the domain in which researchers are required to make themselves accountable for what they intend to do and how they intend to do it. Methodology is the means by which researchers interrogate self-reflexively the hidden assumptions, biases, and institutionalized ways of thinking that might be surreptitiously guiding the work, ways of thinking that even researchers who are native to their research are not immune to. Methodology and the ethical process are intertwined mechanisms of accountability that require the researcher to take a step back and try, as best as possible, to identify potential oversights in an effort to mitigate mishaps that, despite the researcher's best intentions and 'instinctual' sense of care and goodwill, may inadvertently put community members at risk.

One thing I appreciate most about field research, especially at this political moment, when discourse has become so polarized, is that when one is embedded in the field, listening attentively and witnessing a complex constellation of micro movements (competing motivations and commitments on the ground), it becomes increasingly difficult to think in terms of stark dichotomies (e.g. liberation or complicity). I am reminded of the interviews I conducted with Afghan-Canadian immigrants playing the roles of Afghan villagers in simulacra of Afghan villages at Canadian Forces Base Wainwright in Alberta. Daily, the Afghan role-players navigated a complex ethical dilemma: they described how, in an effort to save their people, they were subjecting themselves to the trauma of simulated warfare to serve a nation that had effectively occupied their people. They were also steadfast in their conviction that in the face of a reality that they could not change, they were, at the very least, operating within it to educate soldiers on the basic cultural protocols that could protect their loved ones back home from harm. The improvements they witnessed day by day in soldiers' comportment and attitudes served as evidence to them that their labour was not futile. The practices of embedded field research, which include careful listening, bracketing of judgement, humility, and profound self-doubt (the very opposite of expertise), quickly unveil a complex matrix of realities and lives that blanket positionings of liberation versus complicity cannot accurately hold. It is impossible to step outside of state power. It structures every aspect of one's life. For this reason, I think it's increasingly necessary that researchers question the thrall to the 'liminal norm', to invoke Jon McKenzie (2001: 50), and the idea that unless researchers are examining counter-hegemonic performance practices they are complicit.[1] Researchers often have to embed themselves in sites wherein their own ideological commitments are profoundly at odds, precisely to learn how to 'see like a state', to learn its inner operations and its habits of mind. How can researchers gain a better understanding of how to diffuse and dismantle the grip of state power without this inside view?

Tracy C. Davis: Let's shift to another research challenge. How do you mix methods? Can you think about the moment-by-moment shift between methods, and where some of these kinds of ethical considerations guide the practice?

Patrick Anderson: As attentive as I try to remain to the specific methods I'm using, I tend to follow what works when I'm actually engaged in a particular project. But I have two separate examples where the distinctions between methods matter. One of them is at the level of training. It's important to distinguish between research activities, to call labour what it is while you're doing it, so that you can train other people how to do it, and can help them nurture the skills they need to do the research they want to do. In training for graduate education, undergraduate education, education in the community, or wherever methods education is happening, it's important to be specific and precise. When I am teaching students how to engage in image analysis, close reading, or critical theory, I focus on these practices as *practices*, which is to say as methods.

My second example is not from the classroom, but from my current research site, for which it is absolutely essential that I be able to move between (or 'mix') methods continually. In this work, the most difficult – and often traumatic – part of what we do is watching the body-worn camera footage of shootings and in-custody deaths. We have to watch these videos carefully, and we have to watch them multiple times, often in slow motion. When I am sitting in that claustrophobic room staring intently at a screen as these images of violence stream before me, I'm engaged in methods of reading and analysis that were taught to me in film studies classes, photography classes, and art history classes: how to read a film, how to read an image, how to track perspective. I don't think I've ever felt more practical, methodological respect for Laura Mulvey's (1975) foundational essay 'Visual Pleasure and Narrative Cinema', than I have when engaged in this kind of case review. That may seem like a strange connection to make – body-worn camera footage is not produced or curated in the same way a Hitchcock film is – but the practical value of Mulvey's work, for me, has been its close attention to camera angle, photographic technology, and the relative position of bodies on a screen, and also its close attention to the machinations of power behind the lens. In any case, I'm continually shifting between these modes of analysis and, say, blocking analysis from theatre, or choreography from dance: How are these bodies moving through the space of this scene in relation to one another and in relation to time? And at the same time that I am using these various tools to understand what's happening on the screen, I am shifting back and forth between other kinds of texts: dispatch logs, officer reports, interview transcripts, still photographs, and more. This is detailed work with very different kinds of documentation about a single historical event, and it requires maintaining a relatively strict set of distinctions as to which methods are required for analysing different genres of text.

In other words, while I am constantly mixing methods during the event of case review, the methods themselves do not lose their significance as discrete methods, just as the different kinds of texts do not lose their significance as discrete texts: the camera footage is not the interview transcript; the policy and procedures manual is not the dispatch log. In a sense, the work of case review is primarily a kind of archival recovery of a past event, using texts that cannot, each on its own, represent the fullness of that event. Methods should attend to those distinctions with precision, even as a multitude of methods – and 'mixed' methods – will be necessary in pursuit of the larger goal of archival recovery.

Natalie Alvarez: In the field research I did for the *Immersions* book, the qualitative participant-observer methods developed in situ: listening, observing, and documenting to determine what ideological codes, fields of experience, and discursive and disciplinary fields constitute and impinge upon the world in which I was embedded. Over the course of this field research, I began to think about performance as a hermeneutic method to unveil otherwise invisible and normalized structures of violence, but also as an 'organizing concept', to borrow from Barbara Kirshenblatt-Gimblett (2015), that constellates a host of theoretical concepts and frameworks that can be brought to bear on the scene of analysis. For example, as I was embedded in mock Afghan villages constructed at military training sites in Canada and the United Kingdom, witnessing encounters between soldiers and actors playing 'Afghan villagers', observing soldiers' comportment and bodily behaviours, and attuning my ear to military discourse, a constellation began to form: affect studies, counter-insurgency doctrine, 'warrior science', postcolonial theory, and ethical philosophy, all coming together to allow me to interpret the 'scripts' of these scenarios and identify in precise terms the perceptions and assumptions that were being entrained and habituated in participants. The work required shifting between disciplinary and theoretical vantage points, and these intersecting discursive fields served as interpretive frameworks that helped explain what was happening moment to moment. The mixing of methods can be an effective means of 'triangulation', not necessarily to 'validate' the data, as it's often understood, but to facilitate a deepened understanding of the phenomenon or problem at hand. While I used to feel uncertain about an unbridled mixing of methods, I've come to recognize that qualitative methods are inherently mixed. I appreciate Norman K. Denzin and Yvonna S. Lincoln's idea of the methodological bricoleur-theorist, who moves within and between multiple overlapping paradigms, methods, and perspectives in order to get at competing visions and understandings of a given phenomenon

(Denzin & Lincoln, 2005). The bricoleur's labour produces its own complex, reflexive bricolage, montage, or performance text. In other words, *how* we mix methods is what makes the work unique and singular to the thinker-practitioner-researcher.

Tracy C. Davis: Natalie's experience is not merely a shifting, but a simultaneity of methods. It's not an abrupt 'this then that', but 'this and that and maybe this other thing, too'. Maybe one frame explains one person's behaviour and another frame explains another's, and meanwhile you remain there too, as an observer, or participant observer?

Natalie Alvarez: Thank you for that. I would hate to suggest that it's somehow neatly sequential. There is an overlaying of frameworks. But when it came time to write, I found myself questioning at every step whether this overlaying of theoretical frameworks was serving my efforts to document what I witnessed and whether I was providing an honest account of the encounter. What is the narrativizing and theory accomplishing, and whom is it serving? Coming back to the ethical quandary you mentioned, Patrick, I also struggled with the dyadic positioning of the participant observer (who is at once inside and outside), particularly in the field research for the *Immersions* book, in which I was embedded in immersive simulations that had an ambiguous ontological status to begin with: they were at once 'not real' but 'realer than real', since the modes of engagement habituated in these simulations shaped participants' post-simulation realities. As I began to examine immersive military training exercises, I realized very quickly that I was not innocent of the counter-insurgency strategies I was observing at work: my ethnographic field practices required that I establish relations of trust in order to 'get the intelligence', as it were. But these relationships, and my embedded position in these scenarios as a participant observer, left me uncertain about the extent to which I could intervene in situations that were raising serious ethical concerns for me, or whether I should recede as an observer.

Tracy C. Davis: So, what you do in the moment of doing research exceeds participant observation, in part because you focus on complexity and multiplicity. As performance scholars, what do you think about that?

Patrick Anderson: Changing the question slightly, I would ask: What enables me to do this work in the way I want to do it? *Disciplinary* training, as such, and disciplinary *expectations* about what research within that discipline must look like, have not helped me develop what we've been calling a mixed methods approach. But specific methodological training has proved essential. I have felt empowered, for example, by my training in the precise method of ethnography, the precise method of film analysis, the precise method of close reading, and the precise methods learned in my physical training in theatre, dance, and even (as a child and teenager) competitive gymnastics. The heterodox blend of humanities, social sciences, and arts that came from being a double major in performance studies and anthropology has empowered me to pursue this work. Specific interdisciplinary itineraries are more helpful than broad and generalized avowals of 'an interdisciplinary approach'. And as a field with a specific range of disciplinary and institutional legacies, performance studies has empowered and encouraged me to embrace the mixing of methods with an enthusiasm that many other fields would disavow.

Natalie Alvarez: For me, participant-observer ethnography within a performance studies framework allows for a heightened attention to intersubjective responsibility, which I alluded to at the outset, and to the role of the researcher not as a dispassionate spectator but as a co-performer in the field of 'play'. But to your point, Patrick, about performance studies and specific itineraries of interdisciplinarity, I think what this conversation is bringing to the surface is a way of thinking about performance studies as a mode of investigation that reorients other fields to uncover new pathways of enquiry.

Tracy C. Davis: Do you feel that your use of ethnographic methods is a classic application or that it's more complex than that *because* you're studying performance?

Patrick Anderson: As scholars, we are often called upon to defend our expertise as a superior form of knowledge production, but we are often woefully limited in our understanding of what precisely 'expertise' is. Within any research/field site, there are competing modes of expertise and competing methods: different ways of *doing work* in the interest of producing knowledge. An 'amateur' in scholarly methods is simultaneously an expert in other kinds of work; and an expert in scholarly methods is simultaneously a novice in other ways of working and knowing. Researchers must embody flexibility, must practise good listening, and must approach their work – above all – with *humility*. This is a difficult ask for people who have been credentialed by elite cultural institutions to which very few people ever gain access; but it is an essential one.

Natalie Alvarez: I like that we're coming full circle to underscore the importance of humility in ethical practice. So much of what you're saying, Patrick, resonates with where I arrived at the conclusion of

Immersions: after years of field research, I came to recognize the importance of embracing a position of unknowing, humility, and inadequacy, but also to recognize the challenges of doing so within a knowledge economy and institutional contexts that ask us to perform our intelligence and mastery over given subject areas – 'or else'. There's so little room in this context to self-question or admit doubt. Perhaps this is a way of getting at your previous question, Tracy, about what we do in performance contexts that exceeds classic applications of ethnographic methods: the collaborative nature of performance scholarship lends itself to an upending of researcher-participant knowledge hierarchies and a more collective approach to knowledge creation.

Note

1 I am grateful to Katherine Zien for the generative conversations about our research in relation to McKenzie's notion of the 'liminal norm'.

References

Alvarez, N. (2018). *Immersions in Cultural Difference: Tourism, War, Performance.* Ann Arbor: University of Michigan Press.

Anderson, P. (2010). *So Much Wasted: Hunger, Performance, and the Morbidity of Resistance.* Durham, NC: Duke University Press.

Anderson, P. (2017). *Autobiography of a Disease.* New York: Routledge.

Denzin, N. K. & Lincoln, Y. S. (2005). 'Introduction: The Discipline and Practice of Qualitative Research'. In N. K. Denzin & Y. S. Lincoln, eds., *The SAGE Handbook of Qualitative Research*, 3rd ed. Thousand Oaks, CA: SAGE, pp. 1–32.

Foucault, M. (1975). *Discipline and Punish: The Birth of the Prison.* New York: Pantheon Books.

Kirshenblatt-Gimblett, B. (2015). 'Interview by D. Taylor (2001)'. In D. Taylor & M. Steuernagel, eds., *What Is Performance Studies?* Durham, NC: Duke University Press. Digital book, accessed 11 October 2023. https://scalar.usc.edu/nehvectors/wips/interviews-eng.

McKenzie, J. (2001). *Perform or Else: From Discipline to Performance.* London: Routledge.

Mulvey, L. (1975). 'Visual Pleasure and Narrative Cinema'. *Screen*, 16(3), 6–18.

Tuck, E., & Guishard, M. (2013). 'Uncollapsing Ethics: Racialized Sciencism, Settler Coloniality, and an Ethical Framework of Decolonial Participatory Action Research'. In T. M. Kress, C. Malott, & B. Porfilio, eds., *Challenging Status Quo Retrenchment: New Directions in Critical Research.* Charlotte, NC: Information Age, pp. 3–27.

Turner, V. (1982). *From Ritual to Theatre: The Human Seriousness of Play.* New York: Performing Arts Journal.

PART II

Doing

Research encompasses a wide range of activities, including and exceeding those detailed throughout this book. But when we talk about *doing* research, we most often think about the process of engaging with primary sources or resources, and the practical activities that will generate research data. The word *data* is not widely used in theatre and performance studies (TaPS) research; for some researchers, it sounds depersonalized, abstract, and quantified. But in its most capacious sense, *data* simply names the range of materials generated in the course of research that will subsequently be available to interpretation and analysis. In TaPS research such materials can take many forms and emerge out of a wide array of research activities: archival and other historical investigation, qualitative methods of documentation and discovery, the close analysis of performance events and other cultural artefacts, and the visualization of large amounts of information through computational analysis.

The five chapters that follow explore *the how and the why* of research practice in exemplary yet non-prescriptive ways. The featured approaches are frequently used in TaPS, though the combinations and variants are infinite. Derek Miller uses archival research, digital capture and analysis, and computational visualization. Julia M. Ritter incorporates media content, auto-ethnography, and participant observation in conjunction with performances and their aftermath. Awo Mana Asiedu's main techniques are audience surveys and field interviews. Julius Bautista participates in community performances as fieldwork and thereby documents performance-making processes and performance in conjunction with auto-ethnography and philosophical theorizing. Jonas Tinius also engages in fieldwork, but he does so while embedded within a theatre company, conducting interviews but more often engaging as a participant observer with a keen eye for dramaturgical analysis of situations, including rehearsal observations, meetings, and other encounters. What is distinctive about these chapters is that each demonstrates how methods mediate different treatments of 'performance' across a range of research projects and settings and how the authors think about research as they do it. The prominence of critiques of knowledge stemming from intersectional, Indigenous, and global-majoritarian subject positions that question processes and priorities in the humanities means that ever greater clarity and sensitivity are required to determine the stakes in conducting research in particular ways.

CHAPTER 6

You're Already a Digital Humanist: Why Aren't You Thinking Like One?

Derek Miller

Digital Humanities (DH) uses computer technologies for humanist scholarship, including research, teaching, and archiving. DH research projects include network analyses of dance companies, motion studies of performers, and quantitative explorations of theatre economics (Bench & Elswit, 2022; Escobar Varela & Hernández-Barraza, 2020; Guyot & Ravel, 2020). Teaching-centred DH ranges from the websites that host syllabi and readings to tools such as computer games that interactively rehearse theatre history (Bloom et al., 2016). Digitization of primary and secondary sources sits at the core of archival DH practices, which, as in DH research and teaching, vary from the mundane (scanned documents) to the experimental, such as virtual reality theatre models (Folger, n.d.; Pearson, 2007; Tompkins, 2014). Digital research, teaching, and archiving projects all use computers to work with large quantities of information. We often refer to such information as data. Managing that data – finding it, categorizing it, formatting it, analysing it – requires a method that balances the computer's language of absolutes, of zeros and ones, against the messiness of the real world that data purports to describe. This chapter is about rigorously using data in theatre and performance studies (TaPS).

All scholars should care about data methods because computing underlies most contemporary scholarship. Computing's ubiquity in academic work does not mean it is without sceptics. In particular, the expansion of DH itself over the past few decades has engendered much proper apprehension about the politics and ethics of computerized, data-driven research, with accusations of ill-considered ties to neoliberal technocracy (Allington et al., 2016). But we can use computers and harness their benefits without elevating data-driven methods above others. Indeed, we must not use data methods exclusively: technology and data do not produce truth better than any other human practice; DH should not suggest otherwise.[1] In TaPS, disciplinary discomfort with computers and computing, particularly given the field's intellectual commitment to studying embodied practices, may also inspire suspicion. (Of course, extensive research on theatre's mediatization and the interplay of bodies and non-human technologies represents an important countertrend; see Bay-Cheng et al., 2015.) Most theatre researchers and practitioners, like other scholars, are already engaged in some digital methods, whether they call them that or not. We harness the power of computers to improve our work when we write papers in word-processing applications, send emails, make slideshows, advertise on social media, sell tickets electronically, and otherwise conduct ourselves in digital spaces. All those activities involve data: email addresses, image files, tweets, prices, and so on. Excepting the few scholars who remain firmly in an analogue age, we are all digital humanists, if not DH scholars – the difference is only a matter of degree. I posit digital methods as ubiquitous both to assuage any fears about the unfamiliarity or difficulty of working with data and to demonstrate that most of us have accepted that digital methods, and the data that undergirds them, can help us do our work better.[2] Precisely because most scholarship is already digital, we must all take responsibility for methodically using data.

If computing per se is thus familiar to most of us, thinking about using data is far less typical in theatre studies (but see Escobar Varela, 2021). Data might seem akin to any other type of evidence: close readings rely on quotations; performance reconstructions deploy archival discoveries; ethnographies depend on interviews. Quotations, archival discoveries, and interviews are all evidence that may be transformed into data, but they are not quite data themselves. 'Data' seems to mean something more abstract than the evidentiary base for other methods in theatre scholarship. To become data, evidence must leave its specific context and connect to other pieces of evidence on unfamiliar terms, terms set by the researcher. Data aggregates, accumulates, agglomerates. Data-making and data management thus demand a methodical approach. DH has developed a method for thinking with and about data in a way that is informed by and useful for computers, but also attuned to humanism's values and aims.

This chapter demonstrates best practices for using data methodically, an approach informed by DH scholarship. (For those interested in practical resources for working with data, proliferating textbooks, summer schools, and online tools have made starting a data-driven project easier than ever; see, e.g. Arnold & Tilton, 2015; Jockers, 2014; Montfort, 2016; PH, 2023.) I begin by discussing the life cycle of a DH project, emphasizing the iterative process essential to any data-driven method. I then zoom in on data and the key questions about how we identify, collect, and organize it. The tension between maintaining a usefully rigorous data model and allowing for the uncertainty and 'messiness' present in data sources remains a key theme throughout this discussion. Two examples help specify my description of working with data: a study of early twentieth-century American theatrical venues and the Federal Theatre Project's (FTP's) work in New York City. Both examples use spreadsheets, a relatively simple (and perhaps familiar) digital tool. While I do not provide practice exercises, readers are invited to perform these steps and expand upon them with the sources I cite here (all available for free online), or with their own archives.

There are two further notes on the scope of this discussion. First, this chapter does not dwell on the many techniques one may apply to data in the analysis phase: these include simple mathematical calculations such as averages or distributions, but also more exotic approaches such as network clustering, topic modelling, and ever-evolving forms of machine learning. Application of those techniques (many of them highly complex and specialized) to new domains creates some of the most visible excitement about DH. I emphasize instead the more mundane – but also pervasive and essential – identification, description, and management of data. Second, while 'data entry' has become a byword for mindless busywork, working well with data requires both a methodical approach and a sophisticated grasp of many other methods. Close reading, archival research, digital capture, performance documentation, interviewing, movement notation, and more may all play a part in creating, finding, transforming, and analysing data. I indicate in the following discussion some moments where data-based research demands facility in other methods. Precisely because robust data management requires and invites so many other methods, mastering work with data can improve all of our scholarship, from the organization of files or emails on our computers to the collection and dissemination of new data sets for teaching or research.

A Digital Humanist's Method for Using Data

In outline, a DH research project consists of these stages:

1. Conceive a research question.
2. Locate an archive.
3. Identify a data set in the archive.
4. Shape the data set into a database.
5. Analyse the database programmatically.
6. Create interfaces and/or visualizations to summarize analytic results.
7. Use analyses as evidence to answer the question.

In many ways, these stages differ little from non-DH research. The difference comes in stages 3–6, with the translation of archival material into useful data that then undergoes programmatic analysis and display.

The rest of this chapter emphasizes a method for those steps. Yet I include stages 1, 2, and 7 because the data-focused stages do not stand apart from the rest of the research process. All stages are related, and each includes a set of assumptions – about what counts as a meaningful research question, about what determines the utility of an archive, about how we define data, and so on. This means that despite DH's popular association with objective analysis, no stage of this research is objective. Furthermore, this entire process is iterative. For instance, during programmatic analysis one may discover the need for data that cannot be derived from one's current archive, looping one back to stage 2.

Data-driven research begins like most other humanities research: with a question. For instance, I would like to know how many theatres there were in the United States around 1915, and how they were distributed across the nation. To answer that two-part question, I need an archive, a source of relevant information in the world. My search for that archive may require me to spend significant time and expertise in a variety of obscure collections. It so happens, however, that I have a good archive easily at hand. Julius Cahn, a booking agent who worked with theatre manager Charles Frohman, published a theatrical guide nearly annually from 1898 to 1921. Designed to make theatrical touring easier, Cahn's guide includes detailed information about theatres across the United States. The 1913 edition (vol. 17; Cahn & Leighton, 1913) provides a suitable archive for the question I have posed.

Now comes the first moment that distinguishes data-driven work from other scholarship: we must transform this archive from a messy collection of worldly things into an ordered collection of data, parsable by a computer. Call this organized collection of data from the archive a data set. The data set curates the archive by selecting only some pieces of it, the pieces both meaningful for the data set and useful as data. That process of curation explicitly makes an argument about the archive, an argument that may or may not accord with the original archivist's work. Cahn's guide, for instance, includes venues that he thought useful for theatre producers to know about, ranging in size from the largest theatres of the day to small, local opera houses. If I have methodological expertise in theatre architecture or design, I might wish instead to exclude theatres under a certain occupancy or to use a more specific definition of theatrical venue. By accepting Cahn's definitions, I am creating a data set of Cahn's theatres – a reasonable choice, but a choice nonetheless. Similarly, Cahn includes venue listings for Hawai'i. Sticking with my interest in the United States, should I include Hawai'i, then a US territory, or exclude it because it did not lie along rail networks that facilitated continental North American touring?

If the latter, why not then include Mexico or Canada, which were part of those rail systems? I may choose to focus only on the continental United States, but I must be clear with readers that I have made this decision. The process by which we include and exclude parts of the archive (whether by conscious decision or by ignorant omission) determines the kind of questions we can ask and the answers we can discover. We've begun making arguments about our archive in the process of selecting our data.

At this point in a digital project, most people shape their data set into a formal database. By organizing data in a particular way, the database further refines the data in the data set. In my case, I want to focus on state-by-state theatre counts. I'm going to use a simple spreadsheet, with a row for each state, and columns for the state name, the number of cities with theatres ('playing points' in Cahn's terminology), the total number of theatres, and the state's population in 1910, which Cahn's guide includes. Far more granular information than I will incorporate is also in the guide: details about each theatre in each town. By choosing to focus on states rather than cities and towns, I treat state boundaries as meaningful informational units and ignore, say, the population around New York City in contiguous New Jersey and Connecticut. (I might, at this point, bring expertise in the methods of geography to bear on my work.) Organizing my data into a database, even the rows and columns of a spreadsheet, thus further determines the limits of my study. (There are a variety of forms in which one may store a database. I discuss spreadsheets here because they are easy to learn and ubiquitous. But there exist a number of more flexible, dynamic, and efficient data storage systems and tools, among them relational databases, which minimize redundant storage; JSON (JavaScript Object Notation), which maximizes flexibility at the cost of efficiency; and XML (Extensible Markup Language), which allows for easy data validation and standardization.) The results of my initial data selection and organization may give me a spreadsheet like that excerpted in Table 6.1.

Most digital projects now use some kind of code to analyse the database. Sometimes, researchers write bespoke scripts. (A script is a set of instructions for the computer, written in a language such as Python or R, that sorts through data and parses it in specific ways.) Other times, researchers rely on prewritten packages or graphical applications – anything from functions like AVERAGE in Microsoft's Excel, which calculates the average of a set of numbers, to the networking software Gephi, which offers an array of visualizations – to parse data. Either way, a code base acts on the database to summarize or organize the data in particular ways. Again, such code is an argument. I might simply add up the number of theatres in each state, which

Table 6.1 *US states, playing points, theatres, and population in 1913*

State	Playing points	Theatres	Population
Alabama	37	43	2,138,093
Arizona	17	20	204,354
Arkansas	60	63	1,574,449
Colorado	45	56	799,024
Connecticut	36	42	1,114,756

Note: Only the first five rows of my spreadsheet are included here. 'Playing points' refers to the number of cities in the state with theatres.
Source: Cahn and Leighton (1913).

posits the raw total as an answer to my question. Or I might decide to focus on the number of cities with theatres, and sum instead the playing points column. Or I could group the states into regions by adding more data to my spreadsheet, and look at the number of playing points and theatres in each region. Each of these approaches parses different subsets of the data in different ways to answer different questions. Our arguments are in the code itself, in how the code interprets the information we give it.

My example here reports on the simplest kind of data: a count of the number of theatres or towns with theatres. But our code can increase in complexity with more involved data. (I might calculate the number of theatres per capita, for instance, or, with more precise census data, the average distance between a person and a theatre.) For research on other types of data, other, more complex methods are available. If analysing texts, one may use techniques evolved from stylometry, such as word frequencies and type-token ratios, or more mathematically sophisticated methods such as topic modelling or word embedding. One might use geographic analysis to make maps. One could create networks and study the connections between individuals and among communities. Or one might combine any and all of these approaches, and many others, to suit one's particular object of study and methodological expertise.

With an analysis in hand, it is time to share the results with the world. Digital projects usually summarize their results in some visual form, either a single image or an interactive interface, but tables or simple narrative data summaries are not uncommon. Data visualizations are also arguments. The information you make available through an interface, the way you scale a graph, and the variables you present all alter how people understand your data. Visualization is its own art and science, on which entire sub-disciplines focus (for the classic study, see Tufte, 2001). Producing a clear, legible summary of complex information without letting the visual effect overwhelm or overdramatize the argument is a very particular skill. Finally, one then puts all this work in service of an argument, an argument that may engage multiple other methods and that, one hopes, is of some interest to one's fellow scholars.

A note on the relative technical complexity in all the stages described above: serious intellectual work, along with often time-consuming, tedious, detail-oriented labour, goes into selecting and shaping a data set. But such work often requires little computer expertise, beyond basic knowledge of widely available, often free software. Even data analysis and visualization, for all but the most unique projects, can be conducted without writing a line of computer code. Of course, some projects can benefit from bespoke tools for data entry, data queries, analysis, and visualization. In cases when it does prove valuable to develop specialized platforms or write scripts to perform specialized analyses, one must learn to use new tools and techniques. Whether one is using prefabricated or bespoke tools, however, the method for working with data remains the same.

Wait: What Is Data?

Before we dive more deeply into the middle stages of a DH project – identifying, collecting, and organizing data – let us step back to reflect on what 'data' means. Drawing on ideas outlined in *'Raw' Data Is an Oxymoron*, an essay collection edited by Lisa Gitelman (2013), we might think about data in a few ways. First, data is not facts. Facts are ontological; they exist in the world and are part of the endless stream of phenomena, of real things that we, in our work, seek to understand. Data are not ontological but rhetorical, designed to produce an effect. If this distinction seems blurry, consider that data are not necessarily true: data are not facts yet false data are still data. There is nothing 'given' about data (contra the word's Latin root); data are always already selected, always already rhetorical.

Second, disciplines do a lot of work in defining what counts as data. The load-bearing capacity of a theatre building's walls may never be of interest to a TaPS scholar but is of obvious importance to an architect or engineer. Methodological prioritiess constrain what one does and does not regard as data. One must conceive first of the rhetorical possibilities in a set of facts before translating those facts into data.

Third, data easily provides a false sense of objectivity and innocence. 'I'm just telling you what the data says' is always misleading. Data 'speaks' only because someone has selected what it should 'say'. Data is itself already rhetorical, already an argument, and must be treated as such.

Fourth, data usually undergoes multiple significant transformations. For instance, data often abstracts and aggregates facts. By this I mean that data slots facts into categories that eliminate the specific underlying fact. Furthermore, in DH projects, the data we analyse is often not the document, video, sound, image, or object itself, but rather a digital representation of that thing. Digitization transforms data into a particular digital form – bits storable on a computer – that further delimits and defines the objects of study. In sum, data is: selected from among facts; not ontological but rhetorical; not necessarily true; defined by disciplines; likely to give a false sense of objectivity; and usually transformed by abstraction, aggregation, and/or digitization.

To understand the implications of thinking this way about data, let's consider an example in detail: the FTP and its work in New York City. The FTP was part of Franklin Roosevelt's New Deal, putting theatre artists of all kinds to work across the nation between 1935 and 1939. Much excellent scholarship already exists about the FTP; obviously our research should begin with a careful reading of that literature (e.g. Brown & O'Connor, 1978; De Hart, 1967; Fraden, 1994). Some of that scholarship focuses, to the exclusion of other FTP activities, on controversial productions in New York City. Precisely because of such controversy, 'appraisals of the very genuine accomplishments of Federal Theatre ... outside New York City' have been 'obscured', as one historian put it (Witham, 2003: 5). To fix this imbalance, recent FTP scholarship has often looked particularly at the FTP's national structure (Moore, 2017; Osborne, 2011). Yet the excellent studies that celebrate FTP's national reach and successes sideline another overlooked category: the FTP's work in New York *beyond* its most infamous productions. To complement the national (non-New York) approach of recent scholarship, we can seek to demonstrate the breadth and variety of FTP's New York activity. We may thus take for our example preliminary research questions that seem answerable through data analysis: What, when, and where did the FTP perform in New York City?

Fortunately, the Library of Congress has digitized a tremendous amount of the vast FTP archive – government bureaucracies make terrific data sources. (Note that the Library of Congress's work is itself a data-driven project of archival digitization and dissemination through a public repository, which makes possible our data research.) We can set out to answer our research questions by looking for useful sources in these digitized materials (LOC, n.d.).

Not Everything Needs to Be Data

The library's FTP collection consists of an outstanding array of material: posters, musical scores, costume and set designs, lighting plots, production photographs, scripts, playbills, memoranda, summary reports, catalogues, budgets, and more. Each item, of course, has metadata that names its source, date of production, and relationship to other items in the collection. But we might further parse any kind of item into meaningful, discrete elements, perhaps in conversation with other TaPS methods. For instance, we could explore the use of colour in FTP costume designs by noting the colours and proportions thereof in the Library of Congress's collection of costume sketches. That data might include too the name of the designer, the production name and year, and information about the character. Or we might look at the photograph collection and compare it to a list of FTP productions, to explore which FTP work merited photographic memorialization and which did not. Data is always and everywhere latent in these materials – but how do we learn to see it?

Recognizing data in an archive, we are usually looking for information that is of a certain scale and is amenable to abstraction and categorization. Consider scale: two dates written down in a diary may be literally useful as data, but they do not demand the same resources and techniques as a list of ten thousand dates. We can comprehend two dates easily without even a table, let alone an interactive timeline. Data thus wants to be of a certain size to be worth treating as data. It is harder to identify cases that are absolutely incompatible with abstraction and categorization. (Even in this example of two dates in a diary, I have abstracted and categorized them as 'dates'.) Some things such as affect are particularly difficult to identify in a large data set and to categorize meaningfully – though digital tools exist that can analyse texts for sentiments by measuring the prevalence of words with a positive or negative emotional valence. Yet certainly some archival sources – those involving quantitative information, particularly – are more amenable to sorting into abstract, meaningful categories than others. By contrast, creating categories for a study of colour in FTP costume designs will entail subjective interpretation of the colours in images, and hard decisions about whether to name one or more shades of red, say. As we shall see, all data organization naturally raises such problems, but some cases are more acute than others.

Back, then, to our research questions about when and where the FTP performed in New York City. Among the Library of Congress's digitized collection, we can find (happily) a series of weekly schedules for performances in the five boroughs. The first page for the first week, the 4 January 1937 schedule, appears in Figure 6.1.

PLEASE NOTE
THIS SCHEDULE IS SUBJECT TO CHANGE WITHOUT NOTICE

THE WORKS PROGRAM
WORKS PROGRESS ADMINISTRATION
FEDERAL THEATRE PROJECT
FOR NEW YORK CITY

FOR THE WEEK OF JANUARY 4

FROM: Department of Information
701 Eighth Avenue, N Y C.
MEdallion 3-5962, Ext. 74

WPA FEDERAL THEATRE PROJECT PRESENTATIONS

IT CAN'T HAPPEN HERE-Adolphi Theatre, 54th St.East of 7th Ave. 25-55¢ 8:40 PM

IT CAN'T HAPPEN HERE-Majestic Theatre, Fulton St.& Rockwell Pl.Bklyn.25-55¢ 8:40 PM

BASSA MOONA-Lafayette Theatre, 7th Ave.& 131st Street, 25-40¢ 8:40 PM

MR.JIGGINS OF JIGGINSTOWN-Labor Stage Theatre,106 West 39th St. 25-55¢ 8:45 PM

PIRATES OF PENZANCE-Daly's Theatre, 63rd St.East of Bway. 25-55¢ 8:30 PM

FLIGHT-Heckscher Theatre, 104th St. & 5th Ave. 25-55¢ 8:30 PM Mat.-Thur & Fri-4:00
Sat- 2:30 PM

CIRCUS-N Y Coliseum,E.177th St.Sub.Sta.Bronx, Sat & Sun- 2:30 & 8:00 PM 15-25¢

In addition to the paid admission shows listed above at permanent theatres, the WPA FEDERAL THEATRE PROJECT presents daily in every section of th metropolitan area a variety of dramas,comedies,vaudeville and marionette performances. They follow:

MARIONETTE SHOWS

M A N H A T T A N

(No Admission Charge)

(Mon) THE BIG CITY-NY Foundling Hospital,175 E.68th Street & Lexington Ave. 7:30 PM

(Tues) THE BRASS TRUMPET-St.Judas Chapel,19 West 99th Street, 4:00 PM

(Tues) THE MAGIC BOX-Gulick Plygd. Columbia,Delancey & Sheriff Sts. 3:30 PM

(Wed) THE MIGHTY MIKKO-P.S. 157,327 St.Nicholas Ave. 1:00 & 2:00 PM

(Wed) ZNEE-ZEE-P.S. 11, 320 West 21st Street, 1:00 & 2:00 PM

(Wed) THE MAGIC BOX-Carmine St.Gym, 83 Carmine Street, 3:30 PM

(Wed) PUNCH AND JUDY-P.S.20, 45 Rivington Street, 1:00 & 2:00 PM

(Thur) ZNEE-ZEE-Columbia University Teacher's College(Horace Mann Aud.) 120th St. & Broadway, 11:45 AM

(Thur) THE MAGIC BOX- Rutgers Place Gym, 5 Rutgers Place, 3:30 PM

(Thur) THE BIRTHDAY PARTY-P.S. 2, 116 Henry Street, 1:15 PM

(Fri) ZNEE-ZEE-Christadora House,147 Ave.B.at 9th Street, 4:00 PM

(Fri) THE BRASS TRUMPET-All Souls Church,114th St.& St.Nicholas Ave. 3:30 PM

(Fri) THE MAGIC BOX-Sara Delano Roosevelt Plygd.Christie,Forsythe & Grand Sts. 3:30 PM

(Fri) PUNCH AND JUDY-Utopia Children's Home,170 West 130th Street, 3:30 PM

B R O O K L Y N

(Mon) THE MIGHTY MIKKO-Manhattan Beach Jewish Center,60 West End Ave. 4:30 PM

(Mon) ZNEE-ZEE-Group Club,3109 Surf Ave. 8:30 PM

More # # # #

Figure 6.1 Weekly schedule for Federal Theatre Project (FTP) presentations in New York City, January 1937. Federal Theatre Project collection, Library of Congress, www.loc.gov/item/fpraf.09640001/.

This is it, the data we'd hoped for. It is large: weekly reports through June 1939. It is amenable to abstraction and categorization, with respect to information such as performance titles, locations, performance times, prices, and performance categories. This is our archive, with its mass of information. Now we need to make it useful by transforming it into data.

Data Entry (and Organization): Tedious but Essential

Even the single page shown in Figure 6.1 contains a tremendous amount of information. Starting at the top of the page and moving left to right then down, we find: a warning about possible changes to the schedule, a header for the FTP, the relevant week (the year, though, is provided by our cataloguers, not this document), a source address, a header, and then, finally, production information. As we prepare to reconfigure the production information on this page, we should recognize that not all the facts here help us answer our research questions – though some facts may be useful for answering other questions. For instance, the address of the division that created this list may be of interest for a bureaucratic history of the FTP, but is not relevant to our study of its production work. Our data set will thus include only data potentially relevant to our research questions and exclude extraneous information – even though it, too, may be important information in this archive. Including only information directly relevant to our study is, itself, an act of curation.

Approaching the production information as data requires that we treat each production as distinct and that we distinguish among the pieces of information about each production. That is to say, we must recognize productions as abstract entities, but also see that all productions have certain shared characteristics that we can parse out and treat as their own discrete types. Specifically, each production line in Figure 6.1 includes a production title, a venue name, an address, a price or price range, and a performance time or times. The seven productions at the top of the page follow this format. Productions in the section headed 'MARIONETTE SHOWS' then take a slightly different format, with a day of the week indicated and the productions all organized by borough. Each of these pieces of information – addresses, titles, dates, and times – is a datum. Our work as data researchers involves reorganizing this information into a format easily analysed by a computer, which means structuring the data in a way that groups types together.

Because the authors of this sheet have organized the material so systematically, transforming it into an organized database will not require

Table 6.2 *Extract of spreadsheet of FTP New York productions*

Production title	Venue name	Address	Price range	Curtain time
It Can't Happen Here	Adelphi Theatre	54th St. East of 7th Ave.	25–55¢	8:40 PM

Note: This table includes only the first row of the spreadsheet generated from the archival page in Figure 6.1.

much inventiveness. Indeed, the layout of this page already suggests a spreadsheet, as each production entry presents a roughly similar sequence of information (see Vareschi & Burkert, 2016). Following normal spreadsheet practice, we will treat each entry (i.e. each production line) as a row, and separate the relevant data into columns. Our first entry for the sheet in Figure 6.1 might look like Table 6.2.

This is a good and reasonable beginning, but even now we might recognize some challenges in this data set, and perhaps opportunities to alter our categorization so as to improve its utility later on. Note the address: 54th St. East of 7th Ave. Should we wish to locate this venue on a map, we'll want more precision than this relative address. We might simply look up the Adelphi Theatre's full address (152 W 54th St.) and replace it in the spreadsheet. Or, we may wish to preserve the archival data and add a new column for the full address. Later, we might add geolocation data (latitude and longitude) as yet another column, so as to enable us to digitally map our data set. In this process, we have transformed the facts recorded in the archive into data more amenable to our research by taking the archive's fuzzy geographic information and making it more specific.

Continuing our transcription, we immediately come to a new data problem with the second production, which includes information not listed for the first: a borough. So, let's add that to our columns (Table 6.3).

We could continue in this way for the subsequent rows until we hit the entries for *Flight* and *Circus*. These two productions have unusual curtain time information. The former notes an 8:30 p.m. curtain, followed by matinees on Thursday and Friday at 4:00 p.m. and on Saturday at 2:30 p.m.; the latter specifies Saturday and Sunday at 2:30 p.m. and 8:00 p.m. How shall we record this information? Do we add a column for matinees? Should we add columns for each day of the week and record all performance times? If the latter, how shall we record performance schedules for the first productions, which don't name the productions' performance days? Our archive, typically, includes important information

Table 6.3 *Extract of spreadsheet of FTP New York productions, boroughs added*

Production title	Venue name	Address	Price range	Curtain time	Borough
It Can't Happen Here	Adelphi Theatre	54th St. East of 7th Ave.	25–55¢	8:40 PM	Manhattan
It Can't Happen Here	Majestic Theatre	Fulton St. & Rockwell Pl.	25–55¢	8:40 PM	Brooklyn

Note: This table includes the first two rows of the spreadsheet generated from the archival page in Figure 6.1.

that is ambiguous or confusing. How we record it in our database thus presents not only a practical question about data management, but a historical problem: When, actually, did the FTP perform its *Circus* and other productions?

Leaving the resolution of this issue as an exercise to the reader, I continue down the page to the marionette shows. Our categories once again expand: if we wish to label these as 'marionette shows', we need to create a new column and provide a label for the first set of shows (call them 'permanent', perhaps). We also must create a column for information about the day of the week on which marionette shows played. The spreadsheet has thus rapidly expanded in its set of categories, which we discovered simply by continuing with our transcription. (It is typical of data-driven research methods that the shape of a data set only appears clearly through the process of careful work with the data.) If we move on to the second and third pages of the schedule, we discover still more categories and more questions. How – if at all – should we record the 'Jewish' (i.e. Yiddish-language) performances of *It Can't Happen Here* in our database? Should we create sub-categories for each of the vaudeville shows (2E, 5B, etc.)? Each of these decisions about how to re-present the archive in the database will affect our later analysis. And we will continue to encounter new problems and, perhaps, need to revisit and revise old solutions as we move through subsequent weeks.

By the time we complete our transcription of this first week, we have a large set of categories, some of which may serve us well, others of which may not. This is the moment to remember that our work here is iterative: we must go back, having completed a one-week sample, and reconfigure our categories, perhaps combining some, perhaps adding new ones. Moreover, with additional research, we may wish to aggregate productions into categories not present in the archive. 'Permanent' and 'marionette' are sensible but limited descriptions of these shows. Perhaps we can divide them into comedies and dramas, or musical and non-musical. While those categories are not literally present in the archive, we can infer them from our archival information, and further transform the facts of the archive into useful data. With our final categories, derived from the experience of actual data transcription and our other research needs, we can continue on, transcribing the rest of our archive.

In continuing, we may see further categorization problems that require revision, as well as at least two other problems that necessitate pause. First, what do we do when information changes? For instance, imagine that a theatre venue changes its name, but nothing else. Do we maintain the old name, which we've used up to now, so as to maintain continuity? Do we go back and add the new name, using both throughout? Do we simply change the name without comment? Do we add a new column of some kind, with a note about the name change? Data constantly presents the researcher with these kinds of judgement calls. Answering them may require further research or new data categories, or it may even spur new research questions entirely.

Second, how do we approach errors or inconsistencies in the archive? For instance, one marionette show is listed as *Znee-zee* in January 1937. One year later, a show named *Snee-zee* appears. We can verify independently that these are, in fact, the same play (and the latter title is correct). But having done so, what should we do with our data? Silently correcting the mistake distorts the archive; leaving the mistake uncorrected would make any tally of unique plays performed wrong by at least one. Archives, particularly data-heavy archives, are full of such errors. Part of the necessary work of building a database involves identifying and thoughtfully managing such mistakes. Furthermore, data transcription inevitably introduces new errors into a data set, through mistyped entries, misaligned columns, misreadings of the archive, and so on. It is tempting to regard such problems as minor inconveniences of data-driven research and not the real work. This is wrong: data 'cleaning' not only reveals 'incidental' errors, but also helps us ask deeper questions about what categories we have used and how we have used them (Rawson & Muñoz, 2019). Errors force us to confront, in this work, the trade-off between rigour and uncertainty – a confrontation that encourages us to treat data-based research as both an end in itself and a means for thinking about deep disciplinary questions.

What does it mean to be rigorous and uncertain in data-driven research? First, rigour: in cultivating and sharing their data, the researcher must carefully balance sensitivity to archival nuance with the real benefit of studying data – the ability to pass over minor differences and take in a bigger picture. One could write an entire microhistory of that first page we have just converted into a database. But if we get bogged down in the wrong details, we will not meet our objective of using the archive to garner a big picture of FTP's activity in New York City. We must be rigorous within the context of our research question. But we also cannot lose sight of the uncertainty: data-driven studies must always counterbalance rigour with an awareness of what such 'objective' approaches elide. This means explicating the data categories used, the types of errors treated as inconsequential, and the information excluded. Uncertainty is always present in data-driven scholarship; good data scholarship makes that uncertainty clear and visible. And it is here, in the effort not simply to manage data, but to reflect on our decisions *as* data managers, that some of the most important (and generally applicable) opportunities in data-driven work appear.

Working with Data as a Way of Thinking about Theatre and Performance

Data modelling spurs logical, structural thinking that can counteract disciplinary jargon and ambiguity. Willard McCarty (2014: 27) posits that this is precisely the purpose of working with databases: 'Computational models, however finely perfected, are better understood as *temporary states in a process of coming to know* rather than fixed structures of knowledge.' Method is supreme. Every time we design and use a database, we put our assumptions about theatre and performance to work. And what that database produces sometimes matters less than the writing of the database itself. As McCarty (2014: 27) advises, 'although efficient access to data is an essential function of computing, the greater potential is for computers as modelling machines, not knowledge jukeboxes'.

What does this mean? Consider the problem of *Znee-zee*/*Snee-zee*. I have stated that the titles refer to the same play – and they do. But what is at stake when I claim that a performance in one location in 1937 and then another in a different location in 1938 are the same production? One might, of course, dig into the archives to see whether *Snee-zee* changed its script or production book. Yet by simply accepting that the two performances are one and the same, as I have done, I assert something about a production's ontology, its continuity across time and space, which implies a massive range of assumptions about theatre and performance. In other words, even our category of 'show' is freighted with a set of disciplinary ideas that may not, actually, be the most useful ones for our study.

Modelling data thus requires us to manage information, create categories, and interrogate the categories themselves. Designing a data model, one implicitly asserts fundamental categories that align, for example, performances and works, sex and gender identities, and contemporary and historical vocabularies for performance. Scholars recognized the significance of these issues early in the history of theatre databases. A 1985 conference in London, the first international meeting on theatre and computerized databases, worried over the 'standardization of terminology' across cultures and time periods (Herbert, 1986: 179). The problem, however, extends beyond standardized vocabulary to the organization of that language within the structure of the database. In other words, we must wrestle not only with the 'terminology' of theatre but also with the way a database's model represents (or misrepresents) the ontology of the entities or events it catalogues.

Consider the names we give to theatrical labour. The Internet Broadway Database follows the pattern of contemporary playbills by listing shows as either 'staged by' or 'directed by' an individual (Broadway League, n.d.). If we want to find directors in this database, we need to know about and search for both terms. We could subsume both titles into the modern category of 'director'. (This is called a 'controlled vocabulary', in which the researcher groups like terms into a fixed set of possibilities.) This move would help reveal, for example, that David Belasco both wrote and directed the 1895 *The Heart of Maryland*, a show that the database labels only as 'staged by David Belasco'. But a database that regularizes the two terms would obscure the historical consolidation of directing as a discrete professional role in the theatre, the moment when all 'stagers' became 'directors'. A well-designed database must accommodate the particularity of historical categories while also making possible transcultural and transhistorical analyses that translate – but do not efface – local or archaic practices. Decisions about such controlled vocabularies require careful research and extensive knowledge on the part of data designers and data encoders (see Bollen, 2016).

Moreover, such decisions have not only intellectual but also ethical implications. A given data model may not be inherently wrong. Yet we must recognize that all data models include implicit ideas about theatre and performance – and often other categories such as race and gender – that merit scrutiny. Good data modelling demands conscious attention to the model's complexities and limitations and an effort to explain these choices, and thus not to leave the power of data modelling hidden. Writing of classification schemes generally, Geoffrey C. Bowker and Susan

Leigh Star warn that 'classifications are powerful technologies. Embedded in working infrastructures they become relatively invisible without losing any of that power.... Classifications should be recognized as the significant site of political and ethical work that they are' (Bowker & Star, 1999: 319). Every system of classification codifies power relationships. Classifications define the world, and, in so doing, make present the things we name and erase the things we do not. That power to erase or make visible adds intellectual excitement to much data work, as we interrogate our categories and our assumptions. But it also creates ethical demands to which we must attend with care.

DH raises other moral questions, too. Data-driven research, for instance, favours performance traditions that produce written archives and institutions to sustain them. This is not to say that performance traditions without a written archive are impossible to study with digital methods. But these methods are hard enough with good archives; creating an archive from scratch multiplies difficulties. Digital research is also often more explicitly collaborative than other TaPS scholarship. How best to honour those collaborations and to give and receive proper credit remains challenging for a set of methods that still feel strange to most humanists (see Graban et al., 2019). (And here is the proper moment to acknowledge Jeffrey Careyva, whose own labour transcribing the FTP's data made possible my discussion of it in this chapter.) Furthermore, digital research often relies on grants and funding – and presents sustainability challenges – at a scale unfamiliar to a discipline focused on single monographs (Roh, 2019). For these reasons and others, digital methods are not for everyone or every project.

But what are data-driven methods for? The answer varies widely from project to project. The utility of data-driven research is often most apparent when it is put into conversation with other methods. In the case of our data from the FTP in New York, we might complement the recent historiographical trend of looking beyond New York by demonstrating the FTP's truly astounding accomplishments in the city. As a rough map of our complete data set demonstrates (Figure 6.2), New York's FTP itself was far from monolithic. The controversial productions that made so many headlines and dominated earlier FTP histories were but the tip of an iceberg that extended across the city. Geographically – and, as further data would reveal – artistically, ethnically, formally, and financially, the FTP in New York presented an astoundingly diverse array of work. The turn in FTP scholarship towards regional stories based on archival case studies and performance analysis has occluded New York's variety. (Of course, other data might be used to map and otherwise analyse regional or national FTP studies, too.)

Figure 6.2 Map of FTP performances in New York City, 1937–9. Larger circles indicate more performances.

What else does working with data do? An archivist digitizing rare materials uses DH to disseminate knowledge and to attract in-person visitors. Within a classroom, digital tools might make collaboration easier or allow (through videos or sound recordings) close study of long-forgotten performances. For the researcher, data offers the ability to study information at scale. My own quantitative analyses of theatre history emphasize the massive size of theatrical activity, extending far beyond studies of only one performance or one career (Escobar Varela & Miller, 2002; Miller, 2016). Digital methods give us a handle on this larger universe of theatre – not *Snee-zee*, but all the FTP's performances; not the Adelphi Theatre in New York, but all theatres in the United States – and help us explain the theatrical system within which individual shows, buildings, or careers thrive or fail. But, however you embrace digital methods, thinking consciously about data to study theatre and performance will change how you think about theatre and performance themselves.

Notes

1 And I should bear in mind DH's tendency to repeat disciplinary bias towards white archives (see D'Ignazio & Klein, 2020; Losh & Wernimont, 2019; Risam, 2018).
2 Conversely, Brenda Laurel (1991) posited that user experiences in computing ought to be understood in dramatic terms.

References

Allington, D., Brouillette S., & Golumbia D. (2016). 'Neoliberal Tools (and Archives): A Political History of Digital Humanities'. *Los Angeles Review of Books*, 1 May.
Arnold, T., & Tilton, L. (2015). *Humanities Data in R: Exploring Networks, Geospatial Data, Images, and Text*. Cham: Springer International.
Bay-Cheng, S., Parker-Starbuck, J., & Saltz, D. Z. (2015). *Performance and Media: Taxonomies for a Changing Field*. Ann Arbor: University of Michigan Press.
Bench, H., & Elswit, K. (2022). 'Visceral Data for Dance Histories: Katherine Dunham's People, Places, and Pieces'. *TDR: The Drama Review*, 66(1), 37–61.
Bloom, G., Kemp, S., Toothman, N., & Buswell, E. (2016). '"A Whole Theatre of Others": Amateur Acting and Immersive Spectatorship in the Digital Shakespeare Game Play the Knave'. *Shakespeare Quarterly*, 67(4), 408–30.
Bollen, J. (2016). 'Data Models for Theatre Research: People, Places, and Performance'. *Theatre Journal*, 68(4), 615–32.
Bowker, G. C., & Star, S. L. (1999). *Sorting Things Out: Classification and Its Consequences*. Cambridge: MIT Press.
Broadway League. (n.d.). 'Internet Broadway Database'. Accessed 25 February 2023. www.ibdb.com.
Brown, L., & O'Connor, J., eds. (1978). *Free, Adult, Uncensored: The Living History of the Federal Theatre Project*. Washington, DC: New Republic Books.
Cahn, J., & Leighton, R. V. (1913). *The Cahn–Leighton Official Theatrical Guide*, vol. 17. New York: New Amsterdam Theatre Building.
D'Ignazio, C., & Klein, L. (2020). *Data Feminism*. Cambridge: MIT Press.
De Hart, J. (1967). *The Federal Theatre, 1935–1939: Plays, Relief, and Politics*. Princeton, NJ: Princeton University Press.
Escobar Varela, M. (2021). *Theatre as Data: Computational Journeys into Theatre Research*. Ann Arbor: University of Michigan Press.
Escobar Varela, M., & Hernández-Barraza, L. (2020). 'Digital Dance Scholarship: Biomechanics and Culturally Situated Dance Analysis'. *Digital Scholarship in the Humanities*, 35(1), 160–75.

Escobar Varela, M., & Miller, D. (2002). 'Rethinking the Canon through the Digital'. In L. Mantoan, M. Moore, & A. Farr Schiller, eds., *Troubling Traditions: Canonicity, Theatre, and Performance in the US*. New York: Routledge, pp. 245–56.

Folger Shakespeare Library. (n.d.). 'Shakespeare's Works'. Accessed 25 February 2023. https://shakespeare.folger.edu.

Fraden, R. (1994). *Blueprints for a Black Federal Theatre, 1935–1939*. New York: Cambridge University Press.

Gitelman, L., ed. (2013). *'Raw' Data Is an Oxymoron*. Cambridge: MIT Press.

Graban, T. S., Marty, P., Romano, A., & Vandegrift, M., eds. (2019). 'Invisible Work in Digital Humanities'. Special issue, *DHQ: Digital Humanities Quarterly*, 13(2).

Guyot, S., & Ravel, J. S., eds. (2020). *Databases, Revenues, and Repertory: The French Stage Online, 1680–1793*. Cambridge: MIT Press.

Herbert, I. (1986). 'Computer Databases for Theatre Studies'. *New Theatre Quarterly*, 2(6), 175–80.

Jockers, M. (2014). *Text Analysis with R for Students of Literature*. Cham: Springer International.

Laurel, B. (1991). *Computers as Theatre*. Reading, MA: Addison-Wesley.

LOC (Library of Congress). (n.d.). 'Collection: Federal Theatre Project, 1935 to 1939'. Accessed 25 February 2023. www.loc.gov/collections/federal-theatre-project-1935-to-1939/.

Losh, E., & Wernimont, J. (2019). *Bodies of Information: Intersectional Feminism and the Digital Humanities*. Minneapolis: University of Minnesota Press.

McCarty, W. (2014). *Humanities Computing*. New York: Palgrave Macmillan.

Miller, D. (2016). 'Average Broadway'. *Theatre Journal*, 68(4), 529–53.

Montfort, N. (2016). *Exploratory Programming for the Arts and Humanities*. Cambridge: MIT Press.

Moore, C. (2017). *The Federal Theatre Project in the American South: The Carolina Playmakers and the Quest for American Drama*. Lanham, MD: Lexington Books.

Osborne, E. A. (2011). *Staging the People: Community and Identity in the Federal Theatre Project*. New York: Palgrave Macmillan.

Pearson, R., ed. (2007). 'Victorian Plays Project'. Site discontinued as of February 2023. https://victorian.nuigalway.ie.

PH (Programming Historian). (2023). 'Homepage'. https://programminghistorian.org/.

Rawson, K., & Muñoz, T. (2019). 'Against Cleaning'. In M. K. Gold & L. F. Klein, eds., *Debates in the Digital Humanities*. Minneapolis: University of Minnesota Press. Digital book, accessed 11 October 2023. https://dhdebates.gc.cuny.edu/projects/debates-in-the-digital-humanities-2019.

Risam, R. (2018). *New Digital Worlds: Postcolonial Digital Humanities in Theory, Praxis, and Pedagogy*. Evanston, IL: Northwestern University Press.

Roh, D. S. (2019). 'The DH Bubble: Startup Logic, Sustainability, and Performativity'. In M. K. Gold & L. F. Klein, eds., *Debates in the Digital Humanities*. Minneapolis: University of Minnesota Press. Digital book, accessed 11 October 2023. https://dhdebates.gc.cuny.edu/projects/debates-in-the-digital-humanities-2019.

Tompkins, J. (2014). 'Making the Invisible Visible: Virtual Stage Props and Christopher Marlowe's Dr. Faustus'. In M. Schweitzer & J. Zerdy, eds., *Performing Objects and Theatrical Things*. New York: Palgrave Macmillan, 161–72.

Tufte, E. R. (2001). *The Visual Display of Quantitative Information*. 2nd ed. Cheshire, CT: Graphics Press.

Vareschi, M., & Burkert, M. (2016). 'Archives, Numbers, Meaning: The Eighteenth-Century Playbill at Scale'. *Theatre Journal*, 68(4), 597–613.

Witham, B. B. (2003). *The Federal Theatre Project: A Case Study*. New York: Cambridge University Press.

CHAPTER 7

Analysing Immersive Performance through Lived Bricolage

Julia M. Ritter

A free ticket to a performance turned into a very expensive evening. It was a frigid night in February 2012, and I had just spent three and a half hours in full motion while immersed in the New York City production of *Sleep No More* (*SNM*). Navigating a perplexing, labyrinthine venue designed by the UK-based company Punchdrunk, I followed performers who were enacting scenes drawn from Shakespeare's *Macbeth*, the films of Alfred Hitchcock, and other stories throughout six floors and over a hundred rooms that were curated and decorated with a high-fashion, 1930s aesthetic. Stepping out of the venue onto the cold and empty city street well past midnight, I felt radiant with energy, both excited and somewhat disoriented. I stood for a moment to get my bearings and then walked two blocks to where I had parked my car much earlier that evening. Yet, as I rounded the corner onto Twenty-Ninth Street, I saw not a single vehicle. Where was my car? The disorientation of the evening intensified as my mind raced. It was highly unlikely that my car had been stolen since it was too old and not a luxury vehicle. Towed? Hadn't I checked the street signs? Cursing myself loudly, given that no one was around to hear, I paced back and forth a few times as I absorbed the reality that my night was going to be even longer and, most likely, much more costly than originally expected.

Motion, including walking, helps drive my thinking. Rather than try to hail a cab, I set off on foot in the direction of Pier 76 at Thirty-Eighth Street and Twelfth Avenue, the site of the once infamous, now defunct, Manhattan Tow Pound. Luckily, my phone had full charge since audience participants are forbidden to access their devices during the performance. Opening up a voice memo application on my phone, I talked as I walked uptown, trying to remember and articulate everything that I had just experienced during *SNM*. This particular voice memo would later become a critical component of my data set, revealing an enormous amount of information once I transcribed and coded it. Several times as I was walking and talking, I found myself pausing to play around and experiment with movement. Feeling emboldened on the deserted city streets, with no one to see my improvisational explorations, I was revisiting the sensation of the motion that I had witnessed.

Upon arriving at the Tow Pound, I became distracted by another set of performances. A wide-ranging display of theatrical expression unfolded as a parade of people – whose cars, like mine, had been towed – arrived in various states of indignation and intoxication to beg, plead, gesticulate, rant, and, unfortunately in some cases, verbally abuse the operators in failed attempts to retrieve their vehicles without charge. Three hours and a hefty violation bill later, I was back in my car heading home, with images still swirling in my head and my senses buzzing with the kinaesthetic resonance of two high-adrenaline contexts: the *SNM* performance and, subsequently, the experience of reclaiming my car. Although waiting for my car was time-consuming, those hours were productive in their own way. They became a temporal holding cell through which I remained receptive to my post-performance sensations and reflections while doing my best to act as a bricoleur, or 'an improviser working with what was at hand, cobbling together solutions to both practical and aesthetic problems' (P. Wilcken, quoted in Balzer, 2015: 23). Adopting a bricoleur/improviser stance has served me well over the past decade as I have expanded my expertise as dance artist and movement researcher to become an interdisciplinary scholar with the skills and knowledge to utilize multiple qualitative research methods when analysing performance more broadly as a field of study.

This chapter, like the scenario that frames it, is my story of working out what and how to 'bricolage' in the moment – in other words, how to work improvisationally to draw upon available resources, build on strengths, experiment with strategies, and seek new skills to solve research problems. That initial experience of *SNM* aroused my kinaesthetic, cognitive, and emotional curiosity, prompting me to choose the production as an object of study and its performances as sites for fieldwork. After three more visits to *SNM*, a key research question emerged: What is going on here, choreographically, in terms of both the creation and reception of these *SNM* performances? This question drove the development of a research methodology that supported the publication of several chapters and articles (Ritter, 2015, 2016, 2017) and my book *Tandem Dances: Choreographing Immersive Performance* (Ritter, 2021), which constitute the culmination of my research into *SNM* as an aesthetic event.

It is a rare opportunity, indeed a gift, to be invited to revisit one's research to examine what was done and learned. Now, via this invitation to contribute my perspectives, other research questions have arisen that I attempt to answer. What exactly did I do in the course of this research project? How did the methods that I chose shape and ultimately determine what I came to know and offer to readers in the aforementioned writings? If I claim that my methodological choices were undeniably informed by my creative practice as an improviser, in the doing of bricolage, what is the 'doing' that I did? And, out of that doing, what kinds of questions emerged? How did theory-building manifest? While the story I tell here focuses on my own realizations about the importance of bricolage in my research, it is also interwoven with revelations of how I found others – namely audience participants and spectators – who were researching *their* own experiences of being affected by *SNM* via similar methods and sharing their stories in multiple formats online. Analysing the responses of others alongside my own presented me with degrees of complexity, requiring particular approaches to explore the production and its impact on audiences. A quote from American scholar and arts education champion Elliot Eisner (1982: 49) is helpful here; he states, 'the kinds of nets we know how to weave determine the kinds of nets we cast. These nets, in turn, determine the kinds of fish we catch.' Eisner offered this statement when advocating for curricular reform that would expand the definition of literacy to be inclusive of knowledge gained through the arts and sensorial processes, alongside verbal and mathematical skills. To get a multidimensional view of the production and performances as phenomena, it was necessary not only to cast the nets I knew how to weave (choreographic analysis, for example) but to weave new nets to cast out. Adding research methods, sometimes by overlapping and tangling them, allowed me to expand my 'catch' to include the multiple perspectives of audiences, artistic directors, dancers, and producers that contributed to more comprehensive analysis and theorization.

In putting my iterative, additive research strategy forward as a case study, this chapter details how over several years I drew upon a multiplicity of approaches to examine *SNM*, including ethnographic methods such as bricolage, participant observation, interviews, and spectator participation as research (SPaR), as well as interpretive strategies, including narrative enquiry, creative analysis, audience studies, and analysis of media content. Through writing and publishing multiple essays about *SNM*, I was repeatedly drawn back to the data with different questions – questions that, in turn, called for new nets to be cast. For instance, questions that arose about choreography's paradoxical operation in *SNM*, namely its capacity to both expand the possibilities for and delimit the agency of audiences, necessitated that I cast different 'nets' to gather their perspectives. With these concerns in mind, the aim of the chapter is to make the research process explicit so other researchers might apply a similarly improvisational, compositional approach to the qualitative research of performance, wherein successive questions prompt a mixed methods approach.

Doing Bricolage: Improvisational and Compositional Approaches to Ethnography

Scholars from a wide range of disciplinary practices have linked ethnographic research with improvisational and experimental approaches, the latter being central to bricolage as a method. In his influential text *Tales of the Field: On Writing Ethnography*, organizational theorist John Eastin Van Maanen (2011: 175) writes that ethnography is a 'relatively artistic, improvised, and situated form of social research'. Drawing upon Van Maanen, Anne-Laure Fayard (2017: 142–3), a philosopher studying communication, collaboration, and culture, notes that ethnography 'cannot be procedural. It is more of a toolbox of methods that need to be adjusted, evolved, and adapted to a specific context.' Furthermore, Fayard makes explicit her understanding of ethnography as 'experimental and deeply improvisational' in that the 'ethnographer is a bricoleur' who 'must creatively use and develop tools and methods' and diverge from standard approaches like participant observation when the complexity of a study increases. For instance, my research on *SNM* was initially focused on why and how the creators (Felix Barrett, founder and artistic director of Punchdrunk, and Maxine Doyle, associate director and choreographer) chose dance as the primary medium for communicating the intersecting narratives at the heart of the production. Yet the research scope broadened and increased in complexity as I gained awareness of *SNM*'s impact on audience members and the way they continued to engage before, during, and after performances. In what follows, I break down how my improvisational stance led me to accumulate – indeed, cobble together, as bricoleur – multiple approaches including voice memoing, coding, interviewing, conducting internet-based enquiry, and engaging in creative analysis via descriptive writing. Each approach allowed me to gain insight into participants' lived experiences (including my own), make space for the voices of spectators, develop my reflexivity as a researcher, and share my research. In my experience, bricolage serves a researcher most effectively as a means for adding methods and creating assemblages of different kinds of interdisciplinary data; these assemblages then allow connections to be made, and ideas and concepts to elide in distinct ways that support theory-building. In these ways, creative and scholarly researchers can work both intentionally and improvisationally to be knowledgeable, prepared, and ready to act upon impulses and opportunities (see Knowles & Cole, 2008).

The free ticket affording me my first experience of *SNM* was a gift from Tony Bordonaro, an alumnus of the Dance Department at New Jersey's Rutgers University, where I taught, who, excited about his recent hire as a Punchdrunk performer, sent me a Facebook message about the gig. We hadn't been in touch for several years and his January 2012 message was an unexpected intervention at a critical moment. I had been struggling to identify current productions that served my research interests; namely, those prioritizing dance as the primary mode of expression and offering spectators new models for engagement via non-proscenium settings and multi-perspective viewing angles, with proximity to performers. I had recently found a study commissioned by the James Irvine Foundation and conducted by consultants WolfBrown that listed Punchdrunk, a company unfamiliar to me, as an example of a group of artists who were changing the parameters for audience engagement in the twenty-first century (Brown et al., 2011).[1] Intrigued by the confluence of these two events, I promptly replied to Tony with my congratulations and accepted his offer of a complimentary ticket.

In terms advanced by former dancer and current Professor of Curriculum Donald Blumenfeld-Jones (2008: 176) in a discussion of dance, choreography, and social science research, I am, as a dance artist, both 'analytic instrument and an analyst'. The qualitative methods that I deploy are informed by my point of view as a researcher of dance as interdisciplinary praxis that intersects embodied practice with theoretical and historical research. When experiencing an *SNM* performance, I am a spectator, an audience participant observer, and an ethnographer. Enacting both improvisational and compositional approaches enables simultaneous navigation between the roles of instrument and analyst – and between the planned and the unplanned, the experimental and the structured. Researchers can then examine and analyse their experiences of performance and that of audiences through the widest and most flexible aperture possible. In this way, I came to understand and treat the research process as itself a compositional one that emerges in 'tandem' with the work being researched.

Given this, the ethnographic tool of participant observation was essential when I approached *SNM* as a fieldwork site. Anthropologist James P. Spradley (1980: 145) emphasizes immersion and interactivity in his guidance for individuals engaging in participant observation. I made it my goal to immerse myself as much as possible by attending multiple performances of *SNM* as a spectator/researcher, in order to have 'direct experience with the phenomenon' and to gather data (Merriam, 2009: 25). While I focused on observing the performance, and particularly on tracking the choreography as it unfolded throughout the space, I was aware that my experiences of the total theatrical environment – engaging with performers or audience members as well as interacting with the space and scenography – would be useful data to reflect upon post-performance. Through participant observation, I became attuned to the particular structures, relationships, dynamics, and values shaping how dance and immersive practices interface in *SNM*.

SNM's structure is episodic and non-linear; audiences perceive themselves as having free range of the venue, yet, as I have argued, they are both choreographically constrained and impelled by the dancing of the cast members and by the space itself. Dozens of scenes unfold simultaneously throughout the performance space, making it impossible for an audience member to be everywhere that artistic content is being offered and preventing them from experiencing the entirety of the production in one visit. While encountering scene after scene as participant observers within *SNM*, audiences shift back and forth across a spectrum of engagement ranging from more passive kinds of observation to more physically active, improvisational exchanges with other audience members.[2] For example, one moment in a performance I was simply a member of a group of audience participants who were standing still and watching two dancers perform a duet on a pool table; the next, I came upon another spectator who was admiring a wall filled floor to ceiling with jars of candy. We engaged in a non-verbal, physical dialogue that felt like a kind of dance about whether to open the jars and consume the candy that was displayed, temptingly, in front of us (see Ritter, 2016: 56–7). These types of contrasting experiences, as well as my perceptions of the choreography and performance, featured prominently in the voice memos that I recorded immediately after each performance, as detailed in the next section, 'Voicing Experiences'.

Equally important here is the practice of SPaR, which sensitized my approach as a participant observer and informed my study of how audiences responded to *SNM* via their activity online. Developed by Deirdre Heddon, Helen Iball, and Rachel Zerihan as a means for analysing productions featuring one performer and one audience member, SPaR foregrounds 'the experiential processes of reception' and 'the relational dynamic' of participatory performance (Heddon et al., 2012: 5). Further theorizing by F. H. Babbage (2016) on SPaR as an extension of practice-based research was helpful as I worked to understand how fans of *SNM* repeat their attendance in order to both study the production as art and engage in the practice of art-making – the practice of *being the art* – through their instantiation of the improvisational scores that guided their participation, and their post-performance creation of fan fiction and fan art, discussed later in this chapter.

My first experience of *SNM* was all about movement: not only my own and that of the performers, but also that of my fellow spectators, whom I observed when I wasn't completely engrossed in my own physical, cognitive, and emotional journey through the performance. The choreography of *SNM* involves two distinct and overlapping structures; Maxine Doyle (2013) uses the term *track* to describe the choreography performed by cast members, while I use the term *score* to identify the structure enabling the improvised, individual participatory performances by audience members. Given that the choreography offers possibilities (albeit carefully controlled) for audiences to make their own choices, I found that I was more intrigued by my own impulses to move during the performance, and by the movement of other spectators, than I was by the choreography performed by the cast members. That is, I was intrigued by how the production was structured to impel spectators into motion, and how choreography was deployed to galvanize audience participation and thus affect reception. With this realization came questions about methodology, specifically that of how to dig more deeply. While I ultimately attended *SNM* six times, repeated attendance beyond this was financially prohibitive due to ticket prices. Thus, financial constraints spurred me further towards mixed methods as I sought alternatives to participant observation. How, then, to gather more data?

Voicing Experiences: Memoing, Coding, and Interviewing

One major argument I put forth in my book *Tandem Dances* is that 'immersive performance transforms the spectator into a subject of choreography' (Ritter, 2021: 104). In *SNM*, spectators become such subjects because they follow rules of physical engagement that are aligned to parallel and intersect with the performance *tracks* of the paid, professional cast members. As mentioned at the start of the chapter, the intense, embodied participation of *SNM* coupled with the realization that my car had been towed compelled me to continue being physically engaged by walking and dancing towards the Tow Pound. I also had the distinct urge to talk about and describe what I had just experienced; with no one around, a voice memo was a sufficient proxy for the myriad reflections that surfaced as I, moving along the streets, recalled what had happened over the past three hours.

After transcribing the memos, I used Johnny Saldaña's (2009: 86) analytical strategy of affective coding methods. Saldaña describes affective coding as an initial or 'first-cycle coding' strategy used to 'investigate subjective qualities of human experience', namely by generating lists of recurring keywords and identifying 'emotions and values'. From the four different coding processes Saldaña includes within his rubric of affective coding (emotion coding, values coding, versus coding, and evaluation coding), I chose versus coding. As the nomenclature suggests, versus coding involves identifying binary terms to describe phenomena and processes. This first attempt to analyse the data could involve broad strokes. For example, one of my initial analytic tactics involved grouping data into categories – creators, dancers, audiences – to get at the fundamental questions of 'What is happening here? Who is doing what and why?' while remaining open to other categories and corollaries that might emerge (Saldaña, 2009: 96). Although the boundaries between roles can appear to be blurred in immersive productions – audiences can be both improvisers and spectators, for instance – versus coding allowed me to begin to identify when and how participants were enacting different roles. By taking a 'this or that' approach through versus coding, I was able to isolate different phenomena, processes, and stakeholders (creators, performers, other spectators, myself), and thus analyse them via my questions about choreography and its role in creation and reception.

Coding the raw data from my very first voice memo (Table 7.1) revealed several sensitizing concepts that I decided warranted further enquiry.[3] The concept of risk emerged through acknowledgement of the sensory and physical challenges I encountered. In turn, this concept informed my next steps in research, such as how I crafted the interview questions that I would later pose to artists, performers, and spectators, which then generated new insights of their own. For instance, when I interviewed Felix Barrett, my risk-related questions about the darkness of the corridor and its impact on sensory experience revealed his specific intentions regarding lighting design as a choreographic device for facilitating audience experience. Barrett and his co-creators choreographically conceptualized lighting design as a means of organizing the movement of audiences, with darkness used to slow spectator participants down and light used to activate and direct them to specific scenes within the venue. It was through this interview process with Barrett, which was catalysed through the processes of coding, that I came to understand how he was thinking choreographically, centralizing composition as a methodology intended to facilitate spectator experience (see Ritter, 2015).

Table 7.1 *Sample voice memo data on* Sleep No More *(SNM) with first-cycle versus coding*

Raw data[a]	Preliminary codes	Final codes	Coding memo[b]
The first thing I was, ah, struck by was the element of risk that the company was willing to take by setting up one of the first corridors that audience members had to walk through as pitch black. Keeping my hand on the wall, uh, running my hand along the wall, covered in some velvet fabric was the only way I could find my way forward. And, um, if it had not been for someone walking in front of me, I would have been, ah, really quite concerned about walking through there by myself because I really could not see at all. …	Risk Physical risk Artistic risk Corridor – black Darkness Senses Touch Walk through alone Awareness Someone in front of me Not alone Concern Could not see	Risk vs Security Corridor vs Lobby Space Dark vs Light Sight vs Touch Wayfinding vs Disoriented In Motion vs Stationary Self vs Other Audience My Experience vs Other Experience Awareness vs Unawareness Frontal Orientation vs Posterior Orientation Visible vs Obscured	As an audience member I was immediately confronted with a task, that is, the first corridor, which was unexpected and a surprising challenge to negotiate. As soon as I realized there was someone in front of me, I accelerated my walking a bit to catch up and I announced myself in the form of a joke saying, 'I am not stalking you', and the person laughed, and then said something like they were glad someone else was there too. I agreed audibly. It was reassuring not to be alone, even though I had no idea who this person was. …

Note: This voice memo responds to the *SNM* performance of 2 February 2012 in New York (the performance took place from 7:00 to 11:00 p.m.; the recording was made after the performance and on the drive home, and then transcribed).

[a] 'Raw data' refers to the verbatim voice memo.

[b] 'Coding memo' incorporates reflections on data and the emergent patterns, categories, themes, and concepts from the initial coding (see Saldaña, 2009: 36).

The last column of Table 7.1 represents my application of Saldaña's (2009: 187) 'code-weaving' technique, which he defines as 'the integration of key code words and phrases into [concise] narrative form', used to suggest how data might fit together and inform theorizing. Code-weaving is part of Saldaña's larger rubric of pre-writing, which he frames as a bridge between analysis and finished writings. Code-weaving is particularly helpful for researchers who want to attend to emergent themes and address latent phenomena in future writings. My memoing revealed an awareness of others – being and moving together with other spectators and experiencing empathy for our shared, albeit temporary, struggle. This awareness struck me as significant; up until this point in time, I realized, I had not been particularly attuned to the presence or behaviours of other audience members in traditional (i.e. proscenium) venues, being immersed in a different way in the performance on the stage.

While preparing to interview research participants, I recognized that I might confront issues that exist within participant observation and other data-collection methods in relation to the ontology, epistemology, reliability, and believability of the data. In a paper emerging from the (now discontinued) online project 'Watching Dance: Kinesthetic Empathy', dance and theatre scholars Matthew Reason and Dee Reynolds articulate their struggles with issues of reliability and believability in their research, specifically the methodological problem of how much value or credit to attribute to the 'participants' expression of their own experiences' (Reason & Reynolds, 2010: 51). Ultimately, Reason and Reynolds resolve these issues by accepting that participants' 'construction [of meaning] is contingent, fluid, multiple, and might change according to who they are talking to and over time, but it is nonetheless a significant aspect of their experience'. With this stance, Reason and Reynolds underscore the reality that talking about performance experiences is a process of construction and meaning-making in the moment. Importantly, given that I assert that immersive performance is experienced first and foremost by audience participants via kinaesthesia, creative analysis informed by embodied experiences became critical to my research (Ritter, 2021: 20). Through an additive mixed methods approach, I was able to delve deeply not only into my own experience of improvised performance, but also into that which was recounted by audience members/research participants during interviews and discovered in the writings of fans.

Finding, Following, and 'Fellowing' the Fandom: Triangulation

As my anecdote at the start of the chapter evidences, my experience of immersion continued to resonate after I left the *SNM* venue. Subsequent online research of the production revealed that I was not alone; I discovered an international community, or fandom, of individuals who have attended *SNM* dozens, even hundreds, of times, to experience performances and learn the cultures of its various storyworlds. Finding the fandom meant that I could extend the boundaries of my research landscape beyond participant observation and interviews to include internet-based research. Hundreds of blogs have been dedicated to *SNM*, many actively maintained and serving as archives and resources (see behindawhitemask, n.d.). When turning to the work of the fandom, I was seeking any evidence of dance and choreographic immersion from a population that, in many cases, had already collected far more data via participant observation of the production than I had.[4] Through this internet-based research, I uncovered how fans were making sense of their spectatorship of dance and their experiences during the production, and sharing their research with one another online, a phenomenon I have called *extended audiencing* (Ritter, 2016; 2021). It is at this point that triangulation, described by Norman K. Denzin (1989: 236) as 'the use of multiple methods in the study of the same object', became an essential protocol within my process, a strategy to strengthen the validity of the study by bringing together participant observation, interviews, and analysis of the work of fans.

Evidence of fandom's research on social media platforms included various forms of artistic expression, such as writings and artwork, and revealed to me that these individuals were engaging ethnographically with the production. Indeed, I describe them in previous writings as *incidental* and *intentional ethnographers* (Ritter, 2015; 2017). *SNM* audiences are encouraged to seek out and follow what fascinates them; in this way, they are situated as ethnographers in the field, able to study 'whatever is happening there' and 'to pursue whatever they find to be of the greatest interest', as sociologist Kathy Charmaz (2006: 21) puts it. Yet, the *SNM* fans whom I studied also deployed a range of mixed methods during their returns to the venue. They invested significant amounts of time, energy, and, in many cases, money, to collect, triangulate, and analyse data. Then they created written and visual responses to the show based on their research – auto- and visual ethnographies – to share with cast members, other members of the fandom, and strangers in online communities.

These ethnographies, such as artworks, blog posts, and long-form writings, reveal the impact of the dance and immersive experience on the fans. Research and theory-building around this type of fandom-based audience engagement in immersive performance became a key focus for me, serving my ongoing objective of better understanding the impact of choreography on spectators. Framing the work of fans specifically as ethnographic and pursuing this line of research within the burgeoning field of immersive performance offered enormous possibilities. First, such productions could potentially inform how exposure to and engagement with dance (watching dance as well as being physically implicated and moving through space alongside performers) immerses audiences in contemporary performance. And second, more broadly, acknowledging that fans produce ethnographies presented one way of addressing a concern put forth by theatre scholar Helen Freshwater (2009: 29) that had precoccupied me: 'almost no one in theatre studies seems to be interested in exploring what actual audience members make of a performance'. The enquiry and analysis of fans had not been given their due, a gap I was determined to remedy.

There were several blogs, primarily on the Tumblr platform, that I found myself regularly drawn back to examine. These were the work of fans who were continually posting writings and fan art, doing so in a way that indicated to me their *triangulation* of data as a methodological approach to understanding the production. For example, the blog titled *They Have Scorched the Snake*, created by Evan Matthew Cobb (2022), is one I spent significant time researching. Cobb's blog featured over three thousand posts as of April 2022; while many posts feature Cobb in dialogue with other fans about various aspects of the production, most entries are reposted from the blogs of other fans, suggesting Cobb's triangulation of the writings, artistic collage, and GIFs (as analytical commentary) generated by others as a way to corroborate his experiences of performance (Figure 7.1).

It was while researching Cobb's blog that I first saw the artwork of Chloe Finore and recognized her depiction of a *SNM* scene that I, too, had experienced: what is known by fans as *SNM*'s 'interrogation' scene (Figure 7.2). The discovery of fan artworks, those of Finore and others, was revelatory for me; I understood these drawings, cartoons, and collages as artefacts that demonstrated how fans were analysing their kinaesthetic and choreographic experiences of performance via processes of visual enquiry. Furthermore, Finore's ink drawing, titled *Interrogation* (2013), reinforced my somatic and cognitive recollections of the scene as a highly kinetic, physically aggressive choreographic duet between two men. Finding Cobb's posting of Finore's artwork led me to seek her out on Tumblr; subsequent interviews with Finore yielded valuable data on how she understood choreography to function in *SNM*. In particular, she described the production itself as 'emotion and storytelling bathed in dance' and said that she had learned that the choreography of paid performers in their movement from

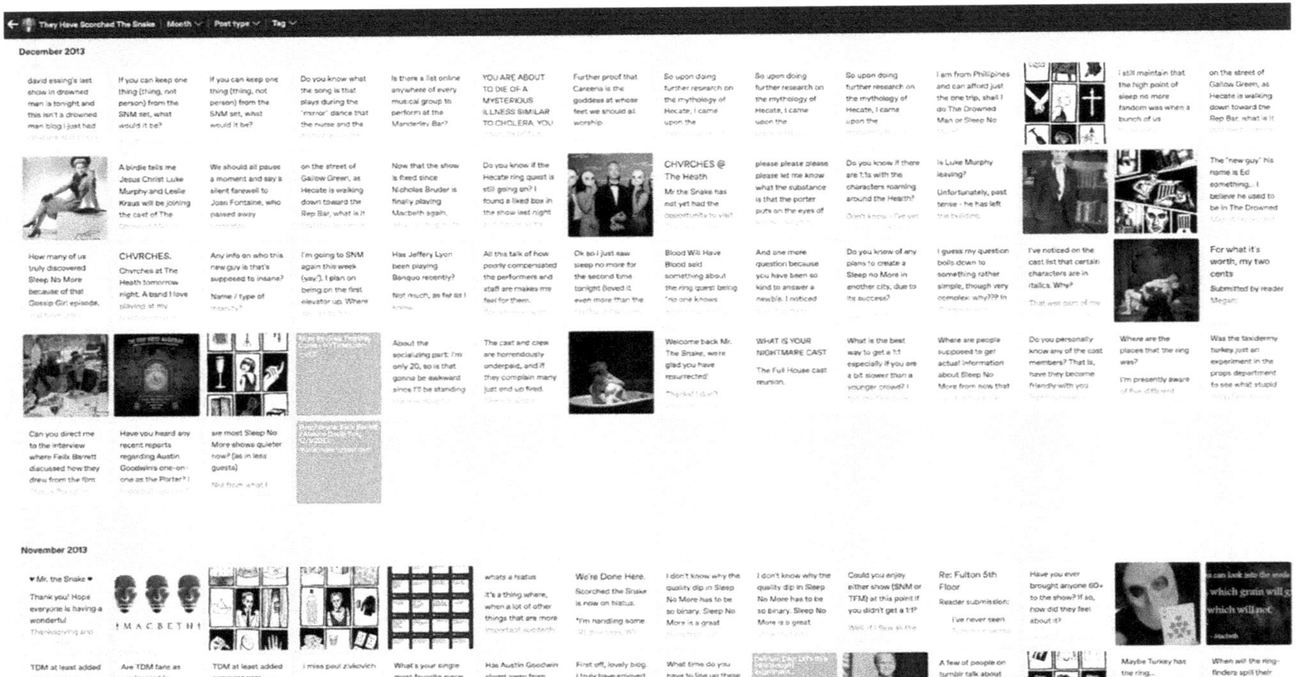

Figure 7.1 Posts *They Have Scorched the Snake* (blog), November and December 2013, created by Evan Matthew Cobb on Tumblr. Screenshot image by the author, April 2014.
The artwork reproduced in Figure 7.2 appears second from the right on the second row from the top.

Figure 7.2 *Interrogation*, ink drawing by Chloe Finore, © 2016 Chloe Finore. See note below Figure 7.1.

room to room had the effect of 'directing [audiences] to certain scenes' taking place throughout the building (Finore, 2014). Finore's art-making is a 'process of construction' towards meaning-making, following Reason and Reynolds (2010). Furthermore, in finding Finore's work, I was prompted to revisit my experience of the interrogation scene via improvised, creative analysis, which I address in the next section, 'Writing Scenarios'.

When I found Finore's *Interrogation*, I understood it to be representative of her visual research methodology; that is, her means for analysing the experiential knowledge she gained from *SNM* performances *and* the medium through which she chose to share that knowledge with the fandom. As Finore recounted during our 2014 interview, when she returned home from her first visit to *SNM*, '[I] whipped out my sketchbook and drew' in order to make sense of her performance experiences. In her depiction of the dancers in *Interrogation* (Figure 7.2), she succinctly captures the antagonistic nature of that scene via multiple approaches. Finore accentuates the angularity of the combative choreography by framing the two dancers within sharp-cornered panels and utilizing to great effect the oppositional intensity of light and dark ink values, which further emphasize the ferocity of their confrontation.

Just as I found the fandom and began to follow fans' blogs, I became aware of how they were finding, following, and 'fellowing' one another by supporting others in their research, sharing their discoveries, and reposting and reblogging content they found useful or exciting in order to amplify its reach to other members of the fandom.[5] Like me, they were immersed in improvisational and compositional (collaborative) approaches to ethnographic fieldwork of performance, with our methods intersecting to reveal insights and new avenues of enquiry.

Writing Scenarios: Creating as Research

Inspired by ways in which the fandom engaged in creative writing or drawing to analyse and express their experiences, I began to write as a form of research analysis aimed towards further understanding of the choreographic workings of the production. Working from my voice memo transcripts, interview transcripts, and recollections of *SNM* prompted by fan art, I developed prose-style writings that I call *scenarios*. These scenarios present my experiences through interpretive and descriptive analyses for the future reader/researcher while also offering a contextualized explanation of the events that occurred during performances. These writings were a way to cast another net (à la Eisner), with the intention of capturing what I experienced as ephemeral and moving it into archived form. Writing the scenarios achieved three purposes. First, through the process of drafting the scenarios, I was able to translate what I experienced during performances into written language for a reader: namely, the sensory, choreographic, theatrical, and scenographic content and the non-verbal, embodied encounters with dancers and other audience members. Second, scenarios connected specific content from each performance to existing theoretical concepts, which then served as tools to assist the reader in following my analysis. Third, when writing the scenarios, I was simultaneously engaged in analytically processing the events and constructing a foundation for future theory-building. Throughout all, the scenarios provided me with opportunities to be self-reflexive about my experiences; at the same time, I was aware of Robert E. Stake's (1995: 128) suggestion that 'reflective moments can detract from the intent of the researcher'. Therefore, when organizing the data and writing scenarios, I worked diligently to balance my perspectives with those of the research participants.

The possibility of becoming imaginatively and creatively involved in my research was enticing as I analysed the work of fans and commenced writing scenarios. Most importantly, however, is the fact that Finore's drawing, indeed her research enquiry through art, sparked my experiential memory and furthered my own physical research; I was prompted, once again, to physically improvise in order to recall sensations. I stepped away from my computer, moved to a wall in my home, and put my back against it in an attempt to recreate how I remembered the placement of my body when witnessing this scene. This act of improvising my memory generated the following passage of 'scenario' writing:

> Another performer appears; he takes my hand and leads me into a small room adjacent to the detective's office. Three other spectators stand against one wall and a male performer sits in a chair at the center of the room. The man who grabbed my hand pushes me firmly against the wall with one arm while lashing out with his other at the man in the chair. It is an interrogation; one dancer confronts while the other deflects, their limbs slicing the air as they skillfully dodge the light fixture swinging violently back and forth in the narrow space. I'm pushed out of the interrogation room and back onto the main street as another man I intuit is Macbeth approaches, his hands bloodied. He disappears down an alley leading away from the main street, dragging his hands along the ridges of its corrugated tin walls to create a deafening noise. (Ritter, 2017: 60)

Finore's art served as a stimulus for me to engage in bricolage based on my embodied experience; my written scenarios are both an example of creative analysis and yet another way of engaging with the data improvisationally and compositionally. In hindsight, I understand how the creation of art as research (fans making their work, me writing scenarios) drove my theory-building, catalysing not just my concept of extended audiences but also my understandings of *insider dynamics* and the various dimensions of dramaturgical practices devised with the intention of eliciting participation from audiences, which constitute the core of my publications on *SNM*.

Continuing, Rather Than Concluding, Thoughts

My first experiences of *SNM* were so resonant with movement and motion it was curious, and somewhat disappointing, that my research revealed how infrequently dance and choreography were mentioned in the extant literature, as well as in the critical press for *SNM* and other immersive theatre productions. While my methods yielded generative data, this omission led me to seek out and add new fieldwork sites where I could both listen to and engage in conversation. These sites included symposia, festivals, and summits dedicated to immersive entertainment and design.[6] The data gathered from these events was similar in type to what I had gathered elsewhere – voice memos based on being an audience member, interviews with key players in immersive design – and expanded my sense that perspectives on dance were indeed marginalized. Yet I also realized that these sites offered opportunities to build knowledge that foregrounded choreographic, kinaesthetic, and embodied understandings of performance. It is my hope that other researchers will consider the role of movement and the many creative ways to analyse it as valid approaches to enquiry.

Identifying and incorporating methods additively encourages flexibility, spurs my intellect, and allows me to remain open to emergent possibilities and to prioritize dance and choreography in the discourse surrounding immersive performance. Limitations and constraints are inevitably part of the academic endeavour, yet my additive approach allowed me to operate as a bricoleur and be inclusive of the voices of a wide range of participants, including spectators, artistic directors, choreographers, dancers, and, of course, myself.

Notes

1 WolfBrown is a cross-disciplinary team of professional consultants dedicated to arts research across public and private sectors.

2 As noted by Torkild Thanem and David Knights, who also reference Spradley (1980), 'different kinds of ethnographic research involve different degrees of participation and different kinds of participation: from relatively passive forms

where the ethnographer is largely a bystander or "fly on the wall", to more active forms where the ethnographer is deeply involved and bodily engaged in the same activities as the people they study' (Thanem & Knights, 2019: 57).

3 Kathy Charmaz, who pioneered grounded theory as a research methodology, has framed sensitizing concepts as 'those background ideas that inform the overall research problem', and 'offer ways of seeing, organizing, and understanding experience' (Charmaz, 2003: 259).

4 While I don't want to be too quick to elide my research with that of the fans of *SNM*, interviews with audience participants revealed a systematic approach to data collection and analysis to augment their understanding. For example, Dee Anne Anderson (2017) stated emphatically her intention to engage in what I understand to be choreographic enquiry, placing herself strategically to get new perspectives on the action unfolding in specific scenes. Using her blog, she analysed her embodied experiences and then distributed her findings by sharing insights with other fans (see Anderson, n.d.; Ritter, 2017: 67).

5 Cobb's blog and several others now serve as archives of the New York production, while new blogs were created when the Shanghai production opened in 2016.

6 For example, my attendance at the 2017 Future of StoryTelling Festival (FoST FEST) in New York yielded data that informed the writing of the introduction to my 2021 book.

References

Anderson, D. A. (2017). 'Personal interview with author'. New York, 11 January.

Anderson, D. A. (n.d.). '*readwithjoy* (blog)'. Last updated 27 February 2023. https://readwithjoy.tumblr.com/.

Babbage, F. H. (2016). 'Active Audiences: Spectatorship as Research Practice'. *Studies in Theatre and Performance*, 36(1), 48–51.

Balzer, D. (2015). *Curationism: How Curating Took Over the Art World and Everything Else*. London: Pluto Press.

behindawhitemask. (n.d.). 'Behind a White Mask (blog)'. Tumblr. Accessed 25 February 2023. https://behindawhitemask.tumblr.com/.

Blumenfeld-Jones, D. (2008). 'Dance, Choreography, and Social Science Research'. In J. G. Knowles & A. L. Cole, eds., *Handbook of the Arts in Qualitative Research*. Thousand Oaks, CA: SAGE, pp. 75–184.

Brown, A. S., Novak-Leonard, J. L., & Gilbride, S. (2011). *Getting In on the Act: How Arts Groups Are Creating Opportunities for Active Participation*. San Francisco, CA: James Irvine Foundation.

Charmaz, K. (2003). 'Grounded Theory: Objectivist and Constructivist Methods'. In N. K. Denzin & Y. S. Lincoln, eds., *Strategies for Qualitative Inquiry*, 2nd ed. Thousand Oaks, CA: SAGE, pp. 249–91.

Charmaz, K. (2006). *Constructing Grounded Theory: A Practical Guide through Qualitative Analysis*. Thousand Oaks, CA: SAGE.

Cobb, E. M. (2022). 'They Have Scorched the Snake (blog)'. Tumblr. Accessed 11 August 2023. https://scorchedthesnake.tumblr.com/.

Denzin, N. K. (1989). *The Research Act: A Theoretical Introduction to Sociological Methods*. Englewood Cliffs, NJ: Prentice-Hall.

Doyle, Maxine. (2013). 'Interview with Julia M. Ritter, 10 October'. Transcript.

Eisner, E. (1982). *Cognition and Curriculum: A Basis for Deciding What to Teach*. New York: Longman.

Fayard, A.-L. (2017). 'Bricolage in the Field: Experimenting in Ethnography'. In R. Mir & S. Jain, eds., *The Routledge Companion to Qualitative Research in Organization Studies*. Abingdon: Taylor & Francis, pp. 141–53.

Finore, C. (2014). Personal interview with author. New York, 30 June.

Freshwater, H. (2009). *Theatre and Audience*. London: Palgrave Macmillan.

Heddon, D., Iball, H., & Zerihan, R. (2012). 'Come Closer: Confessions of Intimate Spectators in One to One Performance'. *Contemporary Theatre Review*, 22(1), 120–33.

Knowles, J. G., & Cole, A. L., eds. (2008). *Handbook of the Arts in Qualitative Research*. Thousand Oaks, CA: SAGE.

Merriam, Sharan B. (2009). *Qualitative Research: A Guide to Design and Implementation*. Hoboken, NJ: John Wiley & Sons.

Reason, M., & Reynolds, D. (2010). 'Kinesthesia, Empathy, and Related Pleasures: An Inquiry into Audience Experiences of Watching Dance'. *Dance Research Journal*, 42(2), 49–75.

Ritter, J. M. (2015). 'Danse en tandem: Étude du mouvement des spectateurs et des performeurs dans *Sleep No More* de Punchdrunk'. *La Revue Tangence: Revue d'Études Littéraires*, 108, 51–76.

Ritter, J. M. (2016). 'The Body of the Beholder: Insider Dynamics Transform Dance Spectatorship in *Sleep No More*'. In J. Frieze, ed., *Reframing Immersive Theatre: The Politics and Pragmatics of Participatory Performance*. London: Palgrave Macmillan, pp. 43–62.

Ritter, J. M. (2017). 'Fandom and Punchdrunk's *Sleep No More*: Audience Ethnography of Immersive Dance'. *TDR: The Drama Review*, 61(4), 59–77.

Ritter, J. M. (2021). *Tandem Dances: Choreographing Immersive Performance*. New York: Oxford University Press.

Saldaña, J. (2009). *The Coding Manual for Qualitative Researchers*. London: SAGE.

Spradley, J. P. (1980). *Participant Observation*. New York: Holt, Rinehart & Winston.

Stake, R. E. (1995). *The Art of Case Study Research*. Thousand Oaks, CA: SAGE.

Thanem, T., & Knights, D. (2019). *Embodied Research Methods*. London: SAGE.

Van Maanen, J. E. (2011). *Tales of the Field: On Writing Ethnography*. Chicago: University of Chicago Press.

CHAPTER 8

*Talking Theatre in an Oral Culture**: *Audience Research in Ghana*

Awo Mana Asiedu

Performance underpins many of our cultural expressions as Ghanaians, and as Africans: whether it is traditional drumming or dancing, or storytelling in communities, people participate. These traditional performances never attracted gate fees and were not commercial. When theatre started to become commercial in Ghana, through the concert party tradition, which began during the colonial period in the early twentieth century and thrived until the 1980s, people participated in that. With the introduction of Western forms of theatre, this participatory tendency became limited, and unlike traditional and popular theatre forms, this kind of theatre often struggled to get audiences.

This factor became a point of research interest for me. I remember watching a magnificent production of Arthur Miller's *All My Sons* (1946) at one of the popular theatre spaces in the late 1990s. There were so few people in the audience, I asked – where *are* the audiences? If the production had been done on the university campus, perhaps it would have had a healthy student audience. Was the fact that it was a Western play a factor? Other Western plays, however – for example, Agatha Christie's *Witness for the Prosecution* (1953) – had been produced at the same venue within the same period, with larger audiences in attendance. This prompted me to ask what kinds of theatre appeal to Ghanaian audiences: what kind of shows would they go and see? A decade later, Roverman Productions, a kind of English-language popular theatre that followed in the steps of the erstwhile concert party tradition, began to draw audiences en masse. If one of our more established playwrights like Mohammed ben Abdallah put on a play at the National Theatre, he would not draw as many audience members as a single Roverman production. This led me to ask: what are these audiences looking for? What are they interested in? These questions motivated my audience research.

* I am grateful to Paul Rae for his assistance in the drafting of this chapter. It was largely developed through a series of Zoom conversations.

Susan Bennett's (1997) excellent book *Theatre Audiences* introduced me to how audiences relate to performance. I became interested in all the debates about the difficulties in *knowing* what the audience experience is. Why do people shy away from claiming that performance *does have* an impact on its audiences? Some scholars say that yes, theatre can have some impact, but it's difficult to measure (see, e.g. Bennett, 1997; Kennedy, 2009). I wanted to take on those sceptics and make a claim not only that theatre has an impact, but that it is knowable. Following Helen Freshwater's (2009) challenge to researchers to engage more directly with audiences, it seemed that the best thing to do was to ask the audiences themselves.

One other consideration meant that this direct engagement was a logical step: Ghanaians are known to be friendly. We love talking. Complete strangers can come up and talk to you, at least generally speaking. We joke that we are such an oral society that people would rather talk about things than read about them. Talk radio is currently very popular, with people calling in to talk about all kinds of issues. The concert party genre itself was born out of the oral tradition: scripts were improvised, and actors relied very much on their oral skills. Roverman Productions is a more contemporary version of that tradition. For example, when Roverman Productions is performing at the National Theatre, there is a guitar band in the orchestra pit and music is integrated into the dialogue: that is, directly from concert party aesthetics.

Researching a performance form rooted in an oral tradition using oral research methods in a predominantly oral culture, therefore, makes a lot of sense, though, with so much talking going on, it is also important to be reflective about how and where those methods are used. In this chapter, I examine the methodological opportunities and challenges this context presents for a researcher. I focus mainly on my own research on Roverman Productions and its audiences, placing it within broader Ghanaian contexts.

Researching Roverman Audiences

In pursuing my interest in researching audiences and their experiences of performance, I needed to focus on methodology. I had to show that the research outcomes were not something I made up or imposed on the data, but were the logical result of doing the research in a certain way. In the literature, researchers appear a bit *mistrusting* of audiences, as if they are going to tell you things they think you are expecting them to say. For example,

Katya Johanson (2013: 163) notes that interviews and focus groups rely on 'the assumption that what people say is what they mean' and warns that 'there are several reasons to doubt the accuracy of the research participants' verbal reports'. Kirsty Sedgman's (2018: 317) article 'Audience Experience in an Anti-Expert Age' also provides an insightful discussion of the unease of some scholars with the use of evidence gathered from 'novice' audiences over those who may be more 'knowledgeable'. As she concludes, however, 'it is not … the research approach itself that necessarily poses a danger but how its findings might be used'.

Then I found Willmar Sauter's (2000) work where he directly engaged with Swedish audiences to find out what their experiences were. Discovering Sauter's research was inspirational and gave me a great deal of confidence that what I was thinking was possible. Sauter's research employed what he called 'Theatre Talks'. He contacted some regular theatre patrons who knew one another to gather and talk about specific performances. Immediately after the shows, Sauter and the patrons would go together to a private place where they would talk about the performance they had just seen. Their conversations were recorded and later analysed. Sauter did not provide any questions but encouraged his participants to talk about any aspect of the performances they wished to.

I found this model useful as it engaged directly with audiences and gave them a chance to describe their experiences of the performances they had watched. The first research project I carried out was during the Roverman Festival of Plays, held from December 2013 to January 2014. As I have discussed in detail elsewhere (Asiedu, 2016), the annual year-end Roverman Festival of Plays brings together all four of the company's productions from that year with an additional play from a previous year, and draws large and appreciative audiences. In approaching this event, I adapted Sauter's 'Theatre Talks' model in several ways to suit my context. Whereas Sauter gathered people who knew one another and who knew ahead of the performance that they would be meeting together afterwards to discuss it, the participants I engaged were complete strangers to me and often to one another, and they did not know they would be called upon to discuss the shows when they went to watch them. Instead, a simple announcement was made after the first show: 'if you're interested in talking about it with a researcher, please go to such-and-such a place'. This could have led to a shortage of participants if people did not feel comfortable talking, but, as I noted earlier, in this part of the world people are often very willing to talk. Refreshments were also provided, which helped create an atmosphere where people felt comfortable. Also worthy of note is that the people who responded to the announcements were enthused by the performances they had just watched. It is doubtful that someone who had not enjoyed the show would have been eager to remain to talk about it. The CEO and director of the plays, Ebo Whyte, was another key factor. Most people who volunteered for the discussions were keen admirers of this man and were eager to express their admiration and support for him.

In terms of how the sessions were run, the largest difference from Sauter's 'Theatre Talks' was that I set an agenda for the post-show conversation, with specific questions around five themes: the participants' perception of what the play was about, the impact of Roverman Productions, the aesthetic appeal of the play, things they disliked about the show, and finally their patronage of theatre and the arts in general. Having these guiding questions allowed us to analyse the data more easily after the fact. In our context, I felt that leaving the discussion open, as Sauter did, would be overwhelming for the research team.

What my approach had in common with Sauter's was that the number of participants at each discussion was kept to a maximum of ten, to facilitate easy conversations and free-flowing contributions, and that the conversations took place immediately after the shows in a private space over refreshments. At times we had more people than we needed and had to turn some away. These discussions were video-recorded and later transcribed and analysed. I attended two rehearsals leading up to the festival and then, on the days of the festival, was present at the theatre from about 3 p.m. until past 10.30 p.m, watching both performances. This allowed me the opportunity to participate in and observe the whole festival.

In addition, with the help of research assistants, questionnaires were distributed to people as they came in to watch the shows. About 60 per cent of these were completed and returned to us. My main aims in this research were to find out to what extent audiences engaged with the shows they watched, how what they watched affected them, and what forms their aesthetic experience and appreciation of the plays took. I was also interested in knowing who these audiences were and whether they were regular patrons of the arts. The questionnaires thus engaged with the same themes as the post-show discussions and corroborated the information gathered in these conversations.

Overall, then, my methods were mixed, combining participant observation, questionnaires, and group discussions, along with my own analyses of the performances. The major outcomes of this initial research project were drawn largely from the group discussions, which yielded a lot of data on audience views but were only able to capture their immediate impressions. In subsequent research on Roverman audiences, I wanted to dig a bit deeper to find out whether there was any real, enduring impact of the shows on audiences. My main approach in this follow-up study was to conduct in-depth one-on-one conversations with selected regular Roverman audience members. I asked the administrator of the group for names and contact details of regular patrons who were willing to talk to me for an extended period about their experiences of the shows. I found three women and two men who were willing to engage with me. One woman was only prepared to answer questions via email, which was quite limiting and not very useful in the end, as there was no opportunity to ask follow-up questions and probe deeper. The conversations with the other four, however, proved insightful, shedding light on the long-term impact of the shows on audiences. The interviews were transcribed and analysed based on themes that emerged. The results of my research into these audiences and their experiences have so far been published in two book chapters and one journal article (Asiedu, 2014, 2016, 2022).

The Broader Context of Research in Ghana

My audience research at Roverman Productions did not happen in a vacuum. As I have indicated, Ghana has a strongly oral culture and it is popularly said that Ghanaians love to talk. This influences research in many different settings, in terms of *what* is researched, *how* it is researched, and what governs the relationship between researchers and those they are researching. The context in which research is done, and the people's understanding of what research stands for, necessarily has a large influence on the methods used.

For example, as a young research assistant, I worked on a series of social science research projects that involved administering questionnaires in rural communities with limited literacy. It is only practical that if you are administering a questionnaire to somebody who cannot write, you will need to do the writing for them. So, the questionnaire becomes more like an interview – one where the face-to-face encounter is an important part of the process. In Western countries it may be more common to conduct online surveys, but in our context that route is not always practical or fruitful. So, you go where the research subjects are. This provides you with important context as to how and why they respond as they do, as well as opportunities to develop the conversation. This was also evident in the second project on Roverman audiences. I contacted the people I wanted to speak with, and met them individually in an office setting: I met three in their offices, while one offered to come to *my* office. Even in those relatively similar spaces there was a difference in terms of what we could achieve and the level of interaction that we could have. The interviews were sometimes interrupted by work colleagues; in one instance, a respondent's colleague, who was also a patron of Roverman Productions, offered his views as well.

Least useful in this second study were the answers that I obtained from the respondent who said that she did not have the time to meet and asked for the questions by email instead. She was not very forthcoming in writing, and there was no opportunity to probe some of the things that she said. For example, to the question seeking her views on how well Roverman Productions had affected her and Ghanaian society in general, her response was: 'Very well. A lot of the plays come with information and advice.' Compare this terse and impersonal written response to the oral response that I received on the same subject from one of the respondents who met me in their office:

> I pity Uncle Ebo, the values he espouses, and the level of thought which goes into his work … I think on one leg, they are making an effort, but on the other leg, the status quo is the same. But I think in the context of marriage, they are making an inroad. Every play has something about relationships, and I think in that respect they are making an impact. But this thing about national life and patriotism … it is too tall a mountain.

I probed further, asking for his personal response to Roverman. He stated:

> You know, I have had plans of not living in Ghana, one of the things that make me rethink that is Uncle Ebo. Frankly, every time I have thought of migrating, he is the only person that comes to mind why I should stay and not leave, and be a part of fixing Ghana. Nobody can come and do it for us, you can be here and create excellence and project it out there. I see that only in him and what he does, original, right from here, and it is world class and can compete on any platform … He gives me that confidence.

The face-to-face conversations, the oral encounters, enabled more spontaneous answers and offered opportunities for me to read the body language of respondents and to ask follow-up questions. These also provided indications of the genuineness of the responses offered.

The *time* of the encounter is equally important. I met with the focus groups for the Roverman project in a private space within the National Theatre just after the shows. There were no interruptions: there was a space where we could sit and relax and chat over refreshments, and that gave it a certain quality that it would not have had if, for example, we had met a day after, in a different space. On two occasions when I met with respondents in their offices, there were some restrictions as to how long we could talk; they were still at work and could not spend so much time with me. In the case of the meeting in my office, it was after working hours, and there was no pressure of time, so we had a more relaxed and extended conversation.

If the place and time of oral research are important, so too are the dynamics of the situation and the way the people being researched perceive it, and the researcher. For example, if one goes into more rural areas as an educated person with paper and pencil or a computer, one is apt to be seen by people as an agent of the government. In the past, when I did Theatre for Development work, I would go into the communities I was trying to engage with, to discover what might be performed or how to perform *with* them. Locals would often assume that I was sent by the government, and they would expect that what I was doing would bring some government intervention to them: there was no real perception of me as an independent academic researcher. This perception could lead to a refusal to provide information, or instead a response of 'cooked' information, rather than the true picture.

So, we know, at least in a Theatre for Development context, that you cannot just go to a community for a day or two and get the right information. You need sustained engagement; you need to live and be in the context of the people for some time to gain legitimacy before they are willing to speak to you openly. And you also need to observe certain protocols. For instance, in some places, a researcher might need to bring some drinks (hard liquor) to the chiefs or people. This is a way of engaging with a community's gatekeepers, who can in turn grant the right to engage with the community. For example, a colleague of mine has recently been studying the funerals of chiefs in a rural community. These funerals are huge and elaborate, and can take days. My colleague goes into the community with their crew and camera operator to record the proceedings, but they had to get the consent of the people involved before they could enter and take video recordings of the event.

These issues about access and the understanding of research also give rise to considerations about ethics, and about the differences between researchers. Sometimes people demand to be paid for participating in research. Or they want to know how they will benefit from what the researcher is doing. And rightly so. Especially in the social sciences, researchers have complained about people being research fatigued. The same communities are bombarded by all kinds of researchers, and they may become reluctant to participate, saying: 'people have done this several times, and they didn't bring us anything, so why should we engage with you?'

At the same time, research can bring legitimation to a community, a sense of valorization of a tradition or culture. Members of a community think that if educated people want to study what they do, it must be important. For example, some colleagues have been going to rural communities to learn about traditional dance forms that are not currently taught in our Department of Dance Studies (at the University of Ghana), and that they would like to see introduced into the curriculum. Sometimes they go and live in the communities, or bring a member of the community to the university to teach those dance forms. In such circumstances, the people see this as a valorization of their tradition: the tradition is being given a new life. Clearly, however, an alternative view would be that 'they're stealing our traditions'. This happens too, even to me. I go to church and see tourists come, and they are intrigued by the way we worship – and when they take out their cameras, I personally feel offended. I feel they should ask first. There should be respect. You need to ask, 'is it okay for me to do this?' Otherwise, there is a feeling of being taken advantage of.

This gives rise to another issue that has an impact on research. Ghanaians love to interact with foreigners, at least superficially. I have a white American friend who has learned some key phrases of local languages. And any time I am with her and she uses the language of people we encounter, she immediately gets their attention – they are very happy, and barriers just fall because she has made the attempt to speak their language. There is a limit to this, of course, and it is tempting to say that researchers from Ghana would have much less trouble than foreigners in terms of their access to the research situation. Certainly, if I went to my own ethnic group in the Volta region, where I would have no language limitations, I would find low barriers to acceptance. But that ease of access is not always the case for non-foreigners. If I went to the northern parts of Ghana, for example, I would have the same difficulty in terms of access as a foreigner would have, because I would need an interpreter to be able to do that. If I went somewhere where I had learned a few phrases of the language, or if I were to visit a Muslim community, say, and wear a headscarf as a sign of respect, that would break barriers. When people see an outsider (whether foreign or local) wanting to learn more about their culture and traditions barriers are naturally erected, but a demonstration of respect for these cultures and traditions would minimize these barriers, if not remove them completely.

A final point here on the researcher's positionality and its implications for the research: there are foreign researchers that I personally admire for how they make so much of so little. I always say that it is a skill that we as Ghanaian researchers, or African researchers, need to learn, and maybe it is because we (and not only Ghanaians) do not recognize the value of what is ours as much as people from outside do. There are performance traditions that we take for granted. Outsiders see the research potential better than we do, and they come and take it and write about it in ways that startle us. On the one hand, I think: 'Okay: I didn't see that!' But on the other, some interpretations are not quite what I think they should be, and of course some things that get written are never read by the people who are being written about.

The Linguistic Landscape for and of Research

Underpinning some of my comments in the previous section is the linguistic complexity of Ghana. Because Ghana is a former colony of Britain, English is our official language. If you do not pass English exams at school, you cannot move ahead in your education. But we have forty-four different languages and dialects in Ghana. So, many Ghanaians are polyglots. I speak two other languages, and I have working knowledge of a third. People switch between languages all the time. Most people speak their mother tongue at home, and switch when they go to the market or to work.

This is a dynamic and fast-changing environment. There is a certain class of Ghanaians who think that since English is the language of mobility, their children should focus on English, and, in the process, they neglect to teach these children their own mother tongue. At the same time, radio talk shows have liberated people to use the local languages, especially Akan, which is the dominant local language – the mother tongue of approximately 44 per cent of Ghanaians. Many more people feel comfortable calling in to radio stations when they know they are free to speak in a language that they are comfortable with. There is a recent upsurge of soap operas and drama series from Asia and Latin America on our television screens, and the dominant trend now is to have local language (mainly Akan) voice-overs. That is phenomenal: everywhere you go, you see white people, Latin Americans, and Asian people speaking Akan on the screen. I come home, and my niece is sitting there watching it, and I'm surprised because that is not our language. We speak Ewe. Does she understand the Akan that they are speaking? I'm sure she does because many people do.

One gets a sense in Ghana today that there is a growing resistance to English as a dominant language. And although English is the language of politics, and of the public sphere, many people also feel more comfortable speaking their own languages in performance. For example, one of our students decided to do a concert party theatre show for his project. He did it in Akan, the language of concert party. And our students, who normally look official and stiff when performing in English, were so fluid onstage. It was like they had been *freed* somehow, and it was beautiful to see. I wanted to explore this with some colleagues. Using focus group discussions again, we asked our students why it was that they seemed to perform better when speaking Akan? The interesting thing is that not all the actors were native Akan speakers. But our languages are closely interrelated, so sometimes the words are different, but the thought processes are similar. This study was published in *Contemporary Theatre Review* (Asiedu et al., 2011).

There is also the question of the status of English in the academy, and in research *on* Ghanaian performance practices. Within the Department of Linguistics at the University of Ghana, there is a big push to have local-language scholarship, but the amount produced is minimal. There is a lot of code-switching in informal academic settings, but I would not allow it in my graduate class, for example. And I would insist that my students write their assignments in English because if they did it in Akan, I would not be able to read it. This points to the fact that it is easier to operate multilingually in the oral register than the written. Even though somebody might be able to express themselves better by speaking in Akan, Ewe, or another language, many would be sorely challenged to write an academic paper in their mother tongue, because they are not literate in it. I can read a hymn, or read the Bible to my mother, in my own language, but I would not be able to read an academic article written in it.

This is a hindrance to scholarship in all parts of the world where people are challenged in having to channel local information into an acceptable international language. Our training has all been very Western in that regard, and even though there is a lot of talk about developing African methods or African ways, it is clear one cannot reinvent the wheel. One does not set out to do research in an African way; one sets out to do research in an African context, using available tools. As one progresses and as ideas form, one adapts them to suit the context – and I think as we do that we will discover the African way.

References

Asiedu, A. M. (2014). 'Constructing Social Realities on Stage: Ebo Whyte at the Ghana National Theatre'. In A. Budde, ed., *Fiebach: Theater. Wissen. Machen.* Berlin: Verlag Theater der Zeit, pp. 67–72.

Asiedu, A. M. (2016). '"The Money Was Real Money": Talking with Audiences about Corruption, Domestic Violence and Aesthetic Values during the Roverman Festival of Plays at the Ghana National Theatre'. *Theatre Research International*, 41(2), 151–67.

Asiedu, A. M. (2022). 'Audience Engagement and the Production of Efficacious Theatre: A Case Study from Ghana'. In M. Reason, L. Conner, K. Johanson, & B. Walmsley, eds., *Routledge Companion to Audiences and the Performing Arts.* London: Routledge, pp. 217–28.

Asiedu, A. M., Dorgbadzi, S., & Ekumah, E. (2011). 'Language and Body in Performance: Working across Languages in the Ghanaian Production *I Told You So*'. *Contemporary Theatre Review*, 21(1), 50–9.

Bennett, S. (1997). *Theatre Audiences: A Theory of Production and Reception.* London: Routledge.

Freshwater, H. (2009). *Theatre & Audience*. Basingstoke: Palgrave Macmillan.

Johanson, K. (2013). 'Listening to the Audience: Methods for a New Era of Audience Research'. In J. Radbourne, H. Glow, & K. Johanson, eds., *Audience Experience*. New York: Intellect, pp. 159–71.

Kennedy, D. (2009). *The Spectator and the Spectacle: Audiences in Modernity and Postmodernity*. London: Cambridge University Press.

Sauter, W. (2000). 'Theatre Talks: How to Find Out What the Spectator Thinks'. In W. Sauter, *The Theatrical Event: Dynamics of Performance and Perception.* Iowa City: University of Iowa Press, pp. 174–86.

Sedgman, K. (2018). 'Audience Experience in an Anti-Expert Age: A Survey of Theatre Audience Research'. *Theatre Research International*, 42(3), 307–22.

CHAPTER 9

Painful Fieldwork? Radical Empiricism and Ritual Performance in the Philippines

Julius Bautista

In the Philippine province of Pampanga, to the north-west of Manila on the island of Luzon, hundreds of men and women undergo ritual acts of self-inflicted pain during Holy Week, the annual commemoration of Christ's Passion. My anthropological research examines the expression of heartfelt sentiments of pity, empathy, and trust that are cultivated through these acts of self-mortification, which, while physically painful for the practitioner, facilitate and strengthen a sense of personal intimacy with the divine (Bautista & Bräunlein, 2014; see also Cannell, 1995). Over four years of conducting fieldwork on these rituals, I was granted the opportunity to spend time with ritual nailees, or *namamaku*, as they are known in Pampanga. In proximity to them, I watched, listened, smelled, and felt the scene as ritual facilitators hammered five-inch steel nails through the hands and feet of the *namamaku*, penetrating deep into the wooden cross beneath. A typical *namamaku* response to this excruciating experience is a sense of calmness and serenity. This moment has frequently been described to me as marked by a powerful and profound sense of connection with God that could not be attained without the experience of ritual pain.

In their analysis of Western society's 'general aversion and sensitivity to pain', sociologists of religion Chris Shilling and Philip A. Mellor have demonstrated the pervasiveness of a paradigm of polypharmacy (Shilling & Mellor, 2010: 521). This worldview, rooted in medicine and science, precludes any acceptance of the concept that self-inflicted physical pain, even when religiously framed, might contribute to a sense of contentment, much less human growth and edification. From my conversations with those who witness nailing rituals from afar, this would seem true in the Philippines as well. I am often told by those I encounter during fieldwork that the mere sight of nailing is incomprehensible and off-putting, causing many to recoil and distance themselves from the pain experience. Contrary to this apparently instinctive response, however, and in recognition of the disconnect between how participants report their experiences of nailing and how more distant observers perceive it, I argue that the deliberate cultivation of a sense of proximal intimacy to the body/subject in pain is important for purposes of ethnographic observation. This is predicated upon the central contention of this chapter: only when one harnesses and actually embodies the complexity and contradictions of the fieldwork experience can meaningful insight into otherwise counter-intuitive realities expressed by our research interlocutors emerge.

In order to make this argument, I correlate my fieldwork on religious practices in the Philippines with that of phenomenologically inclined anthropologists who have endorsed an embodied and radically empirical response to the problems and challenges of ethnographic participant observation.[1] Rather than cultivating objective empirical distance, as the pioneers of anthropology advocated, radical empiricism seeks to productively channel 'the arduous conditions of fieldwork, the ambiguity of conversations in a foreign tongue, differences of temperament, age, and gender between ourselves and our informants, and the changing theoretical models we are heir to' (Jackson, 1989: 3) towards what anthropologist Stephen Tyler (1986: 127) has described as an ethnographic praxis in which 'the form itself emerges out of the joint work of the ethnographer and his native partners'.

From Detached Engagement to Radical Intersubjectivity

Although fieldwork is considered a central rite of passage for anthropologists, important questions remain about the empirical value of getting 'too close' to the research subject. The anthropologist Rebekah Cupitt (2018) has described ethnographic fieldwork as anthropology's chimera, with a lion's head representing the act of going out into the field, a snake-like tail representing the researcher's insinuation into other people's lives, and a goat's body depicting the task of writing as one that 'has us consuming our fieldwork experiences, masticating and digesting them into the more palatable documents that we then publish and share'. This description aligns with the impressions of many anthropologists, among them Talal Asad (1986) and Glenn Bowman (1997: 83), with the latter noting that in doing ethnography, one is effectively 'dismembering the world … through dialogue and participant observation in the field so that it can be reconstituted in the text to accord with analytical categories foreign to those whose world is there represented'.[2] What we can draw from this bodily metaphor, as well as from the vast literature on the critique of ethnographic practices (e.g. Behar, 1996; Clifford & Marcus, 1986; Rosaldo, 1989), is the complexity of the methodological relationship between the act of observation, the act of recording, and the final written output. The pioneers of anthropology as a discipline, including Bronisław Malinowski (1922), advocated stepping back from full engagement with the anthropological Other so as to best confront the challenges of ethnographic fieldwork. The British ethnographer E. E. Evans-Pritchard, whose analysis of Azande rituals has been widely cited as a watershed in the movement away from scientism and towards an understanding of the 'meaning' of social structures, personified the classical withdrawal from ethnographic intimacy. Since 'an anthropologist gains little by obtruding himself into the ceremonies as an "actor"', Evans-Pritchard (1976 [1937]: 67) endorsed the use of an informant (his 'personal servant') as a covert key witness who would ostensibly reveal inner secrets for the benefit of the researcher's ethnographic agenda.

In essence, this imperative of withdrawal presumes that the anthropologist's body is irrelevant – indeed, that it is counterproductive – to the production of ethnographic knowledge. This view, as anthropologist Kristy Nabhan-Warren (2011: 385) describes it, is 'a prioritizing of mind knowledge over body knowledge'. This classical aversion to participating as an actor in the field is based on at least three premises: first, that an anthropologist is, by default, an excluded outsider who 'is never seriously regarded as a member of an esoteric group'; second, that in imposing their presence, an anthropologist risks contaminating 'authentic' cultural experience; and third, that full immersion would adversely affect the ethnographer's critical empirical faculties, since it is 'difficult to use the ordinary methods of critical investigating when one is actually engaged in ceremonial and is supposed to be an eager member of an institution' (Evans-Pritchard, 1976 [1937]: 67).

Anthropology's crisis of representation (Marcus & Fischer, 1986) emerged from a critical approach to 'writing culture' (Clifford & Marcus, 1986), which entailed a concerted effort to decolonize its practice through examination of professional positionality, empirical agency, and self-reflexivity. This constituted an ontological crisis for anthropology as a discipline, a crisis that was manifested in the increasing scrutiny placed on the relationship between the anthropological 'eye' and the imperial 'I' (Rosaldo, 1989: 41). These critiques were driven by the increased participation of the Other in anthropological research, not only 'speaking back' to but also 'speaking as' the anthropologist (Nordling, 2020). Such efforts have entailed a renewed conception of participant observation as less a context for scientific data-gathering and more one of 'deeply engaging moments of ethnographic encounter; moments of dilemma and insecurity, often outside the comfort zone of scholarly methodologies, but nevertheless inherent to practice-based research' (Harrop & Njaradi, 2013: 18).

A distinct approach that has emerged from anthropology's disciplinary renewal, particularly in counterpoint to classical anthropological detachment, is that of 'radical empiricism'. As endorsed most prominently by anthropologists such as Michael D. Jackson (1989), Robert R. Desjarlais (1992), and Kirsten Hastrup (1995), radical empiricism takes inspiration from the nineteenth-century American philosopher William James, who stipulated that the intersubjective relationship between people is just as significant in our understanding of the world as the things/people of culture themselves. Further inspired by the introspective and reflective phenomenology of philosophers such as Edmund Husserl, Theodor Adorno, and Maurice Merleau-Ponty, radical empiricist anthropology posits that ethnographic knowledge should be grounded in and derived from the direct embodied experience of everyday practice. For Jackson (2007: xx), radical empiricism channels the physical, emotional, and mental difficulties of fieldwork towards productive analytical insights. Instead of retreating from ethnographic engagement, it is an approach that 'gives incompleteness and tentativeness the same analytical weight as the finished and the fixed, and refuses to privilege and reify an epistemology that is based on mind knowledge'.

The ethnography that emerges from this approach is not so much an anthropologist's account of the Other, but rather a co-created dialogue that emphasizes the intersubjectivity between interlocutors. If classical ethnography focused on identifying the 'nature' of the Other through detachment, radical empiricism seeks to examine the intersection of lives, including the dialectical tensions and anxieties that are inherent in the anthropological encounter, through a fully immersive, embodied approach. This refocusing sought to move empiricism away from the linguistic turn of post-structuralist discourses and towards a phenomenological ontology that places primacy on somatic experience and feeling.

A rapprochement between theatre and performance studies (TaPS) and the radical empiricist programme is demonstrated by the emphasis of both on intersubjectivity. As the performance scholar Devendra Sharma (2012: 171) points out, performance, like radical empiricism, is inherently interactive in that 'the communication between performers and audiences during performance can create important moments of understanding, where information, knowledge and points of view are exchanged'. Just as radical empiricism channels a renewed sensitivity to embodiment, advocates of this approach endorse a shift in how fieldwork is understood: rather than being limited to data collection, it becomes an intersubjective channelling of the researcher's affective and sensual experience, with the body both the instrument and the key to understanding.

Among the most famous exponents of this convergence is performance studies scholar Dwight Conquergood (2002: 147), who argued against knowledge paradigms that ignore 'knowledge and meaningful action that is unlettered'. As a corrective to this 'textocentrism', Conquergood (1991: 187–8) proposed a programme of 'co-performative witnessing', in which the ethnographer 'moves from the gaze of the distanced and detached observer to the intimate involvement and engagement of "co-activity" or co-performance with historically situated, named, "unique individuals"'. What performance studies offers to the practice of ethnography is that it can take anthropology away from logocentric epistemology, making it a field of 'sensuous scholarship' in its own right. Consistent with radical empiricism, the ethnographic encounter inflected by performance calls for what performance scholars Peter Harrop and Dunja Njaradi describe as 'an embodied, affective and sensory ethnography that privileges encounters between ethnographer, participants and practices as key to understanding and knowledge' (Harrop & Njaradi, 2013: 18). Examining the work of phenomenologically inclined anthropologists and performance scholars reveals how the sensory and bodily proximity that is inherent in performance practice might add to our understanding of the larger challenge of doing fieldwork.

Painful Observation

A radical empiricist approach to ethnography, especially one that involves co-performative witnessing, would uphold the principle that effective interpersonal and intercultural communication is grounded in the deliberate harnessing of the body's sensual capacities as a way of dealing with the inherent anxieties of the fieldwork encounter. If we extend this principle further, we could say that harnessing sensual capacities entails enduring the physically demanding bodily *hardship* that fieldworkers encounter, particularly in areas outside of their comfort zones.

Indeed, an encounter with (and perseverance amid) the physically arduous conditions of fieldwork is a professional rite of passage that is seen as both a prerequisite to and an indicator of ethnographic authority and legitimacy. As Conquergood (1991: 180) observes, 'letters of recommendation often refer approvingly to bodily hardships suffered by the dedicated ethnographer – malarial fevers, scarcity of food, long periods of isolation, material discomforts, and so forth, endured in the field'.

The prospect of subjecting oneself to bodily discomfort brings up questions about how far a researcher should go in doing what their 'objects of enquiry' do, in order to understand their lives and convey it authentically. These are particularly challenging questions, especially in situations that involve the experience of extreme discomfort or even pain. In *The Body in Pain: The Making and Unmaking of the World*, Elaine Scarry (1985) influentially argued that pain and suffering obliterate and deconstruct the self. As she explained in a later interview, they are thus the 'radical opposite[s]' of creation and agency (Scarry, 2000). Social theorist Stephen Larocco (2016: 345) observes that Scarry conceives of pain as 'a form of bodily silence' that eludes language and communication. However, this raises complex methodological questions, since, as Larocco explains, on the basis of Scarry's view of language and corporeal semiotics, pain becomes, in essence, 'a desubjectifying solipsistic experience'. Would this mean that radical empiricism in the course of observing painful experiences becomes impractical, if not altogether impossible, because of the capacity of radical sensory experience to dominate one's empirical faculties?

In addressing this question, we could consider the experience of Nabhan-Warren, who pursued intensive fieldwork among Mexican American Catholics while facing a bout of illness and dealing with a knee injury. Rather than derailing her research process, the pain and discomfort proved to be 'an auspicious outlet' that resulted in her becoming the subject of many prayers, and 'prayings-over' by her interlocutors. Nabhan-Warren (2011: 386–8) knelt through lengthy rosary sessions, suffering the intense pain in her ligaments, and all the while gained a greater appreciation of others' capacity to persevere: 'The thin carpet remnant I kneeled on did little to cushion the pain and I marveled at those beside me who knelt without using any cushioning whatsoever.' For Nabhan-Warren, the experience of pain was 'worth it' from an empirical perspective. Enduring the pain was a way of 'challenging her body' towards achieving a greater empathetic understanding of her interlocutors' perceptions of healing and of 'the thin line between my own body and theirs'.

This perspective might also be shared by the anthropologist Douglas Farrer. Drawing upon the logic of performance ethnography, Farrer (2009: 7) conducted fieldwork among *silat* martial artists in Malaysia by participating as a practitioner. This involved Farrer performing *mandi minyak*, an initiation rite that follows a forty-day period of prayer and training and culminates in the practitioner dipping their palms in a vat of boiling coconut oil as a way of strengthening the body's resistance to pain. Like Nabhan-Warren, Farrer (2007: 23) decided to subject himself to this rite as a way of cultivating an intersubjective commensurability with his interlocutors, which only a demonstration of physical prowess could achieve: 'it took a certain level of violence for me to earn the informants' respect, and only after these painful encounters would they open up to me, taciturn grunts and stormy brows lifting to be replaced by smiles, laughter and valuable information'.

Nabhan-Warren's and Farrer's decisions to assume the ethnographic interlocutor's pain constituted a cultivated and embodied intimacy in which the anthropologist relates to the Other by way of sharing in the experience of extreme sensation and affect. This sharing had the effect of dissolving the barriers between emic and etic, or the insider/outsider dichotomy upon which anthropology is traditionally premised. In the radical empiricism they deployed through interacting and performing with their ethnographic subjects, they positioned their bodies as a crucial part of the research dynamic. In a way that goes against Scarry's classification of pain as de-subjectifying, pain was constitutive of a particular observational and empirical subject position for the ethnographer – a position that would not have been possible if they had remained withdrawn and distanced from the experience being analysed.

In my own fieldwork, I have similarly cultivated a position of proximal intimacy, subjecting my own body to at least some of the hardships encountered by those who conduct ritual nailing (*pamamaku king krus*). One main benefit of this approach of embodied proximity is that it treats those we encounter in research as spatio-temporal contemporaries, or 'coevals', as the anthropologist Johannes Fabian (1983) puts it. In principle, the proximal intimacy prioritized by a radically empirical approach avoids the objectification of research subjects by directly sharing in their temporal and sensory world, thereby shifting the anthropological gaze 'from the retrospective towards the inherently prospective and temporally correspondent' (Gatt, 2015: 338).

A Proximally Embodied Approach to Observing Passion Rituals

Ritual nailing in Pampanga is conducted in the context of a street play called the *Via Crucis o Pasion y Muerte* (*Way of the Cross, Passion, and Death*), a dramatization of the fourteen stations of the cross, depicting the various ordeals Jesus Christ underwent leading up to his crucifixion. The production involves a cast of about forty local, non-professional actors who, upon arriving at each station, deliver lines from a Passion story script written by an amateur dramatist in 1955.[3] The participation of all cast members (whether or not they are nailed) is predicated upon a *panata*, or what was described to me by one long-time cast member as 'a vow to repay God for the good things he's done for me' (Bautista, 2019: 70). The Passion rituals function as the reciprocal act of the *panata*, which might be made in response to (or in prayerful anticipation of) a loved one's recovery from illness, the successful securing of employment, the completion of a long voyage, or other such outcomes that are considered indicative of God's magnanimity. *Panata* in this sense is not just about embodied performance; it entails a deep sense of personal gratitude, which would be the driving motivation for one's ritual agency. As many as twenty to twenty-five thousand spectators amass every year to witness the climax of the play: the nailing of the lead actor, 'the Kristo', to one of three crosses affixed on a purpose-built site at the outskirts of the town.

The director of the *Via Crucis*, known locally as 'Direk', was aware of my desire to learn more about the ritual component of the Passion plays. Initially, he suggested that I could be included among the twenty or so men who would be nailed to a cross at the end of the *Via Crucis* play. However, this prospect of nailing was revoked without explanation by the director – the grandson of the original dramatist and son of the previous director – who instead assigned to me the minor role of San Juan (Saint John). Although I had no lines, this role required me to attend all rehearsals in the days leading up to Good Friday. During the play itself, my instructions were to remain within the makeshift cordon created by the centurions' lances to separate the performers and the street audience. It was not an easy task to keep up with the cast as the production moved along the designated stations of the cross in the village. As San Juan, I placed my body in the same physically demanding conditions as the other cast members. Under the blazing sun, I had to contend with the congestion of the crowd, which would surge for photo opportunities or just to get closer to the cast members. During the play itself, I was required to stay in character by not taking any rest or nourishment throughout the performance. The experience of heat and dehydration, and the suffocating congestion of the often unruly crowd, was in itself a physical ordeal. By the time we made it to the Crucifixion mound, I felt enormous mental and physical exhaustion that would only be relieved when the cast was able to disperse after the play's final act.

Referring specifically to anthropologists as theatre-makers, Caroline Gatt (2015: 341) has described a 'distended reflexivity', whereby an 'undifferentiated importance is accorded to balance and visualisation, to conscious awareness and response in the midst of action, to muscular recall and sensorial intelligence'. In my situation, distended reflexivity emerged from the physical and mental challenge of staying in character for the duration of the street play, which went on for four hours. In addition to following the director's instructions, I found myself obliging the numerous requests from the crowd to pose for photographs, all the while being touched, groped, shoved, and pushed. As part of the production, however, it felt natural to talk to fellow cast members about our common experience of exhaustion, as well as of the jubilation upon finally achieving relief and respite. This shared, embodied intersubjectivity brought what Joni L. Jones (2002: 14) has described as a 'new authenticity' predicated upon 'what audiences and performers share together, on what they mutually construct'.

What I found most valuable in this mode of 'intuitive, body-centered, and richly ambivalent' intersubjectivity (Jones, 2002: 14) is that it enabled a privileged view into the visceral, intimate spaces of the cast members' performance. Assuming the role of San Juan afforded me not only a theatrical persona but also a unique observational and epistemological perspective on how the cast members' theatrical personae were predicated upon personalized evocations of divine intimacy. This included, for example, minute details like how those playing Roman centurions would puff cigarettes in the course of performance in a way that channelled the tough, rugged persona consistent with the biblical story. It enabled me to see how the actor playing Mary Magdalene would recite a silent prayer during challenging moments of the play, as though evoking Mary's persona and intimate communication with God. The Kristo himself would frequently suspend the recitation of his lines while he knelt on one knee and wept, evoking Jesus's lamentations on his own mortality. These snippets reveal a personalized cultivation of intimacy in the performative personae, giving insight – even to those who were not granted the privileged embodied proximity of performing San Juan – into the complex ontological layers of performing in the *Via Crucis*.

It must be emphasized that I did not experience the same kind of pain that *namamaku* experienced through nailing. Nevertheless, my role in the play encouraged a more acute and expansive sensitivity to the nature of their pain, particularly in the process of its ritual sacralization. In the context of Via Crucis, the pain that namamaku undergo is experienced as meaningful – in important ways, it is edifying of their own religious subjectivities – only when it is interpreted within the language and sentiment of divine vow fulfilment. This is a language in the literal sense, expressed verbally between the *namamaku* and their ritual facilitators – the nailers, the centurions – and those cast members that are part of the ritual frame, myself included. There is, therefore, an aural component that was possible only through the proximal intimacy of a radically empirical encounter. While it might have been intuitive to think about pain as an experience that is only de-subjectifying and solipsistic, my embodied proximal positionality as a coeval of the *namamaku* placed me in an ideal position to understand that pain is shared, projected, and multimodal; that it both disarticulates and rearticulates subjectivity, especially in religious domains.

Conclusion: Embodied Proximity as Empirical Practice

In this chapter, I have discussed how anthropologists and TaPS scholars have confronted bodily discomfort in the course of doing fieldwork, even up to a point where the ethnographer's body becomes subjected to the pain that is experienced by their research interlocutors. In doing so, I have examined how the adoption of a radically empirical embodied proximity is most effective when ethnographers reframe their observational faculties away from words and writing and towards feeling and experiencing. I advocate an embodied method that privileges a first-hand, direct, intersubjective engagement with Passion ritual protagonists as an effective paradigm for understanding the nature and experience of the visceral components of ritual action, in this case with pain. Empirical distance and proximity are major themes in this discussion. In the classical regimens of participant observation, fieldwork is an act of theorization and writing, in which the ethnographer is sequestered in a privileged and distanced realm of conceptualization, effectively excluding the research subject. At its worst, this exclusion reduces the latter to what Harold Garfinkel (1967: 68) described as 'cultural dopes': objects that are presumed to live their lives within culture but that do not understand, and cannot exert any agency in, the processes that purportedly influence their lives. Radical empiricism, particularly as executed and deployed by performance studies scholars, goes against this in its endorsement of the ethnographer's emplaced body as 'the epistemological and ontological nexus upon which the research process turns' (Spry, 2001: 711). In this propagating of the 'return of the body', a first-person experience of the physical and emotional sensations that our research interlocutors go through is conceived of as the main instrument facilitating the production of anthropological knowledge.

The sustained physical proximity and 'distended reflexivity' that radical empiricism advocates enable a more nuanced understanding of pain. Radical empiricism is fundamentally a privileging of human sensation and proximal zones of affect as the observational conduits through which we learn about others and their world. This means that as an existentially demanding holistic body-and-mind learning experience, fieldwork is about learning to harness the productivity of 'taking part' as opposed to 'remaining apart' (Droogers & Knibbe, 2011: 297). When they are 'taking part', the ethnographer 'unlearns' their own logocentric empirical conditioning, which is manifested in the hallowed tradition of taking down field notes and recording data as a transcriber of experience. When a visceral and embodied methodology is prioritized, conversely, the ethnographer is enjoined to 'stop asking for more explanations at more or less the same point her respondents did' (Droogers & Knibbe, 2011: 291). Ethnographers may well enter the 'flow' of the ethnographic encounter, described by the psychologist Mihaly Csikszentmihalyi (1990) as a state of concentration and complete absorption in the activity at hand. The 'flow' of co-performative witnessing can only occur when one deliberately places oneself in a position of proximal exposure, in a manner consistent with what a radical empirical methodology advocates. My role as a minor cast member entailed a physical and, to a degree, emotional intimacy with *namamaku*, particularly at the play's climax. Only in such proximity would I have been able to observe the Kristo's minute facial twitches and expressions, his otherwise inaudible gasps of anguish and relief, the varying rhythms of breath, and the visual cues of sensation on his muscles. My performing-observing presence at the point of nailing – so close as to see and hear the raw facial and bodily expressions of the Kristo's moment of anguish – enabled me to experience pain as 'an array of multimodal semiotic forms, [that] riveted my attention, achingly, on a body in pain' (Larocco, 2016: 356). In pursuing a radically empirical approach that involves co-performing and bodily investment, I was able to gain a more acute understanding of the productive, relational, and *performative* valence of the pain experience.

Notes

1 In terms of the possible degree of ethnographic participation by a researcher, R. L. Gold (1958) and Buford H. Junker (1960) promulgated a typology of fieldwork roles as follows: (1) the *complete participant*, or the researcher who

does not divulge their research agenda and who immerses completely in the social or cultural context; (2) the *participant as observer*, or the researcher who is explicit about their intentions but still becomes involved in a way that contributes to the social reality; (3) the *observer as participant*, or the researcher who maintains an observational standpoint that is physically embedded, but intellectually detached; and (4) the *complete observer*, or the researcher whose research agenda is not known and who is completely detached from that which is being examined.

2 As the anthropologist Johannes Fabian (1983) has argued, this is one way in which the researched Other is relegated to a different temporality, having been denied coevalness with the ethnographer in the course of ethnographic writing.

3 The performance takes place along a five-kilometre (three-mile) route around the streets of the village of San Pedro Cutud, in the city of San Fernando, Pampanga. The play progresses to a purpose-built hill, called a *burol*, at the outer rim of the village.

References

Asad, T. (1986). 'The Concept of Cultural Translation in British Social Anthropology'. In J. Clifford & G. E. Marcus, *Writing Culture: The Poetics and Politics of Ethnography*. Berkeley: University of California Press, pp. 141–64.

Bautista, J. (2019). *The Way of the Cross: Suffering Selfhoods in the Roman Catholic Philippines*. Honolulu: University of Hawai'i Press.

Bautista, J., & Bräunlein, P. J. (2014). 'Ethnography as an Act of Witnessing: Doing Fieldwork on Passion Rituals in the Philippines'. *Philippine Studies: Historical and Ethnographic Viewpoints*, 62(3), 501–28.

Behar, R. (1996). *The Vulnerable Observer: Anthropology That Breaks Your Heart*. Boston: Beacon Press.

Bowman, G. (1997). 'Radical Empiricism: Anthropological Fieldwork after Psychoanalysis and the "Année Sociologique"'. *Anthropological Journal on European Cultures*, 6(2), 79–107.

Cannell, F. (1995). 'The Imitation of Christ in Bicol, Philippines'. *Journal of the Royal Anthropological Institute*, 1, 377–94.

Clifford, J., & Marcus, G. E., eds. (1986). *Writing Culture: The Poetics and Politics of Ethnography*. Berkeley: University of California Press.

Conquergood, D. (1991). 'Rethinking Ethnography: Towards a Critical Cultural Politics'. *Communication Monographs*, 58(2), 179–94.

Conquergood, D. (2002). 'Performance Studies: Interventions and Radical Research'. *TDR: The Drama Review*, 46(2), 145–56.

Csikszentmihalyi, M. (1990). *Flow: The Psychology of Optimal Experience*. New York: Harper & Row.

Cupitt, R. (2018). 'We Have Never Been Digital Anthropologists'. *Anthro{dendum}* (blog), 3 February. Accessed 11 October 2023. https://anthrodendum.org/2018/02/03/we-have-never-been-digital-anthropologists/.

Desjarlais, R. R. (1992). *Body and Emotion: The Aesthetics of Illness and Healing in the Nepal Himalayas*. Philadelphia: University of Pennsylvania Press.

Droogers, A., & Knibbe, K. (2011). 'Methodological Ludism and the Academic Study of Religion'. *Method & Theory in the Study of Religion*, 23(3), 283–303.

Evans-Pritchard, E. E. (1976 [1937]). *Witchcraft, Oracles, and Magic among the Azande*. Oxford: Clarendon Press.

Fabian, J. (1983). *Time and the Other: How Anthropology Makes Its Object*. New York: Columbia University Press.

Farrer, D. (2007). 'The Perils and Pitfalls of Performance Ethnography'. *International Sociological Association E-Bulletin*, 6, 17–26.

Farrer, D. (2009). *Shadows of the Prophet: Martial Arts and Sufi Mysticism*. Dordrecht, Netherlands: Springer.

Garfinkel, H. (1967). *Studies in Ethnomethodology*. Englewood Cliffs, NJ: Prentice-Hall.

Gatt, C. (2015). 'The Anthropologist as Ensemble Member: Anthropological Experiments with Theatre Makers'. In A. Flynn & J. Tinius, eds., *Anthropology, Theatre, and Development: The Transformative Potential of Performance*. Basingstoke: Palgrave Macmillan, pp. 334–56.

Gold, R. L. (1958). 'Roles in Sociological Field Observations'. *Social Forces*, 36(3), 217–23.

Harrop, P., & Njaradi, D. (2013). *Performance and Ethnography: Dance, Drama, Music*. Newcastle upon Tyne: Cambridge Scholars Press.

Hastrup, K. (1995). *A Passage to Anthropology: Between Experience and Theory*. London: Routledge.

Jackson, M. D. (1989). *Paths toward a Clearing: Radical Empiricism and Ethnographic Enquiry*. Bloomington: Indiana University Press.

Jackson, M. D. (2007). *Excursions*. Durham, NC: Duke University Press.

Jones, J. L. (2002). 'Performance Ethnography: The Role of Embodiment in Cultural Authenticity'. *Theatre Topics*, 12(1), 1–15.

Junker, B. H. (1960). *Field Work: An Introduction to the Social Sciences*. Chicago: University of Chicago Press.

Larocco, S. (2016). 'Pain as Semiosomatic Force: The Disarticulation and Rearticulation of Subjectivity'. *Subjectivity*, 9(4), 343–62.

Malinowski, B. (1922). *Argonauts of the Western Pacific: An Account of Native Enterprise and Adventure in the Archipelagoes of Melanesian New Guinea*. London: Routledge.

Marcus, G. E., & Fischer, M. M. J. (1986). *Anthropology as Cultural Critique: An Experimental Moment in the Human Sciences*. Chicago: University of Chicago Press.

Nabhan-Warren, K. (2011). 'Embodied Research and Writing: A Case for Phenomenologically Oriented Religious Studies Ethnographies'. *Journal of the American Academy of Religion*, 79(2), 378–407.

Nordling, L. (2020). 'Who Gets to Study Whom?' *SAPIENS: Anthropology Magazine*, 17 July. Accessed 11 October 2023. www.sapiens.org/culture/anthropology-colonial-history/.

Rosaldo, R. (1989). *Culture & Truth*. Boston: Beacon Press.
Scarry, E. (1985). *The Body in Pain: The Making and Unmaking of the World*. New York: Oxford University Press.
Scarry, E. (2000). 'On Evil, Pain, and Beauty'. Interview by J. L. Geddes. *Hedgehog Review*, 2(2). Accessed 11 October 2023. https://hedgehogreview.com/issues/evil/articles/on-evil-pain-and-beauty-a-conversation-with-elaine-scarry.
Sharma, D. (2012). 'Indigenous Performance Art Forms as Spaces for Social Reflection and Participatory Communication in Directed Social Change'. In S. R. Melkote, ed., *Development Communication in Directed Social Change: A Reappraisal of Theory and Practice*. Singapore: Asian Media Information and Communication Centre, pp. 169–96.
Shilling, C., & Mellor, P. A. (2010). 'Saved from Pain or Saved through Pain? Modernity, Instrumentalization and the Religious Use of Pain as a Body Technique'. *European Journal of Social Theory*, 13(4), 521–37.
Spry, T. (2001). 'Performing Autoethnography: An Embodied Methodological Praxis'. *Qualitative Inquiry*, 7(6), 706–32.
Tyler, S. (1986). 'Post-Modern Ethnography: From Document of the Occult to Occult Document'. In J. Clifford & G. E. Marcus, eds., *Writing Culture: The Poetics and Politics of Ethnography*. Berkeley: University of California Press, pp. 122–40.

CHAPTER 10

Fieldwork as Method in Theatre and Performance Studies

Jonas Tinius

> The steps of participant observation, like those of life itself, are contingent on the circumstances, and advance towards no end. They rather tread ways of carrying on and of being carried, of living life with others – humans and non-humans all – that is cognizant of the past, attuned to the conditions of the present and speculatively open to the possibilities of the future.
>
> – Tim Ingold, 'That's Enough about Ethnography!'

Problematizing Fieldwork

It is commonly assumed that fieldwork is what anthropologists *do* when they are in the field. While this may seem tautological, it reflects a long-standing and often rather macho assumption that not much can be said about fieldwork except 'not to be a bloody fool', as the British social anthropologist E. E. Evans-Pritchard (1976: 240) recalls being told by Bronisław Malinowski. It is Malinowski who bequeathed to the field of anthropology not just his work on the kula exchange in the Trobriand Islands (Malinowski, 2005 [1922]), but some of the most foundational and problematic modern formulations of early twentieth-century scientific fieldwork (Malinowski, 1989 [1967]). Anthropology's own critique of these inevitably partial truths of fieldwork, encapsulated in the striking proposals of the *Writing Culture* debate – which underscored the poetics and politics of ethnography (Clifford & Marcus, 1986; Thornton, 1988) – has done much to open up and explain the black box of anthropological methods. Yet fieldwork's enigmatic aura remains. Writing about his own early studies in Morocco, the late Paul Rabinow (1977: 3) even spoke of the 'alchemy of fieldwork'. Musing on his time as a graduate student in the Department of Anthropology at the University of Chicago in preparation for this research, he recalled that 'the world was divided into two categories of people: those who had done fieldwork, and those who had not; the latter were not "really" anthropologists'.

Fieldwork, in other words, is an authorizing and transformative rite of passage: both in terms of what is expected to happen to the presuppositions, ideas, and even corporeality of the researcher, and in terms of the credibility we attribute to the research undertaken. Much of this credibility relies not merely on the level of accurate and plausible description achieved in the ethnographies (or films, or sketches, or even theatre pieces; see Irving, 2007) that anthropologists produce after and about fieldwork, but also on the mere fact that they claim to have been there. Fieldwork is about *situating* situated knowledge. Michael Taussig (2011) captures the tensions involved in this negotiation in the title of his book of fieldwork sketches: *I Swear I Saw This*. The thickness of anthropologists' artful descriptions helps retrospectively construct the credibility of their fieldwork as an experience that led to insight and transformation. Fieldwork is also an educational transformation in the etymological and poetic sense. As Tim Ingold (2014: 388) argues, 'anthropology is a quest for education', not in the modern, institutionalized sense of 'instilling knowledge *in*', but in the sense of leading us *out* into the world, 'pulling us away from *any* standpoint', and bringing us to attend to things, people, and relations of trust. Depending on whom one's interlocutors are and what they know (about anthropologists), one needs to adapt one's ways of conducting research: turn off the recording device and rely on memory or, conversely, generate scenarios with interlocutors and record for and with them (Boyer & Marcus, 2021).

Thus, there is more to fieldwork than the exacting execution of predetermined methods; fieldwork assembles a nexus of commitments to research, including an ethics of interlocution and a pervasive understanding of and fidelity towards what happens, what is experienced, rather than what is being said about what happens. Fieldwork *implies* the researcher and their presence, yet at the same time it is always about more than just *being there*, which is why writing about fieldwork – ethnography – is so complex. For Laura Nader (2011: 211), ethnography is not merely 'a description but a theory of describing'. Likewise, fields are not naturally 'out there' waiting to be discovered but they are instead co-performed, witnessed, constructed before and after fieldwork; and this recognition changes the power dynamic of the research situation. To echo Dwight Conquergood's (1991: 188–9) turn of phrase, fieldwork is a kind of '"coactivity" or co-performance with historically situated, named "unique individuals"', or what he elsewhere called a form of 'co-performative witnessing' (Conquergood, 2002: 149; see also Donkor, 2007: 822). Fields are envisaged and circumscribed when we devise fieldwork; to a strong degree, we construct fields based on the questions we ask in our research proposals and outlines (Marcus, 1995). The temporality of fieldwork is thus more elliptic, recursive, and looped, since we constantly recalibrate our methods, assumptions, and ways of working depending on what *happens* in a field. The methods we employ necessitate in turn a constant methodological feedback loop since the fields we study also change while we are studying them, or perhaps precisely because of our presence. Our writing about this recalibration often glosses over the messiness implied in this process: hence the importance of being aware of what *field materials* are and of what constitutes an *ethnographic text*.

A single, uniquely anthropological method does not exist, not least because there is not a single unique tradition of the discipline; rather, we employ and assemble a series of known techniques for eliciting, recording, and analysing information and experience. And these techniques are, as even early anthropological enquiries acknowledge (e.g. Malinowski, 2005 [1922]), compromised by the partial positionality of any researcher: their moods and background, gender and language, but also the power structures they embody or evoke, along with their capacities, limitations, and impairments (Rosaldo, 1986). After all, central dispositives about the fieldwork rite of passage, not least the emblematic phrase *participant observation*, reify a problematic, ableist assumption of future researchers' physical and cognitive capacities (Devlieger, 2018; Muñoz, 2006).

While a great deal has been said about the poetic and political ways in which we write and document our experiences of fieldwork – this writing being the strong sense of the word *ethnography* – the term *ethnography* has also been used in a rather unhelpful way to denote the practice of fieldwork in general (Carrithers, 2007 [1996]; Howell, 2018). The term has misleadingly come to be associated with *the* method of anthropological research. *Ethnographic*, Ingold (2014: 383) contends, 'has become the most overused term in the discipline of anthropology'. This has, for him, not only led to a great deal of conceptual confusion among those interested in understanding methods of anthropological research, but also caused the term itself to become somewhat meaningless, obfuscating distinctions and preventing cross-disciplinary conversations about methods.

But often crises of traditions are signs of their vitality, and so it is here, with implications for the methods of both contemporary anthropology and theatre and performance studies (TaPS). In recent years, interest in expanded research methods has multiplied in TaPS, prompted by the realization that contemporary theatre and performance have changed and taken on new forms that require different means of research (Balme & Szymanski-Düll, 2020; Kershaw & Nicholson, 2011; Madison, 2010; Wihstutz & Hoesch, 2020). The discussion of multimodal methods in anthropology, too, has boosted interest in artistic forms of research and their expression, expanding into fields long explored by TaPS scholarship, such as embodiment, impairment, design, museums, and curation (Collins et al., 2017; Sansi, 2020). As noted, a recalibration of methods follows shifts in the questions asked and the affordances of these fields.

This chapter rescales this debate by clarifying terminologies for scholars and practitioners working with theatre and performance who are interested in understanding more about the methods of anthropological research. It seeks to render more graspable the distinctions among ethnography, fieldwork, and methods, before analysing fault lines between anthropology and performance research. It suggests some possible lines of research in three fields of performance where anthropological methods of research may usefully be engaged (project-based labour, institutional traditions, and rehearsals), and contributes to a renewed dialogue between performance research and anthropology more broadly.

After all, anthropology and performance research face the same problem. If, as the editors of this book put it in their original brief to authors, 'research practice might be said simply to reflect the expansive scope of the field', and, moreover, the 'expansionist impetus' of performance (studies), then anthropology has faced that problem all along, for its scope is the diversity of human existence. While anthropology and performance research share a concern about how to grasp potentially unlimited fields of study – perhaps 'by any means necessary', as Tracy C. Davis and Paul Rae posited in their brief – it is helpful to trace some debates, to try and understand some of the rather surprising reasons for why the fields have bifurcated in recent decades, and to find new modalities of crossover.

The Anthropological Dilemma of Performance

Throughout the modern and contemporary development of social and cultural anthropology as disciplines, theatre, dance, and performance have repeatedly featured as central modes of being through which to understand culture and society (Baumann & Briggs, 1990; Beeman, 1993; Bloch & Heimböckel, 2016; Kendon, 1997; Morris, 1995; Reed, 1998). Indeed, foundational texts of the disciplines grappled with the role of gesture and habitus (Mauss, 1936, 1990 [1923]), dance and play (Huizinga, 1950;

Spencer, 1985), ritual and performance (Gennep, 2004 [1909]), and performativity and power (Geertz, 1980). However, a systematic and comparative anthropology of performance and theatre did not take shape until the 1980s, with the formation of performance studies (e.g. Schechner, 1985; Turner, 1970, 1986), and even then, theatre/theatricality and performance/performativity did not become key fields in anthropology.

What this 'performative turn' did herald for anthropology was an extrapolation of theatre and performance terms for general metaphors of cultural and social practice, which caused, first, their indistinct and ubiquitous use, and, second (as also happened with prefixes like 'the politics of'), an emptying of their significance (see Korom, 2013). Writings such as Johan Huizinga's (1950) analysis of 'homo ludens' and the role of play, or Victor Turner's (1986: 187) programmatic definition of man as 'homo performans' – Conquergood's (1989: 85) 'culture-inventing and self-making creature' – have inspired a series of influential studies on the processuality of cultural practices *as* performance and performatives.

These approaches permeated the study of gender (Butler, 1990), politics (Alexander, 2011), intellectual life (Baert, 2015; Baert & Morgan, 2015), and the general make-up of symbolic worlds (Goffman, 1959), suffusing, as it were, an enriched understanding of our shared world in general: everything became performance. Interestingly, a parallel development took place in theatre studies, especially in Germany, where the expansion of the scope of what theatre is, where it is enacted, and what counts as staging or acting has likewise led towards a general acculturation of such terms into the fabric of life itself (Fischer-Lichte et al., 2004). But though methodologies of qualitative research can grow in tandem with the expansion of the conceptual and theoretical scope of TaPS, focus is lost if fields are endless and undelineated. The realignment of practice and research can lead to forms of 'genre blurring', where life is no longer distinguishable from art (Geertz, 1983). This realignment characterizes proposals by artists seeking to counter the institutionalization and formalization of art in schools and academies, but it has also inspired anthropologists and scholars of art to propose an analogization of art and anthropology (see Sansi, 2015). After all, this line of thought intimates, anthropology itself can become a practice of life (Ingold, 2014). Such an analogization makes it almost impossible to conceive of a difference between the *study* and the *practice* of art, anthropology, and life, which can be frustrating if one seeks to distinguish forms of awareness or reflexivity, or simply wishes to mark the position of the anthropologist-scholar as different from that of the performer-artist. Marilyn Strathern addressed this with a pointed outburst in a conversation on the topic: 'I can't be the only person who thinks we still want critical observers – "artists" and "anthropologists" – in the mix' (Sansi & Strathern, 2016: 434). Whether we consider ourselves artists, anthropologists, or both, practice does not mean not-thinking or reflecting. Quite the contrary. As Pierre Bourdieu (1977 [1972]: 72) argued, practical activity is always composed through the 'dialectic of the internalisation of externality and the externalisation of internality'.

The gradual dissolution of performance and theatre into generalized metaphors for social and cultural life could be understood as an aspect of the scalability of performance, which extends from the micro level of interaction to the political negotiation of communities, or even cosmologies and worlds (see Davis & Marx, 2021). However complex this scale, methods of study need to be calibrated across these genres. Somewhat ironically, the attempt to bring anthropology, theatre, and performance together through performance studies has caused greater blurring rather than distinctiveness of categories, notwithstanding the condition of 'setasidedness' that separates performance and that is created through performance itself (Davis, 2020). The practice of distinguishing performance and performativity, or theatre and theatricality, from each other and from other forms of everyday or extra-ordinary social practices in adjacent fields and within performance studies has not necessarily become more accurate; likewise, a systematic understanding of the value of such distinctions in anthropology has not refreshed the conceptual and methodological vocabulary. We are still in a state of blurring, rather than conscious mixing.

Conquergood (1989) poignantly captured two further reasons for the sidelining of an open comparative engagement between anthropology, theatre and theatricality, and performance and performativity in his essay 'Poetics, Play, Process, and Power: The Performative Turn in Anthropology': on the one hand, the marked scepticism towards Western, institutionalized, and professionalized art traditions that social and cultural anthropology developed in the 1960s and 1970s; and, on the other hand, anthropological scholarship's attention to the subaltern, suffering, or marginalized subject. I will take each in turn.

In terms of the former, the anti-Western and anti-institutional tendency that Conquergood (1989) ascribes to anthropologists (he disregards traditions that have always focused on fields in the Euro-American West, such as the German-speaking *Volkskunde* or European ethnology) echoes a broader mistrust towards aesthetics and contemporary art and theatre in the West as forms of bourgeois classist expression (Weiner, 1996). Alfred Gell (2006 [1992]: 161), who otherwise translated across these spheres of Western aesthetics and Indigenous art cosmologies (e.g. in his essay 'Vogel's Net': Gell, 1996), parroted this mistrust so as to critique the tacit dogma of a Western philosophical tradition that elevates aesthetics and art in a system of valuation:

> Aesthetics is a branch of moral discourse which depends on the acceptance of the initial articles of faith.... In so far as such modern souls possess a religion, that religion is the religion of art, the religion whose shrines consist of theatres, libraries and art galleries, whose priests and bishops are painters and poets, whose theologians are critics, and whose dogma is the dogma of universal aestheticism.

Gell (2006 [1992]: 159) was concerned with the dominance of an assumption that art was somehow inherently 'a Good Thing', which is why as researchers we are advised to practise a 'resolute indifference to the aesthetic values of art', that is, a 'methodical philistinism'. Gell's observation is emblematic of a wider problem in the anthropology of 'Western' worlds: professional, extra-ordinary settings (such as bourgeois art, aesthetics, and institutionalized Western art institutions) were left out of anthropological study. The study of such fields was thus moved from performance studies and anthropology to sociology, where analyses of Western bourgeois aesthetics formed an important canon (Becker, 1982; Bourdieu, 1984 [1979]).

Anthropological scholarship's attention to the subaltern subject (Conquergood, 1989; Nader, 1974 [1969]; Ortner, 2016; Robbins, 2013) has led to methods of fieldwork designed for the study of non-professional, non-institutionalized, and subaltern or tacit forms of cultural and social expression. It also created a dichotomy in the field, with researchers assumed to be experts while interlocutors were viewed as incompetent to speak for themselves (Spivak, 1988) – a presumed backwardness that was illustrated by covers of undergraduate manuals featuring hiking boots and backpacks in preparation for rural fieldwork in a tent (cf. Breidenstein et al., 2015). Rarely do such investigations, to give one example, include the idea that fieldwork may also take place with an academic dramaturg working in a national theatre.

While most expansive sketches across performance studies and anthropology point to the pervasive presence of performance/performativity and theatre/theatricality as cross-cultural categories of human existence (Davis & Postlewait, 2003), thinking about the relation to anthropological methods is fuzzy. A key factor here is the continued tendency to view fieldwork as way of rendering *intelligible* tacit forms of knowledge that need to be explained by the researcher (Jackson, 1996), translating *unknown* forms of performance and theatricality, or considering *ordinary*, non-professional contexts. As I have argued elsewhere (Tinius, 2020), this tendency has had a significant impact on the continued divides between performance research (and studies), theatre scholarship, and anthropological work.

Extra-Ordinary Fields of Performance and Art Scholarship

Most prominent and problematic among these divides has been the divorce between the study of *extra-ordinary* forms of theatre and performance, by which I mean institutionalized, professional contexts in which theatre and performance are deliberately set aside, no longer immersed in ritual or everyday contexts (Tinius, 2017b, 2023), and the study of those that are marked by the quotidian normality of the ordinary (see e.g. Das, 2007; Lambek, 2010). These extra-ordinary fields – which are not distinct to modern society or the West – are interesting because they pose different kinds of problems to fieldworkers. Among these problems are the complex role of organizational research and interlocution, with expertise on the part of practitioners (dramaturgs, directors, actors, choreographers) as well as academics writing about and thus constituting these fields; the role of theory and intellectuals (Boyer, 2019); negotiations of access into professional environments; forms of contestation; and the collapse in distinctions between researcher and interlocutor.

Two examples drawn from my own field research with migrant theatre-makers in the western German Ruhr region illustrate the problems that arise from a narrow understanding of fieldwork that does not consider the setasidedness of theatre work. The first involves a talk I gave at a prominent theatre studies department in Germany, in which I spoke about 'deep hanging out' at German public theatres (see Geertz, 2000: 107–17). While the host professor was well disposed to my arguments, he insisted on me telling him how I defined theatre. He argued that my understanding of the field of 'theatre' was too all-encompassing, since I included in it practices of theorization of theatre by scholars, critics, and directors, and he asked me to limit myself to a strict definition of the field as including only the artistic practices onstage, and not what is being said about theatre beyond the stage. In other words, I was supposed to restrict my anthropological perspective to theatre performances, and not the production of the field of theatre as a whole. To me, this seemed both too narrow and patently absurd, especially since his own work framed theatre as a discursive field. The field, I argued, was co-constituted in this act of discussion between us, and neither of us occupied the 'Archimedian point from which to represent the world' that we assumed in our discourse (Clifford, 1986: 22). The discussion offers a variant on the question of how to do fieldwork on self-reflexive fields as posed by Jenny Sundén (2003: 18): 'How then to start writing a culture that is already written?'

A second example involves an encounter in which I perceived hesitation on the part of a dramaturg in my field study to open up to me the nitty-gritty details of his daily work (an aspect I had been told would be central for in-depth, thick fieldwork). For him, such nuts and bolts constituted mere 'privatissimi' (originally a reference to particular types of small-scale university seminars, here meaning private and intimate details), letting me know at the end of the conversation that what really interested him was theory (in particular, anthropological theory). Curious, I wrote this in my notebook. Before looking up again, I was handed a slip of paper that included, as the dramaturg commented, 'a few names of my anthropological references'. The names were Kant, Hegel, and Freud. In other words, I had to shift my understanding of fieldwork away from the tacit, under-theorized practices that we are trained to study, to focus instead on the presence of theory as a co-constituent feature of the field I had so carefully (and naively) devised from afar. I understood this suggestion as a rebuttal of my attempted access to his particular practice of dramaturgy as well as a comment on the coexistence of observers in the field (here, dramaturg and anthropologist), something that became manifest to me at a much later stage of fieldwork.

These situations show that our understanding of a field – in this case the expanded extra-ordinary understanding of theatre as co-constituted by scholarly writings about it – must attend to ways the field describes and situates itself, or how practitioners within it understand the scope of what they do. This is not to say that we must always adhere to the definitions and demarcations of those practitioners, which may be particular kinds of performance orchestrated in the moment for the researcher. I would, therefore, like to turn away from classic descriptions of fieldwork methods, such as interviews, note-taking, and visual documentation. These are individual means by which to respond to research contexts, and do not constitute particularly *anthropological* methods. The misconception that they do so has led to the great levelling out of the differences between field sites and the particular methods they afford (decried by Tim Ingold (2014) in his article 'That's Enough about Ethnography!') and has given the false impression that once such methods are in play, any observation will be *more* ethnographic. My anecdote serves as an example to the contrary. Ingold rightly points to the overuse of the term *ethnographic* as a qualifier for certain encounters or methods, as if these are magically thicker, or yield different observations, because they are deployed by an anthropologist: after all, the broad range of methods we use as anthropologists are shared across most disciplines that do qualitative research, and they are described in a wide range of guidebooks and toolkits, online and offline (Boellstorff, 2012; Faubion & Marcus, 2011; Sanjek, 1990). Rather, I wish to explain some elements of what in my opinion constitutes the anthropological mode of *fieldwork as method*, and ways these can be integrated with the study of particular and extra-ordinary settings of theatre and performance.

Fieldwork as Method

Instead of referring to a single method of anthropological research, the anthropologist Daniel Miller (1997: 16) writes of fieldwork as 'a series of commitments' we make to a field and people. This perspective helps ground an understanding of fieldwork as an *approach* to the fields we construct as we conduct research in them, and it is pertinent to understanding theatre and performance as fields. For Miller, among these commitments, four elements are noteworthy.

The first commitment Miller (1997: 16) names is 'to be in the presence of the people one is studying, and not merely of the texts or objects they produce'. That is, we conduct fieldwork in the co-presence of those whom and with whom we study. Such study is not exhausted by a formal analysis of the products (films, texts, objects) that emerge from their practices, and cannot be reduced to them either. We are reminded again of Conquergood's (1991: 188–9) salient point that we are, as researchers, co-performative witnesses. Our presence in fieldwork co-produces the encounter, and we construct the fields we research by our very presence in them. This does not minimize the realness of these encounters or what we write about these fields, but it recognizes the dynamics of work with other human beings. We attend to human interaction and the co-constitution of fields through our presence as witnesses, and sometimes as instigative 'sparring partners' (Tinius, 2021).

Second, Miller (1997: 16–17) points to a commitment to 'evaluate people in terms of what they actually do, that is, as material agents working in a material world, and not merely of what they say they do'. As Sharon Macdonald (2001: 78) points out in an article on museum fieldwork, this leads us to think critically about how social realities cannot be taken for granted. Things may turn out to be different than they are narrated, and talk of reality may obscure the realness of their effects (Rae, 2018). Jokes are told in fields, and anthropologists are, as 'dilettantes' (Rabinow, 1977: 3), often in awkward situations, frequently deliberately so (cf. Oswald & Tinius, 2022). We may even become part of mockeries in performance rituals, as William Sax (2002: 31) recounts of his fieldwork on rituals and dance (see also Cole, 2001). Furthermore, this commitment points to the role of self-narration. Identities are *told*, recounted, narrated in ways that may not always represent how events and actions *really* unfolded. This renders them no less truthful, but it may point to how positions are performatively established and how such positions are negotiated even through performance – something crucial when dealing with charismatic public figures, such as theatre directors and professional actors. Or, as Jane Cowan (1990: xi) describes with regard to 'the ordered sensuality of dancing' in her book *Dance and the Body Politic in Northern Greece*, it captures 'my awareness of myself as body and my awareness of others' awareness of me as an embodied female self'.

Third, Miller (1997: 17) argues that fieldwork is a 'long-term commitment to an investigation that allows people to return to a daily life that one hopes goes beyond what is performed for the ethnographer'. Anthropological fieldwork is often understood as something that requires the researcher to commit to extended periods of time in a particular field site. Just how this length is measured, however, is relative. No one time frame can be universally and determined a priori for fieldwork, and it would instead be more helpful to consider the idiosyncratic time frames, calendars, and rhythms of theatre and performance as fields. There are temporal affordances depending on how one defines the field of performance research. Undergraduate fieldwork in theatres, for instance, is usually conducted over the summer break and thus has only limited scope if theatres close. Rehearsals, depending on the type of performance institution or theatre considered, may take weeks or months, if not longer, with some traditions and rituals developing over years or sedimenting over generations. In other words, the 'long-term' in 'long-term commitment' refers not to a predefined period but to an attentiveness to a given field. Any chosen time frame crafts an artificial window of research out of a field, and we do our best to understand in our design of a field its affordances and timescales.

To pause a bit longer on this third commitment: Miller's proposal points towards the supposed artifice of performance in the everyday. Being with people, however much time is spent, will never reveal a true window into anyone's deepest inner self (not least because this may indeed not exist *inside* us). Anthropological fieldwork is not psychoanalysis (even though it may be about it or study aspects of it); rather, in the best of worlds, we build relationships of trust and mutual care that reveal something beyond appearance, that attain social, psychological, and emotional depth, and that go beyond the constructed phases of work. And yet, even trust is a performance, not unlike theatrical rites of initiation, comradery, or even extended kinship. If we walk into a performance of a theatre piece without having been there for the rehearsal, or without having hung out during a coffee or cigarette break to participate or become the centre of gossip, we will get only a partial picture (Clifford, 1986; see also McAuley, 1988: 79). The positivist assumption that we can somehow get to the 'real' essence of a field – as if it were something natural out there to be discovered, rather than something we co-construct as we observe, write, and speak about it – is misleading. Long-term commitment to a field implies that we are willing to extend our research from the formal survey perspective to a trusting immersion, which oftentimes may become apparent only when we hang out 'deeply', that is, allowing for meandering paths and uncertain times, as James Clifford notes (quoted in Geertz, 2000: 110).

A fourth commitment in Miller's (1997: 17) definition is to 'holistic analysis, which insists that such behaviours be considered within the larger framework of people's lives and cosmologies'. There is a difference between the pretence of capturing a totality of social experiences (the holistic objectivist rhetoric of ethnographic writing that Thornton, 1988, criticizes) and the recognition that anthropological fieldworkers never look at isolated practices or discourses; their object of study is always interrelated to other scales of life. It is the latter that Miller points to with his fourth commitment. I remember a dismissive comment arising from a colleague during a public seminar on fieldwork as a method in theatre studies: 'why do I need to do long-term fieldwork if I can just do one interview?' This perception epitomizes the problem that Miller (1997) and Ingold (2014) caution against, namely, the tendency to speak of ethnography but without the contextualizing and transformative practice of fieldwork (cf. Kreuder, 2016; Kreuder et al., 2012). In my own fieldwork, for example, it is evident that the scope of autobiographical narratives of migrant actors in Germany is connected to traditions and ways in which such lives are framed. There is always a broader social or cosmological frame within which actors live out their lives, however drawn from (but not overdetermined by) repertoires of being that are borrowed, learnt, or sometimes only improvised. Pierre Bourdieu's (1977 [1972]) elaboration of the habitus captures this tension, and as I have sought elsewhere to analyse (in relation to actors' conduct and shaping of their comportment during rehearsals), there are extra-ordinary social settings in which such scalar negotiations of self and cosmos take place (see Tinius, 2018).

Fieldwork loses its anthropological sense if it does not concern the possibility of repositioning our assumptions as researchers: that is, if we do not *learn* while being in the field. It loses that sense, too, if we fail to attend to the temporal, social, and political affordances of the fields within which we work, and if we do not acknowledge that we co-construct these fields (from the moment we conceive of them in a project application or research project to the point at which we write them up in our ethnographies). I return to the epigraph at the beginning of this chapter, in which Ingold (2014: 390) argues that in contrast to a scientific understanding of method as a series of steps, fieldwork is 'contingent on the circumstances': it is 'cognizant of the past, attuned to the conditions of the present and speculatively open to the possibilities of the future'. He urges us to think of fieldwork as a commitment to other people. Before we ask how to deploy a method, we should ask ourselves what we want to know and what is it we are studying (see also Latour, 2003). In other words, mixing methods in performance research implies that we come equipped with a toolkit of possibilities but do not consider anything a one-stop shop. Fieldwork needs to adapt to interrupted rhythms. Depending on where we work, what we study, and what we seek to understand, we may misconstrue fields or block access to understanding and correspondence with our interlocutors if we adhere too strictly to certain protocols that are simply not fit for or emergent from these fields.

Possible Pathways, Extra-Ordinary Fields

Anthropological methods do not come as ready-made tools that can be deployed, like a microphone or a pen and notebook. What makes fieldwork anthropological are the commitments that go with it, grounded in the discipline's multifaceted debates and discourses. If we are interested in mixing methods across fields for the purpose of doing research on performance and performativity, theatre and theatricality, we can do so without being trained in these traditions. And yet whether we decide to do longer-term fieldwork, including participant observation, interviews, or note-taking, fieldwork as method goes along with a set of commitments and approaches to understanding fields and the practices therein. What is outlined in the preceding section, 'Fieldwork as Method', can be considered among ethical and methodological questions that researchers should address before they embark on fieldwork. What do I consider my field, and how do I construct it? What temporalities are implicit in this field, and when, for how long, and how often does it make sense for me to do fieldwork? Whom do I need to approach in this field to address my central research questions?

In my work on professional theatre-makers and lay migrant theatre groups in Germany's post-industrial Ruhr region, many of these fields have *looked back* at me, asked me to recalibrate the methods I thought useful, and thrown me into ethical conundrums that I had not foreseen (Tinius, 2016, 2023). This process ended up being central to my understanding of the core questions that my interlocutors asked themselves. How to build a theatre tradition? How to craft a legacy of transnational work in largely national traditions? How to educate and collaborate with non-institutional theatre groups while maintaining the institutional privileges afforded by public funding? How to negotiate personal artistic autonomy in a tradition of strong individual direction and charismatic authority?

Certain fields of practice open themselves up more than others for anthropological fieldwork. The centrality of theatre and performance as fields of practice for my interlocutors has made me rethink my fieldwork throughout many of its phases, and led me to conceptualize these fields as particularly pertinent zones for thinking about fieldwork modalities and temporalities. Three examples can serve for scholars, students, or those interested in combining fieldwork as method with theatre and performance scholarship.

The first such example involves the creation of 'projects', which strikes me as particularly pertinent. This applies to freelance theatre and performance endeavours dependent on project-based funding for realization. In the German-speaking theatre context, this relates to the so-called free scene (*freie Szene*). As theatre scholar and actress Annemarie Matzke (2012b) puts it, artists working in this field have to design 'the conditions of productions' with every new project. In other words, the labour and design are constructed anew for each project, and thus the artists are working in what could be called a *future perfect* temporality of production: every project has to imagine how it *will have happened* at a future moment. This implies, for a researcher, that fieldwork necessitates an understanding of the kinds of projections made, the stories told about future work, and the assumptions of value. After all, each project has to undergo a self-evaluation of how, with whom, and where productions will take place before any work is even done.

This condenses questions of preparation, anticipation, and projection in the arts, but also issues of valuation, structures, and hierarchy – or, as Karin Barber (2000: 11) puts it, forms of 'generative materialism' – within the field. My own work in this regard has focused on the professionalization and precariousness of such labour conditions (Tinius, 2015a); as well as on the way that such a field opens possibilities for collaboration between anthropological, academic, and artistic expertise (Tinius, 2017a) where the researcher and the process of fieldwork, interviews, and later documentation and ethnography actually become a funded and integrated element in an artistic project. This possibility bears on how to define the field for an artistic project, and thus runs parallel to the construction of fieldwork as method. Funding applications will often ask for a conceptualization of *what, how, and where* artistic work will take place, which often includes phases of archival study and related forms of research, and thus is involved in constructing a field for future fieldwork. In other words, the field we may choose to study will most likely already have positioned, constructed, or circumscribed itself – a feature even more marked in professional, independent, and project-based artistic labour.

My second example involves the study of frames and traditions of institutional theatre and performance production. In contrast to the often temporally finite and relatively shorter period of preparation, rehearsal, and performance in freelance project-based productions, institutions (with public funding) may allow fieldwork to unfold along broader temporal scales (see Born, 1995; Tinius, 2015b). Archival records, the transmission of knowledge, and an institution's negotiation of its values are processes that require longer-term attention, often include narratives of inclusion and exclusion that need a different kind of trust between interlocutors, and frequently reveal the passing on of roles from one person to another.

In my fieldwork, for instance, the work of the theatre pedagogue responsible for youth work, education, and outreach became an interesting 'field' to observe. This person's role was to lower the threshold for the transmission of knowledge by working with local schools to mediate between theatre and pedagogy, but he had become so identified with the work that, shortly before his retirement, he worried about how his role could be continued by someone else. In another case, an actress revealed a previously unknown dimension of an institutionalized tradition. Having been artistically socialized in the institution as a founding ensemble member, where she remained for over three decades, she felt too close to leave yet too remote to work in the same routines. Such autobiographical narratives are less directly pertinent to understanding how project logics and the *future perfect* temporality of work affect performance production, but they are central to understanding the institutionalization of performance traditions. They open up further questions about individual narratives of self (see Herzfeld, 1998; Tinius & Wewerka, 2020) that may become interesting avenues for understanding ageing, archiving, cultural memory, and institutionalization.

My third example involves a field of practice that has become one of the most widely studied across performance research: the rehearsal. Rehearsals encompass all forms of preparatory modes *and* spaces in which a performance, performative iterations, a theatre piece, or a theatrical event are created. Where a rehearsal begins or ends depends on the kind of practice encompassed: it can extend to an entire lifetime in some skills and crafts, while in others it may double as the actual performance. In *Arbeit am Theater*, Annemarie Matzke (2012a: 205) explores the relation of labour, rehearsal, and theatre, arguing that rehearsals have long been misconceived only as forms of preparation; instead, she shows, (anthropological) knowledge about bodies, performance, and collectivity is negotiated and created *through* rehearsals. Matzke points to Carl Weber, formerly an assistant and dramaturg for Bertolt Brecht, for an example of how negotiations within rehearsals incorporate the *perception* of labour, and what it means to attend to such processes and *not* understand them. Writing years after it happened, Weber (1967/8: 102–3) recounted his first visit to a rehearsal of the Berliner Ensemble, in 1952, as the company was rehearsing the *Urfaust*:

> I walked into the rehearsal and it was obvious they were taking a break. Brecht was sitting in a chair smoking a cigar.... Some of the actors were on stage and some of them standing around Brecht, joking, making funny movements and laughing about them. One actor went up on the stage and tried about 30 ways of falling from a table.... This went on and on, and someone ate a sandwich, and I thought, my god this is a long break. So I sat naively and waited, and just before Monk [director of the production] said, 'Well, now we are finished, let's go home', I realized that this *was* rehearsal.

This vignette (see also Matzke, 2012a: 237) is relatable to any novice fieldworker, not just in such specified rehearsal contexts. Precisely because rehearsal practices are such focalized extra-ordinary settings, they can be extremely exclusive and closed, or by contrast open to collaborative practices of observation. Literature on this field abounds (Banu, 2005; Harvie & Lavender, 2010; Hinz & Roselt, 2011; McAuley, 2012). Rehearsal lends itself to anthropological fieldwork not least because it is such a scalable practice that exists in professionalized as well as entirely unformalized settings (Barber, 2007). In every rehearsal, however, what counts as meaningful, ethically relevant work on the process of theatre and performance, and who is considered a meaningful mediator for such selections, is negotiated (Tinius, 2018). Rehearsals are, in some ways, microcosms of any performance-related field, and they mirror many of the key conundrums of trust, artifice, commitment, duration, and design of our fields pertaining to fieldwork as method.

A Short Concluding Note

In this chapter, I have tried to work my way around the all-too-easy equivalence of ethnography with fieldwork and the identification of a particular set of tools that could be considered anthropological methods. Instead, I embraced the complexity of the term *fieldwork* and the reasons it can be considered a method, encompassing the kinds of commitments that mark fieldwork as anthropological. I hope this shifts the conversation away from a quest for ready-made toolkits and towards reflexive conversations on the ethics and affordances of fields, from which we develop ways of assembling methods. Most importantly, fieldwork implies the terms *field* and *work*. When we design, envisage, or eventually conduct fieldwork, we are implicit in forms of construction, fabrication, and labour that make a field a site for work undertaken by ourselves and others. This differs from processes of discovery or revelation of things that are entirely unrelated to the design of our fields. Fieldwork is intrinsically laborious: labour is needed to design, prepare, and fund, processes that in turn involve psychological and emotional labour. Fieldwork is not a technique (like conducting an interview, writing a diary, or using an app or a camera); it is an approach to *working out* how to work in a field. In the end, however, no method can always ensure access to a field, prop open a context for investigation, or guarantee that research yields meaningful results. That is also not always a problem. After all, any fieldwork includes failures and miscommunication, recalibration, and returns. These are processes from which we learn about our (in)abilities and the make-up and politics of the fields we have chosen, designed, and learnt from during our research. Fieldwork as a method is thus more than the straightforward elicitation of information: it is a way of approaching the creation of research projects, reflections on knowledge production, and a commitment to practices, people, and values negotiated through complex fields. Nevertheless, a researcher's desire to find out something about someone may not be reciprocated. Just because we know *how* to do research, it does not follow that we *should* and *can* expect to be allowed to do so.

As a method for investigating theatre and theatricality, performance and performativity, fieldwork is generative precisely because it implies the core aspects of preparation, rehearsal, staging, and reception. Fieldwork crafts set-aside situations: performances of skill and expertise along with ignorance on nearly every level. Last but not least, it is performative as an experience – it transforms – and, at some point, tasks us with responsibility for what we do with the fieldwork material we may have written, filmed, or recorded, or otherwise assembled. Because fieldwork – not just in the field of performance-research – is based on interactions with other human beings, we enter into the complex negotiation of intersubjective relations, collectivities, hierarchies, and trust. As such, fieldwork, in theatre and performance fields, inevitably leads us back to anthropology and to life itself.

References

Alexander, J. C. (2011). *The Performance of Politics: Obama's Victory and the Democratic Struggle for Power*. Oxford: Oxford University Press.

Baert, P. (2015). *The Existentialist Moment: The Rise of Sartre as a Public Intellectual*. Cambridge: Polity Press.

Baert, P., & Morgan, M. (2015). *Conflict in the Academy: A Study in the Sociology of Intellectuals*. Basingstoke: Palgrave Macmillan.

Balme, C., & Szymanski-Düll, B., eds. (2020). *Methoden der Theaterwissenschaft*. Tübingen, Germany: Narr Francke.

Banu, G. (2005). *Les répétitions: de Stanislavski à aujourd'hui*. Arles: Actes Sud.

Barber, K. (2000). *The Generation of Plays: Yorùbá Popular Life in Theater*. Bloomington: Indiana University Press.

Barber, K. (2007). *The Anthropology of Texts, Persons and Publics: Oral and Written Culture in Africa and Beyond*. Cambridge: Cambridge University Press.

Baumann, R., & Briggs, C. L. (1990). 'Poetics and Performances as Critical Perspectives on Language and Social Life'. *Annual Review of Anthropology*, 19, 59–88.

Becker, H. S. (1982). *Art Worlds*. Berkeley: University of California Press.

Beeman, W. O. (1993). 'The Anthropology of Theatre and Spectacle'. *Annual Review of Anthropology*, 22, 369–93.

Bloch, N., & Heimböckel, D., eds. (2016). *Theater und Ethnologie: Beiträge zu einer produktiven Beziehung*. Tübingen, Germany: Narr Francke.

Boellstorff, T. (2012). *Ethnography and Virtual Worlds: A Handbook of Methods*. Princeton, NJ: Princeton University Press.

Born, G. (1995). *Rationalizing Culture: IRCAM, Boulez, and the Institutionalization of the Musical Avant-Garde*. Berkeley: University of California Press.

Bourdieu, P. (1977 [1972]). *Outline of a Theory of Practice*. Cambridge: Cambridge University Press.

Bourdieu, P. (1984 [1979]). *Distinction: A Social Critique of the Judgement of Taste*. London: Routledge.

Boyer, D. (2019). 'Foucault in the Bush: The Social Life of Post-Structuralist Theory in East Berlin's Prenzlauer Berg'. *Ethnos*, 66(2), 207–36.

Boyer, D., & Marcus, G. E., eds. (2021). *Collaborative Anthropology Today: A Collection of Exceptions*. Ithaca, NY: Cornell University Press.

Breidenstein, G., Hirschauer, S., Kalthoff, H., & Niewsand, B., eds. (2015). *Ethnografie: Die Praxis der Feldforschung*. 2nd ed. Konstanz, Germany: UTB.

Butler, J. (1990). *Gender Trouble: Feminism and the Subversion of Identity*. London: Routledge.

Carrithers, M. (2007 [1996]). 'Fieldwork'. In A. Barnard & J. Spencer, eds., *Encyclopedia of Social and Cultural Anthropology*. London: Routledge, p. 262.

Clifford, J. (1986). 'Introduction: Partial Truths'. In J. Clifford & G. E. Marcus, eds., *Writing Culture: The Politics and Poetics of Ethnography*. Los Angeles: University of California Press, pp. 1–26.

Clifford, J., & Marcus, G. E., eds. (1986). *Writing Culture: The Politics and Poetics of Ethnography*. Los Angeles: University of California Press.

Cole, C. M. (2001). *Ghana's Concert Party Theatre*. Bloomington: Indiana University Press.

Collins, S. G., Durington, M., & Gill, H. (2017). 'Multimodality: An Invitation'. *American Anthropologist*, 119(1), 142–53.

Conquergood, D. (1989). 'Poetics, Play, Process, and Power: The Performative Turn in Anthropology'. *Text and Performance Quarterly*, 1, 82–95.

Conquergood, D. (1991). 'Rethinking Ethnography: Towards a Critical Cultural Politics'. *Communication Monographs*, 58(2), 179–94.

Conquergood, D. (2002). 'Performance Studies: Interventions and Radical Research'. *TDR: The Drama Review*, 46(2), 145–56.

Cowan, J. (1990). *Dance and the Body Politic in Northern Greece*. Princeton, NJ: Princeton University Press.

Das, V. (2007). *Life and Words: Violence and the Descent into the Ordinary*. Berkeley: University of California Press.

Davis, T. C. (2020). 'Setasidedness'. In T. C. Davis & P. W. Marx, eds., *The Routledge Companion to Theatre and Performance Historiography*. London: Routledge, pp. 118–40.

Davis, T. C., & Marx, P. W. (2021). 'Introduction: On Critical Media History'. In T. C. Davis & P. W. Marx, eds., *The Routledge Companion to Theatre and Performance Historiography*. London: Routledge, pp. 1–39.

Davis, T. C., & Postlewait, T. (2003). 'Theatricality: An Introduction'. In T. C. Davis & T. Postlewait, eds., *Theatricality*. Cambridge: Cambridge University Press, pp. 1–39.

Devlieger, C. (2018). 'Disability'. *Open Encyclopedia of Anthropology*, 14 June. http://doi.org/10.29164/18disab.

Donkor, D. (2007). 'Performance, Ethnography and the Radical Intervention of Dwight Conquergood'. *Cultural Studies*, 21(6), 821–5.

Evans-Pritchard, E. E. (1976). *Witchcraft, Oracles, and Magic among the Azande*. Oxford: Clarendon Press.

Faubion, J., & Marcus, G. E., eds. (2011). *Fieldwork Is Not What It Used to Be: Learning Anthropology's Method in a Time of Transition*. Ithaca, NY: Cornell University Press.

Fischer-Lichte, E., Risi, C., & Roselt, J., eds. (2004). *Kunst der Aufführung. Aufführung der Kunst*. Berlin: Theater der Zeit.

Geertz, C. (1980). *Negara: The Theatre State in Nineteenth-Century Bali*. Princeton, NJ: Princeton University Press.

Geertz, C. (1983). 'Blurred Genres: The Refiguration of Social Thought'. In C. Geertz, *Local Knowledge: Further Essays in Interpretive Anthropology*. London: Basic Books, pp. 19–35.

Geertz, C. (2000). *Available Light: Anthropological Reflections on Philosophical Topics*. Princeton, NJ: Princeton University Press.

Gell, A. (1996). 'Vogel's Net: Traps as Artworks and Artworks as Traps'. *Journal of Material Culture*, 1(1), 15–38.

Gell, A. (2006 [1992]). 'The Technology of Enchantment and the Enchantment of Technology'. In *A. Gell, The Art of Anthropology: Essays and Diagrams*, ed. E. Hirsch. Oxford: Athlone Press, pp. 159–86.

Gennep, A. van. (2004 [1909]). *The Rites of Passage*. London: Routledge.

Goffman, E. (1959). *The Presentation of Self in Everyday Life*. London: Penguin.

Harvie, J. & Lavender, A., eds. (2010). *Making Contemporary Theatre: International Rehearsal Processes*. Manchester: Manchester University Press.

Herzfeld, M. (1998). *Portrait of a Greek Imagination: An Ethnographic Biography of Andreas Nenedakis*. Chicago: University of Chicago Press.

Hinz, M. & Roselt, J. (2011). *Chaos und Konzept. Proben und Probieren im Theater*. Berlin: Alexander Verlag.

Howell, S. (2018). 'Ethnography'. *Open Encyclopedia of Anthropology*, 18 February. http://doi.org/10.29164/18ethno.

Huizinga, J. (1950). *Homo Ludens: A Study of the Play Element in Culture*. Boston: Beacon Press.

Ingold, T. (2014). 'That's Enough about Ethnography!' *HAU: Journal of Ethnographic Theory*, 4(1), 383–95.

Irving, A. (2007). 'Ethnography, Art, Death'. *Journal of the Royal Anthropological Institute*, 13(1), 185–208.

Jackson, M. (1996). 'Introduction: Phenomenology, Radical Empiricism and Anthropological Critique'. In M. Jackson, ed., *Things as They Are: New Directions in Phenomenological Anthropology*. Bloomington: University of Indiana Press, pp. 1–50.

Kendon, A. (1997). 'Gesture'. *Annual Review of Anthropology*, 26, 109–28.

Kershaw, B. & Nicholson, H. (2011). *Research Methods in Theatre and Performance*. Edinburgh: Edinburgh University Press.

Korom, F. J., ed. (2013). *The Anthropology of Performance: A Reader*. Oxford: Oxford University Press.

Kreuder, F. (2016). 'Schauspieler_innen als Ethnograph_innen'. In M. Cairo, M. Hannemann, U. Haß, & J. Schäfer, eds., *Episteme des Theaters: Aktuelle Kontexte von Wissenschaft, Kunst und Öffentlichkeit*. Bielefeld, Germany: Transcript, pp. 539–50.

Kreuder, F., Bachmann, M., Pfahl, J., & Voz, D. (2012). 'Vorwort'. In F. Kreuder, M. Bachmann, J. Pfahl, & D. Volz, eds., *Theater und Subjektkonstitution: Theatrale*

Praktiken zwischen Affirmation und Subversion. Bielefeld, Germany: Transcript, pp. 11–18.
Lambek, M., ed. (2010). *Ordinary Ethics: Anthropology, Language and Action*. New York: Fordham University Press.
Latour, B. (2003). 'A Dialog on Actor Network Theory with a (Somewhat) Socratic Professor'. In C. Avgerou, C. Ciborra, & F. Land, eds., *The Social Study of Information and Communications Study*. Oxford: Oxford University Press, pp. 62–76.
Macdonald, S. (2001). 'Ethnography in the Science Museum, London'. In D. Gellner & E. Hirsch, eds., *Inside Organisations: Anthropologists at Work*. Oxford: Berg, pp. 77–96.
Madison, D. S. (2010). *Acts of Activism: Human Rights as Radical Performance*. Cambridge: Cambridge University Press.
Malinowski, B. (1989 [1967]). *A Diary in the Strict Sense of the Term*. Stanford, CA: Stanford University Press.
Malinowski, B. (2005 [1922]). *Argonauts of the Western Pacific: An Account of Native Enterprise and Adventure in the Archipelagoes of Melanesian New Guinea*. London: Routledge, pp. 1–20.
Matzke, A. (2012a). *Arbeit am Theater: Eine Diskursgeschichte der Probe*. Bielefeld, Germany: Transcript.
Matzke, A. (2012b). 'Hildesheimer Thesen V: Das Freie Theater gibt es nicht'. Nachtkritik.de, 21 November. Accessed 11 October 2023. https://nachtkritik.de/index.php?view=article&id=7472.
Mauss, M. (1936). 'Les techniques du corps'. *Journal de Psychologie*, 32, 3–4.
Mauss, M. (1990 [1923]). *The Gift: The Form and Reason for Exchange in Archaic Societies*. London: Routledge.
McAuley, G. (1988). 'Towards an Ethnography of Rehearsal'. *New Theatre Quarterly*, 14(53), 75–85.
McAuley, G. (2012). *Not Magic but Work: An Ethnographic Account of a Rehearsal Process*. Manchester: Manchester University Press.
Miller, D. (1997). *Capitalism: An Ethnographic Approach*. London: Routledge.
Morris, R. C. (1995). 'All Made Up: Performance Theory and the New Anthropology of Sex and Gender'. *Annual Review of Anthropology*, 24, 567–92.
Muñoz, J. E. (2006). 'Feeling Brown, Feeling Down: Latina Affect, the Performativity of Race, and the Depressive Position'. *New Feminist Theories of Visual Culture*, 31(1), 675–88.
Nader, L. (1969). 'Up the Anthropologist: Perspectives Gained from Studying Up'. In D. Hymes, ed., *Reinventing Anthropology*. New York: Pantheon Books (Random House), pp. 284–311.
Nader, L. (2011). 'Ethnography as Theory'. *HAU: Journal of Ethnographic Theory*, 1(1), 211–19.
Ortner, S. (2016). 'Dark Anthropology and Its Others: Theory since the Eighties'. *HAU: Journal of Ethnographic Theory*, 6(1), 47–73.
Oswald, M. & J. Tinius, eds. (2022). *Awkward Archives: Ethnographic Drafts for a Modular Curriculum*. Berlin/Dakar/Milan: Archive Books.

Rabinow, P. (1977). *Reflections on Fieldwork in Morocco*. Los Angeles: University of California Press.

Rae, P. (2018). *Real Theatre: Essays in Experience*. Cambridge: Cambridge University Press.

Reed, S. A. (1998). 'The Politics and Poetics of Dance'. *Annual Review of Anthropology*, 27, 503–32.

Robbins, J. (2013). 'Beyond the Suffering Subject: Toward an Anthropology of the Good'. *Journal of the Royal Anthropological Institute*, 19(3), 447–62.

Rosaldo, R. (1986). 'From the Door of His Tent: The Fieldworker and the Inquisitor'. In J. Clifford & G. E. Marcus, eds., *Writing Culture: The Poetics and Politics of Ethnography*. Los Angeles: University of California Press, pp. 77–97.

Sanjek, R. (1990). *Fieldnotes: The Making of Anthropology*. Ithaca, NY: Cornell University Press.

Sansi, R. (2015). *Art, Anthropology and the Gift*. London: Bloomsbury.

Sansi, R. (2020). 'Introduction: Anthropology and Curation through the Looking Glass'. In R. Sansi, ed., *The Anthropologist as Curator*. London: Bloomsbury, pp. 1–16.

Sansi, R., & Strathern, M. (2016). 'Art and Anthropology after Relations'. *HAU: Journal of Ethnographic Theory*, 6(2), 425–39.

Sax, W. S. (2002). *Dancing the Self: Personhood and Performance in the Pāṇḍav līlāof Garhwal*. Oxford: Oxford University Press.

Schechner, R. (1985). *Between Anthropology and Theatre*. Philadelphia: University of Pennsylvania Press.

Spencer, P. (1985). *Society and the Dance: The Social Anthropology of Process and Performance*. Cambridge: Cambridge University Press.

Spivak, G. C. (1988). 'Can the Subaltern Speak?' In C. Nelson & L. Grossberg, eds., *Marxism and the Interpretation of Culture*. Basingstoke: Macmillan Education, pp. 271–316.

Sundén, J. (2003). *Material Virtualities: Approaching Online Textual Embodiment*. New York: Peter Lang.

Taussig, M. (2011). *I Swear I Saw This: Drawings in Fieldwork Notebooks, Namely My Own*. Chicago: University of Chicago Press.

Thornton, R. (1988). 'The Rhetoric of Ethnographic Holism: "Postmodernism" and the Social Reproduction of Texts'. *Cultural Anthropology*, 3(3), 285–303.

Tinius, J. (2015a). 'Between Professional Precariousness and Creative Self-Organisation: The Free Performing Arts Scene in Germany'. In N. Dockx & P. Gielen, eds., *Mobile Autonomy: Exercises in Artists' Self-Organisation*. Amsterdam: Valiz, pp. 171–93.

Tinius, J. (2015b). 'Institutional Formation and Artistic Critique in German Ensemble Theatre'. *Performance Research*, 20(4), 71–7.

Tinius, J. (2016). 'Rehearsing Detachment: Refugee Theatre and Dialectical Fiction'. *Cadernos de Arte e Antropologia*, 5(1), 21–38.

Tinius, J. (2017a). 'Anthropologische Beobachtungen zu künstlerischer Subjektivierung und institutioneller Reflexivität: Das Theaterprojekt Ruhrorter mit

Geflüchteten am Theater an der Ruhr'. In M. Wartstat, F. Evers, K. Flade, F. Lempa, & L. Seuberling, eds., *Applied Theatre: Rahmen und Positionen*. Berlin: Theater der Zeit, pp. 205–35.

Tinius, J. (2017b). 'Art as Ethical Practice: Anthropological Observations on and beyond Theatre'. *World Art*, 7(2), 227–51.

Tinius, J. (2018). 'Capacity for Character: Fiction, Ethics, and the Anthropology of Conduct'. *Social Anthropology/Anthropologie Sociale*, 26(3), 345–60.

Tinius, J. (2020). 'Die Ethnografie als Methode der Theaterwissenschaften?' In C. Balme & B. Szymanski-Düll, eds., *Methoden der Theaterwissenschaften*. Tübingen, Germany: Narr Francke, pp. 315–36.

Tinius, J. (2021). 'The Anthropologist as Sparring Partner: Instigative Public Fieldwork, Curatorial Collaboration, and German Colonial Heritage'. *Berliner Blätter*, 83, 65–85.

Tinius, J. (2023). *State of the Arts: An Ethnography of German Theatre and Migration*. Cambridge: Cambridge University Press.

Tinius, J., & Wewerka, A., eds. (2020). *Der fremde Blick. Roberto Ciulli und das Theater an der Ruhr*. 2 vols. Berlin: Alexander Verlag.

Turner, V. (1970). *The Forest of Symbols: Essays on Ndembu Ritual*. Ithaca, NY: Cornell University Press.

Turner, V. (1986). *The Anthropology of Performance*. New York: Performing Arts Journal.

Weber, C. (1967/8). 'Brecht as Director'. *TDR: The Drama Review*, 1, 101–7.

Weiner, J. F. (1996). 'Introduction: Aesthetics Is a Cross-Cultural Category'. In T. Ingold, ed., *Key Debates in Anthropology*. London: Routledge, pp. 251–4.

Wihstutz, B., & Hoesch, B., eds. (2020). *Neue Methoden der Theaterwissenschaft*. Bielefeld, Germany: Transcript.

PART III

Interpreting

Pluralistic critical reflection on collected information is often necessary in theatre and performance studies (TaPS) because performance represents and expresses culture, generating new realities, and there are many ways this can be analysed (see Table I.1). Study of performance engages factors that exceed or elude direct experience, individual observation, immediate understanding, and 'capture' or recording for posterity (whether by film, digital tools, writing, or memory). The characteristics of a given performance may be conducive to specific approaches (such as semiotics or discourse analysis), but to address anything about who made the performance, why they made it as they did, who attended and what their reactions mean, and how location impinges on what is made and how it is received begs a host of approaches. These include critical race theory, Indigenous studies, feminism, and queer theory in combination with methodologies such as materialism, philology, phenomenology (reception), and affect studies. Performance research scales up and down quite readily, but regardless of whether a micro or macro study is being pursued, the ways that research is conducted are complicated by cultural transfer, shifts in power and authority to define performance, and the precarity of peoples. Methodologies will modulate and combine accordingly.

Additionally, when aesthetic traditions, cultural situations, and economic and political elements are important to contextualizing a performance, interpretive traditions may call for analysis that re-engages *through* performance, thus multiplying the skills, methodologies, and means of engagement needed to account for elusive registers. As the discussion on 'archives and embodiment' in Chapter 11 shows, archival research is always already interpretive, yet researchers can creatively engage with and remediate sources, in both exploratory and performative phases of research. As a trained classical musician, Adrian Curtin scored what he heard on a recording so it could be studied at leisure. Prarthana Purkayastha used reconstructive methods when studying nineteenth-century English images of nautch dancers, moving her body in a dance-based enquiry to 'experience the limitations' of a moment incongruously represented by visual sources. And in meLê yamomo's performative presentation of the ontology of European collections of early twentieth-century Southeast Asian sound recordings, he performed as one of two 'museum guards' in an installation of sonic playbacks: this continued his act of interpretation in public performance, 'decolonizing' archival holdings by featuring ways that their interpretability depends on cultural insiders. In each case, and at all phases of research, ontologies are questioned, juxtaposed, and expanded through methodologies that explore critical difference. These approaches, by performance-trained specialists who subvert the overdetermination of archival collection, storage, and access, underscore history as a critical practice and avoid connecting dots in any way that is inevitable. Such remediations require creativity and ingenuity in tandem with ongoing self-awareness and evaluation to ensure rigour and fidelity. In yamomo's terms, they allow for flexibility in exploration, especially suited to performance researchers with skills in music, dance, and acting or directing; languages and dialects; and cultural knowledge.

Researchers themselves are not necessarily the (re-)performers. Anke Charton describes efforts to assemble primary and secondary accounts of a 'lost' practice with a fragmentary and disputable performance genealogy that entangles Black identity with a history of slavery and cultural appropriation by whites. The *canario* originates in a period before the Canary Islands were colonized, was possibly created on the islands and then eventually (presumably) carried by enslaved populations to Europe, and later transformed into (or perhaps inspired) an early modern European court dance of the same name. This court dance was an exoticization of both slave and peasant cultures, the formal characteristics of which may be traceable in texts, images, and scores. This case study emphasizes how the methodology of performance genealogy can be fraught: sources devolve from sites of power *about* a subaltern diasporic people. Charton's parallel case features choreographer Bintou Dembélé's company Rualité performing in *Les Indes Galantes*, a French baroque *opéra ballet* revived in 2019. This recapitulates the framework of seeking Black identity in a different context, allowing the modern subjectivity of Blackness to speak back through hip-hop. Charton combines content analysis and formalist readings of early evidence to investigate degrees of felicity in performance contexts where the performance makers' standpoints are paramount for conveying claims about cultural specificity and fidelity.

Tony McCaffrey was initially a performer in the Christchurch-based Different Light Theatre, and remains a company member. From this stance, he is a participant observer in preparatory and performance processes at the theatre, which identifies itself as a 'mixed ability theatre company'. The central provocation from neurodiverse participants is that the company generates *beformance* (writing before performance): positionalities of knowledge and the immanence of research in group activities and solo improvisations. This challenging methodological problem of the time or timing of the instantiation of performance and interpretation in relation to the moment of research/encounter/insight may pervade all performance, yet it is acute in this case because different processes of participation run simultaneously among learning-disabled actors and other company members. Neurodiverse company members' positionalities of knowledge are open-ended in time and in the process of co-production. For McCaffrey, the methodological challenge is to account for the truth or reality of the call and response of bidirectional lead-taking that occurs when generating performance, and that is complicated by the temporal disjunction between performance and the research situation.

Katerina Teaiwa's trans-pacific engagements with dance guide her understanding that neither embodied experience of a cultural form nor archival research precede or take precedence over the other. Performative knowledge is coextensive/co-emergent with life as a member of the diasporic Banaba people, whose island at the westernmost point of Kiribati was devastated by corporate phosphate mining. Teaiwa describes how her study of the mining engaged field methods, but she radically critiques the premise of ethnographic anthropology. She makes a compelling case for what it is like to live in the cosmology of the Pacific, undoing a differentiation (established elsewhere in this book) of research processes, sitedness, and exteriorized loci of knowledge that is inimical to her practice and worldview. Her practice is collectively inscribed, even if she pursues it alone: it is informed by Pacific values of reciprocity and is *for* the Pacific. All the complexity of memory, culture, and place is held within dance and the transmission of dance. Thus, she teaches culture through dance and has curated an exhibition that is part of her ongoing experiential, performative, and interactive research.

The final conversation concerns 'complexity' in the sense of conveying and interpreting information through language. Ruthie Abeliovich, Leo Cabranes-Grant, and Soo Ryon Yoon emphasize that what is seen or heard in an archive, or what is collected as oral history, is embedded in and with kinds of knowledge that the researcher attempts to broach. There can be many kinds of fissure between performances, their documentation, the documentation's preservation, and other lines of transmission. As in

Abeliovich's work on early sound recordings of Jewish artists, the aftermath of genocide can make the work urgent, just as the objects' metadata in multiple languages can complicate identification. For Yoon, being a Korean studying the work of West African dancers who have appeared in Korea can mean that oral testimony reaches her through multiple translations, and 'fragmentation that demands other sensibilities' guides her approach. Leo Cabranes-Grant describes working with multiple languages on a document that is translocational and heavily freighted as a version of colonial Mexico, a syncretic culture mediated in a syncretic way. Finding a way to scope these types of complexity results in multiple, and mixed, approaches.

CHAPTER 11

Methodologies Dialogue: Archives and Embodiments

Adrian Curtin, Prarthana Purkayastha, and meLê yamomo

Suggested Reading

Curtin, A. (2014). 'Hearing Affectively: The Noise of Avant-Garde Performance'. In A. Curtin, *Avant-Garde Theatre Sound: Staging Sonic Modernity*. New York: Palgrave Macmillan, pp. 177–98.

Purkayastha, P. (2019). 'Decolonising Human Exhibits: Dance, Re-Enactment and Historical Fiction'. *South Asian Diaspora*, 11(2), 1–16.

yamomo, m. (2019). '"Sometimes You Only Have to Listen…": About the Sonic Entanglements of Our Colonial Past'. Interview by S. Donath. *Textures*, 10 December. Accessed 11 October 2023. www.textures-platform.com/?p=4975.

Paul Rae: Why did you choose the writings you did, and what do they tell us about you as researchers, and about the things you research?

Prarthana Purkayastha: I research dance and performance practices that are either from or connected to the Indian subcontinent. This often involves visiting archives in India or the United Kingdom to conduct dance-based analysis of written or documented historical records, including dance-drama texts, films, letters, and performance reviews. It also includes conducting ethnographic fieldwork in India, which involves meeting with or interviewing performers and other respondents who are associated with the areas of my research, and observing dances both on and off the stage. Sometimes, the lines between ethnography and archival research get blurred. For example, in my current research (Purkayastha, 2021), I have studied the personal archive of a twentieth-century Bengali courtesan, Indubala Dasi, by visiting her home in the red-light district of the city of Kolkata. My research method therefore requires an openness to finding archives within the ethnographic site and as part of the ethnographic encounter, outside of formalized or institutionalized archives.

I've also relied on embodied memories of dancing some of the repertoires I've written about: this was the preferred method employed in my first book, *Indian Modern Dance, Feminism and Transnationalism* (Purkayastha, 2014). In my current book project, which incorporates the 'suggested reading' article on decolonizing human exhibits, the process of researching has been quite different. It has involved a lot of spectatorial wonder and curiosity in encountering the visual traces of dancers, when faced with the impossibility of either witnessing embodied repertoires that may have survived or reading written evidence of such repertoires. I'm discovering and writing about minoritarian figures in India in the nineteenth and early twentieth centuries, which is quite challenging because their practices were either erased by or submerged within dominant historical narratives. Again, there is dance-based analysis of primary resources, close reading of images found in visual and material archives in India and Britain, but also some imaginative leaps when faced with archival silences: working out through the body, and through *my* body at times, the possibilities that the historical figures I've been encountering in the archives mobilize.

meLê yamomo: I've been thinking a lot about the formats through which we relay information and the knowledge that we gather, and that is the reason I chose a conversation for my selected reading. My research project is about sounds – specifically, conducting sound history as a decolonial strategy. The standard model in our discipline of single authorship provides insight from a very specific position that we sometimes universalize: the individual whose observations arise in the silence of their own thoughts. I thought that showing this conversation as a modality could provide insight not just into the way that I'm thinking but also into what transpired between myself and Stefan Donath, who interviewed me. Similarly, I authored an article with Barbara Titus, a historical musicologist, where we specifically designed the layout so that there are two texts running in parallel, and we gave some introduction to readers about their role in deciding how to read this as a kind of decentring of the linear, single-author format (yamono & Titus, 2021).

Adrian Curtin: The writing I selected is from my book on avant-garde theatre sound. I research how sound and music are textually encoded in play texts, how theatrical productions sound, and how audiences hear and interpret performance as part of their holistic experience. My project on avant-garde theatre sound was my first major attempt at this kind of work. I focused on the historical theatrical avant-garde of the late nineteenth and early twentieth centuries, determining how their aesthetic experimentation – with regard to sound and language, noise and music – was connected to the modernity of the period. This involved consideration of audio-phonic technologies, such as the telephone and the gramophone, and the noise of the urban metropolis. Following that project, I have researched more recent examples of theatrical sound design, other elements of 'modern/ist' drama and theatre, and, more recently, the representation of Western classical music and its connections with theatrical performance. There are methodological constants in all my research projects: historiography, textual analysis, performance analysis, reception analysis, close listening.

Paul Rae: Do you all do performance history, period? Or do you do something that other theatre and dance historians do not?

Adrian Curtin: My approach is similar to that of other theatre historians – working with archives, analysing sources, questioning received narratives, proffering alternative accounts of the theatrical past. As sound and music are often my principal objects of study, I draw on my musical education to analyse scores and recordings, when these items are available. I think some theatre scholars shy away from analysing musical elements of performance because they lack formal musical education or training, so they're afraid of 'getting it wrong', which is unfortunate. This has led to musical aspects of theatre being relatively under-researched. The same is true of theatre sound. Until the last few decades, we haven't had a sophisticated vocabulary for analysing sonic phenomena. I would say that methods for analysing theatre sound – especially examples that pre-date sound-recording technology – are still being tested, and some are still being dreamed up. Can we meaningfully reconstruct the sonic environments of theatrical performance? Can we 'listen back' to what audiences in the past might have heard, perhaps using historical phenomenology or what Konstantinos Thomaidis (2021), in his current research project on ancient Greek theatre, is calling 'vocal archaeology'? What kinds of evidence can we use? Can we use our own bodies, our own voices? What other disciplines can we engage with? How can we use the evidence at our disposal – including, but not limited to, scripts – to 'sound out' past performances as well as a play text's imaginative potential? In doing the latter I try to think like a sound designer: What possibilities does a dramatic text afford? How can I access a play text's 'acoustic imaginary'? This involves analysing a dramatic text as a literary object, which is something I think theatre historians have tended not to do on the whole. My modus operandi has typically involved combining literary analysis with performance historiography and analysis of sound recordings, musical scores, visual artwork, and other archival materials.

Tracy C. Davis: Adrian, I think you've thrown down a gauntlet because it's true there's been a shift away from doing dramatic analysis: we kind of forgot to educate a generation to do it. Yet I think there's an assumption that if one is studying the history of theatre, one knows how to do dramatic analysis and then other things on top.

Adrian Curtin: One might assume that dramatic analysis is straightforward, but play texts are ontologically complex, even if the ideology of print makes them seem stable. There is a lot to consider about the text-performance relationship that is missed unless one attends to the multiple ways in which play texts can be conceived (e.g. as a blueprint for performance, as a potential record of performance, as a compositional score, as a literary document, as an 'intertext', as a work in progress, and so on). Our approaches to analysing dramatic text are not always as sophisticated as our approaches to analysing performance, but they should be.

Tracy C. Davis: You all conduct research in archives. What happens when you're there?

Prarthana Purkayastha: The archives become spaces of encounter with historical subjects, and those encounters are often incomplete or tantalizing, particularly when minoritarian figures such as unknown nautch dancers are the focus.[1] Information on these figures can be extremely hard to locate, or when present can be slight (even with keyword searches). For my current research, I drew on the historiographic work of African American studies scholar Saidiya Hartman (2019). She uses the method of 'critical fabulation' in conjunction with archival research on African American figures from the period of transatlantic slavery or in US ghettoes at the start of the twentieth century. Hartman identifies archival silences and then builds fictional narratives that address them. Dance scholar Melissa Blanco Borelli (2016) uses a method close to Hartman's in her book *She Is Cuba: A Genealogy of the Mulata Body*, where she crafts a genealogy of the *mulata* body through historical fiction. This is done by paying close attention to the corporeal possibilities presented by the *mulata* in the archive. I am also deeply indebted to and inspired by dance studies scholars such as Priya Srinivasan (2012) and Ann Cooper Albright (2007), who bring embodied approaches to historiographic research in their books *Sweating Saris* and *Traces of Light*, respectively.

When in the archives, I try to find as much as possible on a particular historical subject, but sometimes I also meet fictional characters, such as archetypal courtesans represented in nineteenth-century visual print culture. I assemble these diverse kinds of information, factual and fictional, and start looking for transversal connections. I identify gaps. There has to be something missing that intrigues you, that pulls you into the archive in the first place, and that often doesn't satisfy you even *after* you've been to the archive. This dissatisfaction can actually be quite productive later in the research process, when one starts to write.

meLê yamomo: I conducted my doctoral project as part of Christopher Balme's 'Global Theatre Histories' project, which emphasized theatre history as a global enterprise intrinsic to colonial, imperial, and commercial realms. This provided me with an opportunity to question the fact that many archives are built within a nationalist frame, and most histories are based on what exists first in the national archives. We tend to talk about 'Philippine musicians', for example, but the word 'Filipino' did not exist until the twentieth century, when the Philippines became an independent nation. Prior to 1946, these musicians disappear from the archive because they were not called Filipinos: you have to think according to the colonizers' logic, which was based on systems of documentation and border control. During the nineteenth century, most musicians who travelled overseas were called 'Manila musicians' because they were logged in to official documents based on their last port of exit. Realizing this, I could start to listen in-between imperial structures. In passport applications held at the National Archives of the Philippines, many indicated their birthplaces and hometowns (listed separately) to be villages or municipalities in provinces or islands hundreds of kilometres from the city of Manila. The other place where I found musicians was the colonial police archives. The police constantly raided the theatres, and in the police records I could hear the subaltern trying to respond to the imperial forces.

So I asked myself: If subalterns are absent from the written archives and text-based 'history', would they be present in sound? This is why I wanted to include recordings among my sources. This is also why I ended up locating different sound archives around the world: listening to colonial recordings became a strategy to listen to how the subalterns performed their agency.

Tracy C. Davis: meLê, let's say you have an object – a recording – you can hold up and proclaim as a material object. It has, perhaps, a closer relationship to the artist who's recorded on it than some of Prarthana's chromolithographs might have, or certainly a digital print of a chromolithograph iterated over several generations of successive technologies. Please describe how this 'closeness' is still complicated.

meLê yamomo: I found sound recordings in Berlin; they ended up in there because Germans had both the technology to make recordings and the capacity to store them. A postcolonial historiographic strategy therefore requires a comparative approach: being able to speak both the language of the empire (the colonial epistemology) and the language or languages from which these cultures are taken, to broach their conditionality. This sitting in-between is a *différance*: I try to understand the materials yet postpone arriving at conclusions about them. In doing so, I also ask what this purposive interruption to my cognitive haste (and intellectual habits formed by my Eurocentric academic training) reveals in the colonial entanglements of my own knowledge-making processes. This also accounts for why I have taken my archival materials onstage to perform *with* them. For example, in the 2019 *Echoing Europe*, which I composed and directed, I created a 'museum' of historical sound equipment, media, and recordings in the main hall of Berlin's Theatre Ballhaus Naunynstraße (Figure 11.1). In an attempt to listen, I didn't speak at all; I just let the material 'speak' so as to see what happened with the audience. In most Western European cities, many of the security guards who take care of all these ethnological objects are people of colour who are not allowed to speak about these objects, even though they are probably the best suited to speak. Costumed as a security guard, I performed this act of being in (silent) proximity to the objects, and in this silence something transpired. It was usually the white male audience members who couldn't stand the silence; they wanted to at least click their tongues, to speak over something. For me, these were moments of historical but also philosophical reflection on how I relate to the archive.

Tracy C. Davis: To sum up, using performance within a research process can lay bare a relationship of historiographic thinking, awareness, reflection, and intervention in relation to the work done in an archive. One might think about this *while* working in the archive. One might think about this *after* researching in the archive. Our remit in this conversation is to focus on research as if it is a discrete phase, though that's not always how it works: the research phase isn't always neatly demarcated from the writing up – or, as meLê highlights, *presentation of insights*.

Adrian Curtin: I think back to my project on avant-garde theatre sound, which involved some archival work. As it happened, I didn't find many relevant sound recordings for the particular performances I was researching. I initially found that vexing because I thought recordings would necessarily be superior sources of information about the sounds of performance than would information provided in play texts, reviews, and other

Figure 11.1 A scene from *Echoing Europe – Postcolonial Reverberations*, created by meLê yamomo, 16 May 2019, and produced by Kultursprünge at Ballhaus Naunynstraße gemeinnützige GmbH, financed by the State of Berlin, Senate Department for Culture and Europe. Photo by Zé de Paiva.

documentary evidence. The few recordings I was able to use were also challenging because I realized how easy it was to misinterpret the evidence, or to imagine that just because I was listening to recordings that I knew were used in a production seventy or eighty years ago, I was then able to understand what a historical audience might have made of them. Ways of hearing – how we interpret what we hear – are as much cultural as they are physiological: we have a habitus of listening by which we are encultured and entrained. I can't hear something in the way that someone heard it eighty or ninety years ago because I've heard jazz and they haven't, or because I am familiar with the work of John Cage and they weren't. My parameters for what constitutes sound and music or noise could be very different from those of a historical audience.

I remember listening to the recording of music and sound cues composed by Roger Désormière for Antonin Artaud's production of *The Cenci* (Théâtre des Folies-Wagram, Paris, 1935). I have a vivid memory of sitting in the Bibliothèque nationale de France (BnF) and wondering to myself: What am I hearing? It wasn't clear how the cues related to specific parts of the production. But also, how could I interpret it, especially in the context of how the cues might have been received originally? I had only budgeted a day or two at the BnF and hadn't planned what I would do once I heard the recording (a rookie error). I didn't have access to the recording outside of the archive, and I wasn't allowed to make a copy of it. I thought, 'well, I'll just write down whatever comes to mind'. And then I thought: 'how can I annotate this in a way that's going to be useful to me when I leave?' I had to somehow record data in a way that was going to be useful for me later, so I made written observations and used music manuscript paper (which, thankfully, I had with me) to transcribe cues.

While there, I intuited that there was something about one cue in particular that was curious and provocative, but it wasn't until I created my own version of the cue later on, using a music software program, that I began to get a better sense of what had caught my ear. My reconstructed version of what I had heard in the archive and transcribed onto paper (therefore, twice mediated) brought Balinese gamelan music to mind. I think that's what caught my attention in the archive, but I didn't identify it upon first hearing it. And perhaps I needed to recreate the cue for myself, afterward, in order to make the connection (I had played in a gamelan ensemble as an undergraduate). Doing something creative with my research notes – 'musicking' (with) them – was instrumental to my analytical process. I hadn't realized that until now (Small, 1998).

I don't know for sure that Désormière was trying to evoke Balinese music with this cue, but Artaud was famously inspired by a performance of Balinese dance theatre he witnessed at the Paris Colonial Exhibition of 1931, so it seems like a reasonable hypothesis (assuming conversation between them). And it helped me make an argument about the production's sound design, which was that the audience's 'habitus of listening' likely did not allow them to make sense of the designed sonic elements in the way Artaud had intended. Would they have heard gamelan music or gamelan-inspired music before? Not necessarily and probably not. I don't claim to have offered a definitive interpretation of the sonic components of the production. I don't think one can ever do that. I agree with meLê that archival items, such as sound recordings, invite perpetual re-hearing by differently situated listeners. We should resist the urge to pin down their meaning authoritatively, once and for all, as though semiosis is always stable and decipherable. But that shouldn't dissuade us from speculating about potential meaning.

Ultimately, the paucity of relevant, specific recordings from this period forced me to look for traces of sound and aurality elsewhere. Could I analyse the 'sight' of sound in visual illustrations, the sight of hearing in paintings and illustrations? Richard Leppert's (1993) book *The Sight of*

Sound: Music, Representation and the History of the Body was instructive in this regard. Could I analyse examples of how people interpreted what they heard in literature or other kinds of texts? (Schweighauser, 2006). Broadening the scope of my research forced me to be more imaginative about the sources I could use. When you're investigating topics such as sound and voice, you can find traces or correlates of their existence and operation in different and unexpected places. You have to follow the trail and (strategically) depart from it.

Tracy C. Davis: Adrian described how mediating the sources he engages can approximate historical specificity yet also clock awareness about distinctions in his habitus. Prarthana, how might that pertain to your thinking about the social meanings of movement? How do you negotiate the habitus when corporeality – including your own corporeality in approaching dance forms – is central to your thinking process?

Prarthana Purkayastha: When I was poring over an illustrated sketch of two nautch dancers within a human exhibit in nineteenth-century London, it was my habitus – my training in Indian dance – that allowed me to see the stark differences between them. My eye was caught not only by the dancer holding her veil and turning (she seemed to be in North Indian kathak-style attire, in gathered leggings, a long flared skirt, and a long scarf), but also by the one seated (who was in a sari). I had made a note that this looked a bit odd. Many weeks later, it was at the City of Westminster Archives, when I was staring at a document titled 'List of Indian Natives', that my suspicions were confirmed. For the first time, I had the names of the exhibited Indians, and the nautch dancer in the veil (Sahina Jayabanoo) was from North India, while the one in a sari (Sheeta Thayi) was from the South. So the habitus allows for certain intuitions in the archival research process.

The habitus also helps me invest in the durational process that constitutes archival work. It can be physically taxing, disorientating, and exhausting to trawl through archival material, whether textual or iconographic. It's really hard to assemble an image of what the movements might have looked or felt like in the reading rooms of the British Library or the National Archives at Kew. I often have to curb the urge to get up and embody a gesture or posture. But rehearsing the gestures or postures in the privacy of my home is very much part of the research process. My intention in assembling these moments of the subaltern nautch dancer's performance is not to represent her movements in any 'authentic' way: I don't think I can, and I don't think I want to, because that would mean appropriating and aestheticizing a traumatic moment from the subaltern subject's history. Instead, embodiment becomes a process of sense-making, without the desire to turn this into a show or spectacle.

Adrian Curtin: I'm interested, Prarthana, in when you go from having surveyed what is available in the archive, being confused or disoriented by what you are seeing and aren't seeing, and then deciding that the best move is to undertake embodied engagement yourself and create performance as a way of finding out more. I've had the impetus to create something in order to understand archival material better, and to reconstruct it for myself, but I have wondered whether my creative act is telling me something I can reliably use as part of my scholarly enquiry. I'd be interested to know more about the embodied research you have done.

Prarthana Purkayastha: I was working with a visual sketch of the nautch dancers, and it did not match the written record, which stated that spectators in London were disappointed because the Indian dancers wore winter wear while performing. I was attracted to that mismatch. I'd read Saidiya Hartman and had come across the idea of the colonial archive as a place of fiction at times, which can be quite liberating for a woman of colour scholar because then the archive can become a site of possibility, of creativity. Thus, a part of my research method – which in hindsight perhaps may be called kinaesthetic approximation – involved wearing similar items of clothing to understand and experience through my body what the nautch dancers would have felt like in that exhibition space in London and how they could have moved. When I put on boots and a heavy coat it was impossible to do a *chakkar* (a pirouette or spin). I was not trying to recreate the nautch performance or attempting to give an air of authenticity to a history of violence. It was primarily to experience the limitations of that moment, and to present a different visual image than what the nineteenth-century illustration gives us of the nautch dancer.

I normally recreate discovering this insight in a lecture that I present by reading from a written paper, alongside a presentation with visual illustrations of the dancers, archival images of the letters from their legal battle against their producers in London, and newspaper articles featuring these dancers. I wear a layered costume and take off items as I proceed. Performance as a research method reveals what the image doesn't tell us.

Tracy C. Davis: You've all described things that we might all recognize, having worked extensively in archives: that the expectation upon entry is often thwarted; how exhausting it is to research in an archive all the hours that you are allowed in; and the need to redirect oneself, so that what one thinks one is seeking is never found. You also alluded to archival breakthroughs: not so much the 'aha, now it's all clear', but rather that sense of sweeping away one's expectations and needing to start fresh. Perhaps archives make us confront our own assumptions?

meLê yamomo: We assume that how we want to tell history now is how the archive organizes its materials. I kept assuming there would be a theatre history section in national archives, but that never exists. Only once you fully internalize how the colonial structure operated can you think beyond it. For example, while working on my dissertation, I was researching at the National Archives of Singapore for three weeks, getting more and more frustrated. I was going through microforms, some of which are digitalized, so I would use keywords to search. The last day that I was there I got desperate. I thought: 'I cannot go back to my dissertation supervisor in Munich and say I spent this much time and money without any discovery.' There were certain corridors of the archive that I did not enter because I just assumed that I would not find anything useful there – the fire department, the police department – yet out of desperation I decided to give them a try. It was in the police records that I finally found a lead: the state was trying to control the theatre artists. Looking in the fire department I realized that theatres were among the most flammable buildings of the nineteenth century, and therefore most of the reports about the theatre would be with the fire department. These are things that you learn by going to archives and creatively persisting. So after I found one clue in Singapore I could fly back to Manila with a name and a date; then I could go to the archives in Manila and find another clue there; then go back to Singapore or to Kuala Lumpur.

I returned to Germany with two terabytes of scanned materials. Yet I couldn't simply start writing, because how do you now work with all this? The process continued. I realized I did not want to tell the colonial history of theatre and opera in Southeast Asia essentially as a footnote to opera and theatre history. First and foremost, I was interested in how this was experienced by the subaltern. My question shifted towards sound epistemology. How did they hear these performances? By examining the police and fire control archival documents, I found a window into how the visiting European theatre and opera performances were being perceived by the locals. In Manila, I learned that policemen were being hired by the opera companies to patrol around the opera houses in Manila because the *indios* (I cannot call them Filipinos because back then they were *indios*),[2] who could not afford tickets, would stand outside and listen to the performances through the windows and 'cracks' in the tropical buildings. Thus, I could hear (and see) them listening.

This insight is also informed by my own embodiment as a Filipino. I did not come from a bourgeois family that went to the theatre. I also experienced this othering, so I could draw from my experience accessing theatre in Manila.

Paul Rae: I wonder, where do methods come in *as* methods? Methodological practice has been inherent to what you've talked about so far. But is 'method' ever a 'thing'? Does it ever come in as a distinct entity either to help or to hinder you?

Adrian Curtin: Practical considerations are worth acknowledging: specifically, time, ability, track record, and confidence level. I have wondered whether I have become more cautious, or perhaps more pragmatic, about the kinds of research methods and methodologies I am willing to employ or propose since finishing my PhD, especially in a grant application. Say I apply for several months' funding to work on a research project. What am I confident I can achieve within that time period? How ambitious should I be? Is it prudent to propose research methods with which I am not familiar? Will assessors believe I am equipped to use the methods I am proposing?

It makes sense to employ research methods one knows well and to refine them continually. This is not to say that one should only ever do what one has successfully done before, because, clearly, that would be limiting and dull. But there is a danger of chasing your tail, so to speak, and not achieving your goal, or not doing so sufficiently well in the time available. I think it's important to identify the research methods one does well (or thinks as much), that one has an instinct for, and that one enjoys, rather than employing new methods on a whim. I say this to PhD researchers. I give them licence to formulate their own methodologies, but I also strongly encourage them to use methods they feel confident with, because the time they have to complete their projects is quite short, especially in the United Kingdom.

Paul Rae: We often take our methods for granted, especially over time. Simply put, we *do* our methods. But every now and then, especially in institutional contexts, we are called upon to explain our methods. What is the relationship between the practice of methods, and their formal articulation?

meLê yamomo: Sometimes we define our methods retrospectively. When we are in archives or are pressed for a deadline, we just let things flow, and much later look back and say: 'that was what I did'. I would like to be able to explicate my methodology for my current research, but I am still developing the strategies for that. The question actually is *when* do you know the method is already being applied? This is important because if we want to decolonize epistemology, we also need to change the methods.

Perhaps the method that I'm looking for is something that I don't have but that a colleague does, and by us sitting together, discoveries arise because of their expertise. I can give an example for this. All over Europe, there are many sound recordings from the colonies, including Southeast Asia. Early in my current research project, I wanted to just go around and collect these materials, but I realized that what I should be doing is using funds to bring in colleagues from Southeast Asia so they could learn what exists. We went on an archival tour. In the Lautarchiv (Berlin) there are sound recordings made during the First World War by Germans recording Malayan, Cambodian, and Indonesian prisoners of war. In one case, a file was labelled 'a Javanese story', despite the shellac disc containing a recording of a man singing. I wondered whether the metadata was in error because the Germans didn't know what they were listening to. I listened to it with Sri Margana, a history professor at Universitas Gadjah Mada in Yogyakarta, Indonesia, and in the middle of the recording he started singing along. It was not a song but a recitation of a fourteenth-century Panji story, which is sung to accompany *tari topeng*, a mask dance from Malang, East Java. I imagine that the recording, when occasionally played by archivists or researchers, might be vaguely understood by its listener, but through Margana's embodied archive the context and meaning of the sound recording were resuscitated and made understandable to us. His grandfather was a *dalang* (shadow-puppet master), so he grew up having been trained to sing these songs. This training enabled him to decode some of the materials.

I call this the *sonus* (yamomo, 2018). To explain this succinctly: sonus is what transpires between a material sound (which can be spoken language, acoustic signals, or music such as an archival audio recording) and a human body, similar to Hans Belting's (2005) notion of the image as what transpires between a picture and a human body. For example: the sonic processes of perception, understanding, and emotion surrounding the US national anthem as it is heard by an American body produce its sonus. When the same song is played to a Filipino, a Russian, or an Iraqi, different soni (plural) transpire. In reflecting on the experience of listening to the archival sound recordings at the Lautarchiv, I think perhaps our bodies do not always have the sonus to interact with the object, and we sometimes need another body – a collaborator – to enable animation of the sonus.

Adrian Curtin: Can that be anybody? Does it have to be a person who has cultural kinship with the historical subjects or objects under investigation?

meLê yamomo: The theory that I've been testing is specifically a cultural connection as a kind of embodied archive. The archive is not just the object, but it requires another embodied archive to reside there for these things to interact, for the understanding to transpire.

Tracy C. Davis: Possibly another way to say that is that different skill sets, and different knowledge sets, allow different methods to be engaged. Earlier in our conversation, the three of you respectively used terms like close reading (e.g. of texts and pictures); close listening (of sound and of scores); and listening in-between. I wonder if we can return to closeness as a method. My position is that while close reading feels like a particular kind of activity, it has to be predicated on certain kinds of knowledge that structure the closeness or structure the reading. For example, does one close read in the tradition of Freudian psychoanalysis? Does one close listen in relation to a subaltern subject position that allows for certain kinds of doubt and questioning about the fidelity of an account or recording? Prarthana and Adrian have backgrounds respectively in literary analysis and performance analysis that predicate traditions that are much more specific than literature or performance: What does that equip you to do?

Adrian Curtin: I think it's about setting up a relationship between you as a researcher and the texts, materials, and objects you are analysing, and particularizing that relationship. Close reading or close listening can't be neutral. You are the one who is doing the interpreting, and everything you bring to it informs your reading. In my case, close listening of a recording will be informed by the musical training I have had in Western classical music and by the reading I have done in sound studies. It will uncover a set of data that I think is valid even if I have interpreted it. It is quite possible that other people with similar training and cultural experiences will derive similar conclusions, so it's not as though my reading is only valid for me, which would be of limited value. This can also involve embodied knowledge: in my case, someone who knows how it feels to play certain musical instruments, to perform for an audience in certain contexts, to have been disciplined and encultured in various ways. All of this can help me get close to whatever it is I am analysing, but, as I've said before, I don't simply suppose that I can directly translate what a historical subject may have experienced. I don't remove myself from the equation. This relates to what meLê was saying about sonus. I know what I bring to the analysis, and I seek to make it transparent.

Tracy C. Davis: You're arguing that close reading/listening is done in relation to the epistemology or epistemologies that an individual brings to the 'doing'. It's equally as disingenuous to say that one 'just' close reads, without necessarily saying what predicates that, as it is to say that one is going to 'decolonize' without having the theoretical knowledge and other kinds of epistemic understanding to bring that about. I think Adrian's, Prarthana's, and meLê's examples demonstrate this distinction.

Paul Rae: I wonder: are methods there to keep us close, or hold us at a distance? Prarthana, in your project there's an intimacy with, sometimes absorption in, the 'objects' of enquiry. When you do your research, is that a breach of some sort – of the membrane that methods are supposed to maintain between us and our materials?

Prarthana Purkayastha: I was also thinking about the words aligned with closeness, and intimacy came up for me as well. Why do I wish to be close to the historical subjects of my research? Why do I desire to breach the distance between me and nautch dancers? There is a gap between the subaltern Indian dancers I am writing about and my own position as a South Asian historian. While I occupy a minoritarian position in my current country of residence (the United Kingdom), I have benefited from some privilege based on class and caste affiliations when growing up in India. In speaking for another subaltern subject, in assembling their history, I am guilty of not shifting the terms of representation.

Yet I desire intimacy with my subaltern subject, which comes from a need to express and act in solidarity with minoritarian struggles such as caste justice movements in India. What I call *corpo-activism*, a concept I am currently developing for my next book, is a use of the body to activate what's hidden in the archive, and I see it as an act of adjacency. Gayatri Chakravorty Spivak's (2010) warnings around ventriloquism point to a danger that I can't ignore: the danger is that in recovering subaltern subjects from the archive, I must recall that bodies like mine were historically used as a weapon to keep those very subaltern subjects in subordinate positions.[3] There is a membrane (between embodying a violent archive and completely representing it as a dance or performance), an ethical concern with power and positionality, that I have to invoke during the research process in order to stop complete absorption. I want to think of my body as a tool that exposes processes of subjugation and the nautch dancer's agency. I return to the archive to search for her insurgent acts, her rebellion, so that we can hear a different historical narrative for nautch: one that doesn't necessarily end in minoritarian tragedy and obliteration but rather highlights moments of sublime minoritarian recalcitrance.

So, the desire for intimacy isn't about absolving myself and my responsibility, but actually about recognizing the role I must play to ensure that subaltern subjects propel and mobilize historical methods and writing. The difference between my research methodology and the other historiographic projects mentioned earlier (from Srinivasan, Hartman, Blanco Borelli, or Albright) is that I have to contend with my own position as a caste-privileged author in recuperating a history of nautch dancers, many of whom came from caste-oppressed backgrounds. In addition to race-based colonialism, Indian cultural nationalism has been responsible for keeping nautch dancers such as Sahina Jayabanoo, Sheeta Thayi, and others like them marginalized in archives.[4] I contend with this history of subjugation, for which the Indian national state is as equally responsible as British colonialism. Therefore, one has to improvise and think about new methods that can allow this complicated set of relationships of intimacy, closeness, and distance to emerge.

Tracy C. Davis: In the lineage of reading closely that devolves from formalism and New Criticism, the claim is to be able to speak on behalf of a self-referential aesthetic object such as a poem (Empson, 1930; Leavis, 1932; Wimsatt & Beardsley, 1946; 1949). 'Closeness' brought the critic to the text, independent of authorial intention (the intentional fallacy) and reader response (the affective fallacy). In contrast, what you're saying is that closeness brings insight into different subjectivities and awareness of how authorship of various kinds intervenes and occludes as well as reveals meanings. Perhaps that is why it is necessary, in all your projects, to look at multiple kinds of evidence (and its generation and preservation history) and be open to places that you'll find it, and ways that evidence will combine, in order to enable you to better distance yourself while seeking that closeness. You strategically regard closeness as a way to reach understanding, yet also the necessity to stand apart.

Adrian Curtin: Like Diderot's paradox of the actor! This reminds me of the fuzzy logic of the research process. One sometimes has to proceed intuitively, without full knowledge or confidence that what one is doing is right. One can begin the writing process without full knowledge of how it will proceed and end; indeed, sometimes one has no choice but to do this. My habit is to plan quite carefully, but usually I find things will only properly 'click' once I begin to write. (And, as a colleague of mine, Kate Newey, likes to remark: writing can be a research method. Or, to put it another way, one continues to 'do' research while figuring things out in writing.) I then wish I were able to re-enter the research phase and re-examine things from the new perspective I have gained. It's not always a linear experience, though: it can be iterative and circling. I am okay with being in a fuzzy state for a while, intuiting that I am bringing things into alignment and making connections.

This is akin to a creative process: it's not all known in advance, pre-planned, and organized. You put yourself into a headspace that allows for associations, and they happen when they happen (*if* they happen!). The process can be messy, but that's okay. Perhaps the reason some of us are hesitant to talk about methods is that we don't always understand how the process works. I don't mean that we are all artists, but there is something similar to how an artist will say: 'well, I don't totally understand my process, but I trust that I'm able to do it'. Carefully examining the process does not mean we will no longer be able to do it. Instead, getting a better understanding of what we do will give us more confidence to proceed in a way where we can think: 'okay, I don't quite have all the answers yet. But I know there's a procedure I can follow and trust.'

Tracy C. Davis: The three of you are at similar career points. You've had the experience of doctoral work where you didn't know whether to trust certain emotional registers of doing research and putting ideas together. But now that you've had that experience you can think about what trusting certain things involves, what it feels like affectively, and how to run with it. It's a bit like getting on your surfboard and riding the wave: it's exhilarating and it's scary and it's what you're there to do, but you're also definitely going to crash at some point. Discipline and experience let you get back up on the surfboard again, sometimes at the right moment and sometimes not. That's how we get better at it.

Notes

1 Popular in the nineteenth century, nautch was an anglicized colonial corruption of the word *naach*, which means 'dance' in Hindi, Bengali, and several other Indian languages. It collapsed a vast range of subcontinental dance practices, including that of hereditary dance practitioners and courtesans. An anti-nautch movement was launched in India in the 1890s, owing to a conflation of nautch with prostitution. It was prompted by a reform and revival movement inspired by colonial missionary discourse and spearheaded by Indian cultural nationalists, who were mostly educated and hailed from upper-class/caste groups. In 1947, the year of India's independence from British rule,

nautch was criminalized by the Prevention of Dedication Act. While the act mainly targeted the hereditary performing communities engaged in ritual dances in temples (often referred to as *devadasis* or servants of gods), it affected a vast population of Indian professional dancers belonging to minoritarian groups, who constituted the heterogenous nautch scene (Chakravorty, 2008; Srinivasan, 1985).

2 In the Spanish Philippine *casta* system, natives of the Philippine islands were referred to as *indios*. Until 1896, the term 'Filipino' referred only to Spanish citizens of European descent born in the Philippines. Outside the Philippines, there did not exist any clear term to refer to the Philippine *indios*. Filipinos who jumped the galleons (Spanish trade ships) in the Americas were called *chinos* in Mexico. Migrant Filipinos in the Dutch Indies were categorized in the general group of Malays. During the nineteenth century's implementation of modern censuses, especially in the British territories, migrant Filipinos began to be recorded in the immigration records as Manila men. In the absence of a nation-state identifier, migrant Filipinos (even those who came from other regions and language groups) were identified with Manila, the emblematic capital of the colony, as a term of reference recognized outside the Spanish Empire. It is in this same light that the Manila musicians were referred to as such.

3 Critiquing Michel Foucault and an 'unquestioned valorisation of the oppressed as subject', Spivak (2010: 27) writes: 'The ventriloquism of the speaking subaltern is the left intellectual's stock-in-trade.'

4 Priya Srinivasan (2012), in *Sweating Saris*, did pioneering archival work in excavating the narratives of unknown and forgotten nautch dancers touring the United States at the end of the nineteenth century. Another important project that has brilliantly critiqued Indian cultural nationalism with its sanitization of classical dance, and focused instead on minoritarian hereditary dance practitioners, is Davesh Soneji's (2012) *Unfinished Gestures*.

References

Albright, A. C. (2007). *Traces of Light: Absence and Presence in the Work of Loïe Fuller*. Middletown, CT: Wesleyan University Press.

Belting, H. (2005). 'Image, Medium, Body: A New Approach to Iconology'. *Critical Inquiry*, 31(2), 302–19.

Blanco Borelli, M. (2016). *She Is Cuba: A Genealogy of the Mulata Body*. New York: Oxford University Press.

Chakravorty, P. (2008). *Bells of Change: Kathak Dance, Women and Modernity in India*. London: Seagull Books.

Empson, W. (1930). *Seven Types of Ambiguity*. Harmondsworth: Penguin.

Hartman, S. (2019). *Wayward Lives, Beautiful Experiments*. New York: W. W. Norton.

Leavis, F. R. (1932). *New Bearings in English Poetry: A Study of the Contemporary Situation*. New York: G.W. Stewart.

Leppert, R. (1993). *The Sight of Sound: Music, Representation and the History of the Body*. Berkeley: University of California Press.
Purkayastha, P. (2014). *Indian Modern Dance, Feminism and Transnationalism*. New York: Palgrave Macmillan.
Purkayastha, P. (2021). 'Outing Pleasure and Indulgence: Indubala's Scrapbook and the Red-Light Dances of Calcutta'. *Contemporary Theatre Review*, 31(1), 14–33.
Schweighauser, P. (2006). *The Noises of American Literature, 1890–1985: Toward a History of Literary Acoustics*. Gainesville: University Press of Florida.
Small, C. (1998). *Musicking: The Meanings of Performing and Listening*. Middletown, CT: Wesleyan University Press.
Soneji, D. (2012). *Unfinished Gestures: Devadāsīs, Memory, and Modernity in South India*. Chicago: University of Chicago Press.
Spivak, G. C. (2010). 'Can the Subaltern Speak?' In R. Morris, ed., *Can the Subaltern Speak? Reflections on the History of an Idea*. New York: Columbia University Press, pp. 21–78.
Srinivasan, A. (1985). 'Reform and Revival: The Devadasi and Her Dance'. Economic and Political Weekly, 2 November, 1869–76.
Srinivasan, P. (2012). *Sweating Saris: Indian Dance as Transnational Labor*. Philadelphia, PA: Temple University Press.
Thomaidis, K. (2021). 'Training as Vocal Archaeology'. Theatre, Dance and Performance Training (blog), 12 April. Accessed 11 October 2023. http://theatredanceperformancetraining.org/2021/04/training-as-vocal-archaeology.
Wimsatt, W. K., & Beardsley, M. C. (1946). 'The Intentional Fallacy'. *The Sewanee Review*, 54(3), 468–88.
Wimsatt, W. K., & Beardsley, M. C. (1949). 'The Affective Fallacy'. *The Sewanee Review*, 57(1), 31–55.
yamomo, m. (2018). *Sounding Modernities: Theatre and Music in Manila and the Asia Pacific, 1869–1946*. Cham: Palgrave Macmillan.
yamomo, m., & Titus, B. (2021). 'The Persistent Refrain of the Colonial Archival Logic / Colonial Entanglements and Sonic Transgressions'. *World of Music*, 10(1), 39–70.

CHAPTER 12

Non-linear Methodologies for Researching Early Modern Performance: The Case of the Canario

Anke Charton

The question of how to approach and speak of the past is essential for any historian, yet in theatre and performance studies (TaPS) historians often research embodied practices that have left few to no conventional traces. For the historian of premodern time periods, the challenges of interpreting scarce, scattered, and poorly accredited sources can be compounded by differences of sensibility and by meaning unique to distant cultures. Dance, in particular, is ephemeral and privileges embodied over logocentric knowledge; it is difficult to notate and even more difficult to reconstruct. How can researchers write about a past that has left little to no direct evidence? How can the little knowledge at hand enlighten a practice rather than further obscure it? I propose methodological approaches to meet this challenge. My example is the *canario*, a popular European court dance of the sixteenth to eighteenth centuries (known by this name in Spain and Italy, as *canarie* in France, and as *canary* in Britain). The *canario* offers a terpsichorean metaphor for researching early modern dance history: non-linear, it is full of twists and turns, leaps and stomps.

The *canario* has left behind few traces, yet by combining approaches that foreground different temporal tethers – present-day experiences, historical sources, and a contextualizing synchronous gaze – I propose modes of access that are unconventional within academic frameworks, kick-starting a connection via a current-day assonance that enhances our understanding of earlier practices. It may even be possible to find non-continuous trace continuities of knowledge in and about embodied practices that people have unwittingly transported across generations. The methodological suggestions I advance address the importance of context and pertain to the self (materiality, positionality, assonance, and resonance), sources (gaps and archives), and time (temporality, historicity, *durée*). As methods, they do not necessarily mix well, but my point is that they do not have to do so.

Different angles, even contradictory ones, can highlight different aspects of a practice and ultimately allow for a different understanding to emerge.

The *Canario*

Canario research is not devoid of sources. Starting with single entries on the *canario* in music encyclopaedias, one can move to dance treatises of the sixteenth and seventeenth centuries, then references in play texts and letters. This builds up a context. Using this, one can then consider historical and geographic scenarios as providers of further, inferred, information on the *canario* and its history.

Indicatively, the *canario* receives three entries in the *New Grove*, the largest Western music encyclopaedia. The longest of these focuses on the *canario* as a musical form, not as a dance practice (Hudson & Little, 2001). Another brief entry defines the *canario* as 'a villancico from the Canary Islands. It is called a Negrilla when it depicts the music, song and dance of the black people of the islands' (Stanford, 2001). The third entry states:

> An old dance from the Canary Islands. It is characterized by jumps, *zapateado* (stamping of the heels) and abrupt, violent choreographic movements, accompanied by fast music with energetic and highly syncopated rhythms. The dance was introduced into Spain as early as the 16th century and became popular on the Continent as the Canary. (Grove Music Online, 2001)

The *New Grove* entries build on preserved music scores, the notated rhythm of which serves as a clue to motion patterns. Specific dance moves are documented in several early modern dance treatises, which allow for current-day reconstructions (Arbeau, 1596; Caroso, 1581; Lupi, 1609; Negri, 1604). These scores and treatises are flanked by copious mentions of the *canario* in other texts, some of which pre-date the treatises and thus enable insight into the *canario*'s trajectory prior to becoming a court dance. In 1594, renowned composer Emilio de' Cavalieri described a performance he witnessed in Rome that featured a priest dancing the *canario* 'in the style of Pedrolino', a famous commedia actor. This letter offers insights into the dancers, audiences, and milieus of the *canario*.

Frequent mentions of the *canario* also appear in play texts (Cotarelo y Mori, 1911: 237), with the earliest written record being in the early sixteenth-century Spanish *Farsa de Sancta Bárbara* by Diego Sánchez de Badajoz (1554: f36r). In this *farsa* (farce), the good and bad deeds of Saint Barbara are weighed before Christ, with commentary by a shepherd. The *canario* is mentioned when Barbara's virginity is listed among her good deeds. The shepherd calls virginity a blessed virtue and assures his audience that few like Barbara would exist in his times, when women better know how to dance – 'más saber baylar' – and bend themselves in the *canario* and similar dances. It is the context of these social and gendered associations that gives a glimpse into the *canario*'s unwritten backstory.

The *New Grove* situates the *canario* as a subgenre of the popular *villancico* folk song and as pattern of the so-called *negrilla*, but neither hold up as origin stories 'from the Canary Islands': in fact, the *villancico* is a Spanish genre with medieval roots that was exported *to* colonized locales including the Canary Islands, a strategic stronghold of the transatlantic slave trade. The Black people of the islands did not originate there but were instead enslaved sub-Saharan Africans. The people indigenous to the islands were the Guanches, an isolated, Neolithic civilization.[1] The late 1300s European invasion led to nearly a century of raids and warfare, until the Canary Islands were annexed by the Spanish Empire in 1496. During this century, the majority of the Guanches were killed or enslaved; enslaved Guanche people became a regular presence in early modern cities such as Madrid, Valencia, and Seville (Trapero, 1993: 48). Guanche survivors on the islands were assimilated into the amalgamated culture of European settlers and enslaved Africans. Research on Guanche practices has to address this rupture: there are no first-hand accounts of Guanche voices. Most knowledge about them is mediated through a colonial gaze, and even current archaeological research is carried out in the framework of later settler culture.

The absence of Guanche voices invites speculation. Jehan Tabourot's early dance treatise *Orchésographie* (published under a pen name) argues that the *canario* was not from the Canary Islands, but instead invented in a French masquerade that fantasized about exotic locales (Arbeau, 1596: f. 95v). This argumentation links the *canario* to the early modern European mirage of the 'noble savage', which was tied not to a concrete geography as much as to an assumed status of civilization (Ginzburg, 2005: 125). Later in this chapter, I engage with an imagined American 'noble savage' setting through Jean-Philippe Rameau's *Les Indes Galantes* (1735), which incorporates the rhythmic echo of a Michigamea chief's dance.

The 'noble savage' trope dominated early European narratives of the Guanches and their practices, as conquest chronicles exemplify (Rodríguez Wittmann, 2018). When the Tenerife-born settler descendant José de Viera y Clavijo (1772: 160) described the Guanche 'Bayle Canario' as lively and expressive, with the beat being stomped out by the feet in 'short and violent movements', he relied on earlier chronicles and the later European practice of the *canario* (Trapero, 1993: 64). By the time Viera wrote his account, the Guanches had long since been killed or scattered into slavery.

Knowledge and practice of what the Spaniards named the *canario* might have persisted among assimilated Guanches, but Viera would not have been able to find it by that designation.

Writing nearly a century after Viera, early ethnographer Sabin Berthelot (1849: 141, 266–7) repeated this pattern. He stated, applying a racializing gaze, that, for the Guanches, dancing was 'one of their favourite pastimes'. He then generalized that this would still be true for the Canarians of his day, ignoring the difference between Guanche culture and that of a later population dominated by European settlers. When Berthelot wrote about the Guanches, he wrote about a civilization with which he had neither direct contact nor first-hand sources. His account relies on the same chain of chronicles dating back to the Norman invasion, ripe with 'noble savage' imagery.

Whereas early modern reception of the Guanches was dominated by the 'noble savage' trope, later linguistic and ethnological approaches banked heavily on racialization, emphasizing the whiteness of the light-skinned Guanches (Schmidt, 1996: 7). For example, the unsustainable white supremacist employment of Atlantis as a place of origin – still present in alt-right Templar myth-building – is already quoted in relation to the Guanches by Viera (1772: 120, 124), who cast the Guanches as non-Semitic. It was again at work in the impactful research of ethnolinguist Dominik J. Wölfel during the 1930s and 1940s. Wölfel (1965) was enmeshed in the anti-Semitic and fascist currents of his day and maintained the colonial term 'White Africa'; he hypothesized about the Guanches as a remnant of a white European megalithic culture (see Schmidt, 1996: 87, 172). While Wölfel correctly linked the Guanche languages to the North African Imazighen, a trajectory of settlement recently confirmed by genomic sequencing (Rodríguez-Varela et al., 2017), he made tendentious guesses based on ideological interests.[2] Ultimately, the link to the Imazighen allows us to place the Guanches as emigrating from today's Mauritania towards the then-uninhabited Canary Islands during the desertification of the Sahara, three thousand to five thousand years ago (Schmidt, 1996: 125–31). The Guanche dance practices, shaped by their culture of origin and by life in their new surroundings, would continue until the European invasion in the fifteenth century. But have these practices endured?

There is no dance called the *canario* on the Canary Islands today, though it was reimported from Spain in the seventeenth century in its appropriated form (Trapero, 1993: 63). Yet there are folk dances practised by local groups that are reminiscent of the stomps and slides described in early modern sources on the *canario*. Berthelot (1849: 99–100), observing customs on the islands in the mid-nineteenth century, wrote of still-present jumps in dances among herders on El Hierro. Yet the name *canario* is not helpful in approaching these dances as it post-dates the Spanish conquest of the islands, effectively muting a Guanche perspective.

In what follows, I argue that mixed methods can illuminate such discontinued and superseded cultural practices. Here, they illuminate how the baroque court *canario* was lifted from cultural performance and fitted into a later cultural framework.

Materiality, Positionality, Assonance, and Resonance

Given the history sketched out above, what methods can help us retrace how 'an old dance from the Canary Islands' turned into highly codified European court fashion? The move from folk dance to elite dance, across racialized and nationalized repertoires, points to a rich and layered history. Yet this history is difficult to access: the primary sources (scores and treatises) only document the later court practice. What we can glean from repeated references in the archives is that the *canario*'s appeal lay in its physicality. It was performed in energetic jumps, stomps, and slides: motion patterns at the margins of a court dance culture primarily concerned with showcasing dexterity, control, and virtuosity (Pontremoli, 2017: 167). Court dance frequently appropriated embodied knowledges across national and continental boundaries; the *canario* is but one example. As a colonial politics, court dance tamed and unlinked the physical expression of othered selfhoods and put the Other on display at the same time, at once present and absent.

If we attempt to trace the dance back to the precolonized Guanches, can we disambiguate the trace of Guanche culture before the imprint of its later adoption? Where, how, and among whom would this trace be locatable? If it is possible to access intangible cultural heritage that may have been conserved over centuries by people unaware of having done so, we need to engage with its embodiments across time. The next step is to ask who danced the *canario* before the courtiers of early modern Europe, and how that practice differed from the later court dance. If we consider how the dance fit into the realities of the dancers' lives, the *canario* becomes a window into early modern shifts along the axes of class and race.

Consider a letter from 1594 that describes a dancing priest during a performance of the Medici court singer Vittoria Archilei:

> Vittoria was in the chambers of the honorable Filippo last night, along with Cusano. She sang a Benedictus, but they wanted to hear Spanish songs, and entertaining ones, of which there were many. And at the end, the honorable Filippo had a priest from the Vallicella church dance a canario in Pedrolino's style. And Vittoria told me that he was excellent and would have to have practiced a lot. (quoted in Palisca, 1994: 397)

The setting mixes the clerical and the secular, the elite and the popular, and though describing an event in Rome rather than on the Canary Islands or in Iberia, the letter gives us clues about the possible trajectory of the *canario*. What happened during an evening entertainment in the (private) chambers of Cardinal Filippo Neri was that two people presented highly physical performances from their position on the margins of courtly society. The first is Vittoria Archilei, one of the first professional early modern woman singers. The second performer is an unnamed priest from Santa Maria in Vallicella (Neri's own parish), who danced the secular *canario*. Moreover, he danced it 'in Pedrolino's style', which the writer of the letter (composer Emilio de' Cavalieri) seemed to expect his readers to recognize, as he gives no further explanation.

Archilei, the court singer, is able to judge the quality of the unnamed priest's dancing and comments that his abilities required frequent exercise. Movements and energy that exceed the regular patterns of court dance – as with Pedrolino's *canario* – are clues to a residue of an older tradition of embodied knowledge that persists in this Roman iteration, which remains ephemeral. Yet instead of emphasizing ephemerality, we might instead think of performance as deeply material and consequential: dependent on embodied lives that extend beyond the stage and bear on realities beyond the moment of performance. Performance, and the lives that produce it, in turn affect and inform each other. While the steps included in a treatise such as Fabritio Caroso's (1581) *Il Ballarino* may seem like abstract instructions – turns and bows not attached to specific dancers – reconstruction, always at the risk of renewed appropriation, shows the range of embodied knowledge that is missing. Instead of looking for what is described, we can instead look for what is absent yet implied. Caroso's steps imply a range of movement that in turn indicates styles of dress and the layout of dance floors. Caroso's manual offers etchings of dancing couples as further clues, but movement patterns and their terminology have shifted as differently habituated bodies characterize successive eras.

If we return to the *canario* in the cardinal's chambers, we can imagine the priest struggling with his cassock as he executes the fast, energetic footwork of the dance. The *canario* 'in Pedrolino's style' capitalizes on the theatrical potential of this excess. Pedrolino refers to the popular commedia actor Giovanni Pellesini, whose mask *in arte* was the zanni Pedrolino (Katritzky, 2006: 248–9). The scenario-based commedia dell'arte (a term later coined by Carlo Goldoni) was a public, itinerant theatre form that relied on slapstick routines called *lazzi* (Hulfeld, 2014: 80–108). These were executed by the zanni, trickster characters whose struggles with hunger, poverty, and low social status were their theatrical capital (Henke, 2007). Apparently, Pellesini, often lauded for his athleticism, made the *canario* part of his routine to a point where a particular style was associated with him: Cavalieri, the letter writer, uses it as shorthand.

Non-logocentric forms of theatrical communication can be helpful in assessing other kinds of marginalized early modern communication patterns that echo through print sources yet cannot be distinctly lifted from them. For example, the physicality of Pedrolino's dance, mediated by a priest, enables engagement of commedia research in the Italian anthropological tradition (Münz, 2010; Taviani, 1991). The athleticism of the outcast zanni who coined Pedrolino's dance – differing from the court *canario* – also implies a physical prowess gained through hard labour. In this, we may recognize not only the menial labour generally attached to the zanni of the commedia, but also a bodily refraction of the enslaved Guanches, who may first have carried the *canario* to Iberia: as people from a Neolithic island civilization without vehicles, they relied on mobility on foot over uneven terrain in their daily life. Just as Caroso's treatise implies dance floors, dress styles, and range of movement, the early *canario* reports imply shards of the Guanches' lived reality. Its imprint on their dance practices likely persisted even when they were moved across climates and continents against their will (Figure 12.1).

Writing about the Guanches – a North African people described by their European contemporaries and later researchers variously as 'noble savages', Neolithic peoples, pagans, and Saracens, as well as both white and Black – has ties to the past as well as to the present (Barker, 2019: 58; Fernández-Armesto, 1987: 180–1, 214; Rodríguez Wittmann, 2018: 291; Schmidt, 1996: 7, 172). The past is not separate from the present, and as a researcher I am tied into this topography in a specific way. The showcasing of physical labour on othered bodies, like forced or coerced labour, is still a reality, and I am embedded in a context that enables it. Addressing my own embodied reality as a scholar serves as a reminder that all research emerges from a positional context that will mark its output. Similarly, a researcher will never stand fully outside of such a framework to realize their research questions. My personal experience and knowledge bear on my work and

Figure 12.1 Image taken from the dance manual *Il Ballarino* by Marco Fabrizio Caroso (1526–1605), engraving, 1581, Italy. Bologna, Civico Museo Bibliografico Musicale (Music Museum). Photo by DEA PICTURE LIBRARY/DeAgostini/Getty Images # 159826856.

shape trajectories when I approach and contextualize sources. Instead of understanding this as limiting in the face of a desired objectivity, I suggest a different, productive methodological response: we can understand this positionality as a chance to contribute a precise and reflective perspective, as modelled by recent developments in auto-ethnography (Adams, 2015; Spry, 2016).

Assonance and Resonance: *Les Indes Galantes*

In research on a dance that is linked to a minority situated at the geographic fringe of a colonial empire and styled as picturesque 'noble savages' by that same colonial power, this situatedness may suggest another methodological angle by which to approach lost knowledge through parallel patterns. In 2019, the Opéra national de Paris (ONP) staged Jean-Philippe Rameau's 1735 *Les Indes Galantes*, an *opéra ballet* full of exoticized cultural settings. It imagines the Ottoman Empire and Persia (to the east of Paris), and a post-Columbian America with Peruvian Incans and Native Americans from the Mississippi Delta (to the west), in ways ripe with the colonial tropes of 'noble savages', fanatic pagan priests, and white saviour fantasies. French baroque *opéra ballet* conveys meaning through both song and dance, however the 2019 production gained acclaim in Western media for how it staged dance. ONP employed street dancers, mainly Black people and other people of colour, from French hip-hop choreographer Bintou Dembélé's company Rualité. As a means of expression, the hip-hop dancers prominently used Krump (or 'Kingdom Radically Uplifted Mighty Praise'). A Black style that developed in the early 2000s out of South Central Los Angeles's 1990s Clowning, it is a highly expressive dance form that grew out of experiences of violence and social injustice (Nereson, 2010; Rose et al., 2021: 236–7). The hip-hop dance challenged the ethos of a predominantly white and bourgeois opera audience, exposing the racist mechanisms of the opera industry. The Krumpers' inclusion in the production made evident the exclusion of people of colour elsewhere, as the singers (all with music college degrees) who performed alongside the street dancers appeared to be white and had traditional French-Romanic names.

Within the production, some scenes resonate with a (post)colonial reality beyond the staging. For example, the second entrée, 'The Incas of Peru', sketches a love triangle between an Incan princess, Spanish invader, and Incan priest. When the princess chooses the Spaniard, the rejected priest causes a volcanic eruption and is then engulfed by it. The role of the vindictive priest was cast against race, played by a white baritone who, preceding the cataclysmic eruption, commanded an increasingly frantic dance carried out by two Black women with long braids: two Black women's bodies were thus singled out in heightened physical labour orchestrated by a white male (ostensibly 'Incan') onlooker for the consumption of an overwhelmingly white audience. The fourth entrée, 'The Savages', portrays a Native American chief's daughter who is desired by a fellow tribe member, a Frenchman, and a Spaniard; she chooses her fellow Indigenous suitor for the unaffected naturalness of his love, echoing the 'noble savage' narrative. While the scene is vaguely set somewhere around Louisiana, it is a white European fantasy, a fact reified in the 2019 casting of white French singers.

For the concluding 'Danse du Grand Calumet de la Païx', the singers moved into the background and gave the Krumpers centre stage. The score of this final dance reaches still deeper into a colonial past: Rameau reused a rondeau for piano written in 1725, likewise called *Les Sauvages*. That year, Chief Agapit Chicagou of the Michigamea, an Illinois nation, had visited Paris along with a royal delegation. As a part of this visit, the chief and his entourage performed a set of dances at the Théâtre-Italien. The echo of this event is imprinted in the music of Rameau, whose rondeau audibly references the rhythm and gravity of the footwork of these dances. Hence Rameau created a repository echo of an idiom he did not speak.

Although the 2019 Paris *Les Indes Galantes* is not at the core of my *canario* investigation, it is pertinent to my discussion of methodology since it allows for a dynamic parallel. There is assonance on a phenomenological level – enabled by my situated gaze – that allows me to conceptualize my research through the resonance caused by comparable material. Both the *canario* and *Les Indes Galantes* concern dancers and dances appropriated into different, dominant cultural contexts. My embodied reality both enables and limits comparison with the *canario* sources and the 2019 Parisian production, yet I want to advocate for what this offers methodologically. If research is always linked to embodied lives – of researcher, researched, and carrier – then the location of an investigation matters as much as does that of a given performance, producing varied assonances and resonances of time and space. In different political and social realities, different aspects of past practices will stand out and connect us as researchers to particular facets of the past and present.

As I write this chapter about accessing a dance – and its resilience – that has been appropriated out of its original cultural and geographic context, and as I rewatch the recording of the 2019 *Les Indes Galantes*, thoughts of the *canario* resound in both. Later iterations of a dance affect our understanding of its earlier manifestations. If lost knowledge can be revived through movement, even in a different cultural setting, it is the agency of the dancers – be it of the appropriated *canario* or of Krump – that mitigates the encounter. Yet this agency remains contingent on how dancers' physicality is regulated and consumed by their audience (Bennett, 1990: 101–3). Both dancers and audiences, given their embodied realities, are tied into a history beyond their specific setting and even before their own lives. Those ties can enable the historian to engage with lost voices, akin to a mathematician being able to formulate an equation with variables.

Both the seventeenth-century courtiers and the twenty-first-century Krumpers at ONP changed the configuration of an older dance, adapting it to suit their own realities, though from different positionalities. Whereas sixteenth-century courtiers (as a colonial elite) co-opted an Indigenous form, the Krumpers of Rualité (as a *banlieue* group, from lower-class environs) offered a postcolonial critique of co-optation per se. In both cases, the interaction between older materials (the *opéra ballet* and the rondeau) and present-day dance styles signified an interaction with a prior knowledge through embodiment, yet it was the postcolonial Krumpers that made the early modern Guanches resonate for me.

The similarities between the *canario* and the rondeau lay in their configuration through a colonial gaze. Likewise, modern stagings interact with distorted early modern documentation of prior embodied knowledge. The methodological question is whether the colonized early dancers of the *canario* can be made visible, not by analysing modern reconstructions of the *canario* but by deducing the *canario*'s characteristics from performance settings inscribed in early modern sources. This implies that the fantasies about the *canario*'s origin and its use in later European geographies may carry, even in the situatedness of their gaze, a reflection of earlier stages of the dance not explicitly recorded in dance treatises or elsewhere. While acknowledging the positionality of their authors, these reflections may result in better-informed guesses about the early *canario*.

Gaps, the Archive, and Temporality and Historicity

Judicious linking between historical materials helps us address a scarcity of sources. If we return to the earliest written reference to the *canario*, in Sánchez de Badajoz's *Farsa de Sancta Bárbara*, the provenance of sources is telling. We know that the Canary Islands were annexed in 1496. The compilation of Sánchez de Badajoz's works was published more than fifty years later, in 1554, with the *Farsa de Sancta Bárbara* written sometime between 1525 and 1547 (Trapero, 1993: 66). Sánchez de Badajoz was an occasional playwright who spent most of his life as a parish priest in his small hometown in the Extremadura, an impoverished rural hinterland in Spain. This means that he did not write for an urban audience, where enslaved Guanches were a common part of the population. Still, the *canario* was apparently popular enough by the 1540s to register for a small-town audience even in the Extremadura. Treatises about the *canario* as court dance first appear another forty years after Sánchez de Badajoz's *farsa*. This sequencing suggests that the *canario* was not disseminated from the courts to the hinterlands, but was instead appropriated by the courts from a prior non-elite practice. This is corroborated in the *farsa* by the shepherd's commentary about the *canario* as a dance incompatible with proper, chaste behaviour (specifically regarding women). Spanish play texts of the later seventeenth century likewise use the *canario* as an indicator of loose morals and low social status (Cotarelo y Mori, 1911: 87–8, 133). Though these are only suggestions of an actual practice, as 'a description … of a dance is not the dance itself', they allow us to approach the dance with dancers' realities in mind (Taylor, 2006: 69). In doing so, they bring us closer to the enslaved and freed Guanche communities of early modern Iberia, whose dances might have been copied, imitated, and appropriated in a milieu of lower standing, away from court.

In historical research, it is sometimes productive to understand a gap between sources as a strategy rather than as an obstacle. This can entail not only enquiring after the story that a gap may represent (such as the time lapse between publications about the *canario*) but also stepping back from cohesive narrative altogether. When shards of information are all we have at our disposal, we may be unable to connect them to a cohesive picture. Carlo Ginzburg (1980: 23) speaks of single threads within a weave. We may be unable to reconstruct the entire cloth (so to speak), but a single thread can remind us that – and why – the weave is unattainable, yet present in its absence. Music historian Beatrix Borchard (2003) calls this 'writing the gaps'. As a researcher specializing in women musicians, she grapples with absences, trying to give visibility and agency to practitioners marginalized by mainstream narratives, keeping the gaps evident and addressing their implications instead of trying to 'fill' them. In the context of TaPS, this might mean noting how material about some people was not considered worth collecting, why some practices were not considered as performance at a given time, or why knowledge has not been passed on in institutionalized forms.

Postcolonial critiques have raised awareness about the epistemological implications of archives' positionality, foregrounding evidentiary absence and archival violence. There are practices and people left out of archives as well as archival practices that mark and objectify people: ways by which people were represented against their will, dehumanized, historicized with others' terminology, and caught in the politics of (in)visibility (Fusco, 2007; Kelly, 1999). Archives are first and foremost mindsets with taxonomical implications imbricated in their holdings (Van Deusen, 2021: 1–3).

Archives are not of much help when we look for the *canario*'s origin. The steps of the fashionable court dance that are referenced in archived materials do not cede access to earlier (undocumented) Guanche forms. Archival sources can neither prove nor disprove a hypothesis, yet in their own right they constitute a hypothesis about a past reality. Methodologically, in addition to understanding sources' provenance, we need to read sources against the grain and beyond themselves, looking for that which is palpable as absence and sometimes bypassing written testimony because of its constraints. Considering performance as part of the archive is a productive approach for TaPS research, as is the general inclusion of other knowledges, embodied or popular (Ginzburg, 1980: 21; Henke, 2007; Schneider, 2001: 101–3).

When Berthelot (1849: 141, 266–7) described the embodied knowledge of dancing as one of the 'favourite pastimes' of the Canary Islands' people, past and present, in his ethnographic chronicle, he imagined a continuity that did not account for the violent shift from Guanche to settler culture. Yet by showcasing folk dance, Berthelot aligns with research in trauma and Holocaust studies into how colonial trauma experienced by Indigenous communities has grown to include multigenerational transfers (Crawford, 2014; Denham, 2008; Fromm, 2012; Jacobs, 2016). This allows for a parallel hypothesis: among assimilated Guanches, transfers of intangible, embodied knowledge and social behaviours, especially when tied into persisting local conditions (such as climate, vegetation, and topographies that influence food, dress, and patterns of movement), might have maintained elements of culture otherwise buried beneath a Christian settler narrative that overdetermined Guanches as the 'noble savage'.

Methodologically, the different historical layers represent decisions about knowledge and transfer across linear time. Performance's unavoidable tether to an embodied present implies the possibility of crossing or queering linear time through embodied actualization of knowledge (Freeman, 2010; Rhee, 2021). Paul A. Harris (2014: 140), writing on the Cretan labyrinth, argues for a synchronous approach across temporal layers. He likens the winding walk through a labyrinth to the bodily experience of time doubling back into itself, and argues that 'a reversible path is drawn between past and present, in which the journey into the past coincides with the past being brought into the present. But at the same time, one could extrapolate this logic to imply that the past is alive in the present.'

Likewise, with the *canario*, we 'brush up against something that represents rituals or functions dating to the Neolithic period' (Harris, 2014: 143). The experience of synchronicity – the non-linear overlap of chronological layers, where we, like Berthelot, might look at nineteenth-century dancers in a specific topographical setting and find medieval dancers – depends on a method with rigorous contextualization. Otherwise, we risk 'mapping the mythic past to the material present' (Harris, 2014: 139).

Researchers of early modern and other performances are bound by the historicity of their research objects. If we research the *canario* as a dance practice of the Guanches, methodological concerns immediately arise with the name: certainly, no Indigenous dance practice on Tenerife or any of the other islands was called *canario* prior to the invasion. The dance – whether it was copied from enslaved Guanches, amalgamated from different Guanche patterns, or simply mimicked by Spanish onlookers – was named by the Spanish colonizers in their language (Trapero, 1993: 50). We have no name to go by to look for the *canario*, or the forms preceding it, before it was called *canario*.

Researchers of early modern performance will share the challenge of looking for practices with names that post-date the time frame they are investigating, for example in finding theatre that was not yet called theatre within an archive's taxonomy. This shifts the methodological attention to the historicity of assigned designations, which concerns the terminology of source materials as much as that of methodological approaches. Meanings and frameworks of terms still familiar have shifted over the course of the past centuries, leading scholars like Quentin Skinner (2002) and Reinhart Koselleck (1979) to formulate a methodology that traces a history of concepts (what Koselleck terms *Begriffsgeschichte*, conceptual history). The historicity of designations, theories, and agendas reminds us that knowledge is a continuous, constituting motion as opposed to a static item that can be collected, added to, and stored away. The following section suggests a way to deal with such shifts.

Durée

With the challenges posed by historicity, research into early modern practices seems daunting. Not only is there a long time period to bridge, but bridging has seemingly no firmly tethered end if the alignment of research objects, taxonomies, and tools is processual instead of fixed. Faced with the question of how we can still grasp the past, we could cite the classic 1975 horror film *Jaws*: 'You're gonna need a bigger boat.'

We might not be hunting a shark that turns out to be much bigger than we expected, but we might be trying to discuss a particular source – a shard, a thread – that turns out to be tied into a much bigger framework. Indeed, one approach is not to narrow our objective down to a single, isolated moment, but to widen the field. If there are only a few sources across a wider time span, we may need to take a step back to find connections on a larger circuit. Widening our gaze – be it in terms of chronology, discipline, or types of evidential material (or experience) – allows us to hypothesize changes and their causes. We can link such an approach to twentieth-century historians Jacques Le Goff and Carlo Ginzburg, whose methodologies are particularly apt for a historiography at the margins. Le Goff's (1994) work with *durée* (coined by Fernand Braudel and disseminated by the Annales school) employs long time spans – the *longue durée* – as a foundation to question the taxonomy of historical epochs. In an opposite move, Ginzburg's (2013: 91) work centres limited geographies, time spans, and even single, everyday biographies – an approach termed microhistory – to investigate people and practices as historical informants about the contexts in which they were embedded. Ginzburg pioneered his approach in work on pre-Christian folk cultures, accessed through the mediated gaze of inquisitorial dossiers.

Both the work with mediated accounts and the concept of *durée* are helpful in historiographical work on marginalized practices. I have established that the *canario* will not reveal its origins through the obvious early modern context of dance treatises and music scores, or their encyclopaedic documentation. However, reading accounts for possible Guanche echoes, and the adoption of a longer time span can return precolonial existence to visibility: late medieval travelogues from Atlantic expeditions that speak of 'naked' people from 'faraway islands' who were singled out for their singing and dancing skills might point to the Guanches (Boccaccio, 1830: 58, 61–2; Rosa Olivera, 1977: 661). But the *longue durée* shifts yet another connection into view: the desertification of the Sahara (Schmidt, 1996: 125–31). It was this geological element that pushed some of the Neolithic proto-Amazigh tribes of Northwest Africa to sail off the coast of Mauritania three thousand to five thousand years ago, resulting in the Guanche culture on the Canary Islands.

The question of how much of an actual Guanche dance was still present in the court *canario* will remain unresolved, but the lack of a first-hand Guanche account does not mean that the Guanche culture has left no traces or cannot be addressed: remnants of Indigenous agency may survive in the *canario*. The medieval travelogues illustrate how readily enslaved 'noble savages' were put on display as a spectacle: European courts consumed their native cultural performances as theatrical and musical idioms, which then entered Western knowledge through appropriated practices and circulated reports. These reports offer an echo, however distorted, of the Indigenous dancers of the *canario*'s antecedents. A combination of broad multidisciplinary corroboration across a large time span (all the way back to the Neolithic age and the desertification of the Sahara) and microhistorical attention to single, everyday mentions (such as the description of the unnamed dancing priest in Rome) allow us to approach those dancers' specific embodied reality.

Long before court dance music scores were written down, the *canario* travelled as embodied knowledge from the Canary Islands to Europe through enslaved Guanches, who are documented in Europe from the fourteenth century. Considered as performance-as-history (Taylor, 2006: 68), the dance might have allowed cultural knowledge to be stored and passed on through bodily practice, maintaining epistemic agency and overriding European logocentrism, even in later forms removed from Guanche dancers.

The array of approaches presented here advocates for a historiographical engagement with the early modern period that positions gaps, temporal distance, and individual embodiment not as obstacles but as viable investigative tools and opportunities. It maintains that research into marginalized and silenced practices does not start by trying to neatly link accounts. Instead, it involves looking at what emerges between the gaps and cracks of official records, reading against the grain of what is there, and thereby making way for a more nuanced and contextually sensitive history.

Notes

1 Guanche is the self-given name of only the Indigenous people of Tenerife, the largest of the Canary Islands. It has been incorrectly applied to the populations of all seven inhabited Canary Islands (Gran Canaria, La Palma, Tenerife, Lanzarote, Fuerteventura, La Gomera, and El Hierro), who, at the time of the Spanish conquest, had distinct cultures based on a shared North African origin. The Guanches formed a civilization of island-bound, non-seafaring Neolithic people with cultural and genetic ties to the Imazighen. Since 'Guanches' has been adapted by Canarian researchers as a collective term, I follow this use.

2 The racialization of the Guanches was widely instrumentalized by researchers, with changing objectives that depended on positionality and interest. Records of differentiated slave labour between domestic service and the sugar mills on

the Canary Islands exemplify, however, how enslavement of the 'noble savage' Guanches was entangled with early modern Black enslavement in the Atlantic, at the same time that the court *canario* offered an exoticist projection space for a majoritarian white European elite (Phillips, 2011: 326).

References

Adams, T. E., ed. (2015). *Autoethnography*. New York: Oxford University Press.

Arbeau, T. (1596). *Orchésographie, métode, et téorie en forme de discours et tablature pour apprendre à dancer*. Langres, France: I. de Preyz.

Barker, H. (2019). *That Most Precious Merchandise: The Mediterranean Trade in Black Sea Slaves, 1260–1500*. Philadelphia: University of Pennsylvania Press.

Bennett, S. (1990). *Theatre Audiences: A Theory of Production and Reception*. New York: Routledge.

Berthelot, S. (1849). *Ethnografia y anales de la conquista de las Islas Canarias*. Santa Cruz de Tenerife, Spain: M. Miranda.

Boccaccio, G. (1830). *Monumenti di un manoscritto autografo e lettere inedite di messer Giovanni Boccaccio il tutto nuovamente trovato ed illustrato da Sebastiano Ciampi*. Milan: P. A. Molina.

Borchard, B. (2003). 'Lücken Schreiben. Oder: Montage als Biographisches Verfahren'. In H. E. Bödeker, ed., *Biographie Schreiben*. Göttingen, Germany: Wallstein, pp. 211–42.

Caroso, F. (1581). *Il Ballarino*. Venice: F. Ziletti.

Cotarelo y Mori, E. (1911). *Colección de entremeses, loas, bailes, jácaras y mojigangas desde fines del siglo 16 a mediados del 18*. Madrid: Bailly-Baillière.

Crawford, A. (2014). '"The Trauma Experienced by Generations Past Having an Effect in Their Descendants": Narrative and Historical Trauma among Inuit in Nunavut, Canada'. *Transcultural Psychiatry*, 5(3), 339–69.

Denham, A. R. (2008). 'Rethinking Historical Trauma: Narratives of Resilience'. *Transcultural Psychiatry*, 45(3), 391–414.

Fernández-Armesto, F. (1987). *Before Columbus: Exploration and Colonisation from the Mediterranean to the Atlantic, 1229–1492*. Philadelphia: University of Pennsylvania Press.

Freeman, E. (2010). *Time Binds: Queer Temporalities, Queer Histories*. Durham, NC: Duke University Press.

Fromm, G. (2012). *Lost in Transmission: Studies of Trauma across Generations*. London: Karnac.

Fusco, C. (2007). 'Fantastic Reconstruction: Postcolonial Artists and the Colonial Archive'. PhD diss., Middlesex University London.

Ginzburg, C. (1980). 'Morelli, Freud and Sherlock Holmes: Clues and Scientific Method'. *History Workshop*, 9, 5–36.

Ginzburg, C. (2005). 'Hybrids: Learning from a Gilded Silver Beaker (Antwerp, c. 1530)'. In A. Höfele and W. von Koppenfels, eds., *Renaissance Go-Betweens*. Berlin: De Gruyter, pp. 121–38.

Ginzburg, C. (2013). 'Some Queries Addressed to Myself'. *Cromohs: Cyber Review of Modern Historiography*, 18, 90–6.

Grove Music Online. (2001). 'Canario (ii)'. https://doi.org/10.1093/gmo/9781561592630.article.53723.

Harris, P. A. (2014). 'Tracing the Cretan Labyrinth: Mythology, Archaeology, Topology, Phenomenology'. *KronoScope*, 14(2), 133–49.

Henke, R. (2007). 'Representations of Poverty in the Commedia dell'Arte'. *Theatre Survey*, 48(2), 229–46.

Hudson, R., & Little, M. E. (2001). 'Canary (Fr. *canarie*; It., Sp. *canario*)'. Grove Music Online. https://doi.org/10.1093/gmo/9781561592630.article.04713.

Hulfeld, S. (2014). 'Einführung in die Lektüre der Scenari più scelti d'istrioni'. In S. Hulfeld & D. Quadri, eds., *Scenari più scelti d'istrioni: italienisch-deutsche Edition der einhundert Commedia all'improvviso-Szenarien aus der Sammlung Corsiniana*, vol. 1. Göttingen, Germany: Vandenhoeck & Ruprecht, pp. 9–112.

Jacobs, J. L. (2016). *The Holocaust across the Generations: Trauma and Its Inheritance among Descendants of Survivors*. New York: New York University Press.

Katritzky, M. A. (2006). *The Art of Commedia: A Study in the Commedia dell'Arte 1560–1620 with Special Reference to the Visual Records*. Amsterdam: Brill.

Kelly, M. K. (1999). 'Performing the Other: A Consideration of Two Cages'. *College Literature*, 26(1), 113–36.

Koselleck, R. (1979). *Historische Semantik und Begriffsgeschichte*. Stuttgart: Klett-Cotta.

Le Goff, J. (1994). *Die Rückeroberung des Historischen Denkens: Grundlagen der Neuen Geschichtswissenschaft*. Frankfurt am Main: Fischer.

Lupi, L. (1609). *Libro di gagliarda, tordiglione, passo e mezzo canari e passeggi*. Palermo: G. B. Maringo.

Münz, R. (2010). 'Il sesso degli angeli und der Weg nach Pomperlörel'. In G. Baumbach, ed., *Auf dem Weg nach Pomperlörel: Kritik 'des' Theaters*. Leipzig: Leipziger Universitätsverlag, pp. 39–74.

Negri, C. (1604). *Le gratie d'amore*. Milan: G. Bordone.

Nereson, A. (2010). 'Krump or Die: Krumping and Racist Ideologies in the Production and Reception of Rize'. *Gnovis Journal*, 11(1). Accessed 11 October 2023. https://gnovisjournal.georgetown.edu/category/journal/2010/.

Palisca, C. V. (1994). *Studies in the History of Italian Music and Music Theory*. Oxford: Clarendon Press.

Phillips, W. D. (2011). 'Slavery in the Atlantic Islands and the Early Modern Spanish Atlantic World'. In D. Eltis & S. L. Engerman, eds., *The Cambridge World History of Slavery, AD 1420–AD 1804*, vol. 3. Cambridge: Cambridge University Press, pp. 325–49.

Pontremoli, A. (2017). 'Trasmissione della danza fra oralità e scrittura nell'Europa di antico regime'. In R. Flick, M. Koch, & R. Rekatzky, eds., *Erinnern – Erzählen – Erkennen: Vom Wissen kultureller Praktiken*. Leipzig: Leipziger Universitätsverlag, pp. 151–71.

Rhee, J. (2021). *Decolonial Feminist Research: Haunting, Rememory and Mothers*. London: Routledge.

Rodríguez-Varela, R., T. Günther, M. Krzewińska, J. Storå, T. H. Gillingwater, M. MacCallum, J. L. Arsuaga, K. Dobney, C. Valdiosera, M. Jakobsson, A. Götherström, & L. Girdland-Flink. (2017). 'Genomic Analyses of Pre-European Conquest Human Remains from the Canary Islands Reveal Close Affinity to Modern North Africans'. *Current Biology*, 27(21).

Rodríguez Wittmann, K. (2018). '"Ciertas islas que por allí se encuentran": El contacto entre europeos y nativos en las miniaturas de Le Canarien'. *Revista de Historia Canaria*, 200, 285–99.

Rosa Olivera, L. de la. (1977). 'Bailadores canarios en unas bodas reales europeas en 1451'. *Anuario de Estudios Atlánticos*, 23, 661–3.

Rose, V., Barrick, S., & Bridel, W. (2021). '"Pretty Tough and Pretty Hard": An Intersectional Analysis of Krump as Seen on *So You Think You Can Dance*'. *Journal of Dance Education*, 21(4), 236–46.

Sánchez de Badajoz, D. (1554). *Recopilacion en metro del Bachiller Diego Sánchez de Badajoz en la qual por gracioso cortesano y pastoril estilo se cuentan y declaran muchas figuras y autoridades de la sagrada escriptura [...]*. Seville: J. Canilla.

Schmidt, B. (1996). *Die Ureinwohner der Kanarischen Inseln: Ihre Geschichte, Herkunft und Hinterlassenschaft*. Münster, Germany: A. T. Edition.

Schneider, R. (2001). 'Performance Remains'. *Performance Research*, 6(2), 100–8.

Skinner, Q. (2002). *Visions of Politics*, Vol 1: *Regarding Method*. Cambridge: Cambridge University Press.

Spry, T. (2016). *Body, Paper, Stage: Writing and Performing Autoethnography*. London: Routledge.

Stanford, E. T. (2001). 'Canario (i)'. Grove Music Online. https://doi.org/10.1093/gmo/9781561592630.article.04712.

Taviani, F. (1991). *La commedia dell'arte e la società barocca: la fascinazione del teatro*. Rome: Bulzoni.

Taylor, D. (2006). 'Performance and/as History'. *TDR: The Drama Review*, 50(1), 67–86.

Trapero, M. (1993). 'Lengua y cultura: sobre las definiciones de canario, "baile antiguo originario de las Islas Canarias"'. *Disparidades: Revista de Antropología*, 48(1), 47–79.

Van Deusen, N. E. (2021). 'Indigenous Slavery's Archive in Seventeenth-Century Chile'. *Hispanic American Historical Review*, 101(1), 1–34.

Viera y Clavijo, J. de. (1772). *Noticias de la historia general de las Islas de Canaria*, vol. 1. Madrid: Blas Román.

Wölfel, D. J. (1965). *Monumenta Linguae Canariae. Die Kanarischen Sprachdenkmäler. Eine Studie zur Vor- und Frühgeschichte Weißafrikas*. Graz, Austria: Akademische Druck-und Verlagsanstalt.

CHAPTER 13

Taking Your Time: Research in Learning-Disabled Theatre

Tony McCaffrey

I have spent eighteen years researching and making learning-disabled theatre, one of whose distinctive characteristics is a complex relationship to time and temporality. A relationship to time, of course, underpins all performance, but learning-disabled theatre has a particular set of relations to temporality that offers distinctive and interesting challenges to any consideration of performance research methods and methodologies. The historical nomenclature, diagnostic labels, and cultural tropes of learning disability – 'retardation', 'developmental delay', and 'slowness' – all categorize the relationship with temporality as deficient or divergent. They all refer to people who do not meet the milestones, norms, and standards of education and development within expected time scales. In addition, learning-disabled people have been historically discounted in a kind of temporo-spatial stasis: segregated in institutions and placed in holding patterns of occupational therapy, set apart from economic, developmental time.

Practitioners and researchers of learning-disabled theatre have sought to address this temporal inequity by paying careful attention to two key areas. First, there is the amount and quality of time allocated to the processes of making learning-disabled theatre. This necessitates a fluid and supple notion of temporality that encompasses giving time *to* time, ensuring that non-disabled facilitators and allies pay careful attention to the creative contributions and needs for appropriate care and support of learning-disabled participants and collaborators: not only listening to them but listening them *into* speech (Lipari, 2014), providing the kind of theatre-making environment in which non-verbal offers and forms of rhetoric other than verbal fluency might be attended to and respected. This involves a commitment to being there for the learning-disabled artists over extended periods of time: the engagement of multiple temporalities and the temporal looping that learning-disabled theatre prompts in the encounter between outcome-based temporalities of narrative, achievement, and efficacy, and slower, processual, and contemplative practices of consideration.

These latter practices involve caring for and supporting the participants, allowing for the vagaries and non-linearity of 'crip time' (McRuer, 2018) and the time needed to afford 'access intimacy' (Mingus, 2011). It includes simply spending time together in what Jasbir Puar (2009) and others term 'conviviality' (see also Calvert, 2020), and what Stefano Harney and Fred Moten in *The Undercommons* call 'study': 'talking and walking around with other people, working, dancing, suffering, some irreducible convergence of all three, held under the name of speculative practice' (Harney & Moten, 2013: 110).

The second mechanism for addressing temporal inequity is a reconfiguration of the kairos or 'good timing' in performance to afford or suit the capabilities of the performers. Conventionally, kairos concerns the condensed and pressurized time of performance before an audience. It encompasses cueing, dramatic pausing, the marking or weighting of specific speech or gestures, and the ready and fluent to and fro of dialogic and gestural actions and reactions that audiences associate with being 'in the moment' of virtuosic acting. These are marks that many learning-disabled performers do not hit, unless such marks can be reconfigured in a radically new pragmatics and aesthetics of performance, of the kind that has been developed over decades of practice by innovative companies such as Australia's Back to Back Theatre (see McCaffrey, 2019). Such techniques include problematizing verbal fluency by dislocating and diffusing speech acts through strategic delaying or echoing of voice-over and captioning, framing verbal or physical incapacity as a challenge to the spectator's expectations, and deploying exaggerated performances of 'disability' by disabled actors.

As these areas of focus demonstrate, however, the temporalities of learning-disabled theatre have to date largely been determined by a relationship between learning-disabled and non-disabled practitioners premised on what Miranda Fricker (2007) calls a formative and epistemic inequity: a disparity in access to the mechanisms of social inclusion, including education and theatre training and experiences. Indeed, even the key terms of enquiry that form the subject of this book are potentially in danger of replicating this inequity. For learning-disabled people, research is something they are far more likely to be subjected to, rather than to engage in as active researchers themselves. The concepts of 'method' and 'methodology' can be traced back to pre-Enlightenment medical or curative discourses and, later, to 'rational' procedures of maximizing efficiency and managing or eliminating aberrance. These meanings are highly problematic in the context of juridical, educational, and linguistic efforts to manage, marginalize, or erase learning-disabled people.

As such, learning-disabled theatre presents distinctive challenges to the conceptual frameworks of performance, research, and, in particular, method and methodology. In many ways the approaches to performance research that emerge out of learning-disabled theatre can be seen as jamming or scrambling systems of intentionality, signification, and hierarchy. This process *slows down* the rush of performance so as to provide opportunities for participants to seek political, aesthetic, and ethical commonality, revealing both the efficacy and limitations of what Fernand Deligny, a unique 'anti-researcher' amongst learning-disabled participants, characterizes as the 'thought-out project' (*le projet pensé*) (Deligny, 2008: 6). In so doing, it requires the researcher to account for a multiplicity of temporalities within the experience of performance creation.

That said, this process, too, presents challenges. Following an increased emphasis on inclusion in such domains of activity, learning-disabled artists are now beginning to take their place in the space of the stage, whether it is the stage of a therapeutic institution, a commercial venue, or an international arts festival. Inclusion can be seen as compensation or reparation for the historical wrongs of exclusion, marginalization, and neglect. However, inclusion itself can presuppose a particular temporo-spatial, conceptual, and practical relationship and hierarchy, within which those who are non-disabled lead those who are disabled. The well-meaning voices of inclusion say: 'We will include you. We will admit you into our spaces and practices.' These voices are caught up in regret over the neglect of the past and yet at the same time avow to make good on such neglect at some unspecified time in the future. The promise that informs initiatives in which the inclusion of learning-disabled artists is viewed as timely or now due means that such a form of 'inclusion' can easily be co-opted into broadly fashionable, progressive, or liberal agendas that emphasize tokenistic and temporary engagement rather than sustained and meaningful inclusion.

Matt Hargrave, who in 2015 authored the first full-length study of learning-disabled theatre (Hargrave, 2015), referred to this inequity in temporality when he characterized the development of such theatre as 'disabled artists … playing catch-up' (Hargrave, 2009: 53). If this inequity is not addressed in terms of a reconfiguration of the temporal aspects of learning-disabled theatre-making and performance, inclusion becomes a journey that only reveals further levels of exclusion or that may in fact, despite its stated aims, facilitate exclusion. The question also remains as to what will happen when disabled performers *do* 'catch up'.

In my experience, the relationship between non-disabled and disabled people in making learning-disabled theatre is complex, beyond simply a reversal of expected knowledge positions in an inclusion/exclusion binary. Over time, the relationship proceeds as a call and response that goes in multiple, unforeseen directions as participants switch between taking the lead and following. Through processes of imitation, deference, misapprehension, sympathy, empathy, misunderstanding, and working at cross-purposes, the 'something else' of learning-disabled theatre emerges. The result is a complex interplay of efficacy and inefficacy, and any attempt to consider learning-disabled performance research methodologically needs to take these complexities into account. In order to do so here, I will make reference to some specific moments in my experience of making theatre and conducting research with Different Light Theatre, an ensemble of learning-disabled performers in Christchurch, New Zealand. This approach is necessary because research is immanent in all that the group does, even if it is not always evident at the moment of its emergence: there is no point at which the creative activities of Different Light stop and the researching of the company starts.

Ben Ellenbroek: Resisting the Rush to Theatre

Ben Ellenbroek, a young man with Down syndrome, was an original member of Different Light Theatre at its launch in 2004. He stayed with the company for six years, participating and performing in all the group's self-devised productions. His most intense engagement with performance was, however, in what might be termed the downtime of the group's processes. During breaks in rehearsal, in the dressing room before and after performances, and onstage after a performance, he would launch into intense improvisations. These consisted of lengthy verbal and quasi-musical extemporizations accompanied by exaggerated movements performed at a deliberately slow and thoughtful tempo. Similarly, offstage he could engage in extended verbal improvisation that ranged across a variety of characters, accents, situations, flights of fantasy, and absurd tangents, switching, mixing, and matching the rhythms of celebration and anger. He seemed to delight in jokingly disrespecting me in particular, as if he were engaging in a kind of freestyle rap battle. These moments were fascinating to watch due to Ellenbroek's sustained intensity and imagination, but they never seemed to be reproducible in performance. When required to speak onstage, he invariably missed the mark of verbal comprehensibility. However repetitively rehearsed, his lines generally came out in a rush of over-breathing, or at a volume or pitch that rendered them difficult to understand. In fact, he often struggled even to make it to the stage.

Immediately before each public performance he would habitually disappear, winding himself up in the black stage curtains and not emerging, even in the face of copious amounts of cajoling, imprecation, and pleading, until the last possible moment.

It was as if Ellenbroek was out of time with performance. But it is perhaps more accurate to say that he was out of time with performance as we at Different Light Theatre then understood and practised it. At that stage in the group's development, performance meant attempting to devise and reproduce conventional representational theatre that would lead to public performance resembling theatre a non-disabled audience would recognize as such. This was part of a wider phenomenon I would describe as 'the rush to performance' by Different Light and other learning-disabled theatre companies. The first few years of the company's development were characterized by the imperative to prove that learning-disabled artists could produce theatre that would engage audiences, who were presumed to be non-disabled. Rehearsal and performance processes were caught up in temporalities of truncation, condensation, and haste, which characterize the common desire in community theatre to see participants' efforts rewarded in public performance, itself indicative of a powerful impetus towards the expedient affirmation of commonality.

In the case of Different Light, early attempts to develop such a sense of community amongst the primarily male participants were caught between a kind of caring, sharing, tactile, physical theatre ethos of ensemble and chorus; and a group dynamic inflected with a kind of blokeish banter, characteristic of stereotypical New Zealand male environments such as sports teams or groups of manual workers. This was deeply ironic in that neither I nor the male learning-disabled performers could in any sense be described as typical New Zealand men. It was as if we sought to redress the perceived uselessness and frivolity of improvisation and theatre games with a pretence at masculine labour. We combined a commitment to theatricality with a suspicious anti-theatricality, an uncertainty over the gendering of what we were doing that was masked by the adoption of stereotypical male personae.

The ambivalence towards theatricality that characterized the group at its emergence was exemplified in Ellenbroek's resistant and complex attitude towards performance. At one and the same time he professed a great desire and love for performance and radically resisted the conventional public practice of it. He in fact produced his own word for what he understood as performance: *beformance*. This was a conscious neologism. He knew and used the word *performance* in other contexts, but for him *beformance* was something he could *be* rather than something he needed to *perform*. It was something he needed to do to feel grounded, even though, paradoxically, it allowed him to make light and floating extra-daily movements that belied his stocky body type, and to find a mode that was intensely personal and imaginative. It covered a range of activities that included his impromptu vocal and physical improvisations, imbued with their own musicality. These he would only produce in the downtime of process, rather than in the kairotic time or requisite 'good timing' of theatrical performance onstage in front of an audience. These inevitably derailed conventional mimetic characterization and character interaction. In contrast to the cueing and the responsive back-and-forth tempo of 'naturalistic' dialogue and movement, they inhabited an entirely different temporality.

At that stage in the company's development, I and the other non-disabled facilitators were requiring the learning-disabled performers to fit the vocal and physical templates of conventional dramatic theatre, along with its temporalities of narrative, characterization, meaning-making, and solicitation of audience response. In terms of Different Light Theatre, Ellenbroek was ahead of his time. He was ahead of how we conceived and made theatre and of what we expected from it. He was in a research and development phase whilst we were still trying to make a repeatable theatrical product.

Being Called Out by Learning-Disabled Collaborators

A watershed moment in terms of the development of the theatre-making and research methodologies of the group occurred in 2007. This took place backstage at the Awakenings Festival, in the Australian town of Horsham, as the company was warming up before going onstage. As was his custom, Ellenbroek was making an impromptu speech calling on the group to do their best and represent New Zealand well. During this speech he directed everyone's attention to me, singling out my presence as 'the world actress here called Tony'. Leaving aside the interesting gender confusion, he called me out. He 'called me out' in the North American sense of the phrase: he drew attention to my behaviour, and to my presence as a non-disabled person at a disability arts festival in a 'mixed-ability' ensemble of fifteen performers. He called out my taking the role not only of actor, but of director and deviser. The play was titled *Ship of Fools* and, as if to testify to the fact that I had just embarked upon a PhD in theatre and film studies, it opened with a physical theatre sequence set to an extract of Michel Foucault's (2005 [1961]) *Madness and Civilization*. The play ended with two white-coated doctors, one of them played by me, running through the audience, sprinkling glitter, and chanting: 'Fluoxetine Paroxetine Escitalopram Citalopram Sertraline Venlafaxine Duloxetine Bupropion Mirtazapine Reboxetine Quetiapine Risperidone Olanzapine Clonazepam Carbamazepine' (DLT, 2007).

I had googled Prozac derivatives and come up with a list of names that sounded like incantations or spells. Their function was to represent the (neo)liberal use of depot (slow-release) medications that underpins the 'care in the community' (deinstitutionalized) model of treatment of the neurodiverse. The play traced a historical journey of treatment from the ship of fools to the asylum to deinstitutionalization. The play was performed to a majority-disabled audience. After their noisy reception of the piece, several audience members came up to me and told me they were currently taking some combination of those same antidepressants and serotonin reuptake inhibitors, the names of which we had sprayed out around the auditorium. They likewise called me out. What for me had been superficially undertaken research for a performance in the rush to meaning or the rush to a crude kind of agitprop 'political' theatre represented for them lived experience: prescribed, circumscribed, painfully painless experience.

This experience of being called out emerged as a moment of clarity that led to my ceasing to perform onstage in the group's public performances. I switched to employing only learning-disabled actors in subsequent performances, which in turn required a far more careful cultivation of, curation of, and listening to the voices of the performers. The crude attempt at agitprop in *Ship of Fools* in 2007 was later superseded through the participation of another Different Light performer, Louise Payne. She was a survivor of the New Zealand psychiatric system, and in the 2010 production *The Wizard of Oz* she created an improvisation on the 'yellow brick road' of medication, tracing how what had been restricted at first to institutionalized patients later found its way into the general population. A transcription of her improvisation could serve as a detailed rebuttal to the 2007 text:

> The first one on the market was Prozac manufactured into 20 capsules 1940s sort of green tapering down into a beautiful cream colour. Made the cover of *Time* magazine because it was so beautiful. With this starter booklet which accompanies it where you have black and white trees but after a few weeks on this you can walk into the colour with the daffodils apparently. And even the checklists for your so-called depression anxiety are in the shape of Prozac pills. You can get Prozac beanies, Prozac lamps,

> you can get junkets to Bali, or you can't your doctor can, the stationery I save it, the tee shirts. The next SSRI – Venlafaxine [*sic*] – originally brought out as 75 mg per capsule – so fast, so heavy they reduced it to 37.5 mg. Venlafaxine – it'll take you there. But will it get you back? And I really do mean that. It's a kick-arse drug. Olanzapine. Anti-psychotic. If you're taking this (Venlafaxine) you might need this to bring you back. White wafer like communion. Gone before you know it. No non-compliance, you can't spit it. Truly make you feel like Muppets. Will knock you out 8–12 hours. And here we have the anti-psychotic when you're not really having an anti-psychotic – the Clayton's effect – Quetiapine: innocuous tiny tiny orange, put you on your butt maybe 3 or 4 hours but they like to tell you that that will dampen down your anxieties. It's more like hammering them. Me I prefer your good old-fashioned 5 mg YELLOW VALIUM. (DLT, 2010)

The rush to agitprop political theatre of the early years of development of Different Light Theatre was superseded by a more sustained, meaningful, and collaborative engagement and participation by the members of the company. This was a methodological switch that occurred almost by accident. This development would probably not have eventuated, however, without the misstep of the rush to a superficial theatre-making method and the subsequent catch-up, but this time, crucially, it was the non-disabled facilitators catching up with the learning-disabled artists.

Ellenbroek subsequently, and amicably, left the company, but his word *beformance* has stayed with us. It might stand as a suitable term to account for the radical challenge of learning-disabled performance: both its plasticity and its temporality. The former denotes its ontological uncertainty, its need to *be*form and reform amid reiterative mechanisms of exclusion, and the way that it is constantly forming its own being and becoming. The latter denotes its relationship to temporality and futurity, and the way that non-disabled facilitators (re)discover that they need to play catch-up with the learning-disabled artists, that they have been repeatedly 'discovering' new instances of the aptitude and creativity of learning-disabled artists that have long been there, evident but unnoticed. Ellenbroek's word might also stand as a tribute to what Different Light Theatre was not able to achieve for him in exploring performance with him. It represents a memory of process never realized in public performance. In my experience of learning-disabled theatre, development over time is not always teleological; it does not recuperate what is lost along the way, or what might have been. Ellenbroek was, in effect, theorizing before the fact the research methods that the company subsequently used.

In Search of a Different Light Performance Research Methodology

Since 2005, Different Light has pursued and presented research across a range of contexts, from research by means of performance, through research that aligns with members' own practices of caring for the company's archive and repertoire, to research as it is performed or presented at academic conferences. This is the spectrum of research that underpins everything that we do: an exploration of how theatre can be devised, practised, and presented by learning-disabled artists seeking a place within a burgeoning learning-disabled culture or poetics.

During the nearly two decades of Different Light Theatre's existence, I have attempted to get the learning-disabled performers to engage in performance by playing catch-up with different forms of (non-disabled-led?) theatre and performance. These included community, dramatic, post-dramatic, site-specific, immersive, ecological, new materialist, and post-human forms of theatre and performance-as-research. These were initially intended to be *progressively* different practices, moving towards the emancipation of the voices and creative potential of the learning-disabled performers. With each successive development, however, it became clear that an ideas-led approach to devising and theatre-making – Deligny's 'thought-out project' – came up against the elusive, resistant, and obdurate presence of the learning-disabled performers themselves, calling into question the efficacy and limitations of each successive theatrical form. These performers changed the goalposts in a myriad of practical, technical, material, unimagined, and imaginative ways, shifting the paradigms, and sending us back to the drawing board to reconfigure what constituted theatre.

For example, at the time of the series of earthquakes and aftershocks that shook the New Zealand city of Christchurch in 2010–11, company members expressed a desire to explore performance grounded in the comfort, familiarity, and repetitive routine of daytime television soap operas. I introduced them to the Dutch TV web series *Downistie*, which is modelled on the 1980s US series *Dynasty* but which features only actors with Down syndrome. The representation of this world became an exercise in utopianism for Different Light members, as the conditions do not yet exist in New Zealand to allow for learning-disabled doctors, drivers, and politicians. As with the web series, the genre of soap opera became something else in the encounter, a performance mix that included (and exceeded) the strategies of social critique, parody, and pastiche. In subsequent performances, improvisations and explorations of characters and situations from the narrative archive and repertoire of a self-devised soap opera, *The Lonely and the Lovely*, recurred when the performers were not yet done with them or realized something about them after the fact.

In 2013 the company performed a twenty-minute version of *The Lonely and the Lovely* at the opening of the Disability Studies in Education conference at the University of Canterbury in New Zealand, the first time the conference had been held outside the United States. At the end of the performance, the actors went amongst the audience, largely composed of academics and teachers, with a short questionnaire: '1. What is your disability? 2. Who are your support workers? 3. What makes you lonely? What makes you lovely?' This was an attempt to flip the script on the expected research relationships between non-disabled researchers and disabled research subjects (see DLT, 2012, 2012–13).

Later that year, Different Light took part in a much bigger, site-specific project entitled *Canterbury Tales*, which was organized by Free Theatre Christchurch as part of FESTA (the Festival of Transitional Architecture), and which featured Pacific Underground, the Christchurch Symphony Orchestra, and a number of other Christchurch artists and organizations (Falkenberg, 2013). A Different Light crew set up outside the damaged Anglican cathedral in Christchurch with cameras and microphones to interview passers-by. They intended to prompt people to tell stories of their encounters with the earthquakes and with disability as a nod to Chaucer's pilgrims. The performers had come up with a number of questions, variously generic, pithy, and pointed. We were later able to debrief and discuss with the whole group the ways in which people sought to avoid the encounter with the camera crews or their reactions to being interviewed by disabled interviewers. We also discussed the difference in responses between those who acknowledged the experience of disability in their lives and those who, for whatever reason, did not.

This integration of research activity has always been immanent within the work and operations of the company, and has increasingly made its presence felt in performance aesthetics. The 2011–12 production *Still Lives* was intended to explore the difficulties of three learning-disabled young men finding their voices in the 'recovery' from the Christchurch earthquakes, a recovery that, it soon emerged, continued to ignore them. Whereas the earthquakes had been inclusive, the recovery clearly was not. The rebuilding of the city from the ground up neglected the opportunity to include equitable access for all. *Still Lives* explored what constituted the voices of the performers by presenting a polyphony of computerized voices, captioned video, fantasy video sequences, and the contrasting spoken voices of the performers (DLT, 2011–12). When it was presented at the Society for Disability Studies conference in San Jose, California, it was also accompanied by two American Sign Language (ASL) signers and live captioning. The production sought to problematize the presence and expression of the young men's 'voices' in the surrounding stillness of both the earthquake-damaged city and their continuing marginalization as learning-disabled people within it. Computerized voice-overs that positioned them in various narratives – disclosing (incorrectly) their disabilities, idealizing them as fantasy princes, and dismissing their desires – contrasted with the contradictions, nuances, and lacunae of their own spoken voices. The production suggested that the rush to identification and meaning of dramatic or theatrical temporality was in tension with the complexities and contradictions of the performers' experience and their manner of expressing this, which required a more considered and contemplative temporality in order to emerge.

In light of this pattern it is perhaps no coincidence that Different Light operates in the interstices of a tertiary educational institution, the National Academy of Singing and Dramatic Art (NASDA), within Ara Institute (formerly the Christchurch Polytechnic Institute of Technology). This affords access to spaces in the downtimes of the institution as well as the opportunity to repurpose the props, costumes, and partially built and completed sets and lighting plots of the drama school, while respecting the health and safety of the Different Light performers and the drama school performers. The absence of an imperative to perform means that the Different Light performers are able to hold up the techne of conventional dramatic and musical theatre performances, to observe them in a different light and to put them to uses they were not intended for in these other productions. In *The Undercommons*, Harney and Moten (2013: 26) write of the need to 'sneak into the university and steal what one can. To abuse its hospitality, to spite its mission, to join its refugee colony, its gypsy encampment, to be in but not of.' For a time, the praxis of Different Light was an exercise in undercommons 'study': a speculative practice not necessarily pursued as a means to knowledge and qualification. Or, as Jack Halberstam in their introduction to *The Undercommons* articulates it: 'a mode of thinking with others separate from the thinking that the institution requires of you' (Harney & Moten, 2013: 11).

In the time after the quakes, the group studied in the backstage and rehearsal spaces of theatre without the pressure to produce completed projects or perform for a paying public. Objects from one proposed production would temporarily mingle with the scenography of another to create other possibilities. Different Light performers started making appearances in masks in and around civic artworks in the city. A group of performers in larval masks sat outside and interacted silently with one another at the tables of a café abandoned during the quakes. On another occasion, fifteen learning-disabled actors staged walks through the road cones, scaffolding, and fences of the city in transition, adapting their formation to the temporary, often inaccessible, constraints on public space. At times they stood and looked at what had previously been a space occupied by a building that was important to them.

In 2019, Different Light company members took part in another theatrical twist on the temporalities of research. They responded to my prompt to devise a performance for the Christchurch Arts Festival that was intended to be their take on the fifteen years of the company's existence. Company member Isaac Tait's immediate response to the idea of a history of the company was a wish to speak of the 'people who had disappeared' in those fifteen years. This included two key company members who had died (John Lambie and Louise Payne), but also those performers like Ellenbroek who had joined the company and moved on over the years, and others whose family and living circumstances had changed, preventing them from continuing with the group. This idea of disappearance then began to permeate the process and the performance. It led the performers to question what appears and disappears in a 'history' as a series of events, what appears and disappears in memory and in performance, and what disappears only to reappear unprompted at some later stage.

In *The History of Different Light*, then, the performers were encouraged to revisit scenes, memories, characters, lines of text, and objects from previous productions, at times connecting with videos of their younger selves in rehearsal or in performance and exploring what had been gained and what had been lost during fifteen years of working together (DLT, 2019). It was an invitation to examine the life of the company by means of a self-reflexive performance. For some company members this was an uncomfortable or alienating return to their past selves. For others, the promissory note of inclusion in theatrical performance and inclusion in a social life outside the theatre had not been redeemed (Figure 13.1).

In another example of how Different Light's research-informed performance feeds performance research, this in turn led to the decision to create a book, which we proposed to Routledge in February 2020 (see McCaffrey, 2023). The book investigates how Different Light has developed its own ways of working, creating, and being together. It attempts

Figure 13.1 Rehearsal for *The History of Different Light* (Christchurch Arts Festival, 2019). Paul McCaffrey on behalf of Different Light Theatre.

to let learning-disabled artists give and take voice in a range of different ways. The focus on *giving and taking* is an attempt to account for the contradictions inherent in this work to date, including the way non-disabled facilitators both give and take the 'voices' of the artists, and the inequity implicit in the exchange when a privileged group *gives* theatre to a less privileged group. It is an attempt to show how ideas or epistemologies such as liberating the 'authentic' voice of a marginalized group of people, or 'giving voice to the voiceless', are a kind of (neo)liberal chimera that posits 'voice' or representation as markers of fixed, static identity when such concepts as self and identity are context dependent, fluid, and (to borrow a term from Harney and Moten (2013)) 'fugitive'.

Conclusion

Anna Hickey-Moody (2009: xiii) offers an intriguing complement to Ben Ellenbroek's idea of *beformance* by acknowledging the way that the temporal and spatial are conflated in the positionality of non-disabled practitioners and scholars participating in and writing about learning-disabled performance: 'Rather than positioning myself as writing about Company members with intellectual disability, I see myself as writing *before* them.' She was writing in the now with the assumption that learning-disabled performers may do so in the future. She was also writing *before* the learning-disabled dancers in the sense that the accused comes before a judge, or a supplicant comes before the monarch for an audience. In a sense, this conflation of the temporal and spatial uses of the preposition *before* is symptomatic of the awkwardness of positionality for those of us who would seek to reverse the expected hierarchical relationship of learning-disabled and non-disabled collaborators but who do so in linguistic and theoretical frameworks largely inaccessible to the former. My practical experience of making theatre for two decades with learning-disabled artists is that concepts, whether of high theory, low theory, or theatre as theory, are admitted, considered, embodied, and reconfigured as percepts in the room of devising and performance.

The performers about whom Hickey-Moody (2009: xiii) was writing were members of Restless Dance Theatre from Adelaide, and she gives an account of the company's distinctive method of creation or performance-making, which she calls 'reverse integration'. This involves the non-disabled members of the company following the creative lead of the learning-disabled performers rather than the other way round. This strategy appears to offer more control, agency, or autonomy to the learning-disabled performers. But within the temporality of learning-disabled performance, it raises the question of how the learning-disabled performers have been introduced to the practice of making the initial movements or gestural 'offers' that may then be developed in improvisational choreography.

Hickey-Moody (2017: 7) herself acknowledges that 'the methodologies of "cultures of intellectual disability" and "reverse integration" are not rulebooks for practice; they are a way of describing an *ethics of practice*'. This methodology echoes in interesting ways Avital Ronell's (2003: 60) provocative statement about the conditions for an ethical relation: 'If one were to state in ethical terms the only possible position … it would have to be this: I am stupid before the other.' Much theatre and performance training, after Jerzy Grotowski (2002), takes the approach of the *via negativa*: the unlearning of acculturated behaviours to liberate creative energies. The danger of this within learning-disabled performance is that the learning-disabled person becomes fetishized or thematized as the Other, the performer before whom the non-disabled performers must somehow 'reverse' themselves or unlearn their training or become stupid or naive.

I often find myself writing before the Different Light performers: transcribing on a computer screen or paper the script of the performance texts that we eventually finalize for public performance. The script is a material object in time. It is an intended recuperation of past processes of devising to be carried forward into future action and performance. Some of the performers put the resulting paper sheets of the script into clear plastic folders, and some mark the pages with highlighter pens. Some of the pages fall all over the stage in disarray. We each take our copies home and sometimes lose them, but we carry on. The scripts pick up dirt from being dropped on the floor, the imprints of shoes or wheelchair wheels, stains from food and drink, and markings that once meant something and may or may not still. A script is a material object and a complex document in which it becomes unclear who is leading and who is following, who is researcher and who is researched. The script speaks back to us, speaks us back to us, exposing our commonalities and inequities. It marks our time together, the complex temporalities of our mutual involvement.

In *The Undercommons*, Harney and Moten (2013: 126, 128) discuss various ways to resist the 'call to order' that insists people give an account of themselves in order to be recognizable. Moten relates this to his coming into a classroom where people are milling around, and he is supposed to call it to order. He then asks what would happen if he were to refuse to make the call to order, if he were to refuse to 'become an instrument of governance' in that room. What possibilities of learning then emerge? Harney later responds to this theme with the question: 'So the thing that I am interested in is, without calling something to order, how can you still sing?' To which Moten replies: 'Form is not the eradication of the informal. Form is what emerges from the informal.' This dialogue – and the question 'without calling something to order, how can you still sing?' – resonates constantly and deeply in the messy mix of Different Light as an assemblage of activities, the research activity that only exists in the resistance to the call to order: the travelling together, the downtime, the break, the offstage that will not come onstage, the conviviality of helping one another out and calling one another out. This is the *beformance* of Different Light.

References

Calvert, D. (2020). 'Convivial Theatre: Care and Debility in Collaborations between Non-Disabled and Learning Disabled Theatre Makers'. In A. Stuart Fisher & J. Thompson, eds., *Performing Care: New Perspectives on Socially Engaged Research*. Manchester: Manchester University Press, pp. 85–102.

Deligny, F. (2008). *L'Arachnéen et autres textes*. Paris: Éditions L'Arachnéen.

DLT (Different Light Theatre). (2007). *Ship of Fools*. Devised by the ensemble, directed by T. McCaffrey. Awakenings Festival, Horsham, Victoria, Australia, 13–15 October.

DLT (Different Light Theatre). (2010). *The Wizard of Oz*. Devised by the ensemble, directed by T. McCaffrey. NASDA Theatre, Christchurch Polytechnic Institute of Technology, Ignition Creative Festival, Christchurch, New Zealand, 18–21 November.

DLT (Different Light Theatre). (2011–12). *Still Lives*. Devised by the ensemble, directed by T. McCaffrey. Society for Disability Studies, 24th annual conference, San Jose, CA, 15–18 June 2011; Ludus Festival Leeds and Performance Studies International (PSi), 18 Riley Smith Hall, University of Leeds, 28–30 July 2012.

DLT (Different Light Theatre). (2012). *Rebuilding Christchurch: A Different Soap Opera*. Devised by the ensemble, directed by T. McCaffrey. Arts Access Australia conference, Concourse, Chatswood, Sydney, 30 October.

DLT (Different Light Theatre). (2012–13). *The Lonely and the Lovely*. 2 parts. Devised by the ensemble, directed by T. McCaffrey. Arts Access Excellence Concourse, Chatswood, Sydney, Australia, 30–31 October 2012; Disability Studies in Education conference, Jack Mann Auditorium, University of Canterbury, New Zealand, 7–9 June 2013.

DLT (Different Light Theatre). (2019). *The History of Different Light*. Devised by the ensemble, directed by T. McCaffrey. Christchurch Arts Festival. NASDA Theatre, Ara Institute, Christchurch, New Zealand, 1–3 August.

Falkenberg, P., dir. (2013). *Canterbury Tales*. Free Theatre Christchurch, FESTA (Festival of Transitional Architecture), Christchurch, New Zealand, 25–28 October.

Foucault, M. (2005 [1961]). *Madness and Civilization: A History of Insanity in the Age of Reason*. Trans. R. Howard. London: Routledge.

Fricker, M. (2007). *Epistemic Injustice: Power and the Ethics of Knowing*. Oxford: Oxford University Press.

Grotowski, J. (2002 [1968]). *Towards a Poor Theatre*. Ed. E. Barba. New York: Routledge.

Hargrave, M. (2009). 'Pure Products Go Crazy'. *Research in Drama Education: The Journal of Applied Theatre and Performance*, 14(1), 37–54.

Hargrave, M. (2015). *Theatres of Learning Disability: Good, Bad, or Plain Ugly?* Basingstoke: Palgrave Macmillan.

Harney, S., & Moten, F. (2013). *The Undercommons: Fugitive Planning and Black Study*. Wivenhoe, UK: Minor Compositions.

Hickey-Moody, A. (2009). *Unimaginable Bodies: Intellectual Disability, Performance and Becomings*. Rotterdam: Sense.

Hickey-Moody, A. (2017). 'Integrated Dance as a Public Pedagogy of the Body'. *Social Alternatives*, 36(4), 5–13.

Lipari, L. (2014). *Listening, Thinking, Being: Towards an Ethics of Attunement*. University Park: Pennsylvania State University Press.

McCaffrey, T. (2019). *Incapacity and Theatricality: Politics and Aesthetics in Theatre Involving Actors with Intellectual Disabilities*. London: Routledge.

McCaffrey, T. (2023). *Giving and Taking Voice in Learning Disabled Theatre*. London: Routledge.

McRuer, R. (2018) *Crip Times: Disability, Globalization, and Resistance*. New York: New York University Press.

Mingus, M. (2011). 'Access Intimacy: The Missing Link'. *Leaving Evidence* (blog), 5 May. Accessed 11 October 2023. https://leavingevidence.wordpress.com/2011/05/05/access-intimacy-the-missing-link.

Puar, J. (2009). 'Prognosis Time: Towards a Geopolitics of Affect, Debility and Capacity'. *Women and Performance: A Journal of Feminist Theory*, 19(2), 161–72.

Ronell, A. (2003). *Stupidity*. Urbana: University of Illinois Press.

CHAPTER 14

Not Here for the Disciplines: Researching with and for the Pacific

Katerina Teaiwa

When you're in the humanities and social sciences, you often need a door to be opened or a space to be created to feel like you can explore forms of knowledge production beyond the text. Three specific influences have empowered me to do that over the last two decades. The first is my mother and the way she instilled certain kinds of knowledge values within the family. She's African American, from Washington, DC. She came from a family that was very supportive of the arts, and she did ballet from when she was very little, until her early twenties. She came out of it truly valuing dance as a knowledge system and as something that everyone should be doing, like maths and English. When she moved to Fiji around 1970, she continued to teach dance, and of course she started with her girls. We learned ballet from her while we were learning all the Pacific dances. We learned the dances of Banaba Island (where my father was from) and Kiribati, our Cook Islands and Fijian dances, and Chinese dances at our Chinese school. And alongside that, we had all this technique that was coming from our mother, which was very structured, and all about strength and flexibility. So our bodies were able to perform a large range of different movements. Being instilled with that kind of embodied literacy across a broad spectrum of dance was a form of empowerment and fostered a choreographic sensibility that has always stuck with me.

The second influence came from doing Pacific Island studies at the University of Hawai'i, where for the first time I was exposed to interdisciplinary knowledge in a *truly* interdisciplinary fashion, though not without some contestation. Pedagogically and methodologically, interdisciplinarity was well woven through history, culture, politics, and Indigenous knowledges. But even as we were being told to 'decolonize our minds' and 'decolonize our knowledges' and 'decolonize our approaches', I kept asking: then why are we doing all this in *text*, through reading and writing? I felt empowered, exposed to actual Pacific history and Pacific contemporary issues for the first time, but I was then made to write analytical essays and research essays and synthesize and critique texts, most of which were written by non-Pacific people. I found it difficult to reconcile being told to decolonize everything without the *form* being decolonized as well, because we were also learning that Pacific people come from embodied oral cultures, where nothing was written down until Christianity and colonization and Europeans arrived in the Pacific. I started having those conversations with my teachers, and I began submitting comic book strips and other kinds of media for my assessments.

The third influence came when I encountered the audio-visual archives of my ancestral island of Banaba in Kiribati, while doing a PhD in anthropology at the Australian National University. I got the National Archives to transfer film from old Kodak reels onto VHS tape. I would watch the footage, and the lack of voice or commentary inspired me to make my own meaning from what I was watching. I homed in on bodies and what they were doing, and that enhanced my choreographic sense: a way of understanding a corporeal history of Pacific peoples.

My PhD explored the impacts of colonial phosphate mining on Banaba throughout the twentieth century, including the island's despoliation and the mid-century displacement of its population to Rabi Island in Fiji. The original title of my thesis was 'The Political Economy of Pity'. Banaban history as written by scholars and as told to us as Banabans growing up in the 1970s through to the 1990s was a traumatic one, and pity, which is *kawa* in the Kiribati language, was a word that permeated all aspects of Banaban life. When I would go back and visit my family in the village in Fiji, I kept hearing the phrase *e kawa te aba*, which means 'pity the land and pity the people'. So like any researcher who hears a phrase repeated again and again, I thought: 'well, clearly this is a central theme of all people's lives', and I was going to do a political economy of pity because I wanted to know *where* and *how* and *what* caused us to become so *pitiful* about everything: why were we framing history and our present lives through this concept of pity? Then I started doing my fieldwork, which I call homework, because I'm going home and I'm related to every single one of the people that I'm talking to (for me, the field was the archives – *that* was the foreign land). And in the islands, everybody's singing and dancing on a daily basis. And I think: 'you might be saying the word *pity*, but your bodies are doing something else'. The words and the actions were not *in sync*. It was almost like people's discourse was on repeat. We had been trained to think: 'this is awful, this is sad – we are pitiful, damn it. Our ancestors did these things, and those white people took the land, and some people were so silly. And now we've ended up in a state of poverty and corruption and we're lacking leadership'. But in their everyday practices, there was *joy*, celebration, innovation: you could feel it in your body when you sang and when you danced and when you had a gathering, a *botaki*. It was wonderful.

So dance challenged pity. People may have said they were pitiful. Christianity, especially, encourages everyone to see things in sacrificial terms, and if you are pitiful then you need saving, and it is a short step from there to Australian, American, and Chinese aid and development projects for the people who need to be saved. But I chose to focus on what people were dancing and singing rather than what they were *saying* about who they were. Dance became woven throughout my whole PhD journey. I taught people dancing, and people taught me dancing. I danced on all these islands all over the Pacific, on the stage, and in *maneabas* (Kiribati communal meeting houses), lit by just a little kerosene lamp. I made a music video of the dance occurring in all these contexts to a single soundtrack, which we were playing in all these different places.

Dancing is something done in *place*. Not so much in *space*, which is how a universal 'technique' like ballet is conceived. My experience of ballet is from Washington, DC, with all the African American histories that converge in *that* place. That ballet emerged from a particular history, and a desire of Black people to be given opportunities to dance, and to be able to go to a ballet school and be taught by a Black teacher. It's *emplaced*, and that is the genealogy I learned when it then became emplaced in Fiji. My mum is Catholic, so the halls she taught dance in were always attached to a church. We learned in a particular environment with particular floorboards. Anyone else might have said: 'that's not a good dance floor'. But those are the floors that we learned ballet on, and it became emplaced in our family. That way, ballet became like every other type of Pacific dance we were learning, which is, as the I-Kiribati (Kiribati people) say, *e kain te aba*: a thing of our land.

All this means that if I say I write or speak as a dancer, it is not that I write or speak solely about dance, but that the specificities of movement and place shape my thinking. For example, when people are talking about Pacific issues, they often discuss big regional meetings of Pacific leaders and say: 'all the participants gathered to talk about climate change and this is the communiqué that came out of it'. As a Pacific scholar I want to know where, exactly, they were. Where were they sitting? How were they sitting? How were they oriented to one another; which bodies were facing other bodies? What were they hearing as they were speaking? Were they forced to dance; were they asked to sing? – of course they were!

As a scholar, I immediately ask *those* questions. Whether the discussion is politics, security, gender, climate change, or another issue, I am thinking of bodies and places, and I'm trying to figure out how they are forming relationships with one another. In August 2021, then Australian prime minister Scott Morrison *ate* during a Zoom meeting of Pacific leaders to mark the 50th anniversary of the Pacific Islands Forum. That body language is pretty important! And this kind of thinking extends across all the work I do.

The Fiery Canoe: Integrated Approaches to Teaching and Research

I do critical, engaged, interdisciplinary, or transdisciplinary Indigenous Pacific-centred teaching, research, outreach service, and engagement. However, I do not think as much as I could about the concepts and frameworks that guide or drive what I do because they are so integrated with the *doing* itself.

For example, while doing my 'homework' in Banaba, I was more comfortable using a video camera than sitting there with a notebook and a pen, because the video camera was interesting to my relatives and the communities that I went to. Everyone knows video, and now they all have mobile phones, so that made sense to them. I probably have a hundred hours of footage over twenty years, documenting life and activities in Kiribati and Fiji. But somebody sitting there with a book writing everything down is very confronting. So when I am conducting research I almost never write anything down right away. I try to commit everything to memory as I experience it, and I let it settle in my body. Then when I come back into an academic context – like having to write something, or go into the classroom – it bubbles up. I might write something down sometimes, but I won't be able to find the notes again. As long as I've gone through the process of writing a little bit of it, it then settles in my body and I can pull it out of my body when I need to. The embodied and the performative come first. They inform the research, and deepen it, allowing me to explore many contexts and to make *meaning*. The downside is not being methodical in the way I write, or structured in the way I organize information. I tell stories. I organize information intuitively.

So all that I do is there in the research, but it is not research alone or in isolation. This is my way of being: an orientation to the world. I am connected and grounded through my body to other peoples, places, and environments, so the mixed model approach is a creative survival technique as much as an actual method for research or a way of teaching or presenting knowledge. It is my ontological reality: how things are.

This of course also extends to my teaching, where two important elements are woven through all my courses. One is that teaching and learning are a journey, a voyage of exploration: they combine the skills and approaches of navigation and wayfinding through the Pacific *and* through Australia and through all areas in which the Pacific has a presence. Following some of the ideas of my late sister, Teresia Teaiwa, I conceptualize the whole undertaking as a metaphorical canoe. The journey is not about getting from point A to point B, but about the range of options along the way, with a clear focus on process rather than the destination. There will be a destination – you just don't know which one, and you can change your mind and be fluid and flexible along the way.

The concept of the canoe is literally embodied in my and my sister's name, or my grandfather's name: 'Teaiwa' means 'fiery canoe'. If I were to track that image going through my father's family, there are always interactions with the canoe. There's fishing in canoes, survival through fishing methods, building canoes, and launching canoes. There are overturned canoes. There are canoes that somebody put an outboard motor on, then there are outrigger canoes, and there's a lot of journeying and sailing. But 'Teaiwa' can also be translated as 'to agitate', 'to move around', and 'to upset'. These come together visually in this idea of the fiery canoe. Our lives are well embodied by that idea. So it makes a lot of sense in our teaching and learning *practice*: the idea of voyaging and moving meets good solid skills, strategies, and capabilities. To have a journey where everyone survives and no one is left behind is critical to the teaching and learning experience.

In my classrooms I have *metaphorical* canoes: we are far away from the ocean in Canberra, so we have to imagine *us* – the classroom, the group, the collective – *as the canoe*. We are on the canoe together. Everyone knows one another's names and what their roles are. Everybody is known, and there's a kinship, a community, which is overwhelmingly valued in the Pacific. For a semester we're a community, and we notice and we keep track of one another, and there's both collective and individual learning.

The other important element is embodied knowledge, which you need to be on the canoe. From a Pacific perspective, the concept of journeying is something that goes back thousands of years and is a collective survival strategy for finding new homes and connecting to the land while still moving. Pacific Islanders are very good at being grounded and moving simultaneously: *routes* and *roots* are both in operation. In order to have a successful journey, you need some embodied, practical, applied knowledge. The first thing I do in all my classes is teach the students a dance. At the beginning, they are thinking: 'What's this? We were told this is a Pacific studies class; it's area studies. Why are you making us stand up? Why are we dancing in this lecture theatre?' And then I explain to them why dance and embodied knowledge are so critical and are a part of this metaphor of the journey. They have to be learning in a fully embodied way. We learn a hula that I was taught years ago when I belonged to a hula *hālau* in Hawai'i: a simple hula that anyone can understand, because it maps onto an island landscape. There's the sun, the moon, the mountains, the waterfalls, the valleys, the sea – there's a distinction made in the dance between the shallow part of the sea close to the shore before the reef, and the deep ocean. It talks about all the different features of the Pacific. If you are in a classroom in Canberra, and you are going to be learning about the Pacific, this dance gets you in the right frame of mind and body to be able to *actually* try to connect with Pacific people and Pacific environments and Pacific ways of knowing and being and doing. The students are not allowed to record it or write it down. There is a quiz halfway through the semester where they have to write down all the different features of the landscape that we have been describing. So there's a little bit of reinforcement there. Otherwise, it's a completely oral and embodied practice. They have to remember everything in their bodies, and they have to sing the song simultaneously while they are dancing. Alongside the arms and upper torso movements, there are some complex foot patterns, and I tell them: 'you don't have to do anything fancy with your feet – you can just sway from side to side. But you *have* to describe the oceanic environment through your hands and arms.' And whether they like it or not, they never forget this song or this dance. We dance at the beginning of every lecture and every tutorial, and the students just go *boom*: 'we are here'.

In other words, I always make sure different elements of embodied knowledge are highlighted and featured in this class, which is essentially about politics, history, regionalism, and cultural revitalization. None of the topics involve dance or performance. The words *dance* and *performance* are not present because I don't want people to think: 'and now we're studying the embodied'. It has to be there from the beginning as an orientation, a way of being in the world. It just is. It's how you do politics, how you travel, how you know what you know, how you don't know what you don't know. How you learn. How you keep track of your classmates. How you form kinship with them.

Kinship itself is one of several values that I have distilled in my practice, and that cut across the whole Pacific. It ties in with the values of process and consensus. People will spend hours trying to work through an issue, not rushing. They take time, or they bounce things off others in different ways, or they wait three weeks and then go and talk to somebody in another place, so there's a *process* to decision-making. There's a process to building consensus. Everyone who was watching the political stand-off in Samoa in 2021, when it was unclear who would be the next prime minister, was thinking: 'my God – will there ever be a government?' Well, just leave Samoa to do Samoa's thing.

There is also reciprocity. Even if it takes two hundred years, somebody will expect something to be given back, down the line. Somebody's auntie's mother's uncle's cousin is going to remember, and if there's a favour, somebody's going to have to reciprocate. So even though there is diversity and difference and complexity in the Pacific, there are these basic values that stretch across this whole one-third of the planet: somehow, those things are there.

The last value is being rooted in the land and sea. Maybe in three hundred years that may have disappeared, but we are still Indigenous. We have not lost that long-term connection. In the Pacific if you were to invoke the mana of the land, even your most arrogant and entitled leader could not ignore. They wouldn't. They might behind closed doors, but they would know what the protocol was in that moment. It's something you must *respect*.

It is from this value system that I draw my own values in academia and make decisions about what research is worth pursuing, what ways of teaching are inspiring or meaningful. When I share that with my students, they write the most profound things in their feedback. One Anglo-Australian student who identifies as non-binary and neurodivergent wrote an email to me after taking one of my courses: 'your class made me want to laugh and sing and cry and learn all at the same time. Every single lecture; every single tutorial. When I left, I' – and this is a non-performer – 'I *danced* out of your classroom; I felt empowered to dance.' And I thought: 'and therefore we are successful here'. That is my goal. If you feel amazing when you leave my class then we are successful. But I don't set out to do that. If you teach in this way, then great things happen, and it doesn't matter what your background is. It's not just for Pacific students. These are basic, awesome life skills that make you a better human who hopefully won't cause climate change.

What's Good for the Pacific

It is not a coincidence that if you do *good* for the Pacific – if you're committed to the Pacific, if you write for and with the Pacific – then it is meaningful and significant to people beyond the Pacific. This is because what is good for the Pacific is good for the planet. The Pacific is a massive body of water that absorbs huge amounts of anthropogenic carbon dioxide. It functions like a critical organ of the planet. If you stay true to your own sense of rigour, your own sense of value, your holistic, integrated, interdisciplinary, and Indigenous Pacific methods and approaches and values, good things come out, and interesting things happen for others. For example, I wrote *Consuming Ocean Island* (Teaiwa, 2015) for Banabans. I wrote for Pacific people, and my colleagues in Pacific studies, but I kept it in a storytelling format. By writing for who I wanted to write for, it worked for a broader audience. Banaba has so much to teach; so much to teach about the Anthropocene, for example. But I don't say: 'we're going to do the Anthropocene'. We start from Banaba; we start from the island, and then you work in a multi-scalar fashion to the other scales of influence and impact and agency, and the different kinds of personalities and people.

That said, Banaba is quite unique in that it is a global island: it connects materially to many parts of the world and to a massive global agricultural industry. When I present the exhibition version of my research, *Project Banaba*, in different places, people invariably come up to me and say: 'my grandfather worked on Banaba', or 'my parents lived on Banaba'. Or 'I work in DFAT (the Australian Department of Foreign Affairs and Trade), and I spent time on Banaba as a child because my dad worked there'. Phosphate extraction from Banaba was a major industry for Australia for eight decades. There are Australian families everywhere who have a mythological story about Banaba because this industry was so critical for them. When I had the exhibition in Sydney, and I was interviewed in the *Guardian*, some people wrote and said: 'my family destroyed your island, I'm so sorry'. When we had the exhibition in Napier in New Zealand, a retired doctor showed up and said: 'my father was the New Zealand officer who took back Banaba from the Japanese'. He had compiled all his father's notes and memoirs and newspaper clippings over time, and he gave me four perfectly bound folders of this material. That happens to me all the time: I have been given personal memoirs and other items that families didn't know what to do with. They didn't know who else valued this story. But the fact that there have been so many of them over time tells me that Banaba is not a small and insignificant island in the middle of the Pacific. It is actually a place that connects to many families of many different backgrounds. And if I could read Japanese or Chinese I would be able to go back to Japan and Hong Kong and track the flows of all of these labourers who also worked on Banaba, and all the records associated with their experiences.

Part of my value system is also valuing others beyond the Pacific, in that I'm interested in their stories. And part of my research approach – and this is present in the teaching as well – is always to present a variety of views on the same thing and let people work out what the ethics and politics and issues are around that. It is always really obvious that it was the Evil Colonial Empire that did awful things to people, but you do not have to say that non-stop. I assemble evidence from as many participants as possible: here are the British, Australians, New Zealanders; here's a housewife; here's the pharmacist; here's a hobby photographer; here's some of the Gilbertese men who were working in the mines; here's the Tuvaluans, and the Banabans, and the labourers who came from Hong Kong. I go down those roads, and I read those stories. Yes, there was injustice, devastation, environmental plunder, and ruin. But there are also amazing experiences and perspectives that come out of it and that teach us so much about human life and the whole world and the kinds of political and economic and ethical choices that we need to make going forward to not mess up things again.

Recently I had to reflect on my definition of academic integrity. It is a values-based integrity, meaning: Who is this for, how will it transform people's lives, and to what end? Rigour for me *never, ever* furthers the anthropological project – I couldn't care less if anthropology ended forever today, or many other disciplines either. The discipline is only there to give us back some of the tools the anthropologists learned along the way after hanging out for a long time, staring at natives. So my work is never going to further anybody's genealogy of thought or methods in a particular discipline. I am *not* here for the disciplines. However, I do value *little bits* of the disciplines that help me tell Pacific stories better to transform things; to make our lives better in a colonial and postcolonial world, or in a post-apocalyptic climate change, pandemic-induced, context. Every discipline has some good material, and it is good because its adherents derived it by observing, learning, and stealing all over the world. I can weave that together. But rigour and integrity reside in the values and in my commitment to the region and to a Pacific audience. So if I read a study about climate change written by an anthropologist or a social scientist, I can easily tell who it is for and who it is not for. I think: 'You're not here for the

Pacific. You're not here for Indigenous peoples.' And I tend not to value those sorts of studies in the same way, unless there's *something* in there that I feel will bring people justice, that will right the wrongs of the past, or the present, or the future.

However, the result of my own work cannot be a half loaf stick lolly, as we say in Fiji to describe something that is subpar, because that does not help anyone, or transform anyone's lives. The Pacific has its own standards of excellence. One is something like virtuosity: an *amazing* performer or navigator or fisherman is highly effective and successful in what they do. But then there's always the question of *who is this for?* If it is just for you, it is not helpful. The idea of service to the collective is strong in the Pacific, and it is how we were all raised. It is also a value that is deeply embedded in Banaban and Kiribati societies, even to the point of *getting in the way* of some actual innovation and creativity.

Nevertheless, I am always looking for that. And because I do not see a lot of value for kinship in academia, except intellectual kin along really specific genealogies that always go back to Europe – I do not value that highly. I come back instead to our basic Pacific values, where the most profound and complex thing is held within the most simple, grounded, usually practical, kind of concept. This is why my research on Banaba drilled down to the *rock*. It's a rock. But in this rock is *everything*: the whole universe is in this rock.

Exhibition: The Multi-Sited and Multi-Scalar

In combination with my values and the interdisciplinary way that I draw on elements from different disciplines, I work in a multi-sited and multi-scalar way: multi-sited because one cannot focus on one island all the time, since we are all interconnected; and multi-scalar because I am always interested in the *really small* and the *really big* at the same time. That is also part of the method and the approach. I articulate that clearly in *Consuming Ocean Island*, and some of those dimensions are in the *Project Banaba* exhibition as well: you have to think about small places and big impacts and then have an embodied or emotional response, too.

The exhibition first took place in Sydney, at Carriageworks, in a huge room with high ceilings. If you are a dancer and you walk into that space, you just want to start flying and twirling and inhabiting the space – at least, *I* do. My training tells me to inhabit the room: flow through one corner, go to another corner, leap to another. And because Kiribati dancing is inspired by the frigatebird, when I look at the height of the ceiling, I think: '*Woo!* We need to go *up*!' That space inspired the exhibition because it features textiles hanging from the sky: land from the sky. It is still about place. But place is flipped, and it is flipped in a way that makes sense. In Banaban oral traditions the land – the rock of Banaba – falls from the sky. It falls into the sea and then becomes Banaba, which is the navel of the earth. So, of course, these oral traditions make sense because bird droppings – one of the materials from which phosphate is formed – come from the sky, or when birds nest, but also land comes from the sea because phosphate is also made up of the mineralized remains of crustaceans and reefs and other marine life, and they fuse together under the pressure of the ocean and they become Banaba.

When I walked into that space in Sydney, I started imagining the island and how we could reconstruct it in that space, bringing together what I learned from the archives with this sense of place. So we appliquéd pinnacles, which are the bones of the land, on the backs of the textiles. We put quotations from the archives on the front of the textiles. It was choreographically informed in that you hang the textiles from the sky, but you hang them low enough that people are not just going to walk in a straight line through them; they're going to weave around them, and they're going to look at them in a certain way. We put in an entry *wall* to guide the flow. And as you move from the front to the back of the room, you encounter a three-screen projection of audio-visual moving images. You pause over there as you work out what it is. And there is also a soundscape; a whole soundtrack flowing into the front of the room from the back of the room, from this three-screen projection. So you move through textiles; you encounter the three screens; and then you need a break after that because some of that content is quite heavy. It's a bit sad, it's very poetic. It's powerful. But, you might say: Is everyone okay? You know, after all this mining – everyone all right? And then you get to this wall, which we call a 'photo reef', where everyone's OK. Those who have survived and lived are getting on with their lives. And I have forty-five photographs of my family just hanging out. And when I say my family, I mean my big family: my fifty first cousins and all of their children, and all my eight or nine uncles and aunties. They're just hanging out, getting on with their lives. That's along the back wall. So you *flow* through the land, you flow through the textiles, you flow through the archives; you look at and you hear things in the back of the room; and then you flow out, back to the entry. But you've gone past this family story of creative survival; lots of pictures of dancing, feasting, hanging out, washing clothes, hopping on the boat, hopping off the boat. You move through time: you move through the past. I also have images of ancestors, very large images, blown up on textiles, and they are watching you while you are moving through the other textiles. So they're like ancestral guardians in the space, watching people as they come in and move through and come out.

In a way, the exhibition is a demonstration of everything that I have been discussing. My curator conceptualized it in many different ways, but I already had a really clear picture in my mind of what it should look like. I'd had twenty years for my sense of my embodied, archival, emplaced, sensibilities to coalesce, to become well integrated and percolate out in whatever way is needed, including through this visual arts exhibition. It is a clear manifestation of all these different methods, modes, ways of thinking and being in the world. When it moved from Carriageworks to MTG (Museum Theatre Gallery) Hawke's Bay in New Zealand, I had to quickly reconfigure the work for a smaller space. The ceiling was much lower, and we decided it was okay for little children to be able to touch and run through and around the textiles, which were much lower to the ground. They kept saying: 'the threads are coming out; do you want us to put signs and barriers out so that people don't pull on those threads?' And I said: 'No, it's okay. The ancestors – you can see through them, they're ancestral presences. They're not solid fabric. They're black and white, and they're see-through.' It is an intensely embodied experience. The exhibition is not one you just stand and stare at. As in all my work, it is really the sensibilities, the techniques, the approaches from dance that I now continue to use in my visual arts practice and my other research, rather than *actual* dancing.

Reference

Teaiwa, K. M. (2015). *Consuming Ocean Island: Stories of People and Phosphate from Banaba*. Bloomington: Indiana University Press.

CHAPTER 15

Methodologies Dialogue: Complexity

Ruthie Abeliovich, Leo Cabranes-Grant, and Soo Ryon Yoon

Suggested Reading

Clayton, M., Franko, M., George-Graves, N., Lepecki, A., Manning, S., Ross, J., and Schneider, R. (2013). 'Inside/Beside Dance Studies: A Conversation: Mellon Dance Studies in/and the Humanities'. *Dance Research Journal*, 45(3), 3–28.

Dening, G. (1996). 'The Theatricality of History Making and the Paradoxes of Acting'. In G. Dening, *Performances*. Chicago: University of Chicago Press, pp. 103–27.

Hughes, B. (2020). 'Oka Apesvchi: Indigenous Feminism, Performance, and Protest'. *Theatre Journal*, 72(2), 127–42.

Yapp, H. (2020). 'Intimating Race: Tao Ye's *4* and Methods for World Dance'. In S. Manning, J. Ross, & R. Schneider, eds., *Futures of Dance Studies*. Madison: University of Wisconsin Press, pp. 489–504.

Tracy C. Davis: Please explain why you selected the particular reading or readings that you nominated.

Ruthie Abeliovich: Greg Dening's *Performances* (1996) is the kind of book I pick up when I get stuck because there's something creative in his writing that provokes an 'opening up'. He shows how various interlocutors make meaning – objects, people, scholars – and how the focus of your study is networked to create the story, which he calls the 'historical plotline' or the 'historical narrative'. Every aspect of history-making exposes new actors (in the theatrical sense, not in the Latourian nodal sense) that perform as part of and within a constructed social fiction. He writes about history as the way historians need to perform, in the ethical and in the theatrical senses, and need to compose compelling stories that work *with* and sometimes against social fiction (cf. Latour, 2005: 46). What else did I think of in that respect – oh, the centrality of experience! We tend to forget our bodies in our scholarship, and Dening brings back the experience of a historian as a noble point, a crucial access for history-making, which narrows the gap between practice and theory (but through scholarship, not the practical side of theatre).

Paul Rae: Has Dening influenced your research methods, or how you research?

Ruthie Abeliovich: Yes. Dening writes about historians' encounters not only with unknown archival objects but with unknown content. I find this productive when I work on the theatricality of cross-cultural encounters in relation to Jewish and Israeli theatre history and the ways that the *meetings* between different identities are always ethically and aesthetically charged.

Soo Ryon Yoon: I included two readings. One is a roundtable conversation among dance and theatre and performance studies (TaPS) scholars about ontological and methodological questions that emerged from dance studies in relation to the broader humanities, and the other looks at the concept of world dance and the way Asian choreographers like Tao Ye purposely use universalist and abstract choreographic forms to do what Hentyle Yapp calls 'intimating race': to gesture to the perception and construction of racial schema for dancing bodies without perpetuating the racist narrative about non-Western dancers. When the first of these was published, I was in the thick of doing my fieldwork, looking at West African dancers working in Korea; it was very useful for me to clarify what I was dealing with. That said, the conversation doesn't necessarily come around to a clear definition or layout of what kind of methodologies will be or are in dance studies. Susan Manning mentions that Susan Foster has a clear idea about what dance studies should be and what methods it should use, which is performative writing based on choreographic exploration, and quickly follows up with a comment on what she calls her 'integrationist or assimilationist' model, whereby dance studies and its methods are always already in dialogue with other humanities disciplines. I selected Hentyle Yapp's piece on world dance as an example of these methods.

Leo Cabranes-Grant: I selected Bethany Hughes's essay because it's a straightforward, direct address to scholars: a call to mobilize a different kind of ontological point of view. I think we are open to the idea of different ways of accessing knowledge, but we don't go far enough into understanding that accessing knowledge is also ontological. This essay states at the beginning: I'm going to walk you through how we can start writing from a different, and ontological, point of view. It analyses three very different events, emphasizing the 'politics of citation' at the beginning because the sources we quote, the sources we are using, predetermine which theory of knowledge we work with. Hughes makes a clear decision: I'm going to only use sources from Indigenous cultures. So don't expect the usual approach – Diana Taylor or Rebecca Schneider or what have you – here Indigenous voices are taking the lead. And I'm going to stick to what they have to say; be also aware that Indigeneity is a *multiplicity* of voices, there is no such thing as an Indian Native American *thing*; among themselves there is also this diversity of points of view, of ways of looking at that. And I particularly like how that combination of factors leads to the concept of care. What is caring? We tend to go to Martin Heidegger or Michel Foucault for the notion of care; that's usually the track we go for – or at least I have – and all of a sudden, we find here this idea of caring, this question of embracing the full picture of your circumstance. And then the water – which maybe some people might use as a metaphor for fluidity and transdisciplinarity – is not just a metaphor this time, it's actually an embodied and embedded notion. It has a metaphorical side to it, of course, but it's also a value system inhabited by the bodies of the people that believe in it. The article makes a direct, precise effort to show us how things will look or feel if we truly try to listen to a different ontological voice.

Tracy C. Davis: Bethany Hughes brings us full circle back to Yapp and Dening, in the sense of how the phenomenology of performance generation or history-writing becomes synonymous with recentring oneself. For example, as a non-Indigenous person – and, in my case, as not-a-dance scholar – I am challenged to even be a witness to their writing.

Leo Cabranes-Grant: Yes, both Yapp and Dening address the affective question, our need to excavate what *actually* happened, not only what was *documented*. As scholars we visit many realms that are not part of our experiences as human beings. For example, I deal with colonial Mexico, which was an incredibly multiracial and multicultural place. I deal with several points of view, most of which I have not experienced myself – and they were also in the past, which is another issue. How do I account for that process in my scholarship, and my understanding of what I'm seeing?

Tracy C. Davis: Speaking for myself, I feel much more comfortable making that set of intellectually generous openings with *history* than with the contemporary. In other words, complexity in the past feels like something mappable and approachable, very differently than in the present.

Leo Cabranes-Grant: I agree with you. The other advantage is that the past cannot come and complain to us about our misunderstandings, whereas the present can say 'wait a second, that's not what I mean!'

Tracy C. Davis: I'm not sure that's true, because there are ways that the past speaks back to us through other historians, and through cultural members who feel continuity with a particular path that we broach. I think there are ways that the past does come back to us – it tends to be on a longer time loop, perhaps, but I think it does happen.

Leo Cabranes-Grant: I agree with Tracy that the past talks back to us, of course it does. But what I was trying to say was that when I'm dealing with the past, I always feel my decisions are made by a committee (including some elusive ghosts). While when I'm dealing with the present it's very much about my confrontation with that other person in front of me.

Paul Rae: Ruthie, considering that you research the past, do you agree? Your research on sound is so much more intangible even than most of the archival materials one might otherwise get one's hands on. Is it more elusive to you, and therefore harder?

Ruthie Abeliovich: I was just going to say that I think what the past is to Dening, nature is to Hughes. I mean, the way she addresses nature; water, as *theory*, resonates with my need to recruit imagination in order to understand the past. I work with historical sound recordings from historical theatre performances, and I try to understand ways people listened, spoke, and performed. I've given up on reality: I look for *experiences*, the sort of *effect* and *impact* sound has on people, how it creates communities, delivers a political or social atmosphere, and embodies (in a way) memories of how people speak and sing. I also look at sound recordings as cultural objects, and in that regard, I don't give up on reality.

Tracy C. Davis: How do you think about the historian's fidelity to whatever memory or past is being engaged? I feel like Hughes gives us her own located position very clearly and then, within an Indigenous ontology, situates the three performances in relation to a kind of cosmological ethics. And that's the fidelity. Likewise, I think that the Yapp article, which I'm really glad to have in the mix here, insists on a culturally located fidelity that destabilizes reading practices and dance critical practices that might otherwise be applied there.

Ruthie Abeliovich: For me, fidelity accounts for the cultural basis that I'm working on, for the sort of world that I'm trying to write about: the symbols, melodies, customs, and language that operate. I am also aware of the *limits* of my methods: the fragmentary historical sound recordings I work with have been torn out of their original historical context and handled by archivists and curators, presenting contingent and speculative historical artefacts. Collecting them and bringing them into one coherent story would be wrong because this would work against their story, which is non-linear and follows a network of multiple sites of cultural and theatrical production.

Soo Ryon Yoon: I want to comment on Tracy's point about history as perhaps more mappable than contemporary reality. Part of the reason Yapp's article has been useful for me is that I also work around the questions and representations of race, in terms of performance – or performance cultures – in Korea. At the same time, for me, history has also been very messy in terms of access to the archives of a cultural locale that has been uprooted – due to colonial domination or nationalist domination – because the archives may or may not be there. Even if there is an archive you are always already suspicious of its credibility. My work, which looks at both the historical and contemporary circulation and representation of African diasporic dance in Korea, is never easy precisely because of what Ruthie just talked about: fragmentation that demands other sensibilities. Mapping ethnographic observation of dancing, or whatever, requires my body to be at stake, more present at the archive because it's always already an evolving and fragmented site in a specific cultural locale.

Paul Rae: Perhaps we can refocus these wide-ranging explorations about the idea of complex methods for researching complex phenomena around the following questions: When you deploy methods, what do you use them for? Where is a method a help, and where is it a hindrance in your engagement with complex research environments or situations or phenomena?

Leo Cabranes-Grant: The distinction that is made between methods of gathering information and methodology as interpreting information is merely situational. It's a matter of emphasis at different moments – can we truly separate gathering from interpreting? I don't think so. I think that the idea that there is some kind of distinction between picking up and interpreting what you're picking up is a blind spot, something unavoidable and yet inevitably problematic in the decisions we make as scholars. I prefer to talk about 'narrative intersections' – the idea that I might be dealing with different kinds of storytelling at the same time, narrative styles that intersect and overlap. This gives me options about which kind of story

I want to pay attention to at any particular moment. That doesn't mean that other stories are less relevant or less factual; they just follow a different way of presenting the information.

Of course, this says a lot about me: which intersections I feel more comfortable with, or which intersections I decide to visit. Some people make the distinction between theory and method – I don't. I think that methods are theories that have become naturalized. And we always start from a theory; otherwise, we will not be able to recognize our object in any particular way. I try to listen to my events and my archive as much as possible – and I know that's an exercise, a deliberate 'as-if' moment – and I also know there are unconscious things working in me while I do that. But I try to listen to the event/the object/the situation that is hailing me, and I try to pay attention to all the voices and all their potential sounds or movements that might be expressing themselves at different volumes, simultaneously. I try to re-experience the process, the flow. For me, the most fascinating and amazing moment of research is when I become the listener or the witness, trying to ensure that no figure participating in the event goes unnoticed.

Paul Rae: Could you give an example?

Leo Cabranes-Grant: I'm trying to work with a manuscript written in Mexico in 1763 by a Basque merchant. This manuscript was probably intended for the consumption of his friends, so it was a private thing, never published. It's a very interesting account from someone who has come from Europe of what he sees in Mexico City. Instead of describing any mountain or river he basically starts describing performances. For this person, Mexico was something that *happens*, not something that is just there. What *happens* there is what defines geography for him, and what happens in this book are dances, sports, festivals, weddings; terrible jokes about race, and racial types; uniforms, soldiers; images of fruits side by side with images of *castas* (ethnic groups) (see Figure 15.1). And the book is not only about Mexico – the text includes the Philippines, which were at the time part of the Spanish Empire. Mexico received objects and produce from the Philippines, and China, and Japan – and then those items crossed the Atlantic into Europe, or travelled to the Caribbean and South America. How can I grasp the complexity of this highly mediated vision of a Mexico that is European and Asian and African and Indigenous all at the same time? I have to listen to all these voices through the filter of what the *author* is doing and thinking about them. I'm very aware of the limitations I am going to encounter doing this, but I find this gives me permission to try *other ways* of approaching the subjects, which can be liberating.

Figure 15.1 '*De mestizo e indio sale coyote*' (From a mestiza and an Indian we get a coyote), Casta #53, Joaquín Antonio de Basarás y Garaygorta. From *Origen, costumbres, y estado presente de Mexicanos y Filipinos* (*Origin, Customs, and Present Conditions of Mexicans and Filipinos*), 1793. Courtesy of the Hispanic Society of America, New York.

Soo Ryon Yoon: I feel like I'm struggling to answer Paul's question because it is both straightforward but also not so straightforward.

Tracy C. Davis: Welcome to Paul Rae's mind.

Soo Ryon Yoon: I'm originally trained as an ethnographer, in the Northwestern Performance Studies Department tradition, where Dwight Conquergood's legacy has shaped the approach to looking at performance (see Conquergood, 2013: 41–2; Madison and Hamera, 2005: xi–xxv). In 2016, I completed my dissertation on ethnographic observation and analysis of West African contemporary dances in Korea, or Korean practitioners doing African diasporic dances more broadly. But then I began to notice or rather emphasize the importance of the historical aspect of how circulation happened earlier on, leading up to contemporary circulation, which demanded that I look at much more archival data.

Ethnography is privileged in performance studies. Historically, however, the Korean context has been powerfully shaped by colonial and Western-centric knowledge production. The first anthropological or ethnographic enquiries were made by Japanese anthropologists studying the bodies of Koreans through the colonial period, and so the ways in which I'm also trained in ethnography demand that, one way or another, I interrogate how racialized bodies have been understood. This suspends the smooth deployment of my training.

Tracy C. Davis: Soo Ryon, how do you bring your ethnographic eye to a study that reveals the necessity to engage with a prior history, relative to what you can directly observe? What do you *do* when you do that?

Soo Ryon Yoon: Trying to locate the archive or to verify its credibility takes a lot of time, in which case you also build trust with the archive owners. In the Korean context, the space in which archival materials are housed is also political: it could be nationalistic; maybe it's made in opposition to or in relation to a colonial legacy. So even before trying to collect or analyse texts or materials, I pay attention to what's going on *around* the archival materials themselves. Bringing my ethnographic sensibility to the archive is also included in that process.

Tracy C. Davis: I don't mean this negatively, but this sounds a little pro forma as a reiteration of the critique of the archive. We know institutions are political entities, and they need funding to exist and perpetuate preservation, and that is bound to be ideological. But then presumably at some point, sitting at a table with a folder or a box of materials in front of you – just as Ruthie is sitting with headphones on listening to recordings and Leo has the Basque author's manuscript opened before him – you're sitting at a desk with 'the stuff'. If we come back to Leo's phrase about trying to listen for the small voice, as an ethnographically trained researcher, what do you do?

Soo Ryon Yoon: That's something that I'm trying to figure out as I write. What I do is in alignment with what Leo mentioned: to try to listen to movements that may not necessarily be so obvious or clear in the text. For instance, in one chapter of my manuscript I draw on novels that depict cafés and club scenes in 1930s Korea. They talk about jazz rhythms, but you know the authors don't necessarily talk about the movements or the gestures or the intimate bodily contacts that are involved; they only allude to those moments and never necessarily get into it. The specific dance archives that I hope to find are not really extant. These novels or literary texts demand my ethnographic sensibility to pay attention to *moments* where movements happen, to try to observe the gaps that may not necessarily be articulated in writing text.

Tracy C. Davis: Do you agree with Leo that method – maybe it's close reading, I don't mean to put words in your mouth, but very close attention to clues – is inherently theoretical?

Soo Ryon Yoon: I've always assumed that it *isn't* inherently theoretical.

Tracy C. Davis: Even so, maybe the recorders of those observations are not escaping ideology?

Soo Ryon Yoon: Sure.

Paul Rae: At the same time, bringing an ethnographic approach to textual analysis is one way of understanding how that method might *properly* sit in relation to complex situations is by being *improper*; Soo Ryon applies the 'wrong' thing in order to get at something that the 'right' thing would otherwise oversimplify.

Tracy C. Davis: I would argue that's a move performance scholars from many orientations have made for a long time. Think about Erving Goffman (1959): a sociologist who identified the frontstage/backstage dichotomy of workplaces. Or Zora Neale Hurston (1935): an ethnologist and anthropologist who adapted her field notes of southern US life into drama, dance, and revues.

Ruthie Abeliovich: For me, finding the method is part of what the research is. I try to work out the media relationship – or what Tracy, with

Peter W. Marx (Davis & Marx, 2021: 4–5), calls 'the media ecology' – of the early Yiddish theatre. I try to decipher the relationship between manuscripts about performances, ephemera, and sound recordings. Most of my manuscripts are handwritten in Germanized Yiddish and are collected in multiple archives in the United States and Eastern Europe, and thus the same manuscript can have two different names according to geography. I've just begun trying to work out this mess in order to understand what the appropriate method would be and how to theorize this field of study. As a guideline, I try to find *correlations*: a theory with an organic relationship to sources, circumstances of preservation, and ways to study this mediascape.

Tracy C. Davis: So, for you, some objects are document*ed*, but not documents. Scope and scale are part of the challenge of mess and complexity. How do you work within that mediascape and media ecology to understand the contours of the study?

Ruthie Abeliovich: I'm looking at transformation: moments of change, when an object transformed from a text to a performance (or from a performance to a text) and then maybe simultaneously to a standard recording. Sometimes it's the other way around: a song entered a theatre performance and became associated with it, though it's an old folk song. I'm not trying to be comprehensive: I limit the scope by working only with representative artists, and seek moments of transformation and of impact to see what materials did to the places they performed, and how they created what I call a 'Yiddish Sound Republic' through the same people singing the same songs. I look at how this affected the transnational migratory community at the start of the twentieth century, and how this networked people and communities together: a theory that tries to explain how both archives and the network grow out of this structure because it's transnational, local, and global, according to creative centres and migratory routes.

Tracy C. Davis: It looks like you're letting this get as complex as possible. One might even say that the search for that complexity is a major phase of the research project.

Ruthie Abeliovich: Yes, and I'm also looking at a multidimensional scale in terms of time, so I'm also looking at how these materials operate today. One thing we try to do in the European Research Council-funded 'DYBBUK' research project is to develop a Yiddish handwriting recognition model (see TAU, 2021). To decipher the handwritten Yiddish, we need to feed the model with many contemporary handwritten texts, for example texts from lowbrow Yiddish theatre and personal memoirs and letters with various histories. This is another dimension of the methodology, but it may also convey a central dimension of it: how these materials, of various media, perform across time.

Leo Cabranes-Grant: The challenge is how you do the *parsing out* without *leaving out*. Basically, every methodology and every method will parse things out for you or with you in a particular way, but what bothers me as a scholar is this awareness that by parsing out in a particular way, I know I'm leaving out something. And for me the leaving out is very important because many of my objects of story are about peoples and cultures that have been left out of or erased from the records, documents, or experiences, intentionally or not. No human person will be able to put it all together at the same time. It comes to a moment of decision: Which kind of skill, which kind of practice, will allow me to give more visibility or sound to things that are usually left out? That's the moment when I realize that I might need ethnography. I'm doing ethnography of this manuscript, you're perfectly right! But at the same time, I have to figure out why the person who wrote this manuscript decided to pay less attention to certain things and so much attention to others. I get the feeling that between those two choices something very important was left out. I find myself more and more drawn to theories of affect, maybe to make myself more comfortable with the fact that, as Tracy said, things might be documented even if they are not in the document. I need something that authorizes me to be a little more elastic, at some moments, about what I allow myself to investigate. If I stick to a very rigid understanding of documentation, a lot of my subjects and objects of study will remain unheard. I have not found any solution that works all the time, so I keep trying.

Tracy C. Davis: Whereas Ruthie starts with a globally dispersed set of objects (that is not really a set) and has to track down the recordings – and then think about them individually and in terms of each one's diasporic travel as well as collectively – Leo starts with one manuscript. That *seems* so much easier. Yet that one manuscript then results in a treasure hunt in numerous archives, cities, countries, and languages. Ultimately, processually, do these become comparable projects in terms of historians' labour?

Leo Cabranes-Grant: It's fair, but I would like to add dance to the mix. Soo Ryon, how do you think dance works from that perspective?

Soo Ryon Yoon: For me, it makes research much trickier because things are put into motion all the time, not just in terms of dance movements but also in the way that different languages have to be mobilized to describe and translate dances across cultural differences. Here is a list of the different types of language I work with: academic English, Korean, Korean transliteration of colonial Japanese, Korean transliteration of early twentieth-century English, French (because a lot of practitioners with whom I work come from francophone West Africa), Mande languages (including Dyula and Bobo of Burkina Faso), Igbo from Nigeria, and African American Vernacular English. As someone for whom English is a second language, there's also lengthy training involved for me to decipher the cultural politics and cultural meanings across all these different languages. This becomes a challenge when I have to interview someone from Burkina Faso, for instance, because I'm not able to conduct the interview in Bobo, but the Burkinabe dancers are generous enough to do an interview in French. My French is broken, so we tend to then rely on someone who has much more proficiency in French to help us communicate, while otherwise (outside the formal interview context) we tend to communicate in English. Then what kind of truthful meanings – fidelity, or authenticity – enables the deciphering of *all* these linguistic and cultural differences?

It's not just because the bodies of these practitioners are always in motion, but also because the way they understand that techniques of contemporary dance, or even the concept of 'contemporary dance', might introduce contested meanings. For instance, Korean dancers understand contemporary dance through Americanized Martha Graham-ian language or Steve Paxton's contact improvisation, or postmodern avant-garde dance. The West African dancers with whom I have worked understand contemporary dance through the French institutionalization of contemporary dance that has been disseminated to francophone regions, so even to read or pay attention to how their bodies move becomes complex in terms of the history, culture, and linguistic differences, as well as the way they accrue their expertise.

Tracy C. Davis: Soo Ryon, let's return to a moment in your explanation where you described needing a francophone speaker to be an intermediary. Historians might wish we could invoke such a person to be present and to clarify our understanding of something we read in an archival setting. We can't say: 'is our understanding of this word, or this phrase, or this gesture, or this movement or this moment or this event, right?' Perhaps when you work with archival materials, you have moments where you wish you could invoke such a person? Maybe there are ways that you do?

Soo Ryon Yoon: That is certainly a challenge! When I look at archival materials something always gets lost in translation; I think that's a given.

I relate to the desire for wanting to invoke that presence, even when I'm looking at something that's written in Korean (which is my native language). There are a lot of times I don't really understand what is being talked about – not because I don't understand the *literal* meaning of the sentences, but I have to constantly situate them in a completely different cultural context. The colonial Korean language is actively polyglot, whereby people and their languages are shaped by the colonial Japanese language, English, French, all cosmopolitan influences introduced to 1920s and 1930s Korea, and so that's when I tend to stumble a lot. I ask my historian friends a lot of questions: 'what do you think this means?' Perhaps they're much more familiar with the materials, so that's the only way that I'm able to tap in to these undecipherable or illegible texts.

Ruthie Abeliovich: One of the beautiful moments in 'Inside/Beside Dance Studies', which you gave us to read, touches upon a dance studies model that considers choreography as a mode of theorizing.[1] I think that is what you just described: the feeling that something's happening to your brain, you need to change a programme when you change your language, and that's *your* choreographic gesture.

Soo Ryon Yoon: Thank you for the generous depiction. I don't know if I'm always successful at executing that choreography, but maybe it's a process.

Paul Rae: How do you know when you *have* been successful? When do you know you've got something right, something's working?

Ruthie Abeliovich: I know that it's working when it corresponds with a broader cultural context, broader systems. These might be social or political or even personal.

Paul Rae: Would you say it's like something slots into place, or forms a pattern? Or is that an oversimplification?

Ruthie Abeliovich: It feels more like a key, like I've managed to access an object and to understand its position in time and place.

Leo Cabranes-Grant: That's a very tough question. I call it the 'poetic spark'. It's a moment when I *know* that I understand something. When I'm reading or observing something where the multiplicity of motions starts to become gestural, choreographic – or melodious, in the sense of music – I become able to trace things in a particular way. It doesn't mean that it's a straight line; sometimes it's a complex design, but I start to see how things echo one another. At first, it's more like an image, then I have to translate that into words, and that's where the problem usually starts: language is not necessarily the most flexible instrument to describe simultaneous events and perceptions, so you have to translate, and things get lost in translation. It allows me to reread and revisit everything, all of a sudden, by understanding how that particular story works. Usually, these moments of recognition restart the whole process and bring me back to the beginning. It doesn't necessarily move me forward, it just makes me retrace everything I have done, and in that retracing some of the most fascinating things can become clearer to me. Then I'm immediately traumatized by the next question: Can I be persuasive to somebody else?

Tracy C. Davis: Leo, when you've gone back to reread, retrace, have you ever found yourself to have been mistaken?

Leo Cabranes-Grant: Oh many, many times. I think one has to learn not to be afraid of mistakes. That's fundamental, because in the process of rereading and retracing and going back and starting again, I start to cancel a lot of my previous perceptions and occasionally get very, very convinced that I really have to reconsider everything. It's not a scary moment; I know I'm reconsidering from a precise experience of my own process, as a scholar, at that moment. But yes, usually that's the moment when I have to get rid of a lot of text that I have written; I realize, 'oh my God, I have to start writing this essay, this chapter again, from what I understand now' (*chuckles*).

Tracy C. Davis: That's just tremendously fun, I think.

Ruthie Abeliovich: It is a moment of frustration that calls me to go back to the beginning and start all over again. Sometimes there is no flexibility to do a particular kind of shift because it's a conceptual shift.

Tracy C. Davis: The Yapp essay identifies 'interesting' as a category, and I was intrigued by that because it recalls a lot of experiences that I've had of thinking 'oh, that's interesting'. However, here we're describing something quite different: not 'that's interesting' but 'I think I understand'. As Leo put it, then you need to figure out how to persuade other people, but perhaps a better way to state that is *you need to show other people that understanding*. Isn't that part of a research process: finding something interesting and then after years and years and years and years of effort and learning and dead ends and blunt ends, and some live ends, and some travel, and in Soo Ryon's version consultations, *maybe* what you have is understanding.

Paul Rae: Can you say that there's one aspect of writing that really is key to getting complexity right on the page? For instance, is it at the level of word choice? Is it at the level of the sentence, the paragraph? Is it about structure?

Ruthie Abeliovich: For me, the moment that I can phrase the question clearly and elegantly is the moment in which I understand that I can begin. From there, it gets easier for me to structure my writing and argument.

Soo Ryon Yoon: I feel as though I'm getting it right when I'm able to map out or delineate a particular narrative or a story that ties all the data together. I don't know if that gets at the complexity – perhaps maybe it's more of a cleaning up.

Leo Cabranes-Grant: First, let me acknowledge that I write in two languages: Spanish (my original language) and English (my second language), and in the process of doing my research sometimes I have ventured into other languages, like Nahuatl (an Indigenous language) or even Danish. All my languages are dancing around in my head at the same time. So, in which language is my insight coming to me? What is the internal translator doing? I ask myself how much of what I'm trying to say implies that I have to leave one language out of another, or how much of what I'm trying to say is made possible precisely because I'm wrestling with more than one language. Translation is a fundamental moment in my process of understanding – of grasping the object. Do I keep the translation as part of my writing, or do I just give you that result, the outcome of that translation?

Another thing is the shift from data to unpacking. I'm always thinking: How much of my unpacking is speculation? Can I go back to the data and still be accurate and faithful to it? Sometimes you have to take a little leap here and there. Do I keep that in the writing, or do I leave it out?

Finally, how effectively can I imagine my reader? I think that as scholars we aim to know everything, but our readers don't need to know everything we know. So, we have to make selections; we have to somehow translate for them. For me, the hardest moment of writing comes when I have to decide how much of what I have done should actually be shared with my readers. How much do they need to know, so they can be convinced – as convinced as I am? It's the old question of Greek rhetoric, how to be persuasive. I agonize over that, and that's probably the reason why I have so many drafts of everything, because it's almost like every draft is a reader, but then I imagine *another* reader, and then I have to figure out in the end which reader am I writing for, all over again. Under those circumstances, deadlines are a blessing. It's not about being right or being wrong; it's more about finding the point of access that will allow communication to happen, and that is incredibly difficult and never gets easier. I hoped that maybe after doing this for so many years, I could come to a point when I open the computer and I just go for it. I'm still waiting for that.

Note

1 In another instance within this article, Susan Manning proposes thinking of a method of translating embodied knowledge. Earlier in the same conversation, however, Naomi Bragin and Nadine George-Graves caution against taking the strategy to move and to be fluid for granted, because it may be a privilege and does not always mean 'freedom' for those accessing research sites within a racialized and gendered structure of dance and performance studies (Clayton et al., 2013: 26, 23–4).

References

Conquergood, D. (2013). *Cultural Struggles: Performance, Ethnography, Praxis*. Ann Arbor: University of Michigan Press.

Davis, T. C., & Marx, P. W. (2021). 'On Critical Media History'. In T. C. Davis and P. W. Marx, eds., *The Routledge Companion to Theatre and Performance Historiography*. Abingdon: Routledge, pp. 1–39.

Goffman, E. (1959). *The Presentation of Self in Everyday Life*. New York: Anchor Books.

Hurston, Z. N. (1935). *Mules and Men*. Philadelphia, PA: J. B. Lippincott.

Latour, B. (2005). *Reassembling the Social: An Introduction to Actor-Network Theory*. Oxford: Oxford University Press.

Madison, D. S., & Hamera, J. (2005). 'Performance Studies at the Intersections'. In D. S. Madison & J. Hamera, eds., *The SAGE Handbook of Performance Studies*. Thousand Oaks, CA: SAGE, pp. ix–xi.

TAU (Tel Aviv University). (2021). 'DYBBUK' Project. Launched 1 October.

Conclusion: The Aesthetics of Performance Research – Appearance, Conduct, Design

Paul Rae

Conventionally, theatre and performance studies (TaPS) research involves the specific combination, sequencing, or blending of research activities and the explanatory frames used to interpret the diverse kinds of data they produce. In drawing this book to a close, I propose a different way of thinking about mixing, one that is present in many of the chapters, albeit latently so. This concerns how the activities we think of as 'doing performance research by using methods' mix with those activities and experiences we would not readily recognize as such: the mixing of methods and non-methods. My reasoning is rooted in one of the original motivations for this book: at the level of discipline formation, TaPS scholars have been much more active in establishing the scope of their research and the theories and concepts they might use in its interpretation than in thinking systematically or reflexively about the methods used to generate the data underpinning their insights. This is not to say that TaPS researchers lack methods or methodologies. On the contrary, they are liberal in their use of them, yet this points to a paradox: despite the sheer – and ever-increasing – volume of TaPS research that has been produced during the past half century, TaPS researchers have not been especially methodical in their methodological practices.

A range of explanations for this could be canvassed. One might centre on how the discipline has defined itself at once with and against other disciplines, sometimes through the covert absorption of other disciplines' methodological norms, sometimes through their renunciation, and sometimes both at once. Another might trace how and why some disciplines developed publication conventions requiring statements, or indeed whole sections, on method and methodology, while in TaPS inclusion is optional, at best. Yet another answer might examine the highly varied commitments to method among the relatively small number of innovative thinkers who have influenced the formation of the discipline to date. In this chapter, however, my concerns are less genealogical than formal. I propose that one distinctive feature of performance research is how researchers' activities are configured in relation to the activities researched: namely the creation, presentation, and reception of performances. It is in the nature of this relation that the systematic activity normally thought of as the practice of method becomes absorbed into, obscured by, or rendered continuous with the phenomena under investigation, in a way that hinders a clear and sustained delineation of method and methodology.

What do I mean by this? Much received wisdom about method treats it as a distinct overlay onto the phenomenon being researched, and much debate and on-the-ground problem-solving in research centres on how to maintain an appropriate distance between the two. Many TaPS researchers will know that this is much easier said than done, and both the distinctiveness of the researcher's perspective and the potential of their presence to influence what is being researched are widely acknowledged. At the same time, much language used to account for such phenomena is generic, limited mainly to professions of positionality and the somewhat bashful acknowledgement that the researcher may have distorted the picture they are trying to present by being there at all. Is there a better starting assumption to research than that of a default 'gap' between the researcher and the researched that is then compromised in its bridging? In *After Method*, the sociologist John Law (2004) details the extent to which all activities in a given research situation are continuous with or integrated into one another from the outset, just as they are equally embedded in any number of other conditions and circumstances that inform the situation, without their being readily apparent. Law's arguments have both general and specific relevance to TaPS research, though it will require a bit of explanation to show how.

Introducing his project, Law (2004: 2) writes: 'parts of the world are caught in our ethnographies, our histories and our statistics. But other parts are not, or if they are then this is because they have been distorted into clarity.' Law's concern is with the best way of accounting, as his subtitle has it, for 'mess in social science research': what to do when the world is 'vague, diffuse or unspecific, slippery, emotional, ephemeral, elusive or indistinct, changes like a kaleidoscope or doesn't really have much of a pattern at all'. In response, he advocates what he calls 'method assemblage', which combines conventional research activity, the other activities underway in any given situation where researchers find themselves (including their tacitly informing circumstances), and the resulting research outputs and outcomes. One implication is that any research process is going to involve bringing specific features of a given situation to light (in Law's terms, making them present), with the inevitable knock-on effect of rendering others invisible, or absent. Some absences Law describes as 'manifest' because they are the necessary counterpoint to what is made present in the research. Other absences are 'other' in that they arise through routinization or repression. For Law, established methods standardize what is made present and what is othered by reinforcing and reasserting the boundaries between them. A more dynamic approach to method can disclose non-standard knowledge and ways of knowing about the world through a process not so much of representing 'in here' (in our research) the 'out there' of the world (what we have discovered), but of continuously engaging in 'crafting, allegory or gathering', which treats research as an extension of the situation as the researcher comes to it (Law, 2004: 118).

Within that process, we can see how method-related activity is additive to, and both selective and energizing of, the 'non-method' activity or other phenomenon that is conventionally thought of as the 'object' of research. Of particular interest in the present context is the language Law (2004: 122) uses to describe the process. He writes, for instance, that 'methods in natural science and social science barely catch their own performativity'. By contrast, method assemblage is a process of continuous enactment, in the course of which

> The possibility – indeed the likelihood – that tensions appear between different enactments (and knowledges) of reality is made manifest. And with this [the] possibility that realities may be crafted and acknowledged as indefinite gatherings, coherent or non-coherent, ambivalent, allegorical, and within or beyond language. If we wanted to play games with words we might think of calling this position *enactment realism*. (Law, 2004: 141)

Perhaps 'enactment realism' is wordplay for social scientists because constructivism and realism have conventionally been thought of as contrasting ontologies; their combination may be less novel for TaPS scholars familiar with the world-making capacities of performance.

That being the case, what might method assemblage mean for TaPS research? The general answer would be the same for many disciplines: stated in abstract terms, any research process primarily involves the contingent integration of ramified relations between a multiplicity of phenomena in order to bring hitherto unacknowledged features of the world to our attention and overcome some of the conventional absences or oversights of the discipline (even while recognizing that new absences will be created in the process). More bluntly put, research activity first and foremost adds complexity to any given situation, but in such a way as to produce explanations of some features of it that other researchers may then take up and put to use in other settings.

The more specific answer to the question concerns what is being investigated when TaPS research is underway. The terms Law uses to argue his case, including *presence*, *performativity*, and *enactment*, are hardly neutral when it comes to performance research. Instead, they beg the question of what happens when, say, one takes an enactive approach to the investigation of staging, brings a performative sensibility to performance analysis, or seeks to make present presence itself, as manifested onstage, in a theatre, and beyond. One response is to urge caution: just because Law uses terms familiar to adepts of a specific discipline, it does not follow that these terms mean the same thing as they ordinarily do within that discipline. At the same time, it is in the nature of ramified relations that they do not mean something completely different, either: these terminologies carry their own embedded associations that resonate and reverberate across the different uses in TaPS, in Law's material semiotics, and in the new realist project to which it belongs, as well as the lay uses of the terms in any number of social settings (see Rae, 2018: 2–10). Nevertheless, I see Law's telling use of performance-related terminologies as indicative of one possible reason why method and methodological thinking has remained relatively obscure within TaPS discourse, if not its practice. If research activity, as continuous with the phenomena it investigates, has a performative and enactive quality, then there stands to be an area of substantial overlap between what TaPS scholars research and how they research it, making a distinct method discourse all the harder to tease out.

The sanguine response to the idea that aspects of method and 'object' might cancel or drown each other out is to take this idea as an occupational hazard of performance research, and get on with the process as best one can. But what if we were to take such a phenomenon as sufficiently persistent and distinctive as to be a characteristic feature of performance research in its own right? It might then form the basis of a more thoroughgoing understanding of what performance research *is*. In this chapter, I explore some of the qualities of these areas of overlap or extensivity between research activity and the activity researched by drawing on ideas and experiences offered by the contributors to this book, as well as some of the relatively rare moments in the wider TaPS literature where authors discuss aspects of their research experience. Since such experiences are rarely the focal point of research in their own right, I supplement those references with more detailed accounts from my own experiences of conducting research as part of a project currently underway on island performances.

In order to maintain a sufficiently tight focus on the matter at hand, I limit my examination to one feature of performance where continuities between performance practice and performance research are particularly pronounced: the domain of the aesthetic. Performance is an aesthetic practice, which emerges through the complex integration of many different functions. But performance research, too, has aesthetic qualities. The forms and behaviours it involves have an important bearing on what it is possible to do, how it is pursued, and what the outcomes are. In what follows, I explore this by first considering how the aesthetics of performance are taken up in the aesthetics of research activity, focusing on moments when the researcher becomes distinctively visible within the research process. I then explore how one does research – in particular, what it means to conduct it well – and what role the dimensions of a research project – its scale, size, and scope – play in determining both a project's significance and its viability. I conclude with some reflections on what this discussion may mean for future understandings of TaPS research activity.

How Do I Look? The Researcher's Appearance

While the creation and presentation of performance is an aesthetic activity, the idea of applying methods consistently is based on an assumption that such activity can stand functionally outside of those aesthetic considerations and the intensities and anomalies they produce. In practice, however, the conduct of TaPS research is always going to have an aesthetic dimension: there are different ways of practising it, and decisions made in the process will determine what the research involves, what the qualities of the activity or encounter are, and what that research actually looks like.

Amidst a charged visual field (and with some exceptions, such as in practice-based research), performance researchers might seek to avoid drawing attention to themselves, the better to enable the practice or event under investigation to appear as planned. However, it only takes a moment's reflection to recognize that in any number of research settings, appearance is important. Whether we are attending a performance event, observing or participating in creative processes, conducting surveys and interviews, meeting industry stakeholders, balancing practicality and credibility in 'the field', or presenting ourselves for the first time at an archive or library, we dress the part. This is by no means unique to TaPS researchers. In popular culture, scientists and anthropologists feature most prominently on the academic workwear catwalk, and the heightened sensitivity to self-presentation experienced within the video-conferencing environments that proliferated during the COVID-19 pandemic affected scholars of all stripes. However, where TaPS researchers may encounter a discipline-specific inflection on this question of appearance is when they do indeed find themselves summoned to appear, experiencing a 'plunge into visibility' akin to that described by Peggy Phelan (1993), as a characteristic of the performances they are researching.[1] Like performances themselves, this happens at unique moments, and arises out of specific circumstances. In Law's terms, we might think of it as a moment when features of a research situation that had been latent or backgrounded come abruptly to the fore, at least in part.

This eventuality is perhaps best illustrated with an example from my own experience. The photograph in Figure C.1 was taken in July 2019 in the town of Bairiki, on the Kiribati island of South Tarawa in the central Pacific, where I research *te mwaie ni Kiribati* (traditional Kiribati dance). One dance group I focus on, Te Waa mai Kiribati (The Kiribati Canoe), had won the annual Independence Day dance competition, and was holding a celebration to mark their achievement. As is evident from my video

Figure C.1 Paul Rae as *te iruwa ae rine* (guest of honour) at a *botaki* (gathering) in Bairiki, South Tarawa, Kiribati, June 2019. Photo by Miriam Baraniko.

camera, notebook, and spectacles, I was documenting the event in my capacity as a researcher. However, as is also evident from my plastic garland headdress, new floral shirt, and lavalava (a wraparound piece of fabric worn throughout the Pacific and known in the Kiribati language as *te bee*), and indeed from the fact there is a photograph of this moment, I was also an active participant. This had come as something of a surprise to me: beforehand, I was told only the time and venue of the *botaki* (gathering). When ushered to the pandanus mat I am sitting on in the picture, I realized I might not be able to be the fly on the wall that, despite my clear visible difference as an *I matang* (white person), over time I had come to be in the eyes of the group. This was confirmed when, first, in lieu of the dancers I knew, their parents filed in and sat around in a circle, and second, a dancer performed a dance with the garland, folded shirt, and lavalava before presenting them to me and asking me to put them on before the assembled group. I was *te iruwa ae rine* – the guest of honour, a function as much as a privilege and one that involves performing a predetermined set of actions. This included giving a speech, being the focal audience member in a series of celebratory dances, and being the first to eat. It also involved being the first 'volunteer' in a comical improvisatory dance-based game called *te kabuti bwatika* (the bicycle dance), in which one mimes riding a bicycle around the circle, making outlandish and amusing gestures all the while, before inviting another participant to take on the role and retiring to one's place. Once the parents' celebration was complete, they filed out, the dancers filed in, and I performed the same functions all over again, including eating a second meal and going another round of the bicycle dance. The tone this time was rather more boisterous.

This was a moment in my research when I was required to enter very visibly into the research situation. The research hardly 'ended' at this point. On the contrary, my participation as *te iruwa ae rine* involved being explicitly instructed in a range of activities that would otherwise go unspoken, ordinarily requiring more sustained and acute observation on the part of a researcher to identify. Kiribati dance is a venerable and carefully guarded tradition. Its historical association with magic, and alleged capacity to kill rival choreographers, means that practitioners are slow to disclose more than minimal information voluntarily: trust must be established over a considerable period of time. After the *botaki*, I discovered that my interpretation of my role as guest of honour at a celebration for the dancers and their parents was only half right. I was told it was also a surprise party for me, ahead of my imminent departure for home; and, moreover, a kind of test. As a member of the group explained later, once one has participated in the bicycle dance, one joins the 'circle' of the group, and the extended family at its core. But they decided not to tell me this ahead of time, to see how I would react when invited to participate. Indeed, the fact that the group member only told me this three years later, when I asked about the reasons for the secrecy, is further indication of the complexities of the presentational dimension of performance research. If I had not asked, my performance during this moment would have continued to shape perceptions of me as a researcher by my research 'subjects', while I would have remained unaware that my status in relation to the group had shifted.

Such presentational considerations may or may not sit within the planned research methods: when I formulated my research plan for Kiribati, I had not anticipated such active participation in the *botaki*. Moreover, a white British citizen such as I could hardly be naive about the ways in which whiteness is historically marked in Kiribati, which only secured independence from the British in 1976. But insofar as participation was a logical extension of my research activity – and in keeping with an ethical commitment to reciprocity in research settings – I was happy to join in and lend my visibility to proceedings. As one group member said to me, in somewhat proprietary fashion: 'We've never had an *I matang* before.' By joining in, I learnt something about Kiribati dance culture I otherwise may not have, and it marked a new level of acceptance into a situation I was seeking to understand. I also entered into a more complex visual relation to the research setting. One might have thought, for instance, that the floral shirt I donned as *te iruwa ae rine* made me stand out. But arguably it is the drabber olive cast-off to my left in the photo that marked me out in Kiribati: the floral shirt's brighter colours and pattern (what, in Western terms, would be described as 'loud') enabled me to blend in a little more. At the same time, I must confess that I have yet to re-view my performance of the bicycle dance captured by the video camera visible in the photograph. Even though I understand that making myself visible in that way was consistent with the protocols of the moment, I would be too embarrassed to watch myself. I have no reason to delete the footage. But unless a new research imperative sends me back to the bicycle dance specifically, I am content for the moment to have passed, and for my performance at the time to have served its function. Embarrassment is not unusual in research, but I am in no rush to dwell on it.

One might argue that moments of aesthetic or performative intensification risk compromising the performance research process: the abrupt appearance of the researcher as such blows their cover, erasing the gap between observer and observed that should provide the basis for a disinterested account of the phenomenon under investigation. However, as details of research activity sprinkled throughout the TaPS literature and this book make clear, the experience detailed above is hardly unique, and the meaning and effects of such moments can carry significant complexity.

One aspect of this relates to the political and power-related dimensions that circulate around researcher visibility and its relation to their identity. In *The Politics of Cultural Practice*, Rustom Bharucha (2000: 25) summons the memory of a group of highly visible Western theatre researchers at a Chhau performance in India in 1977: the researchers' 'glittering array of cameras, zoom lenses, videos, and projectors' signified 'at a very visceral level, an image of western technology and power'. Bharucha (2000: 38), a native of Kolkata, goes on to contrast the relative ease of international access to 'the field' experienced by researchers with so-called First World passports with the challenges he faces in securing visas: 'my negotiation to cross the border in face-to-face encounters with visa officers has become a performative act in its own right'. In a later book, *Terror and Performance* (Bharucha, 2014: 71–90), he channels these experiences, crystallized around an offhand remark on his appearance by a publisher, back into analysis through a sustained reflection on 'passing as a Muslim' in a time of terror.

Even when the political stakes of such researcher visibility may be less fraught, ethical relations can still come to the fore. In his contribution to this volume, Tony McCaffrey recounts a moment when, in his telling, he was 'called out' by a member of the theatre company with whom he was working. Different Light largely comprises learning-disabled individuals, and McCaffrey interprets his teasing characterization by company member Ben Ellenbroek as 'the world actress here called Tony' as a playful but telling pastiche of his theatrical aspiration and actorly seriousness, informed by normative expectations of artistic productivity, and a failure to recognize how far the lived experience of company members was being overlooked in McCaffrey's earnest but ultimately superficial critiques of the medicalization of disability. If the 'call out' moment was fleeting, however, McCaffrey's response took a long time to work out, as he became more attentive to company members' accounts of their experiences of medicalization, changed his ideas about the kinds of work the company would create, and decided for his own part no longer to perform with the company.

Moreover, while there is a tendency to presume that where research ethics are concerned the focus is largely on the researcher (what Jonas Tinius, in this volume, calls an 'ethics of interlocution'), the negotiation of visibility may equally implicate others within the situation. Julius Bautista recounts a decision by the organizers of a Catholic nailing ceremony in the Philippines to disallow him from being nailed to a cross; he was instead given a less prominent role that actually enabled him to make nuanced observations about the other participants in the ceremony, observations that would not have been possible had he been the centre of attention. Meanwhile, the role of 'researcher' may take many forms and is rarely reducible to a single, self-contained identity, as an abrupt moment of visibility can make evident. In her contribution to this book, Julia M. Ritter describes a formative moment in the development of her research into audiences for immersive dance when, having had her car towed while she was watching Punchdrunk's *Sleep No More* for the first time in New York, she sought to recover aspects of the work and her experience of it by dancing as she moved through the city on foot towards the car pound.

Ritter goes on to detail how this experience seeded features of the research project she would subsequently develop, reminding us that researcher visibility need not always involve becoming apparent to *others*. Sometimes, in our actions, we become apparent to *things*, or to the situation itself, or indeed to *ourselves*. Under time pressure in the Bibliothèque nationale de France and without the ability to reproduce the sound recording of Antonin Artaud's *The Cenci* he was listening to, Adrian Curtin explains in this book how he drew on his music training to score the avant-garde sounds he was hearing – an active response that adverted him to a more 'performerly' part of himself. Indeed, in such moments, our researcher identity may develop in tandem with our growing sense of what the research enquiry may itself be. In a striking and amusing moment in an article on Marina Abramović, Peggy Phelan (2004: 24) describes how her left buttock began to jiggle uncontrollably after she locked eyes with the artist during one of Abramović's durational performances. 'I became extremely self-conscious', writes Phelan, but this experience inaugurates an extended reflection on the intensity of the encounter, narrated in an epistolary form that seeks to carry over some of the particularity of the animating experience, with the letters addressed to Abramović herself.

If in Ritter's and Phelan's cases, the moment of visibility inaugurates the enquiry (rather than simply illuminating the situation), a logical extension of this phenomenon is represented in this volume by Prarthana Purkayastha and meLê yamomo, who each describe how they carried their research activities over into performative presentations. Purkayastha created a lecture performance seeking to reimagine and restage the experience of a group of Indian nautch dancers at a late nineteenth-century exhibition in London, while yamomo created a performance installation that staged the outcomes of his work with colonial European sound archives from Southeast Asia. In both cases, the researchers sustain into transmission the embodied dimensions of the research process itself, both as a means of making that knowledge visible in a medium appropriate to the ideas being explored, and as an act of historical surrogation, which seeks to recuperate and reclaim – albeit tentatively – experiences that have been occluded or appropriated by the colonial archive.

All these examples remind us that when the TaPS researcher becomes visible within the research setting an understanding of the situation does not cease, but it does change modality. It *can* be hard to hold on to a 'research perspective' in such moments: I have written about moments in practice-based research where the demands of the creative work become absolute and will not admit the reflexivity or scepticism upon which much research activity is predicated (Rae, 2003). But even in those cases, the moment of absorption becomes a point of research interest in its own right, to be recollected (to bastardize William Wordsworth) in tranquillity. The point holds more broadly. It is easy to presume that the emergence of the researcher qua researcher at acute moments within a performance research scenario instantly introduces a blind spot into proceedings. But if the researcher remains attentive to the experience, be it in the moment or subsequently, such eventualities become sources of distinctive insight in their own right. They can reconfigure relations, shaking up otherwise settled priorities. They may disclose latent political and ethical dynamics and point to new possibilities for interpretation. What is important is that the researcher remains as attuned to these complexities as they are able, and that they find a situation- and medium-specific mechanism for documenting the unfolding event in ways that will be amenable to analysis.

At the same time, such moments of visibility or participation, while often unanticipated, rarely come out of the blue. Many factors condition and influence what happens *in* such a moment, and reckoning with this situation requires that we open up our account of where we understand the aesthetic dimensions of performance research to reside.

The Aesthetic Conduct of Performance Research

The preceding section highlights specific occasions when the moment of research becomes aesthetically indistinguishable from or coextensive with what is being researched. But 'aesthetics' is not limited only to qualities of expression or modes of presentation. More broadly conceived, it relates also to formal properties such as scale and proportion and the relations between them, as well as to taste, tact, and discernment, all of which have a bearing on the conduct of research. How, precisely, does one practise one's methods over the duration of the research period? How does one comport oneself as one does so? What are the qualities of one's relation to what one is researching? What makes a well or poorly designed and conducted process or project?

These questions are relevant across the range of research methods deployed in TaPS. They may be most acute in practice-based research settings, where a defining feature of the associated methodological discourse has been how to articulate and answer research questions in environments centrally characterized by often open-ended aesthetic activity (see e.g. Nelson, 2022). In my own case, however, I am prompted to pose these questions in light of my experience researching the work of applied drama company Youth Advocates Through Theater Arts (YATTA) in Dumaguete City, in the Visayas region of the Philippines. YATTA's thirty to forty members, aged between thirteen and thirty-five, produce a wide range of theatrical and other events addressing social issues that are important to them and their generation, including poverty, environmental justice, and human rights. For many, membership in YATTA is a formative experience, and the advocacy ethos alluded to in the name of the group is as present in how the company functions as it is in the positions it adopts. YATTA members think of themselves as a family. They refer to one another as *kapatid* – 'sibling' or 'sib' – and, for many, the prospect of belonging is a primary attraction of the company, at least at the outset. For some, the company provides much-needed structure, support, and even physical sustenance: warm-ups are long and rigorous, expeditions to the surrounding mountains and beaches are part of the group's social life, and meals are served at rehearsals.

It is not possible to research the work of such an organization without the researcher finding or making a place within its structure. Partly, this will be a formal designation, determined by age, status, and a range of demographic and identity-related factors. I was less than ten years older than the oldest group members when I began to work with YATTA, but since they were already referred to by other YATTA members as *ate* and *kuya* (older sister and brother, respectively), I was framed, by dint of my foreignness, grey hair, seniority (as a university teacher), and prior association with YATTA founder Dessa Quesada Palm (known as *nanay*, mother) in a role akin to that of a parent. From a research perspective, such framing can be quite limiting, both because it can overdetermine relations with group members, constraining or pre-empting what they are willing to share, and because such formal designations can be extended to many people, regardless of the extent of their interest or involvement in the group.

To gain a fuller picture of the group's activities and members' understanding of participation, it was necessary to supplement or supersede that formal designation by allowing a series of more subjective qualities to enhance my relations to group members. Broadly speaking, these draw on aspects of the research dynamic that are difficult to articulate or reflect upon, but that undoubtedly play a role in the conduct of much research, concerning the personality, attitude, and abilities of the researcher. Take, for instance, the issue of credibility. It is not possible to understand the ethos of a group like YATTA without participating in the range of activities that define membership. It is certainly a pleasure and a privilege to join in with group members as they hike in the mountains, snorkel in the ocean, jump off promontories into waterfalls, and sing karaoke until late at night. More than that, however, while I never felt I was subject to examination during these regular events, it did feel like my willingness to throw myself (sometimes literally) into such activities enhanced my credibility as someone group members would allow to watch them create and perform theatre, to whom they could talk about their experiences, and whom they would trust to describe and analyse their work for others.

Credibility alone is not sufficient in such settings. University ethics committees increasingly seek evidence of reciprocity in research with other people, in order to address widely acknowledged concerns over the potential for research to benefit the researcher significantly more than it does those who contribute knowledge, time, and other resources. One cannot force reciprocity: that becomes an imposition in itself. Negotiating when and where and what forms reciprocity should take again requires tact and imagination. In my work with YATTA, reciprocity has been varied. I have conducted drama workshops, secured overseas touring opportunities for the group, and acted as mentor to some of the older members. I have provided feedback on rehearsals when requested, and shared my documentation, in particular videos of performances, which the company has used to review its own work. This range of activities is not reducible to the domain of the aesthetic, but, understood as behaviour and comportment alongside representation and expression, each activity has an aesthetic quality that often lies in the gift of the participants and plays an important role in determining outcomes.

As such, when interpersonal relations are at issue, the stakes for research (as they relate to access and opportunities for interpretation) are high, but so, too, is the potential for missteps that can fundamentally compromise a research project. These issues can be hard to discuss, since they concern personal qualities that the researcher may be unaware of, or only partially able to comment on (given that it concerns other people's perceptions of them). However, as other examples from this book demonstrate, such qualities are ever present in research and take many different forms. Some of these examples pointedly and necessarily throw aspects of my own account into relief. Awo Mana Asiedu, for instance, reiterates the aesthetic dimension of research conduct by focusing on the appropriate use of oral methods in a Ghanaian cultural context where talk – from conversation through storytelling to talk radio – is widely practised and well appreciated. Asiedu is careful to note that within the linguistically, culturally, and economically differentiated Ghanaian landscape, she must conduct her research according to the setting, adapting the relationships between talking and writing, conversing and surveying, accordingly. Such variations can easily become an animating factor for research in their own right. In *Defiant Indigeneity*, for instance, Stephanie Nohelani Teves (2018: xiv) discusses widespread feelings of inauthenticity among Kānaka Maoli (Native Hawaiians), motivating her to look to a range of performance practices to assess 'the multiple ways in which we cultivate our indigeneity and defy the expectations colonialism has handed down to us'. Nevertheless, Asiedu does note the 'pass' that foreigners – perhaps, particularly, white researchers – receive relative to local researchers in Ghana, at least in terms of initial entrée to some research settings. Here, we see the aesthetic conventions of research conduct combine with another set built around practices of welcome and hospitality. These can themselves be highly performative: the anthropologist Milton Singer (1955) described the origins of his concept of 'cultural performance' – foundational to performance studies – in his experience of being invited by informants in India to document a diverse range of cultural and religious events because, in his analysis, they intuited that such events encapsulated key features of the wider culture he was seeking to understand (see also Rae, 2010: 68–73). Asiedu withholds judgement on the phenomenon of differences between researchers in her chapter. I would not be alone, however, in taking seriously her observation that in the case of research conducted by foreigners, 'some interpretations are not quite what I think they should be'. The piquancy of the sentiment is hardly belied by the subtlety of its phrasing.

The high stakes in such conduct can be in no doubt, based on any number of other contributions to this volume. Jonas Tinius succinctly summarizes the current state of anthropological debates on such matters and articulates an intriguing paradox: insofar as some of the problematic cultural politics of anthropology may be traced to what Tinius calls 'an extrapolation of [performance-related] terms for general metaphors of cultural and social practice', a corrective may in fact be found in the particularities of researching performance as such. Tinius illustrates his argument by drawing on his own experience of researching theatrical production in his native Germany, focusing on the nuanced negotiations with his subjects around his identity as an anthropologist. Ben Spatz makes a related, albeit discipline-specific, case for a mixed-mode research practice that is consistent with an embodied exploration of identity and difference sensitive to song forms. In approaching performance research, Nicola Mārie Hyland speaks of observing the Māori idea of Titiro, Whakarongo, Kōrero: 'watching and listening before you speak … paying attention to the way that other people are having a first-hand phenomenological experience'.

Inevitably, once one begins to acknowledge the granular level at which research activity varies and negotiations among research participants is pursued, it quickly becomes apparent how consistently attentive and responsive the researcher must remain to the situation as it changes. This process comprises affective modes, various dispositions, the exercise of tact and judgement, and the management of specific situations as they arise. It requires that the researcher is attentive to tone and mood as well as to the impact of their presence, and that they respond accordingly by drawing on the full repertoire of their expertise, experience, and personal qualities. This emerges very clearly in the course of the conversation on ethics between Patrick Anderson and Natalie Alvarez. Anderson – who, like McCaffrey, deliberately refuses conventional boundaries around when research is or is not underway – cites the example of a departmental meeting as a setting in which he is attuned to who speaks, who does not, and why. Anderson and Alvarez both recount how they deploy performative nuance in engaging durably with representatives of institutions or systems towards which they retain a political antipathy, without thereby acting in bad faith. Conversely, Alvarez in particular considers the real-time dynamics of a properly ethical research practice, describing an approach 'that is continuously modified and adjusted based on what's happening in the room, on deepening trust, and on an attentiveness to risks as they emerge moment to moment in concrete practices, which cannot always be accounted for in advance'.

These considerations open onto the broader question of how – or on what terms – one might conceive of one's research project as a whole, and here the question of aesthetic conduct joins with more formal aesthetic preoccupations with dimension, proportion, and internal coherence. What is the shape and size of a research project? How can one ensure that the methods and methodologies deployed are proportionate, both to the resources available and to the phenomenon under investigation? These questions are not routinely posed in the abstract. But they are a common preoccupation of researchers, as well as topics of conversation both in research supervision or mentoring settings and in situations where significant resource commitments or the outlay of social capital are at stake.

Derek Miller's contribution to this volume, for example, lucidly outlines the affordances and challenges of digital methods for performance research. However, in talking the reader through a sample data input and analysis process, he equally underscores how every step in the process requires acts of judgement, discernment, and discrimination that are by no means reducible to the performance of technical protocols. Without such an approach, one stands to have the worst of both worlds: onerous data input that is little more, as Miller calls it, than 'busywork', yielding limited results and insights.

Indeed, as many researchers can attest – though few want or need to do so in writing – the specific contours of elegant research design most often become apparent only in the breach. Several years ago, I attempted to assess the contributions Singapore theatre director Kok Heng Leun had made to the Singapore Parliament during his tenure as a non-constituency MP for the arts. I was particularly interested in gauging how and where Kok's speeches and tabled questions sat in relation to the totality of parliamentary business during his three-year tenure, so I undertook to read the entirety of Hansard (the parliamentary record) for that period. I half-jokingly described my plan to the editors of the book where my assessment was to appear as a 'durational research project', an ambition I quickly came to rue. I had significantly underestimated the time commitment that would be required to do the reading, let alone to summarize the results in a single analysis of eight thousand words for a chapter in an edited volume. With a combination of reluctance and relief I decided to reframe the project, zooming in on the roughly two hundred thousand words that Kok and his parliamentary respondents had uttered. This was just the right size for my purposes: it was still demanding, but after multiple readings, I felt able to inhabit the corpus thoroughly and attentively enough to derive an accurate and persuasive account of Kok's achievements and shortcomings, and to locate them within a broader argument about the relationship between his directorial persona and political contributions (see Rae, 2022).

This is an example of a reasonably clear-cut 'research fail', albeit one I was able to rectify by rescaling the project to match the time available, and the relatively modest scope of the expected outcome. More often, as Maggie B. Gale suggests in this book, overambitious research projects founder because of the many other commitments that university-based researchers face, which consume time and energy, disrupt thought, and routinely present distracting new opportunities that invariably hold out the chimera of a quicker and easier means of meeting institutionally determined research 'outputs'.

That said, some contributors to this volume demonstrate how an aesthetically informed approach to research design can afford both the structure required for there to *be* a research project, and the flexibility needed to adapt to changing circumstances as they arise in the course of it. Like Ritter – whose chapter title 'Analysing Immersive Performance through Lived Bricolage' points to a sympathetic relation between the composition and working-out of her research materials on the one hand, and the choreographic imagination shaping the phenomena she is researching on the other – Anke Charton sees in the elusive historical dance form *canario* 'a terpsichorean metaphor for researching early modern dance history: non-linear … full of twists and turns, leaps and stomps'. Recognizing that the minoritarian *canario* form (practised between the sixteenth and eighteenth centuries) is traceable today only in discontinuous fragments, Charton gathers multiple methods that, as she puts it, 'do not necessarily mix well'. In doing so, she reveals how the different and potentially contradictory angles those methods present on the form are perhaps the most accurate means of bringing it to light.

If Ritter's and Charton's chapters provide good examples of project-specific alignment of design and object, Katerina Teaiwa's chapter articulates a more expansive version of the same kind of thinking. Teaiwa outlines a set of principles that are rooted in a Pasifika epistemology and its manifestations in her lived experience, principles that subtend all her work as an academic, across the often-siloed activities of teaching, research, and service. For Teaiwa, the geography, history, and cosmology of island formations and lives in the Pacific are most explicitly expressed in performance, through dance, speech, and song, including in her own dance education. And yet, what is more important than focusing her research on performance practices is that, regardless of the subject matter, she speaks and writes 'as a dancer', meaning that 'the specificities of movement and place shape [her] thinking'.

Does the aesthetic conduct of research matter only when living people are in the picture? Assuredly not. Time and again in this book, we hear from researchers challenged by their research materials and compelled to come up with imaginative and inventive solutions that have an aesthetic shape or quality of their own. This is well illustrated by the contributors to the dialogue on complexity (Chapter 15). Working across eight languages and linguistic registers, Soo Ryon Yoon creates a collective translation enterprise that draws on multiple interpreters to complement her own distinctive mix of linguistic competencies. Seeking to place handwritten Yiddish archives into a dynamic trajectory that sees them move in and out of performance over space and time, Ruthie Abeliovich aims to trace the migratory routes of such texts while utilizing new software that can recognize and distinguish Yiddish handwriting. Meanwhile, a particularly succinct summary of the performance researcher's disposition in the face of complex and demanding research materials comes from Leo Cabranes-Grant, whose research involves a sustained engagement with how colonial manuscripts document performance practices in eighteenth-century Mexico and yet are connected to global practices:

> I try to listen to the event/the object/the situation that is hailing me, and I try to pay attention to all the voices and all their potential sounds or movements that might be expressing themselves at different volumes.... For me, the most fascinating and amazing moment of research is when I become the listener or the witness, trying to ensure that no figure participating in the event goes unnoticed.

Such practices are not unique to TaPS researchers: Purkayastha cites Saidiya Hartman's (2019) method of 'critical fabulation' in pursuit of a related enquiry (a point also explicated in Tracy C. Davis's Introduction). What *may* be distinctive to TaPS research is how resonant Cabranes-Grant's strategy is. I am not a theatre historian. However, I instantly recognize what Cabranes-Grant is talking about from my own experience of watching and thinking about live performance: it is an informed, critical, highly attentive spectatorial position by which we reciprocate the offer our research materials hold out to us, without simply reproducing their own 'method'.

Such moments of recognition and reciprocation are important. But they can bring with them their own limitations. At any given moment, a consensus prevails around accepted methods and methodologies within a discipline, which plays a significant role in determining what 'counts' as a valid object of enquiry. Michael McKinnie considers this point when he surveys a range of challenges that social scientific perspectives pose to dominant understandings of theatre within theatre studies. He advocates a conceptual shift in perspective that promises to reconfigure and perhaps re-energize how we understand theatre's relationship to politics, society, and economics. Two other contributors to this volume indicate what this might mean in practice. Brandi Wilkins Catanese expresses both hope and concern about the ways in which the concept of reproductive justice – which has largely been articulated within the social sciences – can inform the analysis of contemporary plays and performances by Black female artists. While she states that as a theatre scholar she is 'avowedly … focused on feelings and other reactions that can't easily be quantified', she recognizes that these 'are intimately linked to the kinds of structural analyses of power that undergird much existing scholarship in the reproductive justice arena'. Catanese does not settle on a resolution to this challenge, but its articulation already goes some way to revealing how a combination of methods and approaches might enable a researcher to match the multi-scalar complexity of what they are investigating. Emine Fişek's prospectus for what a large-scale, collaborative research project on migration and performance might require is a good example of how the specific and complex conditions of the field of enquiry can determine a range of methods, some of them more familiar to certain performance researchers than others.

Is it possible to conduct an aesthetically exemplary research project, or to conduct a project in an aesthetically exemplary way? Probably not, although certainly we may feel that a project has gone well or poorly, and if we think about it, we can most likely trace the source of such impressions to those dimensions of the project and the qualities of our conduct discussed: it did or did not *work*, it was or was not done *well*, we are or are not *convinced*. These, of course, are preoccupations that are only too familiar to those with experience of creating performances. What is important is that we are capable of acknowledging the similarities without collapsing one activity into the other.

Conclusion: Performance Research and Medium Specificity

I have argued that there is a distinctive and sometimes intimate connection between *what* is researched in TaPS and *how* it is researched: a connection that, left unexamined, risks obscuring or eliding the conceptualization and enactment of method and methodology within the discipline, such that this process is taken either as self-evident or as unimportant. While, as my invocation of John Law's (2004) writing on social science research makes clear, performance research is not unique in featuring enactive and performative dimensions, the specific ways in which these resonate with the enactive and performative dimensions of performance itself mean that this area of overlap is particularly acute: so much so that it is best understood in aesthetic terms more familiar to us from performance than from research. Under a range of conditions and circumstances, performance research activity can be described in terms of aesthetic presentation, conduct, and form. As such, there is always the possibility that methodological practices in TaPS are absorbed into, or rendered continuous with, those activities being researched in such a way that they become obscure to the researcher, obviating the need for their conscious, separate, and reflexive discussion.

Other disciplines may have had a clearer run at articulating a discourse on method because they have an opportunity *both* to acknowledge the enactive and performative aspects of research *and* to maintain a separate, discipline-specific vocabulary by which they may articulate their relation to their objects of enquiry. While the aesthetic overlap of performance research and performance practice can intensify and energize both activities, it may also produce a blind spot. It would be inaccurate, however, for TaPS scholars to conclude that the medium specificity of their research activity means there is nothing to be done about the development of a clearer discourse on method. My aim has been not to absolve TaPS of its obligations to methodological thinking, but the opposite: to recognize that the distinctive relationship between the design, conduct, and moment-by-moment enactment of performance research on the one hand, and both historical and contemporary performance practices on the other, has methodological implications in its own right. Acknowledging and articulating this may be the first step to a clearer, more consistent, discipline-specific account of how and why performance researchers use the methods and methodologies that they do. The anti-institutional bent of TaPS, whereby creative researchers hold the field open to the disarranging force and emergent innovations of performance, is not going away. But it need not come at the expense of greater methodological transparency, which stands to promote wider, more inclusive participation, more durable and defensible research insights, expanded common ground for comparative research and interdisciplinary engagement, and research that is at once engaged, ethical, and elegant.

Note

1 Phelan (1993: 148) writes: 'Without a copy, live performance plunges into visibility – in a maniacally charged present – and disappears into memory, into the realm of invisibility and the unconscious where it eludes regulation and control.' The broader claim has been widely debated, but the evocative language still captures an intuitive truth about one way in which many people experience a key aspect of live performance.

References

Bharucha, R. (2000). *The Politics of Cultural Practice*. London: Athlone Press.
Bharucha, R. (2014). *Terror and Performance*. Abingdon: Routledge.
Hartman, S. (2019). *Wayward Lives, Beautiful Experiments*. New York: W. W. Norton.
Law, J. (2004). *After Method: Mess in Social Science Research*. London: Routledge.
Nelson, R. (2022). *Practice as Research in the Arts (and Beyond): Principles, Processes, Contexts, Achievements*. 2nd ed. Cham: Palgrave Macmillan.
Phelan, P. (1993). *Unmarked: The Politics of Performance*. London: Routledge.
Phelan, P. (2004). 'On Seeing the Invisible'. In A. Heathfield, ed., *Live: Art and Performance*. London: Tate, pp. 16–27.
Rae, P. (2003). 'Re: Invention – On the Limits of Reflexive Practice'. PARIP: Practice as Research in Performance, conference, University of Bristol, 11–14 September. Accessed 11 October 2023. www.bris.ac.uk/parip/rae.htm.
Rae, P. (2010). 'Wayang Studies?' In J. Harding and C. Rosenthal, eds., *The Rise of Performance Studies: Rethinking Richard Schechner's Broad Spectrum*. Houndmills: Palgrave Macmillan, pp. 67–84.
Rae, P. (2018). *Real Theatre: Essays in Experience*. Cambridge: Cambridge University Press.
Rae, P. (2022). 'The Acknowledged Legislator: A Theatre Director in Parliament'. In R. Gough and C. Rajendran, eds., *Drama Box and Spaces of Encounter*. Aberystwyth: CPR Books, pp. 238–56.
Singer, M. (1955). 'The Cultural Pattern of Indian Civilization: A Preliminary Report of a Methodological Field Study'. *Far Eastern Quarterly*, 15(1), 23–36.
Teves, S. N. (2018). *Defiant Indigeneity: The Politics of Hawaiian Performance*. Chapel Hill: University of North Carolina Press.

Index

For EU product safety concerns, contact us at Calle de José Abascal, 56–1°, 28003 Madrid, Spain or eugpsr@cambridge.org.

www.ingramcontent.com/pod-product-compliance
Ingram Content Group UK Ltd.
Pitfield, Milton Keynes, MK11 3LW, UK
UKHW021922190226
468223UK00008B/62
9781009294881